SEX AND RACE

1. Charlotte Sophia, Queen of England, consort of George III, and great-great-grandmother of George VI.

SEX AND RACE

NEGRO - CAUCASIAN MIXING
IN ALL AGES AND ALL LANDS

By

J. A. ROGERS

Author, From Superman to Man; World's Great
Men of Color: Nature Knows No Color-Line, etc.

Volume I

THE OLD WORLD

J. A. ROGERS

HELGA M. ROGERS   4975 59th Avenue South
St. Petersburg FL   33715

© Copyright by
Helga M. Rogers

All rights reserved
Ninth Edition, 1967

ISBN 0-9602294-0-X
Printed in the United States of America

FOREWORD

This book is dedicated to a better understanding among all the varieties of the human race. The merest common sense calls for such an understanding. Racial doctrines as they exist today negate intelligence. Indeed they furnish a paradox that exceeds any of the extravagances of Gilbert and Sullivan.

For instance, we had the great dictators, Hitler and Mussolini, openly saying that "race" is a fraud but cynically using it to unite their gullible followers. At the same time the two great democratic nations, Britain and America, while condemning Fascist and Nazi doctrines, and proclaiming equal justice for all, were using "race" as a fetish to keep their own citizens and subjects divided. White people were set against black peoples by the bogey of miscegenation.

The purpose of this book, therefore, is to see what and what have gone into the make-up of this fearsome creature.

We shall see that mankind began as a single family; that the family circle widened and widened until it broke into segments, and with that came the illusion that the segments were no longer parts of the circle. But thanks to mechanical progress and the spread of knowledge the segments are coming together again; the various ends are being united; the cycle is being completed; and a single understanding family is once more being formed. Already among men of goodwill in many parts of the world this understanding, this sense of unity, exists.

The second world war began as a fire set by Fascist looters in a black neighborhood (Ethiopia) which then spread into the white one (Europe) where they and the Nazis had more to loot.

Racial understanding, racial sympathy, is the key to permanent WORLD PEACE.

More extensive historical research and current information on this volume will be found in Volume Three of Sex and Race (1944) and Nature Knows No Color (1952) both of which are profusely illustrated with portraits and reproductions of paintings.

New York, N. Y.   J. A. Rogers
August 1, 1952.

CONTENTS

Chapter One

RACE TODAY

"A Charm of Powerful Trouble"

"THE conception of races once so innocent," said Jean Finot, "has cast a veil of tragedy over the earth. From without it shows us humanity divided into unequal fractions... From within this same falsely conceived science of races likewise encourages hatred and discord among the children of the same common country . . . People against people, race against race . . . persecution and extermination on every hand."

One writer has called it a Frankenstein monster. But that comparison is far too feeble. However, it has this point of resemblance: Frankenstein's monster was built of scraps—scraps of corpses, a hand from this one, an eye from that, a patch of skin from this other. The evil genie of race is also created from scraps—scraps of false philosophies of past centuries; a quotation from this or that prejudiced traveller; lines from this and that semi-ignorant divine of colonial days; excerpts from Gobineau, Thomas Jefferson, Abraham Lincoln, the Bible; passages from this or that badly mixed-up ethnologist, all jumbled together with catch-phrases from greedy plantation owners, slave-dealers, and other traffickers in human flesh.

The purpose was to create a "pure" race, a "superior" race, a race that like the philosopher's stone of the ancients, excelled all excellence—a race so meritorious that it had the right to enslave and use the rest of humanity.

Every newly discovered bit of anthropology was twisted into building this doctrine of a "superior" race. A Putnam Weale worked most industriously on this part of it; a Tom Dixon, Madison Grant, and Lothrop Stoddard on that; a William McDougall and a Frederick Hoffman busied themselves with that other, while a host of Southern politicians and other lesser fry assisted.

One can see them at work. Like the witches in Macbeth they "round about the cauldron go" and "in the poisoned entrails throw" to make "the hell-broth boil and bubble." Finally the monster stirred to life, to ravage and slaughter. His name: Adolf Hitler. His purpose: World Domination.

It is a matter of common knowledge that Hitler copied very carefully American racial tactics. For instance, Harold Callender says (New York

1

Times, Aug. 4, 1940), that when he saw the Nazis in their beginnings in Munich in 1931, Rudolf Hess defended his stand by pointing to racial discrimination in the United States and saying, "We are very much like the Ku Klux Klan."

The creation of this monster was the easiest thing in the world. Peoples are governed not by realities but by myths. And of all the myths that of racial superiority is the sweetest. Any number of otherwise intelligent people, some of them of the highest scientific pretensions, can be found who believe that their own particular "race" is elevated far above the rest of humanity, and is actually enclosed in some air-tight compartment that keeps it free from contamination. Any number of writers can be found, like William Benjamin Smith, who will declare that race-mixing does not affect the purity of the white race, since those with the slightest degree of Negro strain are classed as Negroes.

As for the mixed-blood, he ought never to have been. No amount of Christianity or religious training, we are informed, will give him good heredity, and this as late as 1935 by no less an authority than the learned Victoria Society of London, England.[1] In short, the mixed-blood is a creation of Satan. "God made the white man and God made the black man," said Colonial America, "but the Devil made the mulatto."

The white race flowed from "a pure source": Europe. Miscegenation with blacks there was unknown throughout the ages, we are told. "It was not until the discovery of the New World that the races of men strikingly different in appearance came to intermix," says Crawfurd. Before that, he says, inferior races did mix with superior races, but both were white.

Nothing, however, is further from the truth. We shall show in these pages that sex relations between so-called whites and blacks go back to prehistoric times and on all the continents. Furthermore, since it is held by many that it is only the mixing of the black man and the white woman that can affect the "purity of the race" that it is precisely this kind that happened most in Europe.

For instance, Aristotle (384-322 B.C.), the first real scientist, tells of a white woman in Sicily who committed adultery with a Negro and had a daughter by him.[1a] Not that this was an uncommon occurrence in his day but because he was discussing whether a white woman could have a black child by atavism. Adultery was then punished with death.

Plutarch, (46-120 A.D.) first of the great biographers, speaks of "a certain Greek woman, having borne a black child, then being on trial for

[1] "Race Mixture with Some Reference to Bible History," Victoria Soc. Jour., Vol. 67, pp. 43-64.
[1a] Aristotle Book VII, Chap. vi.

adultery discovered herself as being descended from an Aethiop in the fourth generation."[2] Wanley tells of a noblewoman "who though both she and her husband were white had a child the colour of an Ethiopian, whom when she was about to suffer as an adultress, Hippocrates (460-359 B.C.) is said to have delivered her by explaining the causes of such things and by showing the picture of an Ethiop in the chamber where she and her husband lay and with which it seems she was strongly affected."[3]

St. Jerome (340-420 A.D.) says that Quintiliani (35-100 A.D.) had freed a Roman matron charged with adultery when she bore a black child by proving the same had been caused by seeing a black man before she gave birth.[4] Juvenal (60-140 A.D.) evidently did not believe this theory of maternal impression, and advised the Roman husbands not to take away the abortive potions from their wives if they did not want blackamoor children. He said, to the husbands, "Grieve not at this, poor wretch! and with thine own hand give thy wife the potion whatever it be for did she choose to bear her leaping children in her womb thou wouldst, perchance, become the sire of an Ethiop, a blackamoor would soon be your sole heir."[5]

Martial, the great epigrammatist (40-102 A.D.), also satirized this tendency of the Roman matrons to cohabit with Negroes. He speaks of one Roman matron who had borne her husband seven children, none of which is his and all of which are mixed-bloods. "One of them with woolly hair like an African Moor seems to be the son of Santra, the cook. The second with flat nose and thick lips is the image of Pannicus, the wrestler... Of the two daughters, one is black ... and belongs to Crotus, the flute-player . . ."[6]

Shakespeare, drawing on Roman history, makes an empress, the German wife of the Emperor Saturninus, be madly in love with a Negro, Aaron, for whom she has a "blackamoor" child. This empress is the

> "...lovely Tamora, Queen of Goths
> That like the stately Phoebe 'mongst her nymphs
> Dost overshine the gallantest dames of Rome."[7]

Among other records of that time are how "a Princess was delivered of a black daughter by only seeing for the first time a blackamoor while she was pregnant," and of a woman who gave birth to three sons at Epiphany, "one of them born black like one of the Three Wise Men."

So much interest was aroused on this subject that "the attack and de-

[2] Plutarch. Delay of the Divine Justice, p. 58. Trans. Peabody. Boston, 1885.
[3] Wanley, N. The Wonders of the Little World, pp. 104, 105, 106. London, 1774.
[4] Pearson, K. Albinism in Man. Draper's Company Research Memoirs. Text Pt. 1. See pp. 120-121, 234. London, 1911.
[5] Juvenal. Sixth Satire.
[6] Martial. Book VI. Epigram 39.
[7] Titus Andronicus.

fense of a woman charged with adultery for giving birth to a black baby
became a popular topic for declamation."[8] Calpurnius Flaccus, noted Roman
orator of the First Century, has left us an oration of this kind, "De Natus
Aethiops."[9] There was much academic discussion on the whys and where-
fores of the mulatto. Herodotus (484-425 B.C.) had said that the semen
of black peoples as the Ethiopian and the East Indian was black like their
faces. Aristotle disagreed with him, saying it was white like that of other
races.[10] For centuries later, the partisans of the two argued the matter,
pro and con, and how it was possible for a white woman to have a black child.

As regards the white man and the black woman, there is at least one
classic case. Persina, Queen of Ethiopia, had a mulatto daughter, named
Chariclea, which color "is strange among the Ethiopians." The black queen
explained it by saying that at the moment of conception her eyes fell on the
statue of Andromeda, Ethiopian princess, which had evidently been done
in white marble. Her husband, the black King Hydaspes did not believe her.[11]
Perhaps if she had given some more commonplace cause such as that used
by the black wives in our times, namely, that she had drank too much butter-
milk, or had been caught in a snowstorm, she might have had better luck.

This last story was written by Heliodorus in the Third Century and is
said to have been a romance. But the point so far is this: Miscegenation
existed not only in early Europe but was of such proportions as to be a topic
of general discussion. Later we shall show the same in northern Europe,
where the interest grew even stronger after Queen Maria Theresa, consort
of Louis XIV of France, had a mulatto daughter,

In the meantime this important fact about these discussions must be
pointed out: They were conducted without that animus against Negroes
which is so characteristic of English, American, and German writers today,
especially when the white woman is involved. Furthermore, percentage of
Negro population had nothing to do with it as some of the ancient European
cities had Negro populations proportionately as large as some of the principal
northern American ones, and even southern ones. The ancients were much
more concerned with the adulterous aspects of such unions than with the
racial one. Class and religion, not race, were then the legal barriers in
marriage.

---

[8] Pearson K. Ibid.
[9] Quintiliani, M. F. Declamationes, pp. 665-698. 1655.
[10] Herodotus. Book III, Chap. 101. Aristotle. Book III, Chap. 21.
[11] Heliodorus. Ethiopian History. Underdowne, 1587, pp. 107-8. London, 1895. (Sir
Kenelm Digby, (1603-1665), also tells of an Ethiopian queen who had a white son
which she says was caused by her looking at a statue of the white Virgin Mary at
the moment of conception. "Powder of Sympathy," p. 76 London 1660.)

Are White and Black Inherent Enemies?

The ancients, being much more interested in the broad question of human conduct than in race, had a favorite problem of discussion which ran something like this: If a man who had never seen another human being were to meet with one suddenly in the woods would he fight him or make friends with him? The idea was to determine whether human beings were inherently friendly to one another—whether war was natural to mankind.

The old philosophers were never able to solve that question. There was no way of getting at the facts. However, in this day when war and race occupy the centre of the world stage, a similar question could be put and with more profit, namely: Were two men of different races, say a white and a black, to meet suddenly for the first time and alone would they fight or make friends?

There is probably no record of such a meeting in ancient times. The nearest to it was when Ptolemy, son of Lagus, (323-285 B.C.) brought a piebald Negro from Egypt and placed him on exhibition in Greece. The greater part of the audience at seeing a human being, part white and part black, burst into violent laughter, while the rest "was horror-struck as if they beheld a prodigy of mischievous portent."[12]

The old Romans, too, according to Juvenal, thought it unlucky to see a blackamoor before breakfast.

> "One of that hue that should he cross the way
> His omen would discolor all the day."

That great satirist did not say, however, what happened if they saw one after supper, or as we say in America, after night-fall.

The answer to what two men of different races would do in our times if they met suddenly under the above-mentioned conditions is probably this: The more enlightened one of the two would try to make friends, the less enlightened one would take to his heels if he were superstitious, or if he were brave would put himself on the defensive.

As it happens we have a very definite index to this. Livingstone says that when he entered certain villages of Central Africa for the first time the women and children and even the dogs and hens would run away as if the devil himself were at their heels. It was their first sight of a white man and the effect, he said, was precisely as if a mummy in the British Museum were to come to life.

Other white travelers have reported similarly of the South Sea and the Australian blacks. Lady Diana Cooper says that a Negro woman in Timbuctoo laughed at her because of her white skin.

[12] Lucian. Works of. Trans. W. Tooke. Vol. II, p. 624. 1820.

On the other hand, how do the inhabitants of remote villages in Europe act at the sight of their first black man? They usually come crowding around in intense curiosity. I have seen French and German children, three and four years of age go up to the black-skinned, saucer-lipped Ubangi women when they were on tour in Europe and rub their fingers on them and look at their fingers to make sure that the grown-ups were not passing off a burnt-cork comedian on them.

One fact was significant in the attitude of the children. Even under the hideous Ubangi distortion they did not fail to recognize instinctively their bond of common humanity with the black women. Similarly was it with Livingstone. The blacks had run away, not because they had failed to recognize him as human, but precisely because they had. He had eyes, ears, and hands like themselves and walked as they did, but being black, their devil was white. Later, they discovered, however, that he was a very good man, that though "as white as the devil," he had "a black soul," (reverse Anglo-Saxon of course), and when next he visited them they ran to welcome him. The bugaboo of color was entirely forgotten.

In short, the child and the so-called savage have no difficulty in realizing the essential oneness of mankind. Little children are not only free from national and religious prejudices but from racial ones, also.

The royalty of all lands, as we shall see, was singularly free from color prejudice too. Even recent European monarchs adopted Negroes as their sons and daughters. The Popes of Rome, too, were particularly kind to Negroes. In short, the universal thinkers of every race and every land have known but one race—the human race.

On What Do the Mischief-Makers Base Their Doctrine of Racial Superiority?

Of Man's single race, there are scores and even hundreds of varieties. Variational differences are based largely on head-form, hair, and color. Some human varieties have a greater proportion of long-heads; others more of round-heads, but all peoples have long-heads and round-heads in their group. As for hair, some white peoples have frizzly hair and certain black ones, silky hair. Color? That is not even skin-deep. It is only a varnish, so to speak. But since color, whether it be in man, plant, or material, is what catches the eye first, color has come to be installed as the chief racial difference in mankind by the civilized Nordic.

Scientists, who wouldn't dream of classifying dogs, horses, or cats, according to color, claim to see in the color of the human skin something so important as to warrant establishing mankind into separate and distinct races—white race, red race, black race, yellow race, brown race, brunette race, blond race, etc., etc., etc.

For nearly three hundred years they have been dinning "Race, Race, Race," into the ears of humanity. The books they have written on the subject would tower miles into the sky. One does not exaggerate.

Superior races!

Inferior races!

Pure races. High-bred, heaven-sent races, born to command.

Mongrel races. Debased races, born to slavery.

Racial messiahs rose to world prominence. They waxed fat. Mankind became race-conscious as it became bingo-conscious, baseball conscious, or prize-fighting conscious. And when people become conscious about anything they usually strive for supremacy in that particular field, to see who is the world champion.

"Superior" Race Versus "Super-Superior" One

It was inevitable that this should be so too in the matter of race. The battle for world racial supremacy is now on. Superior Anglo-Saxon versus super-superior Aryan!

For centuries the Anglo-Saxon had proclaimed himself the racial cock-of-the-walk. But now the Hitler Aryan has announced that he is "the master race, destined to rule the world." He is looking down on the Anglo-Saxon much as how the latter looks down on the Negro. In a word, he is calling the Anglo-Saxon "nigger."

Of course this is quite in line with the traditions of the "superior" race. In America when one member of the "superior" race wishes to sting another, he either rents his home in the white residential district to Negroes, or broadcasts that his opponent is a Negro. It will be recalled that the political opponents of Warren G. Harding published in many of the leading newspapers that Harding was a Negro on the eve of the 1920 presidential election, reserving their fire till the last, and not giving Harding a chance to reply.

Hitler, too, has adopted these tactics. German propagandists are declaring that white Americans, after cohabiting with Negroes for centuries, are a Negroid people, and are bringing their Negro strain into the British Isles.

In September 1939, Lord Haw Haw, German radio back-biter and a New Yorker by birth, said in his broadcast, "Mr. Winston Churchill, whose mother is an American Negress, and whose father, Lord Randolph

II. Ludwig van Beethoven, at the age of 44. Drawn from life by Letronne; engraved by Hofel
(See notes on the Illustrations).

III. Clarence Cameron White, noted Aframerican composer. Less Negroid in appearance than Beethoven, and resembling him somewhat.
(See notes on the Illustrations).

Churchill, died of an unmentionable disease . . ." That is, he gave the British Prime Minister, the worst ancestry possible on both sides of his family.

After what Hitler has said about French and other European ancestry, this leaves the German as the only "pure, pure race."

Could Churchill, and Even Hitler, Be of Negro Ancestry?

Of course, the English people laughed at Lord Haw Haw. The statement that their Prime Minister was a Negro was obviously only more Nazi propaganda. The purpose was to blacken Churchill morally by blackening him physically precisely as in the case of Harding. But joking apart, was it ab-so-lute-ly impossible for a British Prime Minister to have had a Negro ancestor lurking somewhere in the distant wood-pile?[12a]

The answer to that brings us to the purpose of this book, which is to try to show from the most authentic facts available what and what and what have entered into the family trees of the "superior" and the "super-superior" races; whether in the case of Aryans it may not be a case of the pot calling the kettle black.

Of course, in an undertaking of this sort, one starts with a tremendous handicap. The "pure race" idea has had a start of three centuries. It is as firmly fixed in the popular mind as ghosts or that thirteen is unlucky. Some of the firmest believers of this theory are the under-dogs, the victims, themselves. Say that this or that great man, as Beethoven, whom they have all along believed to be pure white, was a Negro, and you are likely to have even some of their scholars down on you, regarding you as a falsifier, or at best as irresponsible. But we shan't let either the attitude of top-dog or under-dog bother us.

How White Is the European?

The first step is that certain words have to be given their proper meaning. One of these is European. No less an authority than the United States Department of Immigration sets down all Europeans as "white."

Let us remember, however, that Europe is only fifteen miles away from Africa. America, which had had so much race-mixing is three thousand miles away from it. And while America has tried to prevent race-mixing, Europe generally has not. Moreover, while the Negroes came to America largely as slaves, thus permitting race-mixing to be controlled, the Negroes for four times at least entered Europe as conquerors.

[12a] A distinguished European writer to whom I mentioned this said that Lord Haw Haw was right; that Churchill does have some Negro in his American ancestry. I have done no research on that.

What have the European writers, themselves, to say on this subject? The fact is that no reputable European historian or archaeologist will deny that there is a Negro strain in the European.

Here are the opinions of two different schools of thought, both of which happen to be German. The first is represented by Hans Guenther, a Hitler Aryan; the second by Brunold Springer, of the liberal school of the late Felix von Luschan.

Guenther says, "A Negroid strain is found from olden times all over the Mediterranean area (Negroes in the Roman army, Negro slaves) especially in the shipping towns since the Crusades. Negroes were and still are the fashion as servants in the big towns. Marriages with Southern Europeans have brought Negro blood into Central Europe; Italian navvies, particularly, have shown a more or less evident Negro strain. Into France Negro blood has made its way from the French territories in Africa. Portugal, owing to the former importation of slaves from Africa shows a particularly well-marked Negro strain."[13]

Brunold Springer in his book, "Racial Mixture as the Basic Principle of Life" tells of the Negro strain even in the Hitler Aryans. The New York Times in a news article on this book entitled "Negroid Blood in Hitler's Aryans," says:

"Often the Negroid aspect is strikingly evidenced in personal appearance, Herr Springer writes, as in the case of Dr. Schweninger, Bismarck's physician, who had warm, African eyes, or of Beethoven, who possessed in addition a strain of Malay or Alpine blood as well. Once the characteristic Negro features become familiar to the glance, blonde Negroes are often discernible. Gabrielle Réjane, the French actress, had the broad nose and heavy lips of the blonde Negroid type."

The Times quotes Brunold Springer:

"BLACK STRAIN IN SPANIARDS

" 'There is a very large percentage of Negro blood in the Spanish people, brought by the slaves who accompanied the Moorish invaders. The Spaniards then carried the black strain farther into Europe, into France and the former Netherlands. When the Spaniards were driven out of the latter lands, about 3,000 of them settled in Hamburg, and many a Hamburg citizen today bears a striking resemblance to the citizens of Spain.

" 'Portugal was the first example of a Negrito republic in Europe. In the Portuguese runs a deep current of Negro blood, and there the Negro has often risen to the caste of the nobility. Napoleon's army had many small, black Portuguese soldiers, who were nicknamed "the fleas." Sicily, of course,

[13] Guenther, Hans. The Racial Elements of European History, p. 65. London, 1927.

is also profoundly Africanized.

" 'All of this is ancient history. The Romans brought Negro troops to the Rhine and over the Donau. Later merchants purchased the young Negroes as servants; in all large cities of commerce there were several hundred blacks, and many a house was known simply as "at the Moors."

" 'In one circle of people whose members belong to the Russian, English and German nobility there is much Negro blood, inherited from an ancestor who lived at the end of the eighteenth century, and who was the great-grandfather of one of the greatest poets of all lands and of all times, Alexander Sergeivitch Pushkin.' " (July 1, 1940, p. 19, early ed.)

H. G. Wells goes even further. He says, "Everyone alive is, I am convinced of mixed ancestry, but some of us are more white, some of us more Negro, some of us more Chinese."[14]

The good people of Virginia and a dozen other Southern States will hardly be thanking Mr. Wells for this. He'd be putting them all in the jim-crow car. Their "race purity" law is so worded that if it can be proved that even one of a person's ancestors had been a Negro as far back as the Neanderthal age he might as well be born at midnight in the heart of the Congo.

The Total of One's Ancestors Is Astronomical

Everyone has two parents, four grand-parents, and eight great-grand-parents? How many know all of the eight? How many three of them. How many even one? In ten generations the number of one's ancestors, more or less direct, runs into the millions, each one of which in turn runs into other millions. In a hundred generations, the figure mounts into the trillions. Man has been living on this planet for over a million years, and the ancestry of the most insignificant pariah goes back the same distance as that of the proudest blue-blood. Both, too, have an identical number of ancestors. As Professor Einstein says, "All modern people are the conglomeration of so many ethnic mixtures that no pure race remains... It is impossible for any individual to trace every drop of blood in his constitution. Ancestors multiply like the famous seed of corn on the chessboard which embarrassed the sultan. After we go back a few generations our ancestors increase so prodigiously that it is practically impossible to determine exactly the various elements which constitute our being."[15]

And what was the moral calibre of all these millions of ancestors? The race purist never stops to ask. All he knows is that it was glorious. But

[14] World of William Clissold, Vol. II, p. 431. N. Y., 1926.
[15] Saturday Evening Post, October 26, 1929.

AUG. 21, 1937—THE ILLUSTRATED LONDON NEWS—305

A DANDY OF THE EQUATORIAL FOREST : A WEST AFRICAN TRIBESMAN WITH HIS
SIDE HAIR DRESSED IN STIFFENED COILS, TOP-KNOT, AND POINTED BEARD—THE
GENERAL EFFECT RATHER REMINISCENT OF DISRAELI.

IV. (See Notes on the Illustrations).

were it possible for a William the Conqueror, or a Mayflower descendant, and a Daughter of the American Revolution to get a real glimpse of all their ancestors, they would either drop dead or go insane, or forever after remain speechless. What a sight that would be! Cannibals, phallic worshippers, wretched Egyptian peasants, chiefs, kings, pharaohs, philosophers, prostitutes, thieves, thugs, poets, physicians, pirates, convicts, counterfeiters, horse-thieves, a Pope or Rome or two, rogues of the deepest dye, and saints of the most finical honesty. And as for so-called race, they range from coal-black to straw-blonde; and long-heads to round-heads, not to mention pin-heads. Your asserter of race purity is either a psycopathic, or a hopeless ass. The trouble is that he is gnawed by a vast inferiority complex that can be satisfied only when he is looking down on someone else. When there is none such, he becomes a nobody even in his own estimation.

The difference between your very superior white-Southerner or Hitler Aryan and the "Uncle Tom Negro" is like the difference between Mutt and Jeff of the cartoons. One towers above the other, it is true, but to the sane eye, both are freaks.

Once in a hospital for shell-shocked veterans, I saw an unmixed Negro whose mania was that he was a white man. As I listened to this poor lunatic spouting the doctrines of white racial superiority, I could fancy myself back in the gallery of the United States Senate listening to Cole Blease, Vardaman, Heflin, John Sharp Williams, or Theodore Bilbo.

When John IV of Portugal was urged to sign a law compelling all of Jewish ancestry to wear a white hat, he refused. "Better go easy, senors," he said, "We may be having to wear one ourselves." And to quote Wells again, "We have to remember that human beings can interbreed freely and that they separate and mingle as clouds do. Human races do not branch out like trees that never come together again. It is a thing we need to bear in mind this remingling of the races at every opportunity."[16]

British Prime Ministers with a Possible Negro Strain

Returning to the subject of the British Prime Minister, it will be shown that at least two of them were of mixed blood. One was of part East Indian ancestry, the base of which is Negro. The other was the great Disraeli. In his "Rassenkunde des Judischen Volkes," Hans Guenther compares a portrait of Disraeli with that of Abraham Plaatje, a Hottentot. Guenther, it is true, is a Hitler Aryan. His aim might be to belittle the Jew as Lord Haw Haw in the case of Churchill but it must be said that the resemblance is there.[17] As will be shown there is a Negro strain in the Jew. Of

[16] A Short History of Mankind, p. 70. London, 1922.
[17] p. 109. Munich, 1930.

course there are Jews who will consider mention of the Negro in the same breath with themselves as defamatory. But if it be a disgrace to be descended even in part from a people who at any given period are socially unpopular then everyone on earth has been disgraced. Not so long ago the Hitler Aryans were regarded as the scum of the earth, and for that matter are still so regarded by some. Furthermore, certain peoples who were scum rose to the top of the heap, and then sunk back to scum-dom.

Miscegenation is usually spoken of as if it were the latest moral reprobate to be halted at Ellis Island but the fact is that it is more characteristically American than Plymouth Rock. White and black Spaniards were mixing in what is now the United States even before Sir Walter Raleigh, the founder of Virginia, was born.

Moreover, according to Professor Dixon and others, there was a Negro strain in the American Indian, especially those of Massachusetts and Rhode Island. The American family that didn't bring a Negro strain with it from Europe had thus an opportunity for picking up one here.

Albert Payson Terhune in an article entitled, "Mongrels All," declares that there is no such thing as a pure American stock. He says: "Half-breed Jake, the tramp, who was hanged for stealing food from the Continental army at Valley Forge, may be just as much your great-great-grandfather as is Eusebius Van Blanck who signed the Declaration of Independence...

"You may inherit your rich brunette complexion quite as logically from Half-breed Jake's Indian or Negro or Hindu mother, as you inherit your aristocratic aquiline nose from the blue-blooded Eusebius. You can't accept one possibility without accepting both.

"In my own case, even in one of the two direct lines, my genealogy stops short in the fourth generation. For all I know, one of my great-great-grandfathers (the father of a ne'er-do-well who called himself Jesse Hawes) may have been a Turk or a Chinaman or a Negro or a gypsy or George Washington or an Indian... You and I, in short, are mongrels."[18]

Neither age nor custom has been able to make miscegenation respectable. In 1925, when Philip Rhinelander married Alice Jones, a light mulatto girl, it caused a furore of disapproval and held the front pages of the New York dailies for almost a year. Shortly before that a play by Eugene O'Neill, "All God's Chillun Got Wings," which dealt with race-mixing, caused a nation-wide storm and led even the New York World, which was then regarded as one of the leading champions of democracy in America, to demand that the Board of Aldermen suppress the play on the ground that "an act which is illegal in more than half the country and is viewed with disapproval in the other half is to be represented in a manner indicating approval in a

[18] Liberty Magazine. April 30, 1932.

public theatre.**"** (March 4, 1924).

In 1930 in the State of Washington where so-called intermarriage is legal an official refused to issue a marriage license to a mixed couple saying that he "has the right to ascertain whether the mentality of applicants for marriage licenses is sound and I can but question the sanity of a white woman who will marry a Negro." In Boston, Massachusetts, in 1937 there was another tempest when a Negro college graduate married a white girl of good family connections. As for the Southern states, heaven only knows how many are languishing in prison for this "crime" including North Carolina, the supposedly most civilized of them all.

In all the tens of thousands of years prior to the coming of the English to the New World the mixing of black and white was considered, on the whole, perfectly natural, and is still so regarded in nearly all the civilizations of the Old World. But tobacco and cotton, and the desire of one part of the human species, or rather, certain members of it, to enrich itself at the expense of another part, changed the picture.

Fountains of ink have been spilled by racial vultures, as Houston S. Chamberlain, R. W. Shufeldt, E. S. Cox, Lothrop Stoddard, Henri Champly, in predicting the calamity that the darker races and the Negro in particular were going to bring on the white race. Mixing with these peoples meant final ruin for the "superior" race. But now racial calamity is upon us all, white and black, such calamity as the world has never seen before. And it is not the Negro that has brought it about. It is the same "superior" race these writers deified. Mankind is thundering with avalanche speed back to the Dark Ages, and it is not race-mixing that is the cause; it is the doctrine of race purity, underneath which is the fight for money and markets.

Under the horribly false and monstrous doctrines of these right wing anthropologists the darker-peoples became "lesser breeds outside the law." The teachings of early Christianity on the essential oneness of the human race were silenced and instead of talking about human beings, it became the fashion to speak of Caucasians, Mongolians, Mongoloids, Eskimoids, Armenoids; Proto-Negroes, Negritos, Negroids, and Negroes; Polynesians, Micronesians, Indonesians, Melanesians, and heaven knows what else besides.

Legs, arms, ears, noses, hair, genitals, and even the down on the foetuses were classified according to "race." In most learned circles, Man disappeared and centimeters took his place. The craniometrists, the old time phrenologist in a new dress, no longer saw human heads but such outlandish, jaw-breaking names as brachycephalic, dolichocephalic, chamecephalic, orthocephalic, ultra-dolichocephalic, hypereuryprosepous, hyperleptoprosepeus. Had Hamlet looked at the skull of poor Yorick today he would hardly have seen in it a human symbol. Instead of his famous reflection on Alexander the Great dead and turned to clay and being used to stop a hole to keep the wind away, he would have taken out his calipers and made a learned disquisition on orthognatism and prognathism, or on the acute or the oblique angle of the skull and thus deliver judgment whether Yorick was a member of a superior or an inferior race, whether he was of the damned or the elect. As Professor Toynbee has so truly said, "Our modern Western racialists have rationalized their Calvinism by substituting Black and White skins for damnation and grace and expurgated it by omitting the divine cause. The result is not science but fetishism."

A few anthropologists as Finot, Boas, Herskovits, Dorsey and Hooton, it is true, taught the opposite, but their voices were almost drowned by the paranoiac screamings of the false prophets.

It is my opinion based on fairly wide experience that the white race when not agitated by the cunning propagandists of capitalism, is almost totally free from color prejudice, in any case it is less disturbed by it than the black. In the many years I lived in Europe, I did not once see a native European discriminate against a Negro, except in the case of certain hotel proprietors who did it to please Americans. On the other hand I have seen in Africa, ill-smelling natives hold their noses at the approach of white people, saying that white people smelt bad. Later, however, these blacks learnt better.

The dogma voiced by Abraham Lincoln that "there is a physical difference between the white and black races that will forever forbid the two races" from living as social and political equals is one of the biggest and most pernicious lies ever uttered. It has been done elsewhere, as I shall show. Why not in America? "Race" is almost wholly a capitalistic concept. I have met, in my time, almost every "race" under the sun, and I have still found "race" as elusive as electricity or the ether, have still to understand what the racialists are talking about. The most striking thing to me is the similarity in the psychology of the so-called races. The three principal things I notice that will move all peoples from the most benighted to the most cultured are in the order named: money, a smile, and flattery. Humanity instead of being different, is rather too monotonously alike when you get acquainted with its different "races." Such differences as exist are minor and change with the environment. In other words, blacks who have been reared exclusively by whites have a "white" psychology, whatever that is, and whites who have been reared among primitive Negroes or Indians are, except for color, Negro or Indian, Hollywood notwithstanding.

That brings us to the real issue in the matter of race-mixing. The problem is not anthropological. It is ethical. Races have always mixed and will continue to mix; if not in accordance with man-made laws, then against them. The real question is whether the Anglo-Saxon, the Nazi, the

Fascist, shall continue to maintain their fake position on "the purity of race," whether they shall continue to eat their cake and have it, too.

For instance, though so much race-mixing has taken place in the United States, nothing that Alfred Rosenberg, Nazi fanatic, had been able to devise against the Jew sounds half so fantastic as American laws against the Negro— laws which have received the sanction of the United States Supreme Court, which, in the past, has had a most notorious record of appeasement. These laws and cases have been collected by Charles S. Mangum, Jr., in a volume entitled, "The Legal Status of the Negro," and published in 1940, by the University of North Carolina Press. The book is full of Americana so incredible that on read- ing it, one fancies himself in a mad-house. Such twistings, such distortions to rob Negroes and check the impartial administration of justice! But behind these seemingly crazy laws was the cool, calculating idea of the upper class whites tc use the egotism and inferiority complex of the white masses to exploit Negro labor and despoil Negro womanhood and also the white masses.

I am as convinced, as I can be convinced of anything, that it is not the in- dividual murderer, or thief, or liar, that is the real enemy of mankind in this the Twentieth Century but the racial purist. As the war-makers have taken the in- ventions created by Science for the betterment of mankind, as the airplane, and turned them into instruments for mass slaughter, so the politicians have used Ethnology for creating unparalleled discord in the human family.

The supreme creation of the racial purists working for the past three cen- turies, whether they were British, American, Australian, or South African, was, as was said, Adolf Hitler.

Hitler was a stream-lined Machiavelli and past master in behavior psychology. He used race to whip up his people but was no more sincere than he was about Communism, which he opposed or allied himself with as suited his purpose. He said as regards race, "I know perfectly well just as all these tremendously clever intellectuals, that in the scientific sense there is no such thing as a race. . . . But I, as a politician, need a conception which enables the order which has hitherto existed on historic bases to be abolished . . . and for this purpose the conception of race serves me well."[19]

Hitler's attack on Jews was motivated by similar opportunism. As for the anti-Negro part of his program that was to get even with France's use of black

[19] Rauchning, H. Hitler Speaks, pp. 230-31. London 1940 (Rauchning was one of the founders of the Nazi party.

soldiers against Germans in the first World War, as well as to win English and American favor, because while the Anglo-Saxons make a fetish of race, the Germans, as we shall show later, really have no color prejudice.

Nazi race doctrine opposed intermixture even with non-German whites. Its organ, *Neues Volk,* exhorted Germans to preserve their alleged race purity in the conquered lands. It said:

"Every German and every German woman has the duty to avoid association with other races, especially Slavs. Each intimacy with a people of inferior race means sinning against the future of our own people." Thus, if ever the Nazis get to America, they'll give the white Americans a dose of what the latter have been giving the blacks.

But for the myth of race superiority built up by the Anglo-Saxons, and on which Hitler modelled his own racial dogmas, his doctrine of "Aryan" superiority over the rest of humanity, including other whites, could never have attained the extent and the dogmatic force it did. He would have had to find some other fanatical idea to stir his people to war. The nearest idea could only have been religion, and people no longer war over that.

As for Mussolini he turned "race" into an even more barefaced racket than Hitler or the Klan. The Italian, as everyone knows, has long been regarded as an inferior "race." In 1924, the United States amended its immigration laws to exclude as many Italians as possible and to have more Nordics. Consequently, the Italian, like the Negro, is on the racial defensive. Italian ethnologists have taken the lead in proving "race purity" a myth.

No one was more emphatic on the subject than Mussolini, himself. In 1932, he said, "There are no pure races left; not even the Jews have kept their blood unmingled. Successful crossings have often promoted the energy and beauty of a nation. Race! It is a feeling, not a reality; ninety-five percent, at least, is a feeling. Nothing will ever make me believe that biologically pure races can be shown to exist today. Amazingly enough not one of those who have proclaimed the 'nobility' of the Teutonic race was himself a Teuton. Gobineau was a Frenchman; Houston Chamberlain, an Englishman; Woltmann, a Jew; Lapouge, another Frenchman. Chamberlain actually declared Rome was the capital of chaos. No such doctrine will ever find wide acceptance here in Italy."[20]

[20] Emil Ludwig, Talks with Mussolini, pp. 73-74. London, 1932.
On Sept. 6, 1934, Mussolini in a speech from Bari, flung back at his chum-to-be, Hitler, "We can look with contempt on the doctrine of a certain race which did not even know how to write when we had a Caesar, Virgil, and Augustus." Mussolini was then smarting under a book on racial research by Hermann Gauch, Nazi, in which he called the Italians, "half-apes." This book was suppressed. (N. Y. Times Dec. 8, 1934.)

Speaking of a certain professor, evidently a German, who had been preaching the doctrine of the "noble blonds," Mussolini said, he "is a man with more poetic imagination than science in his composition. National pride has no need of the delirium of race."

In fact there seemed nothing else for an Italian who was not an idiot to say. Even the most casual visitor to Italy cannot help but see that it is a land of very much mixed races. Nevertheless on July 13, 1938, the Fascist Grand Council with one stroke of the pen, and without setting up a single face-bleaching or hair-straightening parlor in Sicily, Calabria, or elsewhere, transformed the Italians into "a pure Aryan race."

Among the ten points of the manifesto were the following: That there is such a thing as race; that there is "a pure Italian race"; and that histories that speak of an influx into Italy of other than Aryan peoples are false.[21]

In other words, Hannibal never crossed the Alps and the Latin writers who told of seeing him were liars. As for the Egyptians, the Moors, the Huns and other dark-skinned non-Aryans, they only imagined they had entered Italy. The Negro slaves of Italy from the thirteenth to the seventeenth centuries were white people who had blacked themselves up. So were the Italians with whom Napoleon used to fill up his Negro regiments when the French supply of blacks ran out.

The supreme concocter of human misery—the mass murderer, liar, and thief of this century is the racial purist. Anyone, even the lowest moron, can always believe and declare himself to be better than anybody else.

The race prejudice which originated in Virginia in the Seventeenth Century is as truly the spiritual ancestor of Adolf Hitler as poisonous manure is of toadstools.

But this monstrous fad will pass. An important fact to remember: The present generation of Americans is not responsible for what was done in those days. They will be, however, if they help in perpetuating them.

There is much more anti-Negro prejudice in Washington, D. C., than there is in Berlin now.

The time has come either to treat the Negro better or to stop talking about democracy.

> "United States! The ages plead
> Present and past in under-song
> Go put your creed into your deed
> Nor speak with double tongue.
>
> "Be just at home then write your scroll
> Of honor o'er the sea
> And bid the broad Atlantic roll
> A ferry of the Free."

[21] New York Times, July 14, 1938 et seq. Also La Difesa della Raza, Italian Race magazine.

WHICH IS THE OLDEST RACE?

FOR us of the present day, the earliest history of all peoples and nations is lost in a fog. Our prehistoric ancestors never thought of preserving records for our benefit and even if they did, fire, flood, earthquakes and war, might have destroyed them. Such relics as have been found are accidental, and must be pieced together, often leaving great gaps.

Most of all is this true of the origin of Man and the development of his many so-called races from a single race.

Was the original man black or white? Was his hair frizzly, woolly or silky? Was his nose flattened out or pinched upwards? Frankly we do not know and perhaps will never know. With "race" so much in the air, however, the question seems of the highest importance.

Our earliest ancestors have left no records whatever on this subject. They were too busy worrying whether they were going to eat or be eaten to occupy themselves with such finical things as color of skin, cranial angles, and texture of hair. Primitive men probably accepted racial variety among themselves as horses, dogs, deer, and buffaloes did among themselves.

If, after they had advanced some degree in culture, anyone asked what the first man looked like, they had an easy and assured answer. Pointing to the statue of the god they had erected in their own image, they'd say, "What a stupid question! Can't you see we look like him?"

Of course, that might not have been their exact words, but if they were anything like us that's what they said. Thousands of centuries later that is our answer. The god of primitive Africans is still black. The Eskimo god is an Eskimo, and so on. And ninety percent of civilized white folk still picture their god as a white man with a long white beard. One fact is certain, they do not imagine the god, who made them in "his own image" as being of a "race" other than their own.

But as primitive man developed mentally and the tribes came more and more in contact with one another, they could not help seeing that whether they claimed their god was Osiris, or Jehovah, or Unkulunkulu, or Mumbo Jumbo, or Wotan, that there was something strikingly alike between themselves and the foreigner. Especially were they impressed by such similar uncomfortable traits as wishing to get something for nothing, or the love of flattery, or the desire to get the last word in an argument. The result of all this was that as time went on, the more enlightened peoples, as the Egyptians came to formulate a theory of the common origin, not only of mankind, but of all things, as we find it in the doctrines of Akhenaton.

But even the most enlightened of these peoples had discriminatory laws or customs against the stranger. The Egyptians thought it an "abomination" to eat with their Jewish visitors from Canaan. (Gen. 44, 32). Later the Jews, themselves, as well as the Greeks and Romans came to regard others not of their own nations as barbarians. But, mark you, this distinction was based, not on color or race, but on tribal, national, and religious differences.

The first attempt to found a doctrine of race, based on physical appearance, came with the introduction of Negro slavery in Virginia. Prior to that "race" was used chiefly as meaning a contest. The King James' version of the Bible uses it only in this sense. Shakespeare also uses it in the sense of "family." But the American slave-holders, finding themselves forced to explain how the teachings of Christ could be reconciled with the cruelties of slavery set their lackeys, the theologians, who were the "scientists" of that time to find an explanation.

Turning to the Bible, the leading "scientific" authority of that period, the servile divines, discovered that Cain had taken a wife from the land of Nod. Now according to the story of Creation, which is Jewish folk-lore and nothing more, there were then only three people alive on the planet, Adam, Eve and Cain. Who were these people living in the land of Nod then? They were pre-Adamites! And pre-Adamites could be no other than Negroes, that is, people who had had no part or lot in the creation by God. Moreover, Cain was wicked and low and could have been counted on to marry a Negro. Abel, "the righteous" and respectable would have lived with her in concubinage. Yes, there could be no doubt, whatever, that the people of the land of Nod were Negroes.

Other servants of God, searching the "scripters" found still more "scientific" things about race. The Bible had also spoken of "a beast," the unknown beast of Revelations. What else could this be, but the Negro? Still another theory that came to be accepted was that Negroes were the descendants of Ham, whose son, Canaan, had been cursed by Noah. "Cursed be Canaan, a servant of servants, shall he be unto his brethren." (Gen. ix, 25, 26)

Noah, according to this bit of folk-lore, had been drunk and exposing his person, and Ham had laughed at him, while the other sons had covered his nakedness; accordingly, the eldest son of Ham, mark you, not Ham, himself, was doomed to eternal servitude. Besides, were not the Negroes black—different in color from the whites? Blackness and servitude should go together like ham and eggs, or Siamese twins. Moreover, slavery was so philanthropic. It "made Christians of heathens and useful servants from savages."

The above sounds like a joke. But it is far from being one. Early American literature is full of it, and most Americans of the time believed it.

Indeed, millions of Americans, black as well as white, and British West Indians, too, still cling to this sub-human absurdity. I, myself, was so taught in Sunday school, and by a Negro teacher, who valiantly defended the falsehood, quoting the Bible as an infallible authority. Of course, the Bible says no such thing. As will be shown later, the Canaanites, on whom this alleged curse is supposed to have descended, were Asiatics, while the ancestors of the New World Negroes came from West Africa.

And the Negroes who accept this Ham story are not all illiterate. In 1938, an Aframerican, twenty-six years of age, a graduate of Tuskegee Institute, noted educational centre for Negroes, told me of this curse, and insisted with vigor that it was true because "the Bible said so." Again, I was recently informed by a white friend from Minnesota that two Mormon missionaries there, when asked whether Negroes were admitted to their faith, replied, "Yes, but we do not encourage them. Their race is cursed by God."

Incidentally, the West African Negroes had a rather fitting reply to this. When told the Ham story by the slave-traders and the missionaries, they replied, "You're wrong. All men were originally black, but when Cain killed his brother, Abel, and God shouted at him, Cain was so frightened that he turned white and his features shrunk up, making him the first white man."[1]

Of course, theories like these have an immense advantage. They are economical. They save wear and tear on the brain because Man's origin and his many varieties from a single source still continue to be the most baffling problem for all who use their heads other than as a means of livelihood for the hair-dresser and the hatter.

Man's history, prior to the last 20,000 years or so, trails back into darkness almost as dense as the interior of the earth or the depths of the Atlantic. Try to remember by your unaided efforts what happened to you from the moment of your conception through to your birth and until you were about two or three years old and you will get a faint, a very faint, idea of what even the wisest man is up against when he tries to unravel what happened in the conception and infancy of mankind, billions of years ago.

But even as we may learn something of our earliest individual history from our elders so we may deduce something of Man's origin from the sea, the rocks, rivers, caverns, fossils, trees—such deductions being to the highest degree faulty. It is precisely as if we were to find a very old book with nine-tenths or more of the first part missing and whole pages here and there in the remainder, and then trying to write the whole of the original story. Now

[1] For the origin of the Ham story as drawn from ancient Jewish legends see Sex and Race, vol. 3, pp. 316-17. See also "Nature Knows No Color-Line" for Negro theories on the origin of the whites.

and then we stumble on some of the missing pages, badly torn, which some say, belong to this part of the book, others to that. All knowledge rests on a foundation of ignorance. Truth is but a distillation of error.

Were the First Men White?

Interest in the origin of the so-called races arose in the 17th century when the white "race" was in the ascendant; hence it was naturally assumed that the white race was the original, and that the Ham story was true. In the latter part of the 18th century, however, Blumenbach, a German anthropologist, improved on this theory, declaring that while it was true that the white race was the first, yet the other so-called races were in no way inherently inferior, and that the difference was due to environment. He stressed particularly, the equality of the Negro with the rest of the human race.

For the white race, Blumenbach coined the word "Caucasian," and he did it in a manner characteristic of much of what still passes for science in all matters of race. In his collection of skulls was one of a woman found on Mt. Caucasus in Georgia, Asiatic Russia. It was a shapely, handsome skull, and Blumenbach thinking it was typical of the white race dubbed it "Caucasian."

Later, this proceeding vastly amused Thomas Huxley, who ranks near to Darwin in his efforts to solve the riddle of Man. "Of all the odd myths that have arisen in the scientific world," said Huxley, "the 'Caucasian mystery' invented quite innocently by Blumenbach, is the oddest. A Georgian woman's skull was the handsomest in his collection. Hence it became his model exemplar of human skulls from which all others might be regarded as deviations; and out of this by some strange intellectual hocus-pocus grew up the notion that the Caucasian man is the proto-typic 'Adamic' man and his country the primitive centre of our kind."[1a]

Huxley, on his part, declared that there were only two "races," the ulotrician or woolly-haired, and the lissotrichian, or silky-haired. Color, features, and the rest didn't count, he said. Haddon agreed with him but named a third, the frizzly-haired. Others have named as many as sixty-three races.

And there you are. When you enter the field of anthropology, you are right back in the intellectual bogs of the Middle Ages when learned theologians used to argue where Cain got his wife; or how many angels could dance on the point of a needle; or if Christ was the Son of God how could he be as old as God. In time the theologian came to be regarded as a symbol of boredom and asininity. The word, ethnologist, is rapidly drifting into the same category.

1a Man's Place in Nature. Essay IV, p. 245. London

The so-called races do have points of physical difference, but so also do all the individuals of which these races are composed. Nevertheless, certain professors and doctors of philosophy under the influence of capitalism and also to satisfy their own egos insisted that there were hard and fast and even air-tight divisions. Fair-skinned humanity was then encroaching on the lands of dark-skinned ones and the capitalists had to have some theory to quiet the conscientious victims of their own race and also to keep their own status right with God. Moreover, the colleges were maintained by the richer whites who looked down on the poorer whites. From looking down on poor whites to looking down on darker peoples is but a step.

Color discrimination began thus. Tobacco and cotton were needed in Virginia for sale to Europe. Tobacco was at one time currency in Virginia. White serfs were growing it. These were not succeeding very well. Black men were then imported. They proved capable and willing workers. The doctrine of upper class white superiority over lower-class whites which had been operating alone for thousands of years suddenly moved then into larger quarters so to speak, and took in the Negro, putting him in the lowest rank because of his difference in color. Had the Negro been an incompetent and an unwilling worker, like the Indian, he would never have got the very bad name he did. It was his very assimilability, his capacity for progress that caused the slave-holders to invent the doctrine of inferiority in order to keep him down. Fifty-one years after the Negro's arrival in Virginia, a law was passed to prevent his buying white people. Louisiana passed such a law as late as 1818.

Nevertheless, truth is at its best when tossed among error, ridicule, and ignorance. It always emerges stronger. Out of the clashings of sense and nonsense uttered by the divines and the scholars, the truth has emerged so strongly, so triumphantly, that the man who denies it today is regarded as a freak. This is that Man has a common ancestor; that the points of physical difference between so-called races are almost as nothing when compared with their points of resemblance; that such differences are almost wholly external; in short, that if one were to take the proudest scion of a so-called superior race and the most benighted member of a New Guinea tribe and put them both on an operating table one would find brains, heart, lungs, veins, and other organs in both and so precisely in the same place that even a blind surgeon would know where to find them.

As was said, both Science and the Bible agree on a common origin for mankind. They also agree, by inference, that man originated in the tropics, that is, in an environment where food and shelter were most easily obtainable. The supposed Garden of Eden has been fixed either in India or Persia. In Southern India the tourist will be shown "the graves of Cain and Abel"

IVa. Left: Reconstruction of the Rhodesian Man with the original skull. Lived probably hundreds of thousands of years ago, and was, perhaps, the ancestor of the Grimaldi race of Europe and Africa.

The skull was found at Broken Hill, Rhodesia, almost in the heart of Africa with 160 feet of earth packed above it. The teeth were filed like that of certain Ethiopians today.

Rhodesian Man is supposed to represent a low degree of culture, but there is no proof that he was lacking in intelligence, or that he was less intelligent than millions of Americans and Europeans today.

Centre: Cro-Magnon, or Aurignacian Man, with original skull found in Southern France. Like the Grimaldi, he was probably a descendant of Rhodesian Man. This type is nearer the Caucasian than either the Rhodesian or the Grimaldi. (Vienna Natural History Museum.)

Right: Grimaldi skulls from Paris Museum of Anthropology. For reconstructions see page 27.

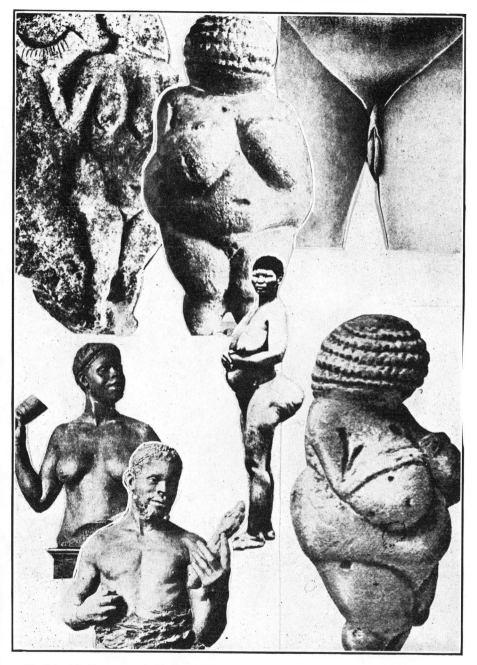

V. Grimaldi Negroes and Modern Bushwomen-Hottentots. See Notes on the illustrations.

and in Ceylon the "foot-print of Adam" on Adam's Peak. The Jews, in writing their account of Man's origin, copied it from the ancient East Indian legend of Hadama and Hava (Adam and Eve). Herodotus, of 447 B.C., said very clearly that the people of all that region of Mesopotamia and India were black. He called them Ethiopians. Moreover, tropical man is never white. He is most often black or dark brown, with flat nose, frizzly or woolly hair, and protruding jaws. Thus when the Christians chose Adam as their ancestor, they really chose a dark-skinned progenitor for the human race, even though the early Christians of Europe knowing no better represented Adam in their paintings as white.

At this point a grain of truth emerges through the mists of untold centuries, as if by a miracle. Most of the ancient skulls so far discovered are Negroid. As a result of this the reconstructions of primitive man in the modern museums are no longer the glorified white man as in the drawings of Michael Angelo and Doré but a dark-skinned, frizzly-haired, heavy-jawed creature, near to the lower animals. Instead of having fallen, Man has been rising. Perhaps the truest reconstructions of primitive man are those in the Field Museum of Chicago.

Increasingly it is being said in the most informed scientific circles that the Negro was the ancestor of the human race. Henry Fairfield Osborn, late head of the American Museum of Natural History, who had himself, a strong tinge of white fanaticism, said, "Negroid stock is even more ancient than Caucasian or Mongolian man."[2] Griffith Taylor says, "A major principle of ecology tells us that the Negrito was therefore the earliest to develop of the five races."[3] Professor W. K. Gregory, in the illustrated frontispiece of his book, "Our Face From Fish To Man," gives the Tasmanian Negro as the first man. Rene Verneau, head of the Paleontological Institute of Paris, says, "Recent discoveries seem to indicate that the Negro element preceded the White and the Yellow everywhere."[4] Griffith Taylor adds in support that the Negritos, or little Negroes, were the first in Europe, after the Neanderthal, a near-human Negroid type, and that the Negritos "introduced" their culture "all over the world." The original color of primitive man was "black," he says.

These earliest known human beings, of whom we have fairly abundant evidence from their skeletons and their art on all the continents, might have lived anywhere from 600,000 to 8,000 B.C. They were of small stature,

[2] Man Rises to Parnassus, p. 201. Princeton, N. J., 1928. Men of the Old Stone Age, pp. 262, 278-79. 1918.
[3] Environment and Race, p. 230. London, 1927. Environment and Nation, p. 87 Chicago, 1936.
[4] Huxley Memorial Lecture for 1924, p. 20.

probably from four and a half to five feet tall. Their nearest living descendants are believed to be the Bushmen of South Africa; the Mincopies of the Andaman Islands off the coast of India; the hill-folk of Southern India; the Tapiro of New Guinea; and the Negritos of the Philippines. Others more or less remote—are the Southern Japanese; certain Indian tribes of northern South America; and the Laplanders of Northern Europe.

The current scientific theory is that the white man is a dark-skinned man bleached out after living for untold centuries in foggy, snowy climes. We shall examine that a little more closely later, pointing out in the meantime, that the present scientific theory on man's color was enunciated by the Ethiopians long before Moses, or whoever it was, wrote Genesis.

Diodorus Siculus of the First Century B.C.. the first world historian, says, "The Ethiopians say they were the first men that ever were in the world and that to prove this they have clear demonstrations. For they say they are natives of the country and not strangers that came to settle there... It is most probable that those who inhabit the south were the first living men that sprang out of the earth. For being that the heat of the sun at first exhaled the moisture of the earth and in the first production of all things. influenced it with a quickening virtue, they say, it is rational to conclude that those places nearest the sun should have been the first parents of all living creatures." (Book III, Chap. I.)

Origin of the White Race

"There is no such thing as a white race, much as this is talked of," said Schopenhauer, "but every white man is a faded or bleached one."

Von Luschan, late of the University of Berlin, said, "We now know that color of skin and hair are only the effect of environment and that we are fair only because our ancestors lived for thousands, or probably tens of thousands of years, in sunless and foggy countries. Fairness is nothing else than lack of pigment and our ancestors lost part of theirs because they did not need it."[5]

Brinton says as regards this theory, "The most completely white communities are found among the Slavonic populations of Southern and Central Russia. Their hair is colorless and their complexion so near a 'dead white' that one anthropologist (Theodor Posche) has selected the vast Roketno swamps as the original home of the white race which he thinks arose by endemic albinism."[5a]

Sergi, of the University of Rome, denied that there was a European race. European man, he said, was African man, changed by the effects of European

[5] In G. Spiller, Papers on Interracial Problems, p. 14. London, 1911.
[5a] Races and Peoples, p. 43.

environment. The correct term, he says, is "Eur-African," which species, he says, "falls into three varieties: The African with red, brown, and black pigmentation; the Mediterranean or brunet complexion, inhabiting the great basin, including part of Northern Africa...and finally a Nordic variety of blond skin and hair, blue or grey eyes, most universally represented in Scandinavia, North Germany and England."[6]

Professor Dorsey said, "Biologically speaking, the white skins of Europe have lost something. When and where they lost their pigment, and why they lost more than the Asiatics we may never know."[7]

There are, of course, objections to the full acceptance of this theory. The Eskimos, for instance. They have lived for a long time in the far North and are not white. This we shall discuss later. In the meantime it may be said that the following broad truth holds good: Fair-skinned humanity lives to the north and dark-skinned one to the south. Blonds predominate in Scandinavia; brunets in Southern Italy and Spain.

Were the Negroes Always Black?

Herodotus said of the Ethiopians, "Now it is certain that the natives of the country are black with the heat." Similarly, Theodectes, an ancient Greek writer, in explanation of the color and the hair of the Ethiopians, said,

> "Near these approaching with his radiant car
> The sun their skins with dusky tint doth dye
> And sooty hue; and with unvarying forms of fire
> Crisps their tufted locks."

Grecian mythology says that when Phaeton attempted to drive the chariot of the sun, he swung too near parts of the south with it, scorching the faces of the people there like bread in an over-heated oven. At the same time, he swung too far away from the north, bleaching the faces of the inhabitants. Shakespeare called the color of the Prince of Morocco, "The shadowed livery of the burnished sun." In other words, the very black people of the Congo and New Guinea have experienced a natural process, the reverse of that of the blonds of Scandinavia. "Kinky" hair probably is due to the same cause. The pepper-corn hair of the Bushman might have once been like the hair of the Fuzzy-Wuzzy of the Sudan. The sparse grains of hair on a Bushman's scalp reminds one strikingly of the sparse growth of vegetation on the American deserts. Generally speaking, the hairiest men, like the hairiest animals, live in cold countries.

[6] The Mediterranean Race, p. 259. N.Y., 1901.
[7] Why We Behave Like Human Beings, p. 45. N. Y., 1925.

The very black man, like the corn-silk blond, therefore, seems to be an extreme type caused from too long living in one environment and with little or no race-mixture. As Professor Dorsey says, "Pure types are extreme types. Blue eyes, flaxen hair, white skin is an extreme type. The huge African with kinky hair, black skin, thick lips, high, smooth brow, hairless body is equally extreme. One is as pure as the other; one is as high as the other."

Was There a Mulatto Race in Europe 30,000 to 50,000 Years Ago?

The theory that the oldest human beings were what in America would be called Negroes is supported by the fact that the oldest known entire human skeletons so far discovered are Negroid, as the Grimaldis of Europe, whose skeletons may be seen in the Paris Museum of Anthropology and the Museum of Monaco, and whose relics may be found from Italy to Russia and as far north as Britain and Scandinavia.

Where did the Grimaldi come from? By many they are considered an African people, and they do show evidences of African ancestry in their physique and their culture. The Grimaldi women, like the Hottentots of South Africa, had huge humps of fat on their buttocks, which were supposed to be a storage of reserve food as are the humps on a camel. Their breasts were also very large and the nymphs, or inner lips of the genitals, so elongated that they seem hardly human. This trait is most apparent in the Venus of Willendorf, a Grimaldi woman, and the most ancient sculpture of the human form yet discovered.

Professor Pittard, speaking of the similarity between these very ancient Negroes and some of the present ones, says, "The Hottentots have what the scientists call 'pepper-corn' hair; the Willendorf Venus has both steatopygy and pepper-corn hair, which are two characteristics peculiar to the Hottentot. The Aurignacian sculptors could not have invented a type provided with these two characteristics... Each day Africa appears, more than ever, as having possessed the whole of our paleolithic and neolithic civilization. Everywhere over the continent, the archaeological finds which have furnished to the pre-historian a comparatively abundant material, multiply. The ancient and middle pleistocene era of Africa had, as in Europe, Chellean, Achellean and Mousterian stone implements."[8]

Professor Hooton says also, "It is interesting to note that the clearest cases of steatopygia occur in the representatives of females from the Aurig-

[8] Les Races et L'Histoire, pp. 81-89. Paris, 1924.

nacian period of the European cave-cultures and among the modern Bushmen-Hottentots."[9]

It also engages the attention of Sir Arthur Evans, who says: "This steatopygous family which in other parts of the Mediterranean basin ranges from prehistoric Egypt and Malta to the north of the mainland of Greece, calls up suggestive reminiscences of the similar images of Aurignacian man."[10]

The Negritos, or pigmies, as was said, are the first known human type. The Grimaldis, who were taller, invaded Europe and mingled with them. Probably the two continued to live side by side for centuries as their modern representatives, the Bushmen and the Hottentot, were doing in South Africa when the white men invaded their lands in the 16th century, A.D. Verneau attributed the small size of the people in certain parts of France to ancient Negrito ancestry. "Among the present day Europeans certain types crop up occasionally which strongly remind us of the African pigmy," says Hertz.[11] Professor Roland B. Dixon said that the Negrito type persisted in Southern Russia until the Middle Ages.[12] There are abundant traditions of pigmy inhabitants in the rest of Europe, including the British Isles. The latter are believed to have migrated there from Spain. A small pigmy-like race was discovered at Gerona, Spain, as late as 1898. Professor Dixon thought that the Negritos developed into the European Alpine stock.

There was once an "uninterrupted belt" of Negro culture from Central Europe to South Africa. "These people," says Griffith Taylor, "must have been quite abundant in Europe towards the close of the Paleolithic Age. Boule quotes their skeletons from Brittany, Switzerland, Liguria, Lombardy, Illyria, and Bulgaria. They are universal through Africa and through Melanesia, while the Botocudos and the Lagoa Santa skulls of East Brazil show where similar folk penetrated to the New World." Massey says: "The one sole race that can be traced among the aborigines all over the earth or below it is the dark race of a dwarf, Negrito type."[13]

What Became of the Ancient European Negro?

As regards these Negroes, Theal says, "What became of the Negroid inhabitants of Europe no one can say. They were there before the Great Ice Age and then they disappeared."[14] Might not the answer be that they disappeared through amalgamation, a very common occurrence? In Europe, during this period, there also lived another race taller and with Caucasian

9 Harvard-African Studies II: Varia Africana II, pp. 93-4. Cambridge, 1918.
10 Proceed. Brit. Ass'n for the Advanc. of Science, 1916, p. 19.
11 Race and Civilization, pp. 100-01. N. Y., 1928.
12 Racial History of Man, p. 478. N. Y., 1923.
13 Ancient Egypt, pp. 230, 251. London, 1907.
14 Theal, G. M. Ethnog. and Condition of S. Africa before 1505, pp. 9-17. London, 1919.

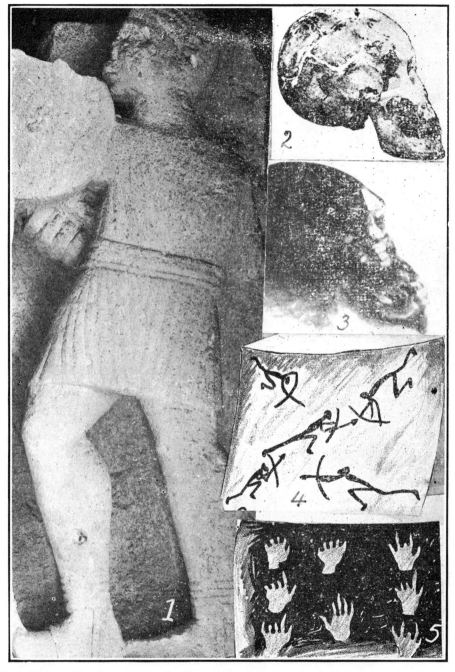

VI. 1. Negro soldier from Ancient Spain; 2. Negro skull from Ancient Portugal; 3. X-Ray of skull
of living West Indian Negro; 4. Prehistoric Battle-scene, Spanish cavern;
5. Prehistoric Bushmen finger-prints.

features, known as the Cro-Magnon. Is it not possible that Grimaldi and Cro-Magnon amalgamated to form a different type? Giuffrida-Ruggeri, leading authority on the origin of the Mediterranean race, evidently thinks so. He speaks of a "strongly hybrid population which must have been derived from the crossing of Cro-Magnon man with the Combe-Capelle and the Grimaldi Negroids."[15]

Professor Osborn after naming five races which were believed to have occupied Western Europe in the Old Stone Age, says, "We must, therefore, imagine Western Europe in Upper Paleolitic times again as a terminal region, a great peninsula towards which the human migrants from the east and from the south came to mingle and super-pose their cultures."

Sir Arthur Evans, excavator of the ruins of Crete, and once president of the British Association for the Advancement of Science, says similarly of this period, "One should never lose sight of the fact that from the earliest Aurignacian periods onwards a Negroid element in the broadest sense of the term shared in this artistic culture as seen on both sides of the Pyrenees."[16]

Sir Harry Johnston also thinks that there was a mulatto strain in the Europeans of this prehistoric period. He says, "Recent discoveries made in the vicinity of the principality of Monaco and others in Italy and Western France...all of them analysed in monograph on the skulls found in the grottoes of Grimaldi, edited by Dr. Verneau of Paris, and published in 1909 by the Prince of Monaco...would seem to reveal even if some of their deductions are discounted erroneous, the actual fact that many thousands of years ago a Negroid race had penetrated into Italy through France, leaving traces at the present day in the physiognomy of the peoples of Southern Italy, Sicily, Sardinia, Southern and Western France, and even in the western parts of the United Kingdom of Great Britain and Ireland. There are even at the present day some examples of Keltiberian peoples of Western Scotland, Southern and Western Wales, Southern and Western Ireland of distinctly Negroid aspect and in whose ancestry there is no indication whatever of any connection with the West Indies or with modern Africa. Still more marked is this feature in the peoples of Southern and Western France, and of other parts of the Mediterranean already mentioned."[17]

But it may be asked where did the whites come from to amalgamate with the blacks? The answer is: Might not a Negrito people have been bleached out into a white or nearly white race after having lived for hundreds of thousands of years in Europe, and then their lands be invaded by a dark-skinned race—the Grimaldi—from the south, that is, Africa? The Paleolithic Age, that is, the period of the earliest human races, which is estimated to have lasted from 500,000 to 1,500,000 years, would give plenty of time for any change in physical appearance. The dark-skinned man, having

[15] Man, Vol. VI. No. 107. Dec., 1921.
[16] Evans. Ibid., p. 15.
[17] World Position of the Negro, etc., in G. Spiller. Ibid., p. 330. London, 1911.

VII. AN IMMORTAL SPECIMEN OF NEGRO ART

The Illustrated London News says: "A masterpiece of Prehistoric Art." "An outstanding Monument in the History of Sculpture — The World-Famous South African Bas-Relief of a White Rhinoceros with a Swarm of Tick-Birds, Hammered Into a Slab of Basaltic Rock, More Probably 50,000 than 25,000 Years Ago By a Sculptor of the Stone Age.

"By virtue of its great antiquity and superb artistic qualities, South Africa becomes the birthplace of real art. No finer page could be clipped out of Nature's grand realm than this truculent rhinoceros, endeavoring to remove some of the all too many tick-birds that seem to annoy it . . .

"How many decisive actions are blended into this unconscious thrill of alarm and speed. The head tossed high, ears cocked, lips wrinkled, tail in the air, two limbs in ambling swing and the others supporting the two-ton body weight, seem all to breathe exultant life. Unrivalled skill has added those points that make this South African petroglyph an outstanding monument in the history of sculpture. The realism of the texture of the hide and the markings of significant features by a few clear-cut lines contribute much to its fine plastic appearance . . . Even in the famous exhibitions of modern art, so unique a piece would command attention. As a foundation stone, engraved with unalterable promise of the forward march of humanity, it will always remain a priceless relic from bygone times. Considering this Stone Age man's pride in accuracy and beauty, have we progressed so much in these many thousands of years? What an achievement when the tools consisted only of sharp edges of splintered rock . . ." ...The Illustrated London News, July 14, 1928, has a double-page reproduction of this work. Later it reproduced it separately in natural colors. The actual length of the slab is 47 inches. ...(Transvaal Museum)

become white, mated with both white and black. Out of this intermingling evolved in time the present thousand and one varieties of the human race as well as the two billion individual types now alive. One fact is evident: The very black man and the very white man are extremes. The former is at one pole of human color; the latter at the other. Between the two types lie all the other varieties as the earth between its poles.

To summarize. A certain portion of the original human race, which had been changed to white by climatic conditions and a change of diet met again after untold centuries another portion of the original stock which had migrated south and made still blacker, and the two mated and produced the different "races" of mankind. Something the like has been true of plants as the rose, orange, apple, wheat; and certain animals as the horse, dog, cat, cow, whose original types were changed by interbreeding.

Of course, the above explanation of the cause of variety in the human race is largely a hypothesis. It will no doubt sound far-fetched to some. But it at least has this merit: *It is not miraculous.*

Even the most ordinary observer will note how white people in the course of a single summer at the beach get darkened and how Negroes after living in cold countries for a winter or two get lighter. It does not require much imagination to see a people becoming permanently black or permanently white after experiencing such climatic effect for hundreds of thousands of years.

Naturally the theory of descent from Negroes will be most unpalatable to many. Far rather would they hear they were descended from apes. As Ellsworth Huntington says, "It hurts the pride of the lordly Nordic to think that he has in his veins the same blood as the Negro."[18]

[18] Character of Races, p. 84. London, 1924.

Among other works consulted on this subject were:

Blumenbach, J. Anthropological Treatise. London, 1865.
Foster, T. S. Travels and Settlements of Early Man. London, 1929.
Churchward, A. Origin and Evolution of Primitive Man. London, 1912.
Sollas, W. J. Ancient Hunters. N. Y., 1924.
Quatrefages, A. The Pigmies. N. Y., 1925.
Moir, J. The Earliest Men. Huxley Memorial Lecture for 1939.
Beddoe, J. Color and Race. Huxley Memorial Lecture for 1924.
Wilder, B. Pedigree of the Human Race. N. Y., 1926.
McCurdy. Human Origins, N. Y. 1924.
Lowe, C. Van Riet. South Africa in the Stone Age. Illus. London News, p. 606. April 29, 1933.
Herve, G. Cranes Neolithique Armoricans de type Negroide. Bull. et Me. de la Soc. d'Anthrop. de Paris. June 18, 1903.
Moulton, F. R. The World and Man as Science Sees Them. 1937.
Verneau R. Les Origines de L'Humanite. Paris, 1926.
Hooton, E. Up From the Ape. N. Y., 1931.
Frobenius. Prehistoric Rock Pictures. Museum of Modern Art. N. Y., 1937.
Parkyn, E. Prehistoric Art. London, 1915.
Perry, W. J. The Megalithic Culture of Indonesia. London, 1918.
Ripley, W. Z. The Races of Europe. N. Y., 1923.
Linton, R. The Study of Man. N. Y., 1935.

Chapter Three

THE MIXING OF WHITE AND BLACK
IN THE ANCIENT EAST

THE great areas of race-mixing in the ancient world were both shores of the Mediterranean; Asia Minor and Arabia; all the territory bordering on the Persian Gulf and the Indian Ocean; the greater part of India; the Malay Peninsula; China; the islands of the Pacific, including the Philippines, Java, New Zealand, and Australia.

Egypt

The records from Ancient Egypt on the mixing of white and black are clear and unmistakable. However, the ethnologists are far from being agreed on what is a Negro. Some writers use the terms, Hamite and Semite, to describe the Egyptians, but these terms, like Aryan, have to do with language and nothing at all with race. A Hamite or a Semite might be white or coal-black just as one who speaks English or French may be of any color.

Again when a European speaks of Negro, he generally means an unmixed black man of primitive type, say the Chankalla; when an American does, he might be including some one who is even fairer than himself. For instance, John Powell, noted American pianist, who was an agitator for white Anglo-Saxon supremacy in Richmond, Virginia, in 1926, was certainly darker than many Virginians who are compelled to ride jim-crow. In fact, he is so dark that if he were to be seen alone in a Negro gathering, he would normally be taken for a "Negro."

Again, the Ethiopians, who both in color and hair, and ofttimes in features, show more of the Negro than the Aframerican, are classed by the ethnologists as white, a fact that most Ethiopians resent.

Instructions to the 1940 census-takers in America were that anyone with Negro strain, however slight, was to be set down as Negro. Someone has rightly described a Negro in America as one not light enough in color to ride in a white coach in America—except, of course, that he happens to speak a foreign language, in which case, no matter how dark, he is classed as white. In short, as was said, when one enters the field of ethnology one steps into an atmosphere of crooked thinking, where the main idea is to prove inferior and superior races. If the kind of science that is in ethnology went into engineering, no automobile would ever run, no air-ship would ever leave the ground, in fact not even a clock would run.

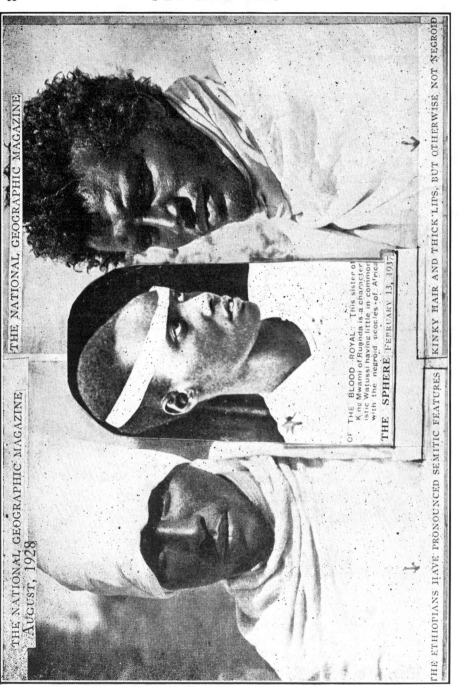

VIIa. These portraits, with their original sub-titles will help to show how capriciously the terms "Semitic" and "Not Negroid" are used. Dress these Africans in American-made clothes, and these same scientists would instantly call them Negroes.

VIII. Two Aframerican types. The average Egyptologist, will call the figure to the left Semitic; that to the right, Hamitic, and will deny there is any Negro blood in either.
(See Notes on the Illustrations.)

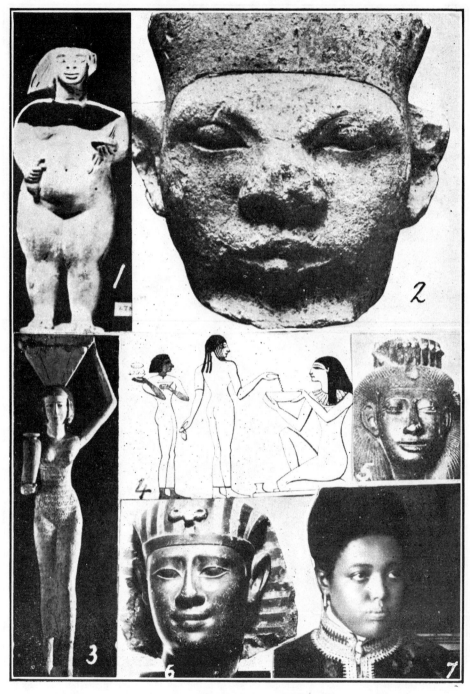

IX. 1 to 6 Ancient Egyptian portraits; 7, a modern Ethiopian woman.
(See Notes on the Illustrations).

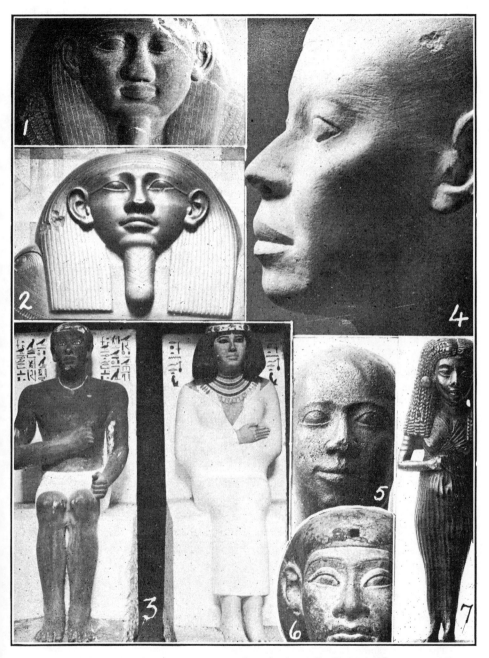

X. Ancient Egyptian Portraits. (See Notes on the Illustrations).

These are those Egyptologists who positively deny that the Negro had any part in Egyptian civilization except as a slave. Dr. Junker, for instance, denies that the Negro was the founder of the earliest Egyptian civilization. In the back of Junker's mind was the conventional picture of the Negro-blubber lips, ape-like face, lark heel, "pepper-corn hair between which the scalp is visible," "thinness of calves" and "long, narrow skull." He says he was able to find none of these characteristics in the graves of the oldest period accessible to us, *i.e.*, roughly from 5,000 to 3,600 B.C."[1] The Ethiopians, or Nubians, who were described by Herodotus, Diodorus Siculus, Ammianus and others as black and woolly-haired, were Hamites, he declares.

It is no wonder that he didn't find any of that type, however, because the kind of Negro created by the right-wing ethnologists is a rarity. It is no more characteristic of the race than the ape-like creature of the bogs that was once used to represent the Irish was true of all Irishmen. Winwood Reade said, "The typical Negro is a rare variety even among Negroes." Frobenius says also, "Open an illustrated geography and compare 'The Type of the African Negro,' the bluish-black fellow of the protuberant lips, the flattened nose, the stupid expression, and the short curly hair with the tall, bronze figures from Dark Africa with which we have of late become familiar, their almost fine-cut features, slightly arched nose, long hair... In other respects, too, the genuine African of the interior bears no resemblance to the accepted Negro type."[2]

Livingstone said that the Negro face as he saw it reminded him more of that on the monuments of ancient Assyria than that of the popular white fancy.[3] Sir Harry Johnston, foremost authority on the African Negro, said that "the Hamite, that Negroid stock which was the main stock of the ancient Egyptians, is best represented at the present day by the Somali, Galla, and the blood of Abyssinia and Nubia."[4] Sergi compares pictorially the features of Ramases II with that of Mtesa, noted Negro king of Uganda, and shows the marked resemblance.[5] Sir M. W. Flinders Petrie, famed Egyptologist, says that the Pharaohs of the X dynasty were of the Galla type, and the Gallas are clearly what are known in our day as Negroes. He tells further of seeing one day on a train a man whose features were "the exact living type" of a statue of ancient Libya, and discovered that the man was an American mulatto.[6]

[1] First Appearance of Negroes in History. Jour. Egyptian Archaeol. Vol. VII, pp 121-32. (1921).
[2] Frobenius. Report. Smithsonian Institution. 1898. p. 637.
[3] The Zambesi and Its Tributaries, p. 526. N. Y., 1866.
[4] The Uganda Protectorate, Vol. II, p. 472. London, 1902.
[5] The Mediterranean Races, p. 243. N. Y., 1901.
[6] Royal Soc. of Arts Jour., Vol. XLIX, p. 594. 1901.

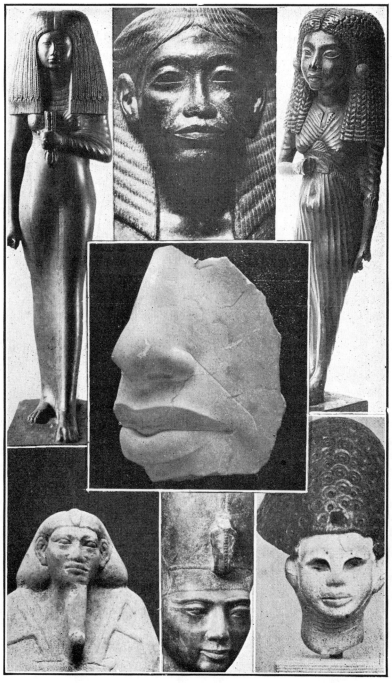

XI. Portraits from ancient Egypt. (Center) Fragment of face of Queen Nefertiti. (See Notes on the Illustrations)

Similarly I met in Harlem a Negro woman of unmixed ancestry, who resembled strongly Amenophis III, the great Egyptian conqueror. I also saw another girl with a face so distinctly like that of Amenophis IV (Akhenaton) that she could have been used as a model for him. The Princess Tsahi, daughter of Haile Selassie, when I saw her in 1930—she was then thirteen, bore a most striking resemblance to one of the daughters of Akhenaton, and the Negro ancestry of the Princess is evident. The Negro features have not changed in hundreds of thousands of years. I once saw in Harlem a very tiny, jet-black woman with an age-old face, who looked so much like one of the gods of Ancient Mexico unearthed by Desiré Charny that she might have stepped off an ancient Mexican monument.

Herodotus, who visited Egypt about 447 B.C., is most precise about the Negro strain in the ancient Egyptian. Speaking of the Colchians who lived in the vicinity of the Black Sea, he said, "There can be no doubt that the Colchians are an Egyptian race... My own conjectures were founded first in the fact that they are black-skinned and have woolly hair, which certainly amounts to but little since several other nations are so too, but further and more especially on the circumstance that the Colchians, the Egyptians, and the Ethiopians are the only nations who have practised circumcision from the earliest time."[7]

Speaking also of the Dodonean oracle in Greece he says: "Lastly by calling the dove black the Dodonae indicated that the woman was an Egyptian."

Match this statement of an eye-witness with that of certain Egyptologists who have come on the scene 2,400 years later and must rely on measuring skulls and leg-bones from the graves, after which they compare these measurements with certain standards fixed by members of their own school, who have determined what a Negro ought to look like. Much bitter argument has waged over what was the race of the ancient Egyptians. The exploiters of Negro labor and the Negrophobes are strongly opposed to the statement that the creators of the marvelous civilization of Egypt could have been Negroes. They were Caucasians, they declare. However, the scholars who have been claiming all these black, woolly-haired people as white, have now lost out to Hitler. The Egyptians, announces the great dictator, were Aryans, that is, Germans.

One who is writing a serious book really feels like apologizing for introducing discussions of this sort, but few laymen have any idea of the amount of nonsense uttered by some of these scientists. For instance, when the Nordic theory was at its height some years ago, the late Henry Fairfield Osborn, head of the American Museum of Natural History, announced quite

[7] Herodotus. Book II, Chap. 104.

XII. 1. Dagon, Fish God of the Philistines; 2. Phoenician deity; 3. Akhenaton, Egyptian Pharaoh and the first Messiah; 4. Egyptian deity; 5. Osiris, the Christ of the Ancient Egyptians.

seriously that all the world's greatest men had been of the blond type, for which he was well trounced by the press.

Sir Harry Johnston comes nearest to a definition of this elusive subject. He says that by Negro and Negroid must be understood "any human race, nationality, or people sufficiently tinged with Negro blood to display the Negroid characteristics of a dark skin and spirally coiled hair." To this must be added the most important sign: length of distance between nose and mouth, and, to some extent, fullness and wideness of the latter as well as the facial angle. Our sign for recognizing the race of the Egyptians will be their portraits.

The Most Ancient Egyptians Were Negritos

Flinders Petrie begins the history of Egypt with the Bushmen or Negritos of before 8,000 B.C.[8] Abundant evidence of their presence has been unearthed. The Ethiopians also claimed, according to Diodorus Siculus, historian of the First century B.C., that they were the founders of Egyptian civilization. He says, "The Ethiopians likewise say that the Egyptians are a colony drawn from them," and that "Egypt was made out of the mud and slime of Ethiopia," meaning the rich silt brought down by the Nile. They further declared, according to this ancient writer, that the Egyptians got their laws, their customs, their burial rites, their statutes, and their system of writing from Ethiopia. Furthermore that the gods were of Ethiopian ancestry and recognized it by the high esteem in which they held the Ethiopians, and their annual return to Ethiopia for sacrifice and feasting. Egyptian history and modern excavations support these assertions.

Egyptian civilization, from its beginning to the Christian era, lasted for more than seven thousand years, that is, about four times as long as from "the birth of Christ" to the present, therefore, most of the records have been lost, and the little that remains must be pieced together. There are often great gaps. Between the Bushman period of 9000 B.C. and the First Dynasty (4477-4514 B.C.) very little is known. Some of the faces of the rulers of this dynasty are clearly Negroid. The founder of the Third Dynasty, Sa-nekht, was a full-blooded Negro, a type commonly seen in the Egyptian army today. Petrie says of him, "It will be seen how strongly Ethiopian the characters of it (the portrait) is. even more so than Shabaka, most marked of the Ethiopian dynasty. The type is one with which we are very familiar among the Sudanese of the Egyptian police and army; it goes with a dark-brown skin and a very truculent character. From the sculpture then it may be inferred that we are dealing with the declining civilization of the

---

[8] Migrations. Huxley Memorial Lecture for 1906, p. 16.

NETEK-AMEN, Nubian Pharaoh, of about 30 B.C. (Lepsius)

NEB-MAAT-RA, a mighty ruler, and builder of the 17th Pyramid (Lepsius)

RA-MER-KA AMEN-TARIT, Nubian Pharaoh of about 100 B.C. (Lepsius)

PTOLEMY XIII (Neus Dionysius), father of Cleopatra, the most beautiful woman of antiquity. This ruler who was black called himself "The New Osiris." Note his African mouth and those of the other Pharaohs also. (Lepsius)

Second Dynasty which was overthrown by an Ethiopian invasion and the great art of the Fourth and Fifth Dynasties arose out of this mixture."[9]

The Ethiopians also declared, according to Diodorus Siculus, that they were the first to give religion to the world. Archaeological research in Egypt has borne them out amply. The earliest Egyptian gods were Negritos, or the little Negroes, mentioned in Chapter II. Ptah, "the Great, the Mighty, the Source and the Head of all the Gods of Egypt—the oldest being that the priests of Memphis could imagine"—was a Negrito. Sir E. A. W. Budge, gives a list of the Egyptian gods that originated in the Sudan, the land of the Negroes, and says there is "little doubt that the great god of Memphis, Ptah, was originally a great handicraftsman and worker in metals who was deified."[10] It was the Negroes from the South who introduced the use of iron into Ancient Egypt. Prehistoric iron furnaces discovered in Northern Rhodesia, almost in the heart of Africa, by Nino del Grande,[11] show that the Negro knew the use of iron untold centuries before the European. Archaeologists generally agree that it was the Negro who first discovered the secret of iron.

Another important Egyptian deity was Bes, the original Tom Thumb. He was the god of laughter, happiness, mischief and war. Paul Marceaux says of him, "He is not the caricature of an Egyptian, or of a Cushite of Ethiopia, nor is he from Arabia. He was a Negro."[12] Budge says, "His pygmy form and his head-dress prove that he was of Sudani origin. There is no doubt that his cult was very ancient... He appears as a dancer, a musician, he played the lyre and the harp and probably acted as tribal singer; as a soldier he wears a short military tunic with belt and he holds a short sword in his right hand and a shield in his left. He symbolized the jolly, good-natured, happy-go-lucky Sudani man who loved and still loves good eating and good drinking and pleasure, jollity and feasting and amusement of every kind and was equally ready to make love and to go fight his enemies."

Professor Breasted, famous Egyptologist, also maintains that the Ethiopians were the first to give religious thought and aspiration to the world. Speaking of the so-called Memphite Drama which is known only through a copy of it on a slab made by order of Sabacon, Ethiopian ruler of Egypt, about 700 B.C., he says, "This pious Ethiopian King of Egypt was interested in preserving an ancient writing of his ancestors.

"The document (the original) is enormously old. We have mirrored in it the oldest thoughts of men that anywhere have come down to us in written

9 Researches in Sinai, pp. 43-4. London, 1906.
10 From Fetish to God in Ancient Egypt, pp. 253-55. London, 1934.
11 Natural History Maga, Sept. to Oct., 1932. pp. 531-39.
12 Revue Hist. t. 47, pp. 1-64 1891.

form."[13]   And here again we find archaeology supporting history in the Ethiopian's favor.   Diodorus Siculus said of this king, "Sabacon, an Ethiopian, came to the throne, going beyond all his predecessors in worship of the gods and in kindness to his subjects."

Coming to the Fourth Dynasty and the building of the Great Pyramid (about 2900 B.C.), we find a Negro on the throne and Negro members of

The serene and beautiful QUEEN NEFERTITI, beloved wife of
Akhenaton (Berlin Museum)

the royal family.   In the Boston Museum are busts of a prince and princess of this family, the latter seemingly of "pure" Negro type.

Beardsley says of these: "There have recently come to the Boston Museum two excellent portraits of an Egyptian and Ethiopian prince and princess dating about 3000 B.C.   Dr. Reisner calls these 'the earliest known portraits of Negroes.' "[14]

[13] The Dawn of Conscience, pp. 30-31. N. Y., 1933.
[14] The Negro in Greek and Roman Civilization, p. 12. Baltimore, 1929.

When Did the Whites First Reach Egypt and From Where?

There is no definite proof of the coming of the first whites to Egypt, or of when race-mixing began. We do know that they came in large numbers, as conquerors, under Alexander the Great, but that was thousands of years after the founding of Egypt by the Negritos. The Nordics very likely first came in as slaves and captives. In 1500 B.C., a horde of white-skinned barbarians landed in the Delta and were promptly made prisoners.

At that time the Nordics were on a social scale comparable with that of the lowest New Guinea native today. Julius Caesar and Tacitus have given us a most precise description of what they were as late as the beginning of the Christian era and St. Jerome as late as the Fourth Century, A.D.

For centuries even after Caesar wrote, London, Paris, Berlin were wildernesses with not the faintest glimmer of what they were to be. As Professor Breasted says:

"On the borders of this earliest civilised world of Egypt and Western Asia lay for some two thousand years the wilderness of savage Europe stretching far westward to the Atlantic, untouched by civilisation, except at its south-eastern corner, where the Greek islands looked south-eastward to the mouths of the Nile and eastward toward Hittite Asia Minor.[15]

"How low the savage European must have looked to the Nile Valley African looking north from his pyramid of Cheops?" says Professor Dorsey. Morris also reminds us that, "Were the white an inherently superior race we should not have found it, at the beginning of authentic history almost lost in the sea of under-life, but its superior qualities would have told at a far remote epoch; the Negro and the Mongolian expansion would have been checked long before, and history opened up with the Caucasian as the dominant element."

Joseph McCabe says, "Primitive man, let us remember, was a colored man, a dusky person . . . Four thousand years ago, when civilization was already one or two thousand years old, white men were just a bunch of semi-savages on the outskirts of the civilized world. If there had been anthropologists in Crete, Egypt, and Babylonia, they would have pronounced the white race obviously inferior, and might have discoursed learnedly on the superior germ-plasm or glands of colored folk."[15a]

But the Nordics, wherever they came from, must have reached Egypt at a very early date as we see their faces, or what look like them, on the monuments of the early dynasties. Mixing between black and white might have begun even before the Fifth Dynasty. Petrie, speaking of the ruling race, says, "There is a coarse type of mulatto appearance; and it is certain that there is much Negro blood in the oldest Egyptians. We have one element of the mulatto in evidence... The Negroes were most likely to have

[15] American Hist. Review. Jan., 1929, p. 219.
[15a] Key to Culture. Book III, p. 26. Girard, Kas. 1927.

SETI THE GREAT, conqueror of Cush and Assyria and a famous builder, as Amen, the most powerful of the Egyptian gods. (Louvre)

NECTANEBO I., statesman and military leader. Opposer of the Assyrian Invaders. 383 B.C. (Turin Museum)

THOTMES III., (1600 B.C.), the Napoleon of far antiquity. Conquered the then known world. Was wise administrator and merciful ruler. (British Museum)

Pharaoh of the 12th Dynasty (Louvre)

mixed with the fair races which bounded on the north..."¹⁶

As the population increased and as more strangers arrived there came to
be four "races" in Egypt, namely, the Rot, or native Egyptian, who is
depicted on the monuments as a reddish-brown mulatto, as Ra-hotep, and
his white wife, Princess Nefert; next was the Nehusi, Nehsi, or Nahsi,
or unmixed black from Nubia; then, the Namu, or Asiatic, a yellow-skinned
race with so-called Semitic features; and last, and least for some time to come,
the Temehou, or Nordic.¹⁷

As for the secondary position of the Nehusi, or blacks, it seems that
as the Egyptians progressed they tended more and more to disassociate themselves from their ancestors to the south, and even to look down upon them
much as the city-dweller is inclined to look down on his people in the rural
districts, or as the Northern Negro on the Southern one in the United States.
We shall find much of this attitude towards the blacks from the interior in
the Mohammedan era.   It was not a question of color but of culture as some
of the native Egyptians were as black as the Nehesu. "They (the Negroes),"
says Weisgerber, "were not considered an inferior race by the ancients since
we see them, on the contrary, figuring in the tablets of Seti I, in the third
rank before the Europeans... One can truthfully say that the Negroes
mixed freely with the Egyptians, either as mercenaries, slaves, or otherwise.
They were not considered an inferior race since several of their queens were
Negroes... On the tomb of Seti the Negroes were better considered than
the whites since we see the whites figuring in the last rank."¹⁸ Seti, himself,
seems to have been a full-blooded Negro.   Rawlinson says, "Seti's face is
thoroughly African, strong, fierce, prognathous, with depressed nose, thick
lips and a heavy chin..."¹⁹   Seti's mummy is coal-black.

Certain of these blacks from the interior reached the highest seats of
power.   Most of the Egyptian soldiery, then, as now, were full-blooded
Negroes.   The Egyptian word for soldier, Matoi, came from an African
tribe of that name probably the present day, Masai.   The god, Horus, includes
them, as equals with the others in one of his pronouncements. "I have been
content," he said, "with the millions who have come forth from me in your
name of Neshesu." A Nehesu figures as the third person of importance in
the realm under Queen Hatshepsut.   He was the commander of the expedition to Punt and is mentioned on the walls of the temple of Deir al-Bahri as
"Chief Treasurer," "Prince Chancellor" and "First Friend."²⁰   Still another
Nehusi ruled Egypt as far south as the Delta.   Petrie thinks he was a "Sudani

¹⁶ Religion and Conscience in Ancient Egypt, pp. 26-27. N. Y., 1898.
¹⁷ Pittard E. Les Races et L'Histoire, p. 508. Paris, 1024. (It is customary to name
the full-blooded Negro as the last of the four. But he came before both the Asiatic and
the Nordic as Prof. Pittard says.)
¹⁸ Les Blancs de l'Afrique, pp. 205-07, 217-18. Paris, 1910.
¹⁹ Rawlinson, G. The Story of Egypt, p. 252. London. 1887.
²⁰ Davis, T. Tomb of Hatshopsitu. p. 29. London, 1906.
  Breasted. Earliest Records of Egypt. Vol. II, p. 119.

A daughter of Akhenaton, and a sister of
Tut-Ankh-Amen (Cairo Museum)

The QUEEN TIYI, mother of Akhenaton
(Berlin Museum)

AMENOPHIS III, father of Akhenaton and a
mighty conqueror (Berlin Museum)

An Egyptian Princess of the 18th Dynasty
(Berlin Museum)

slave or soldier raised to power," while Budge thinks that he was "entitled by law thereto" as he calls himself "royal son, first-born Nehsi."

Race-mixing went on unrestricted in Ancient Egypt until the population became a thoroughly mixed one. The faces of the Pharaohs throughout the successive dynasties showed all types from the Ethiopian of the south who was described by Herodotus and Diodorus Siculus as the "darkest-skinned and most woolly-haired of mortals" to the fair-haired Nordic. Some of the dynasties had a greater percentage of blacks and mulattoes, while others had more of whites.

In the harems of the Pharaohs were women of all colors and races, and it seemed that the white women did not attain the status of the black ones for some time. Rawlinson and Wilkinson say: "Amenophis I is frequently represented with a black queen, Ames-nofri-are, who appears to have been the wife of Ames, and one of the holy women devoted to the service of the god of Thebes.

"...Indeed, it is the marriage of Ames with her which is thought to have united the two families of the 15th and 18th Dynasties. There was also another queen, called Aahatop, a white woman, and an Egyptian, who is represented with the black Ames-nofri-are on the same monuments at Thebes and in the British Museum, but in an inferior position, and this is readily explained by the greater importance of the Ethiopian princess."[21]

The Eighteenth Dynasty was of almost unmixed Negro strain, in fact, its two principal representatives, Amenophis III and his son, Akhenaton, seemed to have had no "white" blood. J. A. Wilkinson says of Amenophis III, "The features of this monarch cannot fail to strike every one who examines the portraits of Egyptian kings as having more in common with the Negro than those of any other Pharaoh."[22] Akhenaton, his son, is still more Negroid, however.

As regards the race-mixing that went on during this dynasty, Birch says, "At the Eighteenth Dynasty the Negress mounts the throne and as will be subsequently seen intermarried with sovereigns whose features as beheld in the sculptures recall their mixed origin... Aahmes-Nefertari was a Negress, and probably the daughter of an Ethiopian monarch."[23] Maspero says, "Such a continuous infusion of foreign material into the ancient Theban stock gave rise to families of a highly mixed character in which all the various races of Egypt were blended in the most capricious fashion."[24] Osburn, speaking of the tomb of King Ai, first husband of Queen Tiyi, says, "The Negro countenance of the King (Ai) was the most remarkable thing in it."[25] Tiyi was also the wife of Amenophis III, and mother of Akhenaton.

21 Rawlinson & Wilkinson. Herodotus. Vol. II, p. 298. London, 1859.
22 Wilkinson, J. G. The Ancient Egyptians, Vol. I. p. 42. London, 1878.
23 Birch, S. Egypt From the Earliest Times, p. 83. London, 1875.
24 Histoire Ancienne des Peuples de l'Orient Class., Les Empires, pp. 170-71. Paris, 1899.
25 Monumental Hist. of Egypt. Vol. II, p. 341. London, 1854.

XVII. Egyptian Portraits. (See Notes on the Illustrations)

The 8th century brought another great amount of Negro strain into the population. The Ethiopians, under their king, Piankhi, invaded Egypt in such numbers that they extended their power as far as the mouths of the Nile and established an Ethiopian dynasty, the XXV, under Sabacon. The latter's nephew, Tirhaquah, or Taharka, carried the Ethiopian power into Syria, Palestine, and Asia Minor, and still more Negro strain into those lands. Breasted says of Tirhaquah, "He was the son of a Nubian woman and his features as preserved in contemporary sculpture show unmistakable Negroid characteristics." His sister became divine head of the Egyptian religion and his mother, a goddess. Maspero says as regards the race-crossing that went on at this time, "The multiplicity of black women in the harems of the rich and even in the huts of the fellahs, changed, not long after the purity of the type, even among the highest classes of the nation so that it came to resemble that of the tribes of Equatorial Africa. Tirhaquah offers a good example of this alteration of the Egyptian type. His face presents the characteristic traits of the black race."[26]

The Ethiopians also brought in something more than a mixture of blood. They brought rejuvenation in physique, art and religion to a people grown effete and decadent. "Egypt," says Petrie, "seemed hopeless until a fresh Ethiopian invasion stimulated it, as in earlier instances."[27] To have any comprehensive idea of the artistic beauty and splendor brought into Egypt by the Ethiopians one must see the display of objects taken from the tomb of Tut-ankh-amen in the Cairo Museum. Nothing superior in art has been produced on this planet. MacIver and Woolley attribute the best in Egyptian pottery to these blacks.[28] The Negro, even from the time of Spanish cave-dweller art, anywhere from 600,000 B.C. to 10,000 B.C. has been an artist of consummate skill.

In the 7th Century, B.C., Asia made its first successful invasion of Egypt, this being its conquest by Esar-haddon, King of Assyria. But Egyptian rulers as Pepi, Amenophis III, Thotmes III, and Tirhaquah had been carrying Egyptian power and Egyptian blood into Syria, Palestine, Phoenicia, and Assyria for nearly two thousand years. With the Assyrian invasion of Esar-haddon there came an infusion of Asiatic strain into the Egyptian population; we say Asiatic because it is impossible to say just how much white strain there was in it. It was in all probability largely a mulatto strain as fair Aryan and black Elamite, as will be seen later, had been mixing in all this Asiatic area for thousands of years. After the Assyrians, came the Medes and Persians, who were also a mulatto race.

The nearest to what was a "pure" white infusion in the Egyptian population came in with the conquest of Alexander the Great in 335 B.C.,

26 Maspero. Ibid.
27 The Making of Egypt, p. 158. Also pp. 135, 155, 168, 182. London, 1939.
28 MacIver. R. and C. L. Woolley, Areika, pp. 1-16. Oxford, 1909.

and the later rule of Ptolemy, one of his generals. Ptolemy was a Greek, and presumably white. In any case the Greeks of that era, though highly mixed, seemed to have been much nearer white than black.

The earliest Ptolemaic rulers are in appearance white; but as time went on their physiognomies changed more and more towards the Negro one. The Negro strain in Alexander II is apparent, and still more so in Ptolemy XIII, the flute-playing father of the most celebrated of the Cleopatras. Ptolemy's mother was a slave. Cleopatra, herself, is known through tradition as having been of a tawny, or mulatto color, and is so described by Shakespeare. Greek and Egyptian intermarried freely and brought another change of physiognomy to the population. Lane-Poole, speaking of the disorders that followed the Grecian invasion, says, "Intermarriages, however, gradually had their effect; after the revolt in the reigns of Ptolemy IV and V, we find the Greek and Egyptian elements closely intermingled."[29]

A still whiter strain came in with the Roman invasion under Julius Caesar, 47 B.C. Roman and Egyptian intermingled their blood, Caesar, himself, taking Cleopatra as a left-handed wife, and having a son, Caesarion, by her. Later Mark Antony, Caesar's best friend, married her, and had three children by her. The portraits from the Graeco-Roman tombs of Ancient Egypt show an undoubted mulatto cast of features in many of them.

So much for the Pharaohs. We shall return later to Egypt where, under Islam, we shall find greater and more precise evidence of the mixing of blacks and whites.

Among other works consulted are:
Thomson, J. Arthur. Man, Vol **V**, No. 38, 1905. Vol. VI. No. 2, No. 63, 1906.
Thomson and McIver. Ancient Races of the Thebaid, pp. 110-111. Oxford, 1905.
Weideman, A. Religion of the Ancient Egyptians, pp. 131, 136-7, 159, 168. London, 1897.
Bryant, Jacob. Analysis of Ancient Mythology, Vol. I, pp. 1-17; Vol. III, pp. 192-275. London, 1775.
Bates, O. The Eastern Libyans. Vol. I, pp. 459-60. London, 1879.
Atlanta Univ. Publications. 1906. No. 19. 1907, pp. 13-14.
Brugsch, H. History of Egypt. Vol. I, pp. 459-60. London, 1879.
Stanley, H. M. **Origin of the Negro Race**, N. Amer. Rev., Vol. 170, pp. 656-665. 1900.

* * * *

Gowland says as regards the Negro and the earliest use of iron, "In Africa so far as metallurgical evidence may be relied on, the extraction of iron from its ore was carried on at a very remote date. The seats of an ancient iron industry marked by accumulations of shag and debris are so widely distributed in that continent that it must date from a very remote period and according to Beck, must have been indigenous. That this early African iron smelting was known in Egypt is well shown by Figs. 8 and 9 which are reproduced from bas-reliefs on a stone now in the Egyptian collection in Florence.

"In Fig. 8, a youth whose head and outstanding ears characterize him as an Ethiopian is working a drum-like skin bellows from which the blast of air is conveyed to a shallow hole in which the ore is reduced to metallic forms." The Metals in Antiquity. Huxley Memorial Lecture, 1912, p. 285.

* * * *

[29] Encyc. Britannica, Vol. VIII, p. 77 (14th ed.).

Chapter Four

SYRIA, PALESTINE, ARABIA, PERSIA

THE Near East was the scene of another vast amalgamation of black and white, evidences of which are offered by both mythology and archaeology. According to Greek mythology, which is a sort of shadowy history, the ancestor of the Persians was Perses, the son of the Greek, Perseus and Andromeda, daughter of Cepheus, King of Ethiopia. Andromeda's mother was the black Queen Casseiopia, whose beauty so aroused the jealousy of the Nereids that they caused her land to be afflicted by a monster that could be appeased only by the sacrifice of Andromeda. From this danger Andromeda was rescued by Perseus, who is also renowned as the slayer of the Gorgon. Perses according to this tradition was therefore a mulatto.

Memnon, another important figure in mythology, was a mulatto, his father being an Elamite black and his mother an Aryan white, both of which races once inhabited Persia.

Bushman art, similar to that of Western Europe, has also been found in this region. According to the London Times, October 6, 1932, the explorers, Neuville and Stekelis, found prehistoric drawings of elephants rhinocerii and other African animals, as well as plants in the cave of Umm Qalifa at Wady Khareitum, Palestine.

The ruins of a splendid Negrito civilization have also been unearthed by Dieulafoy in Persia at Susa, the Shushan of the Bible, where Ahaserus, King of Persia and Ethiopia, chose the beautiful Jewess, Esther, as his wife. Speaking of the mixture that went on in this area between Elamite black and Aryan white, Dieulafoy says, "The Greeks, themselves seemed to have known these two Susian races, the Negroes of the plains and the Scythian whites of the mountains. Have not their old poets given to the direct descendants of the Susian, Memnon, the legendary hero who perished under the walls of Troy, a Negro father, Tithon, and a white mountain woman as mother—Kissia? Do they not also say that Memnon commanded an army of black and white regiments? 'Memnon went to the succor of Priam with 10,000 Susians and 10,000 Ethiopians.'"

Continuing, he says: "I shall attempt to show to what distant antiquity belongs the establishment of the Negritos upon the left bank of the Tigris and the elements constituting the Susian monarchy... Towards 2300 B.C., the plains of the Tigris and Anzan-Susinka were ruled by a dynasty of Negro kings.

"The coming of this dynasty of Medes corresponded perhaps to the arrival in the south of an immense Scythian invasion. Pushed back by the black Susians after having taken possession of the mountains, the whites poured into the plains of the Tigris and remained master of the country until the time when Kudur Nakhunta subdued Chaldea and founded Anzan-Susinka and who added to the territory of the blacks—Nime, Kussi, Habardip —all the mountainous districts once inhabited by the whites of the Scythian race."[1]

Herodotus, who visited this region in the Fifth Century, B.C., mentions the dark skins of the people. He calls them Ethiopians but says their hair was straighter than those of the Western Ethiopians who, he says, had woolly hair. The Elamites, however, seemed rather to have belonged to the more Negroid stock of the west as their hair as seen on the monuments is short and woolly. "The Elamites," says Sir Harry Johnston," "appear to have been a Negroid people with kinky hair and to have transmitted this racial type to the Jews and Syrians. There is a curliness of the hair, together with a Negro eye and full lips in the portraiture of Assyria which conveys the idea of an evident Negro element in Babylonia. Quite probably the very ancient Negro invasion of Mediterranean Europe (of which the skeleton of the Alpes Maritimes are vestiges) came from Syria and Asia Minor on its way to Central and Western Europe."[2]

Elam, or Susa, once dominated Babylon and Assyria. The inscriptions of Assur-banipal reveal that Kudur Nakunta, the Negro king, invaded Chaldea and carried off to his palace at Susa the booty captured there, including the famous golden statue of the goddess, Nana. "Babylon," says F. Gillet, "was subjected to the neighboring kingdom of Elam or Susiana."[3]

According to Houssaye, "The Susian Negritos were in contact with the Mediterranean peoples from the most distant antiquity."[4] Maspero said also that "the connection of the Negroid type of Susians (Persians) with the Negritic races of India and Oceania has been proved."[5] Professor Paul Pelliott also finds that "Negroid scripts of Easter Island in the South Seas have been shown to be similar to those in Southern India and Elam, where flourished more than three thousand years ago, a great Negro civilization." In short, the influence of this splendid Negro culture extended far to the east and to the west. Elamite and invading Aryan later united to form the Persian people of Cyrus, Darius, and Artaxerxes.

For thousands of years before even Cyrus, however, Ethiopians and

[1] L'Acropole de Suse, p. 27, 44, 46, 57-86; 102-115.   Paris. 1893.
[2] Negro in the New World, pp. 24-27.   London, 1910.
[3] Ancient Cities and Empires, p. 87.   Philadelphia, 1867.
[4] Dieulafoy.   Ibid.   Appendix. p. 115.
[5] History of Egypt, Vol. IV. p. 46.

Egyptians had been penetrating into all this region as conquerors and traders and bringing still more Negro, mulatto, and white strain into the mixture already there. To get an idea of the mixed nature of all that ancient Eastern population we must divest ourselves entirely of the current notions of race. The Chaldeans, for instance, the land from which Abraham, ancestor of the Jews, came were Negroes, according to Godfrey Higgins and others. As for the Phoenicians, they also were a very much mixed people, and might have been a composite of Elamite, Aryan, Ethiopian, and Egyptian.

Some of the Phoenician rulers as Tabnit and his illustrious son, Eshmunuzar II, were "pure" Negroes. Eshmunuzar is described as "being Egyptian with large full, almond-shaped eyes, the nose flattened, and the lips remarkably thick after the Negro mold."

Mention of the Phoenicians brings us back to the Ham story. According to this bit of Jewish folk-lore, Noah cursed Ham's son, Canaan. Now, according to this same source, the eldest son of Canaan was Sidon, the ancestor of the Phoenicians and the founder of the great cities of Sidon and Tyre.

The Phoenicians were the greatest explorers and merchants of antiquity. They circumnavigated Africa, colonized Britain, and worked the tin mines there; and founded Carthage and a colony or two in West Africa. Their glory certainly dims that of the ancient Jews.

As for another son of Ham, Mizraim, he was the founder of Egyptian civilization, according to this same Jewish folk-lore source. Now the Bible also says that the sons of Shem, the ones to whom the sons of Ham had been delivered as slaves by Noah, were slaves to the Egyptians for four hundred and thirty years. As for the supposed sons of Japheth—it wasn't so long ago that the Nordics were called the Japhethic stock—they were another people, who, according to the Bible, Ham's eldest son, Canaan, was to serve. But when the Phoenicians, the sons of Canaan, were at the height of their glory, the Nordics were sunk in the depths of savagery and cannibalism, and remained so for a full thousand years after the glory of Phoenicia had faded. These whites were made slaves by the Phoenicians, too. In short, never before had a curse worked so much in reverse as this alleged one of Noah's.

As for the sons of Ham being black because of a curse, we shall see later that in all probability the sons of Shem, from whom the Jews are supposed to be descended, were black, themselves. *According to the Bible, the eldest son of Shem was Elam, and the Elamites as we have just seen were a black people.* Moreover, no one has yet explained how one branch of Noah's family came suddenly to change from white to black. In any case, this tale from Aframerican folk-lore seems as good an explanation as any. The three brothers, Shem, Ham, and Japheth, runs the story were all of the same color—black. But once while travelling in Africa, Japheth woke one morning to see a great, glistening, white pool of water before him. He ran to it and jumped in and was turned white all over.

Anxious to make his brothers white, too, he ran to wake them up. Shem got up, but Ham, lazy as usual, just grunted and went back to sleep.

Shem raced for the water, but before he could reach it, it had nearly all disappeared. There was just enough left to turn him brown. Both called to Ham, who finally woke, but took his own time. When he reached where the pool had been there was just enough left to wet his palms and the soles of his feet. Thus this was the nearest he came to having the color of the elect of the earth.

Maspero speaks of "the little kings, black and white," that dominated Eastern Asia. It is probable even then that these kings imported black concubines from Africa and white ones from the Caucasus for their harems. This, we know, was definitely done in the earliest historic period, and is still being done.

Darius the Great (521-486 B.C.), whose capital was Susa, had wives of many races, and might have been a mulatto or a black himself.

In the Islamic period we shall have more precise evidence of the mixing of white and black in this part of the Near East.

See also:
Sykes, P. History of Persia, Vol. I, pp. 51-2. London. 1930.
De Morgan, J. Mission Scientifique en Perse, Vol. IV, pp. 182-3. Paris, 1896.

Chapter Five

WHO WERE THE FIRST INHABITANTS OF INDIA?

ACCORDING to the distinguished authority, Giuffrida-Ruggeri, the earliest East Indans were "the Negritos." In his "First Outlines of a Systematic Anthropology of Asia" he names them as the first.[1] The next, he says, were the Pre-Dravidians, another Negro type of taller build; and then the Dravidian, who was a mixture of Negro and Aryan, with at times a Mongolian strain.

Thousands of years before the Christian era when these Negroes, or Dasyus, as they are known in the sacred writings, were still the masters of India, the Aryas, or Aryans, a white or nearly white people, swarmed down on them from the north probably through Afghanistan.

The Rig Veda, most ancient of the sacred hymns of India, tells of the fierce struggles between these whites and blacks for the mastery of India. It sings of stormy Aryan deities who rush furiously in battle against the black foe. The hymns praise Indra, the white deity, for having killed 50,000 blacks, "piercing the citadel of the enemy" and forcing the blacks to run out in distress leaving all their food and belongings. "Indra protected in battle the Aryan worshipper; he subdued the lawless for Manu, he conquered the black skin... He beat the Dasyus, as was his wont; he conquered the land for his white friends." The Dasyu was the foe who was "to be flayed of his black skin" and who was dubbed "goat-nosed" and "noseless." "The blacks under their renowned leader Krishna," that is, "The Black," fought back with valor, especially on the banks of the Jumna. "Possessed of magical power these renowned warriors with their families and tribes concealed themselves in the pathless woods and in swamps and morasses made impregnable by the rise of the rivers. From these unexplored wilds they obtained information of the wealth and cattle of the white men living in far villages, suddenly they proclaimed their presence by their uncouth yells and in a moment the work of destruction was done and the fleet plunderers disappeared as suddenly as they had come."[2]

Out of this fierce struggle came what was the first color-line in history. The conquering whites in India did precisely what the European whites

[1] p. 53, Calcutta, 1921.
[2] Dutt, N. K. Aryanisation of India, pp 76-101. Calcutta, 1925.
Dutt, R. C. Ancient India, pp. 12-19. London, 1893.
Hunter, W. W. The Indian Empire, pp. 69-70 London, 1882.

did to the black and yellow men in Asia in our era. Indian caste was founded on color. The Sanscrit word for caste is "varna" which means color.

But as the centuries passed, the two races mixed; commercial relations were established and the color-line faded over the greater part of India. In the Gangetic region, it disappeared until the whites enlisted in the service of the blacks and fought under Negro chiefs. In the famous battle of the Ten Kings, one of the leading Aryan chiefs was a Negro.

Even the Brahmans, the proudest of all Aryans, the originals, whose name has become a byword for all that is haughty and stuck-up, and who would still consider themselves defiled to eat at the same table with a Hitler Aryan, have a Negroid strain. Nesfield says, "The Aryan invader, whatever class he might belong to, was in the habit of taking the women of the country as wives and hence no caste, not even that of the Brahman, can claim to have sprung from Aryan ancestors."[3] Today some of the Brahmans are as black and as flat-nosed as the early Negro chiefs. Max Muller said that some Brahmans are "as black as Pariahs." Nesfield says, "The great majority of the Brahmans are not of lighter complexion or of finer or better-bred features than any other caste" or "distinct in blood from the scavengers who swept the road." Thurston says also, "It is no insult to the higher members of the Brahman community to trace in their lowly brethren the result of mixing with a dark-skinned race."[4] Elliott Smith says, "In India...there are also traces of intermingling with the Negro race to which part of the darkness of the skin so widely prevalent in India may be attributed."[5] In the later centuries caste came to be established on occupation and not on color or race.

The Negro strain is still clearly apparent in large masses of the Indian population, even in the north. There are any number of East Indians who are indistinguishable from Aframerican mulattoes. In Spain, I once saw an Aframerican girl, a dancer, who had dressed herself up to look like a Spanish senorita, and who had succeeded, too. Later she went to India, and returned to Paris where I saw her. In the meantime, she had married an Indian, and was now dressed like an East Indian. This time she looked like an East Indian, while her husband, who wore Western garb, could easily have been taken for an American mulatto. In short, the couple was East Indian, or Spanish, or Aframerican type, according to their dress.

In Southern India are still to be found Negroes of a type almost as pure as those of Africa. On the Andaman Islands not far from Burma are what are probably the purest type Negroes in existence, the Mincopies. "Their hair is so excessively woolly," says Risley, "that when separated from the

[3] Brief View of the Caste System, para. 135. (1885).
[4] Castes and Tribes of Southern India. Vol. I, p. 54. Madras, 1909.
[5] Human History, pp. 136-45. London, 1934.

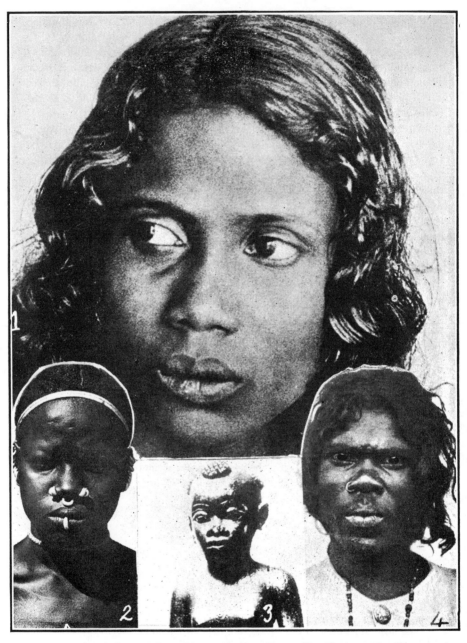

XVIII. I and 4. India; 2. West Africa; 3. Ancient Egypt. (See Notes on the Illustrations)

XVIIIa. Upper group: Indian rulers and notables. Lower group: Three Malay rulers; and one East African sultan. All are contemporary. (For their names see Notes on the Illustrations.)

head it is almost unrecognizable as human hair."⁶   Certain other tribes as the Nayadi, Urali, Kadir, and Bendkar are as Negroid as certain of the natives of New Guinea.   The Dravidians, or mixed bloods, now number between thirty and forty millions, and were the founders of a civilization which in architectural beauty and grandeur equals some of Egypt's most famous structures.   As Professor Hooton says," A large share of responsibility for the great civilization of India must be assigned to Negroes since there is unquestionably a very strong Negroid strain in the Indian population."⁷

In India, as in the Near East, black women were, and are, taken freely into the harems of the rulers.   Burton says, "Women with white skins are supposed to be heating and unwholesome; hence the Hindu Rajahs slept with dark girls in the hot season."   Incidentally, in Africa, white men also choose Negro women for the same reason.   Their skins are said to be velvety and cooling.   As regards skin color, the Kama Sutra, or love precepts of the Brahmans, teaches abhorrence for a very white skin. or a very black one, and places both in the same class with a bad-smelling woman.   The passage reads:

> "Women not to be enjoyed:
> A woman who is extremely white
> A woman who is extremely black
> A bad-smelling woman."⁸

Later, in the chapter on Islam, we shall see how African Negroes came to India in great numbers and mixed their blood with that of the native population.

⁶ The People of India. Plates 23 and 33. Vol. IV. Madras, 1915.
⁷ Up From The Ape, p. 592. N. Y., 1931.
⁸ Vatsayana, Kama Sutra, Love Precepts of the Brahmans, p. 46.   Paris.

Chapter Six

WHO WERE THE FIRST CHINESE?

THE first inhabitants of China seem also to have been the Negritos Unmixed Negroes with no connection with Africa still live in Southern China.

H. Imbert, a French anthropologist, who lived in the Far East, says in "Les Negritos de la Chine," "The Negroid races peopled at some time all the South of India, Indo-China, and China. The South of Indo-China actually has now pure Negritos as the Semangs, and mixed as the Malays and the Sakais. . . .

"In the first epochs of Chinese history, the Negrito type peopled all the south of this country and even in the island of Hai-Nan, as we have attempted to prove in our study on the Negritos, or Black Men of this island.

"Skulls of these Negroes have been found in the island of Formosa and traces of this Negroid element in the islands of Liu-Kiu to the south of Japan.

"In the earliest Chinese history several texts in classic books spoke of these diminutive blacks; thus the Tcheu-Li composed under the dynasty of Tcheu (1122-249 B.C.) gives a description of the inhabitants with black and oily skin. . . .

"The Prince Liu-Nan, who died in 122 B.C., speaks of a kingdom of diminutive blacks in the southwest of China."[1]

Additional evidence of Negroes in China is given by Professor Chang Hsing-lang in an article entitled, "The Importation of Negro slaves to China under the T'ang Dynasty A.D. 618-907." He says, "The Lin-yi Kuo Chuan (Topography of the Land of Lin-yi) contained in Book 197 of the Chiu T'ang Shu (Old Dynastic History of T'ang) says: 'The people living to the south of Lin-yi have woolly hair and black skin.'" Chinese folk-lore speaks often of these Negroes, he says, and mentions an empress of China, named Li, (373-397 A.D.) consort of the Emperor Hsiao Wu Wen, who is spoken of as being a Negro. He adds, that according to the writings of a later period—the Seventh to the Ninth Century—Negro slaves were imported into China from Africa.[2]

In 1933, Dr. Joseph F. Rock, botanical expert of the United States Department of Agriculture, discovered an unmixed Negro people in China.

[1] The Negritos de la Chine. Hanoi. 1928.
[2] Bulletin No. 7. Catholic Univ. of Pekin. Dec., 1930.

the Nakhis, numbering 200,000, who, he says, had preserved their culture for 2000 years.[3] This Negro strain penetrated, no doubt, into the far north and showed itself in the faces of the Tatar. Even the sacred Manchu dynasty shows this Negro strain. The lower part of the face of the Emperor Pu-yi of Manchukuo, direct descendant of the Manchu rulers of China, is most distinctly Negroid. The Chinese of the North, however, incline rather to the Caucasian type and some are almost indistinguishable from whites, due probably to mixture with them.

The Indo-Chinese, Siamese, and Malay

The Negro strain in the above is still more evident than it is in the Southern Chinese. Negritos of pure type still live in Siam and the Malay Peninsula. Photographs of Indo-Chinese and Senegalese in French military caps are almost indistinguishable one from the other, so Negroid in appearance are the Indo-Chinese. The principal difference is in color and hair. A picture of King Sisowath of Cambodia, Indo-China, appearing in Current History Magazine, May 1927, (page 190), is clearly Negroid. The Indo-Chinese were founders of a mighty civilization as may be seen at Anghor Vat and elsewhere. The Siamese are even more Negroid than the Indo-Chinese. Prajadhipok, the ex-King of Siam, has a decidedly Negroid face.

Were the First Japanese Negroes?

There is a very evident Negro strain in a certain element of the Japanese population, particularly those of the south. Imbert says, "The Negro element in Japan is recognizable by the Negroid aspect of certain inhabitants with dark and often blackish skin, frizzly or curly hair... The Negritos are the oldest race of the Far East. It has been proved that they once lived in Eastern and Southern China as well as in Japan where the Negrito element is recognizable still in the population."

Professor Munro, one of the foremost students of Japanese life and culture, says, "The Japanese are a mixture of several distinct stocks, Negro, Mongolian...breadth of face, intraorbital width, flat nose, prognathism, and brachycephaly might be traced to the Negro stock."[4]

Quatrefages,[5] Professor R. B. Dixon, and others also think that the Japanese show a Negro strain. Dixon says, "In Japan, the ancient Negrito element may still be discerned by characteristics which are at the same time

---

[3] New York Times, Nov. 26, 1933.
[4] Prehistoric Japan, pp. 676-8. Yokohama, 1911.
[5] Race Humaine, p. 345. The Pigmies, pp. 27 8. N. Y., 1895. Rapport sur le progrès d'Anthropologie. 1867.

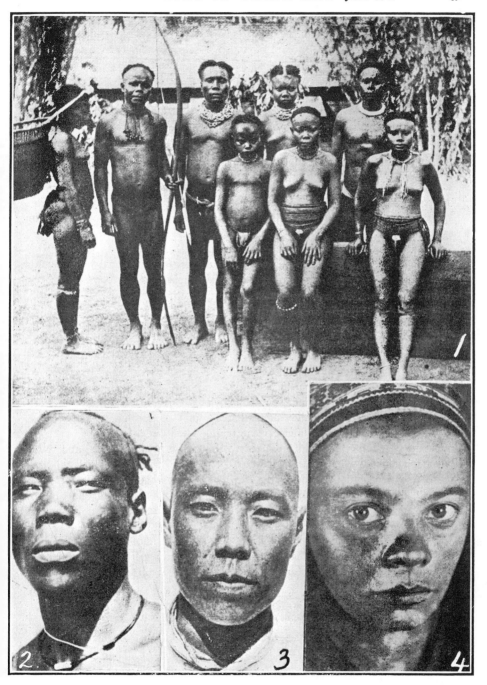

XIX. 1. Andaman Islanders; 2. Central African Negro; 3. Mongolian; 4. Laplander.

exterior and osteologic."[6]

However, no proof of the actual presence of a Negrito people has yet been unearthed in Japan, according to Professor Kyuzo Torii of the University of Tokio, a painstaking scientist. Indeed, he discounts the idea that the Negrito was one of the tribes of early Japan. He says, "Some hold that among the tribes of pre-historic Japan were some Negrito. But I doubt this hypothesis. It is true that this hypothesis will explain away the phenomenon of some Japanese having curly hair in Kyushu and that curly hair is never a feature of the Mongol. But my explanation of the phenomenon is as follows: In Kyushu there lived some Indonesians such as the Hayato and when these Indonesians migrated into that part of the country they had already mixed with the Negritos. And it is probable that some of the Negrito characteristics came out insistently by the law of atavism. The question thus answered you will agree with me that it is not necessary to conclude that the country was inhabited by the Negritos."[7]

In his book "Yu-shi i-zen," published in 1918, he also refers to Negrito skill in archery in contrast to the Indonesians, and says that the use of bows and arrows by the Japanese from the earliest times recorded may have been brought over by Indo-Chinese who had learnt the art from the Negritos. Professor Asakawa of Yale University says as regards this theory that the Negritos may have influenced the Japanese indirectly through the Indo-Chinese immigrants who had intermingled with Negritos before they started from the south towards Japan.[8]

The oldest known inhabitants of Japan are the Ainus, who appear to be nearer the Caucasian than to any other race. But they also show signs of Negro and Mongolian admixture. Batchelor, a leading authority, describes them as being lighter in color than the average Japanese but says that some of them are as dark as American Indians. Their noses, too, are "flattish" and "their mouths wide and lips thick." The hair, which is long and thick, is coarse. "Wavy hair is much prized," he said, "and one who has curly hair is said to be a person having 'the hair of the gods.' "[9] It is this kind of hair which, perhaps more than anything else, indicates a distant Negro ancestry in them. Naturally curling hair may be set down as an almost sure index of Negro ancestry.

That brings us to the question of who were the ancestors of these most ancient known Japanese? Might they not have been Negritos? The Japanese still have Negrito neighbors on the mainland, in the Philippines, and on other

[6] Racial History of Man, pp. 287-92. N. Y., 1923.
[7] Ancient Japan in the Light of Cultural Anthropology. Tokyo, 1935.
    Etudes Anthrop. Les Aborigines de Formose. Tokyo, 1910.
[8] Letter to J. A. Rogers.
[9] Ainu Life and Lore, p. 8. Tokyo, 1927.

Pacific islands. Negrito remains have also been found on the near-by Riu-Kiu Islands as well as on Formosa. Furthermore there are millions of Negroes some of them of the purest type in all this region. Also, the Indo-Chinese, the southern Chinese, and the Malays, though they have straight hair have mulatto complexions and faces that are clearly Negroid. The Ainus themselves as was said, show a Negroid strain more or less distant therefore is it not probable they mixed with some lighter-colored invader or after thousands of years of habitation in northern Japan, were changed to their present type? The Ainus once dominated Japan as Japanese place-names, which are Ainu, seem to indicate.

Significant, too, is the fact that Ainu traditions tell, according to Batche-lor, of "a race of dwarfs," or Koropokguru, which inhabited Japan, before the coming of the Ainu, and which the latter exterminated. Might not these have been the Negritos?

Professor Torii speaks of the Negroid appearance of some Japanese being probably due to atavism. But this seems to be coming dangerously close to metaphysics. Instead might it not be more realistic to say that the Negroid strain has not yet been bred out in such Japanese as show it? If atavism, or a throw-back, were true in the case of color and hair, any number of Americans with apparently white parents ought to be born with Negroid color and hair.

It seems difficult to escape the theory that in the most ancient times a Negrito race found itself cut off in some way in the far north in both hemispheres. Northern Japan, Northern Europe, and Northern America are all inhabited by a diminutive people with hair, which though straight, is black (not blond like that of the whites), and with dark, Negroid faces with a suggestion of the Mongolian.

There is still another important affinity of the Japanese with the Negrito yet to be mentioned, namely, height. The Japanese are only very slightly taller than the Negritos of the Philippines. Again, there are any number of Japanese, who but for color and hair, bear a striking resemblance to the South African Bushman, another Negrito race. There is also a type of Japanese, which in color and features looks more European than Mongolian. But even in some of these, as in the brunette whites, there is a sign, almost infallible, of Negro ancestry to be distinguished, namely, the coloring of the nipples and the genitals. This, and not the supposed half-moons on the finger-nails, is the last of Negro strain to be bred out. As Bloch says, "The penis and the scrotum of the Japanese have a marked coloration. Among the women, the little lips as well as the entrance to the vagina, are frequently pigmented. This is not special to the Japanese because it is also to be found in other yellow races. In the Javanese the large and little lips are not only often of a dark brown color but present black spots." These traits, he says, recall the Negro origin of the Japanese, the Malay and the Indo-Chinese, who, he adds, "are all descendants of a Negro race which occupied all these lands in ancient times."[9a]

Imbert offers what might be an explanation of the present racial types of the Pacific. He says, "The most ancient humanity was composed of white and black pigmies, who, thanks to a better diet, more meat and a gentler climate improved in height and intelligence and finally amalgamated to form the present human type."

The question might never be settled. Archaeological research is recent in Japan, however, and a closer Japanese affinity with the people to the south might yet be discovered.

Negro Strain in the Filipinos, Australians, Hawaiians, and Other Pacific Islanders

As was said there are millions of Negroes in the islands of the Pacific, who, in color, features, and hair, are almost indistinguishable from Africans. These islanders constitute a vast jumble of "races" shot through with a Negro strain in which the Mongolian and the Caucasian sometimes appear.

Is this Caucasian strain ancient? It is difficult to say how much, if any of it, existed prior to the coming of the white man. Europeans have been coming to the Pacific for more than four centuries and have been mixing their blood with the islanders. Magellan, the first, arrived in 1521. The Spaniards came in 1571; the Dutch in 1616; the English under Dampier in 1669; and Captain Cook in 1770. The sailors and other members of these expeditions mixed freely with the native women, and gave them their first visitation of venereal disease which killed them off like flies. Instances like those of the Mutiny on the Bounty where the white men deserted their ships to live among the natives were far from being uncommon. Since those days Europeans have been arriving in numbers and intermingling their blood with that of the natives. One of the first things the white man does on arriving in the South Seas with its dark-skinned, voluptuous. and most amiable beauties is to set up a harem. Some writers who insist that certain Pacific Islanders as the Tahitans are a Caucasian race, and were originally so, forget that they have had nearly four centuries of amalgamation with whites.

A large exhibit in the Museum of Natural History, Paris, France, might serve to throw some light on what the natives of the Pacific looked like before the present great migration of Europeans and Japanese to their lands.

[9a] Bull. et Mem. Soc., Anthrop. de Paris. 5 ser. 1-2, p. 619. Nov. 21, 1901.

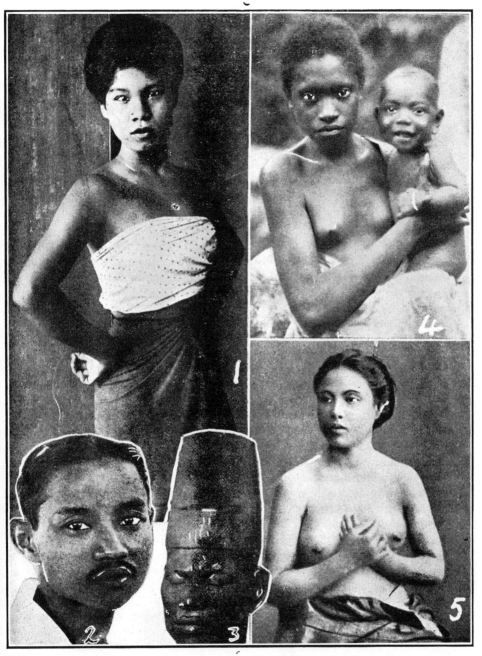

XX. I. Siamese Belle; 2. Prajadhipok, ex-King of Siam; 3. A French Indo-Chinese soldier;
4. South Sea Island mother and child; 5. Japanese beauty.

⅃his exhibit is a large collection of life masks and photographs of the faces of the earlier Pacific Islanders from over a vast range of that ocean. The general aspect of the exhibit is decidedly Negroid, some of the faces being of the deepest shade of black such as the Solomon Islanders and the Marquesans.

These islanders are generally divided into three groups: Melanesian, Micronesian, and Polynesian. The first are unmixed Negroes; the second are a mixture largely of Negro and Mongolian; the third, among whom are some pure blacks, are a mixture of Negro, Caucasian, and Mongolian, with sometimes the last named predominant.

The blacks, themselves, constitute an ethnological puzzle. Some like the Tasmanians, who were killed off by the English settlers, were "pure" Negro; while others, like the Australian Bushman, though jet black and with Negroid faces, had hair and beards that were sometimes more silky than woolly, and with body hair as thick as if nature had given it to them expressly as a coat. This fact may be noted: There are Negro peoples with naturally straight or frizzly hair; others with kinky hair, that is more or less abundant as some of the West Africans; and still others with sparse, tiny beads of hair, the so-called pepper-corn. Malay Negritos who are alike in color and features have, some of them, straight hair, others, woolly hair. How can one explain these caprices, except on the ground of climatic environment?

The original inhabitants of the Philippines were undoubtedly the Negritos, who still live there in considerable numbers. Following the Negritos came the Mongolians and the Malays, a Negroid people; then the white Spaniards; and the Americans. White American soldiers and Aframerican ones, too, had tens of thousands of children by the native women during the American occupation.

The older white Australians also have a Negro strain. The first settlers, a large number of whom were convicts, came without white women and found mates among the black women: "The majority of Australians," says Cedric Dover, "are unmistakably branded by the signs of miscegenation."[10] In New Zealand the mixing of white with Maori, a type that is more Mongolian than Negroid, is still more common. New Zealand is perhaps the only Anglo-Saxon colony on earth where colored and white live on terms of almost perfect equality, including intermarriage. The sharp racial differences that once existed there, and caused much bloodshed, have disappeared. Maori blood may be found in the best white families. One Prime Minister of the islands, Sir James Carroll, was a mixed blood.

Francis J. Sullivan, writing in the Interracial Review, says, "Today and

[10] Half Caste, pp. 178-80. London, 1937.
Davenport, C. B. Australian Aborigines and Black-White Hybrids. Amer. Jour. of Physical Anthrop. Vol. 8, pp. 73-94. 1925.

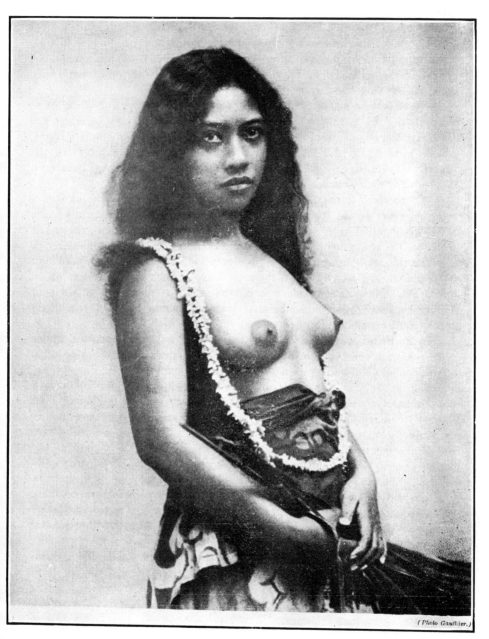

(Photo Gauthier.)

XXI. Belle of Tahiti.

for the past sixty years since the signing of the Maori 'Magna Charta'—
the Treaty of Waitangi—it is no disgrace for a white man to marry into a
good Maori family. It may even be an honor to do so. The percentage of
white blood in the Maori race is rising yearly. Rapidly adapting themselves
to the ways of the white conquerors—but at the same time clinging to their
tribal traditions, of a high order—the Maoris are the most fortunate of
colored races. Instead of facing decrease, so often the lot of natives in
daily contact with white races, the Maoris are increasing.

"New Zealand has solved amicably the problem of brown and white living
side by side. In fact the problem does not exist. Maoris, most of whom are
farmers, have risen high in the councils of the Dominion. Sir Mauri Pomaré,
Sir Apirana Ngata and Sir James Carroll are three great members of the
Maori race who have played able parts in Dominion politics and have been
knighted for their services.

"So accepted is the Maori throughout the Dominion that the idea of a
color-bar never occurs to a New Zealander. If by some unfortunate mischance
a Maori traveling with a white friend was insulted for 'color' reasons it
would be the white man who would be quicker to take offense.

"In the relationship of these two races in New Zealand, the dominant
white and the respected Maori, there is surely a lesson in tolerance for all
the world. New Zealand has proved that color is not incompatible with
democracy, cooperation, and mutual respect for achievement, that the bitterness of racial prejudice can be overcome."[11]

In Tasmania where fierce and bitter warfare waged between the whites
and the blacks, and ended in the extermination of the blacks, the latter killed
off the mulatto children as soon as they were born.[12]

Samoa, Tahiti, Papua, Borneo and the Dutch East Indies all have a
population of mixed Negro, Mongolian, and Caucasian. In the Dutch East
Indies, the mixed-bloods enjoy a degree of equality, which is perhaps higher
than mixed-bloods in any other European colony. Marriages between natives
and Dutch women are discouraged but the offspring of Dutch fathers and
native women become full-fledged Dutch citizens, looking down frequently
on the native, and becoming even more Dutch than the Dutch, themselves.

The old Dutch families of white stock look down, in turn, upon these
mixed-bloods and will snub them when they can, but the mixed-bloods are
strong politically and hold high government posts. Most of the 225,000
whites of the Dutch East Indies have a Malay strain.

R. V. C. Bodley says of the status of these mixed bloods, "It is sufficient for a white man to recognize a child born out of wedlock for it to

11 Interracial Review. March, 1940. N. Y.
12 Bonwick, J. Last of the Tasmanians, pp. 307-23. London, 1870.

receive the same rights of citizenship as its father and have the same opportunity as the sons of the greatest Dutch families. To cite an example, one of the Governors of the Dutch East Indies, in the presence of whom all Europeans must stand while he is standing, to whom ladies curtsy as to Royalty, who has the power of clemency or amnesty, has a Malay grandmother. I know a man bearing one of the most illustrious Dutch names, who is decidedly half-, at any rate, quarter-bred and though he probably would not talk about it to an Englishman, who has different views on the subject, he is not ashamed of his taint." The writer adds that the Dutch criticize severely the English settlers "who live with native women but do not recognize any children who may be born."[13]

In the Pacific, also, to the east of Australia is Pitcairn Island, made famous by the "Mutiny of the Bounty." Its inhabitants are the offspring of the white mutineers and the native black women.

The Hawaiian Islands

The basic strain of the original Hawaiians, as seen in their color and their faces, was undoubtedly Negro, with an admixture of Mongolian. Much

effort is being made today to deny the Negro part of it, yet it is evident to anyone who knows the mulatto type. White Southerners on the islands had a song which ran, "You may call them Hawaiian, But they look like niggers to me."

As a human melting-pot Hawaii ranks second to none in the world, if not in volume, at least in thoroughness. Native Hawaiians, Chinese, Japanese, Koreans, Malay, Portuguese, Negroes from the Cape Verde Islands, white Americans and other Caucasians, as well as Porto Ricans, white and black; and Aframericans, intermarry . Since living conditions are good and intermarriage meets with social approval fine types of human beings are being produced. Margaret Lam traced the offspring of the marriage of a white sea-captain and a Hawaiian chieftess in the early part of the nineteenth century and found that some of Hawaii's leading citizens were descended from them. In the six branches resulting from this union, she found 95 marriages, forty of which were with Caucasians, and twenty-four with Caucasian-Hawaiian.[14]

So firmly is racial intermarriage established in Hawaii that newcomers who protest against it find themselves in a hopeless minority. As Paul Hutchinson said in the Western Christian Advocate: "What chance have

[13] Indiscreet Travels East, pp. 47-8. London, 1936.
[14] Racial Intermarriage in Hawaii. Sociol. and Social Research. Vol. 17.
    Adams, R. Racial Intermarriage in Hawaii. N. Y., 1937.

·uu of sitting down in the face of a racial potpourri of that kind and maintaining that the races can't mix, and wont mix, and mustn't mix, and that general and indescribable evils will result if they do mix. For Hawaii smiles back at you from beneath her palm shadowed eyes and says: 'But they do mix, and so far as I can see to the great advantage of all concerned. Come on, now, don't get so hot over this racial matter about which you really know very little after all. Let's go surf-riding in the moonlight at Waikiki.' "[15]

As might be expected, howev... , there is or was, some prejudice against Africamericans. Racial conditions were proceeding harmoniously until about 1912 when it was reported that the 25th Infantry, Negro, was coming to Hawaii. The white soldiers there, some 8000 strong, at once started a propaganda against them, warning the Hawaiian women not to associate with the Negroes as "they had venereal disease" and would "make them give birth to monkeys." When the Negro troops arrived they found a chilly reception, but since the Negroes were good spender⁵ and good lovers, the situation quickly changed. This caused several riots with the white troops. The Negroes were finally removed.

Officially, too, there is some racial discrimination. Instructions to 1930 census-takers in Hawaii were, "A person of mixed white and Negro blood should be returned as Negro no matter how small the percentage of Negro blood." The 1930 census lists only 563 Negroes—322 males and 241 females —and a total of only 3000 of "Negro" blood.

The Cape Verdians and the Porto Ricans, some of whom are more Negroid than the Aframerican, are listed as white, and barber shops in the tourist districts will serve the former when they will not serve a lighter-complexioned person who is known as an Aframerican. Some magic in the use of a foreign tongue has changed black into white, as the black Portuguese are classed as white. However most prejudiced Americans on the island find themselves in a minority and accept the Hawaiian tempo, sooner or later. Outside of Honolulu, Aframericans are fairly well received by the American whites. Color is forgotten in similarity of culture.

White slavery has introduced a new element of race-mixing in the Orient and the Pacific. We shall speak of it in its proper place.

[15] Quoted in Literary Digest, Oct. 3, 1925, p. 32.

Shapiro, H. L.   Heritage of the Bounty, 1936.
Additional Bibliography on the Negritos: Nippold, W. Rassen-und Kulturgeschichte der Negrito-Volker Sudost-Asiens. Liepzig, 1936.
Geografisk Tidsskrift, Dec. 1937. pp. 110-137.
Evans, I. H. N. The Negritos of Malaya. Cambridge (Eng.) 1937. This book has some excellent portraits of Malay Negritos who look just like Africans.
For the sex life of the Oceanic peoples and data and pictures of mixed-bloods, see: Venus Oceanica, edited by R. Burton. N. Y., 1935. Brinton, D. Races and Peoples. which has abundant illustrations. Zaborowski: Métis d'Australiens et d'Anglais. Bull. et Mém. Soc. d'Anthrop. de Paris, July 4, 1907.

Chapter Seven

THE NEGRO IN ANCIENT GREECE

R ETURNING westward, we come to Greece. Grecian civilization was
the offspring of the Egyptian one. This fact has been clearly proved
by Sir Arthur Evans, who, through his excavations on the island of Crete,
has established that island as "the vital link between the civilizations of Egypt
and Southeastern Europe." Speaking of the Libyan and the Egyptian
factors in the Cretan civilization, he adds that Negroes even from the Upper
Nile might have penetrated to Crete. "The question," he says, "even arises
whether some of the other, in this case, partly Negroized element with whom
the proto-Libyan stood in close relations in the Nile Valley may not have
also found their way to the Cretan district in their wake."[1]

Grecian mythology, which, as was said, is a kind of shadowy history,
proves further this Egyptian origin. The earliest Greek gods, like the Egyptian ones, were black. We shall see more of this in the section on "Black
Gods and Messiahs."

According to this mythology, the Greek people, themselves, seemed to
have come into being as the result of miscegenation. Zeus, the "Father of the
Gods," who is of Ethiopian ancestry, mates with the fair Greek maiden, Io,
and has a mulatto son, Epaphus, who is born in Egypt. Eschylus, great
tragic poet of ancient Greece, says of this union, "And thou shall bring forth
black Epaphus, thus named from the manner of Zeus' engendering... Fifth
in descent from him fifty maidens shall return to Argos (Greece), not of
their choice but fleeing marriage with their cousin kin." Eschylus adds,
"Call this the work of Zeus, and this his race sprang from Epaphus, and
thou shalt hit the truth."[2]

This was the symbolic way of saying that the Argives, or Greeks, were
of mixed blood. One of the titles of Zeus was Ethiop, an Egyptian or
African word, which came later to mean "black."

Further, to show the racial affinity of the Greeks with the Phoenicians,
Epaphus is named as being the ancestor of Danaus, King of Arabia, and of
Cadmus, a prince of Phoenicia, inventor of many useful arts and the intro-
ducer of the alphabet from Phoenicia into Greece. Furthermore, Cadmus
is the brother of Europa, whose sons by black Zeus are the founders of the
European peoples. Underlying this mythology are certain historical and

[1] The Palace of Minos. Vol. II. p. 45-6. London, 1928.
[2] Eschylus. Prometheus Bound, line 850. The Suppliant Maidens, line 859

ethnological truths. As was said several scientists, among them Sergi, declare that the Europeans, especially those of the Mediterranean, are, strictly
speaking, Eur-Africans. Thus we find anthropology supporting mythology.

The religion of ancient Greece, like that of Egypt, was established by
the Negro. Not only were the Grecian gods black, as was said, but the two
most important oracles of Greece were established by Negroes, namely those
of Dodona and Delphos. The first, according to Herodotus, was founded
by two black doves who flew across the waters, from Egypt, the black doves
being symbolic of black priestesses. He said also that the cries uttered in
the Greek temples during the Hellenic rites sounded as if they had come
from Africa.

Delphos was the founder of the Delphic Oracle, whose renown was so
great, that his island became one of the greatest tourist centres of the ancient
world. The Delphic Oracle was the principal rites of Apollo, and it is
significant that though Apollo is shown with Grecian features, his hair is
shown curled in pepper-corn style in imitation of the Negro, or ancient
Negrito. As for Delphos, himself, there is unmistakable evidence from
his coins that he was a Negro.

C. T. Seltman says of these coins, "A type of exceptional interest—the
head of a curly-headed Negro. As a coin-type this head is so extraordinary
that it is only natural to bring it into relationship with the other coins, almost
contemporary, which bear the same type. These are the little silver pieces
of Delphi, with heads of goats or rams and the letters 4 on the reverse, and
with a Negro's head as obverse type. The head has been identified as that of
Delphos, son of Melaina (the black woman), mythical founder of Delphi
and this attribution is certainly strengthened by the time when the Alcmae-
onidae had just completed the temple of Apollo at Pytho. Thus the Alcmae-
onid Cleithenes as the founder of Delphi's temple placed upon the Athenian
money the head of the first founder of Delphi itself. The obverse-die which
accompanies this Negro head is a fac-simile in miniature of the tetradrachm
A218 and for the die I have suggested the date 502 B.C."[3]

Some numismatists think that the coins of Delphos were those of Esop
(that is, Ethiop), the great fabulist, but Esop, it will be recalled visited the
island of Delphos but once and did not leave it alive. The Delphians tossed
him to death from a precipice because of a cutting and very witty remark
he made in depreciation of their island, and which coming from so great
a man, they were afraid would hurt their tourist trade.

Further light on the Negro in Greece has been given by Grace Beardsley
in her book, "The Negro in Greek and Roman Civilization." She gives
pictures of Negroes from Greek vases, tells of the traditions of the black

[3] Athens, Its History and Coinage, p. 97. Cambridge, 1924.

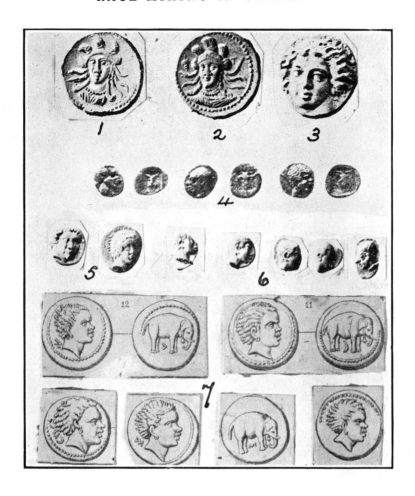

XXII. Greek and Roman Coins. (for details see Notes on the Illustrations)

King Memnon and of Circe, the famous enchantress, who is sometimes depicted as a Negro woman.   This latter fact is true to history because Circe is the sister of another enchantress, Medea, who is the daughter of King Aetes of Colchis, where Jason went in search of the Golden Fleece.   The Colchians, it will be remembered, are described as Negroes by Herodotus. Rawlinson thinks that the Colchians disappeared by amalgamation with the whites.

Still another Negro is mentioned in the Homeric legends, Eurybiates. Homer speaks of his "woolly hair" and "sable skin" and compares him with Ulysses, greatest of the heroes.

> "Eurybiates in whose large soul alone
> Ulysses viewed an image of his own."

In addition to their original Negro strain, the Greeks seem to have had a considerable number of unmixed Negroes among them principally as servants and soldiers.   Black domestics were common.   J. A. St. John says, "It became a mark of wealth and consequence to be served by black domestics, both male and female, as was also the fashion among the Romans and the Egyptian Greeks.   Thus Cleopatra had Negro boys for torch-bearers and the shallow exclusive in Cicero is anxious to make it known that he has an African valet.   Juvenal, in his sarcastic style, alludes to this practice. (Satire V. 52).

"The Athenian ladies like our Indian dames, affected, as a foil, perhaps to be attended by waiting-maids rendered 'by Phoebus' amorous pinches black.' "

This custom, in fact, persisted throughout Europe, as we shall see, down to our own century, and there were never any restrictions against the cohabiting of these blacks with the whites.

Alexander the Great

Alexander the Great, as may be supposed, had Negroes in his armies. One of the most illustrious of the latter was Clitus, his best beloved, whom he made King of Bactria, and commander of his cavalry.   In fact, Alexander and Clitus nursed at the same breast.   Clitus' mother, Dropsica, was Alexander's nurse.   Clitus is mentioned by Plutarch and others as Clitus Niger, that is, Clitus the Negro.[4]

˺Alexander undoubtedly sent to Greece numbers of Negroes and mulattoes from Eastern Asia and Egypt after his conquests of those lands. He encouraged intermarriage of the Macedonians with the conquered peoples

[4] Plutarch: Alexander the Great. Diodorus Siculus, Book XVII, chap. 2. Clavier in Biog. Universelle. Vol. VIII, p. 461 (1844).

XXIII. I. Hair of Apollo; 2. Ptolemaic Pharaoh; 3. Graeco-Egyptian lady; 4. Greek head—said to be Memnon; I. Negro Sibyl in the Cathedral of Sienna, Italy.

and took wives from among them himself, which greatly incensed the Macedonians. Indeed, there was even a tradition that Alexander was of Ethiopian origin, and that he was the son of Nectanebo, King of Egypt.[5] Ethiopian lineage was then considered "tops." Were not the gods, themselves, of Ethiopian origin, and did they not return annually to Ethiopia for feasting and sacrifice?

Two of the most illustrious writers of Greece are mentioned as Negroes: Esop and Sappho. Socrates, too, might have been of Negro origin. He has the small, flat nose and bullet head of the Bushman. His features are most certainly not Grecian.

The facts as given by Planudes and others on Esop's race are precise. And as was said, Zundel, Champfleury and others think that the "woolly-haired Negro" on the coins of Delphos was Esop.[6]

As for Sappho, Ovid makes it clear that the ancients did not consider her white. She is compared with Andromeda, daughter of Cepheus, black King of Ethiopia. Ovid says,

"Andromede patriae fusca colore suae."

In Epistle XV of the Heroides of Ovid (translated by Ridley), she says to Phaon, "I am small of stature but I have a name that fills all lands. I, myself, have produced this extended renown for my name. If I am not fair, Andromeda, the daughter of Cepheus, was swarthy though the complexion of her country was pleasing to Perseus. White pigeons, too, are often mated with spotted ones and the black turtle-dove is often beloved by a bird that is green."

Paul Lacroix, in his "History of Prostitution," says of her, "Although Plato graces her with the epithet of beautiful and although Athaenus is persuaded of her beauty on the authority of Plato it is more probable that Maximus of Tyre who paints her for us as little and black is in conformity with more authentic tradition."[7]

Sappho lived about 600 B.C., and was a native of the island of Lesbos, from which comes lesbian, or sapphic love, although there is no proof that Sappho was a lesbian, herself.

At least one ancient Greek poet, Asclepiades, (270 B.C.), sang the praises of a Negro woman. He says, "With her charms, Didymée has ravished my heart. Alas, I melt as wax at the sight of her beauty. She is black, it is true, but what matters? Coals also are black; but when they are

---

[5] Budge, E. A. W. Life and Exploits of Alexander the Great. (Trans. from the Ethiopic Texts). Vol. II, pp. 3-32. London, 1896.

[3] Zundel. Revue Archaeol. March, 1861. Hist. de la Caricature antique, pp. 101-2. Paris, 1867.

[7] History of Prostitution, p. 150. N. Y., 1926. Pope's translation of Ovid reads as regards Sappho, "Brown as I am an Ethiopian dame." (Sappho to Phaon, line 41. 1807).

alight, they glow like rose-cups."[8]

Asclepiades is noted for his erotic verse, and gave his name to a metric form used among the Lesbian poets.

When we come to the Byzantine and the Islamic periods of Grecian history we shall have more precise information on Negroes in Greece as well as on race-mixing.

[8] Deheque. Anthologie Grecque, Vol. I, p. 48. Paris, 1863.

Note: On page 80, para. 5, line 3, for "island of Delphos" read "city of Delphos."

Chapter Eight

NEGROES IN ANCIENT ROME AND CARTHAGE

THE earliest known natives of Italy were Negroes, as was said, thus making the base of the Latin race, Negroid.

D. Wilson, basing his observations on the earliest Etrurian pottery refers to "Well-known examples of Etruscan vases moulded in the forms of Negroes' heads and of Greek pottery painted with the same characteristic features and woolly hair. Specimens of both are preserved among the collections of the British Museum and furnish interesting evidence alike, of the permanency of the Negro type and of the familiarity both of the Greek and Etruscan artists with the African features long prior to the Christian era."[1]

As regards race-mixing in Rome, Juvenal, Martial and other writers. were cited in Chapter One. An oration by the noted orator, Calpurnius Flaccus, of that time was also mentioned. Judging from the interest manifested, miscegenation, or more precisely speaking, adulterous unions with Negroes, must have been fairly common.

Rome, like Egypt and Greece, had no color distinctions. Her extensive literature reveals none. Rome's attempt at a color-line begins with Mussolini thousands of years later. Peoples of all races and colors were brought to Rome from her far-flung provinces—Sudanese, Ethiopians, Egyptians. Moors, Greeks, Parthians, Gauls, Celts, Belgians, Saxons, Britons and thrown into a vast melting pot. We find proof of the absence of color prejudice in the word, Niger. Like Ethiop, it crept into the Roman language, having been brought there from Africa. The word comes from the River Niger. and Nigritae means the people from the River Niger. "Ni" probably means "great" and Ger, or Geir, is African for river. At first Niger had nothing more to do with black than the waters of the river itself. "Ater" was the Latin for black.[2] Some of the most illustrious Romans bore the surname "Niger" or "Negro" as Pescennius Niger, one of their greatest emperors. Another "Niger" was counsellor to the royal family and accompanied Octavia, sister of Caesar Augustus to Greece when she went there to try to win back her husband, Mark Anthony, from Cleopatra. A later "Niger" was Henry III, Emperor of the Holy Roman Empire (1017-56 A.D.), who married

[1] Prehistoric Man. Vol. I, pp. 369-70. London, 1876.
[2] For Biblo. see No. 91 in Rogers, J. A., 100 Amazing Facts About the Negro, (18th ed), N Y. Revised 1940.

XXIV. The young Roman Emperor Honorius. (After Jean Paul Laurens, distinguished French painter)

the daughter of Canute, King of England."[3]

Another most distinguished Negro was Terentius Afer (Terence the African) an ex-slave, whose complexion was described by Suetonius, a contemporary, as "fuscus" or dusky. Terence is the greatest of the Latin stylists, and the author of six plays. He is famous mostly, however, for what is one of the finest civilized utterances ever made: Homo sum humani nihil a me alienum puto—I am a man and nothing human is alien to me.

Septimus Severus, another great emperor, was born in Africa. Macrinus and Firmus, other emperors, were Moors. Macrinus came of most humble parentage and was probably an ex-slave as his ears were bored in slave fashion.[4]

Hannibal and his African troops must have brought a great deal of Negro strain into the Roman population. For thirteen years they dominated the peninsula from the Alps to Naples. Hannibal, himself, was a full-blooded Negro with woolly hair, as his coins show.[5] His wife was Spanish, and perhaps white.

As in Egypt and Greece, the blacks also wielded considerable influence in religion. They established the cult of Isis which spread through the Roman empire as far as Paris, France, and Britain. This cult received additional prestige when Julius Caesar brought Cleopatra and her son, Caesarion, to Rome and set them up in magnificent style.

Carthage and North Africa

The earliest North Africans were, as was said, the Negritos. Bertholon and Chantre, leading authorities on the anthropology of North Africa, also place them as the first, a position, which, it appears, they continued to enjoy to a high degree well into the historic period as finds from the ancient graves have revealed. Bertholon and Chantre say of the skeletons from these graves, "Some characters possess marked Negroid traits. And such are not always persons of no importance. Indeed, the celebrated priestess of Tanit showed numerous Negroid traits, marked prognathism, flat, wide nose, long forearm, and had the physical traits of the Neolithic Negroes..." In still another sarcophagus with rich belongings they found the form of a woman who

---

[3] Wanley. Wonders of the Little World, p. 465. 1774.

[4] De Serviez. J. B. Lives of the Roman Empresses. Vol. II, p. 271. London, 1896.
  Crevier. History of the Roman Empire, Vol. VIII, p. 201. London, 1814.
  Gibbon. Decline and Fall of the Roman Empire, Vol. I, p. 200; Vol. IV, p. 273, Dublin, 1781.

[5] Garrucci, R. La Monete dell'Italia Antica. Parte Secunda. t. LXXV, 11, 12, 13, 14, 15. Roma, 1885.

"presented marked Negro characteristics."[6]

Ratzel and Reclus have also spoken of the marked Negro strain in the North African peoples. The former says, "Negroes crossed the Alps with Hannibal and fell at Worth beside McMahon. Whatever their original nature may have been all this population must have been alloyed with a strong Ethiopian element... The entire Semitic and Hamitic population of Africa, has, in other words, a mulatto character which extends to the Semites outside Africa."[7] Hannibal, most famous of all Carthaginians, was a Negro, as was said.

This North African region was once known as Barbary, and its people the Berbers, or Barbarians, who despite the bad use to which their name was put by the Europeans, were once leaders in culture. The Berbers claim descent from the Mazoi, or Negro soldiery, that was the backbone of the Egyptian army. Today these Berbers range from coal-black to white. One of the latter group, the Kabyles, have lived in the fastnesses of the Atlas Mountains, the Djurdjura and the Tizoussi, from the time of the Vandal invasion in the Fifth Century, A.D. The Kabyles are often said to be "pure" whites, but, they, too, are mixed. As Weisgerber says, "Slavery brought an infusion of black blood into the Kabyles... All the Kabyles of the Riff, of the Grand Kabyle, of the Aures, and of the Enfida, belong to the Mediterranean white race, and are to a greater or less degree mixed with blonds, Ethiopians, and Negroes."

Elisee Reclus, noted geographer, also says, "A large strain of Negro blood may everywhere be recognized among the inhabitants of Algeria. Whole tribes even among the highland Kabyles betray clear proofs of crossing between the aborigines of the sea-board and the Sudanese Negroes. Perhaps more than half of the Algerians who pass for Arabs or Berbers are of mixed descent."[8]

The Numidians of classic antiquity were a Negro people. Sir William Smith, says that the word "Mauri" from which comes Mauritania (Morocco), means "black" and adds "These Moors must not be considered a different race from the Numidians, but as a tribe belonging to the same stock."

The most noted figure of Numidia was King Massinissa, who provided the balance of power whereby Rome was able to defeat Hannibal. Massinissa, it will be recalled, deserted his natural ally, Carthage, because the beautiful Sophonisba, with whom he was in love, was given as a bride to Syphax.

---

[6] Bertholon, L. and E. Chantre. Recherches Anthrop. dans la Berberie. Vol. I, pp. 279-80 for Carthage; p. 241 for Negrito origin; and Vol. II for 171 portraits of North Africans, showing the Negroid strain in the majority of them. Lyon, 1913.
See also Harvard-African Studies, Vol. X, 1932, on "The Natives of Siwah Oasis."
[7] Ratzel, F. History of Mankind. Vol. II, p. 246. Lond., 1896-8.
[8] The Earth and Its Inhabitants, Vol. II, p. 286. N. Y. 1893

In Cabiria, Gabriel D'Annunzio's moving-picture, Massinissa, is portrayed as a Negro. The ancestors of the Carthaginians were the Phoenicians, who, as was said, were Negroid, their founder being Queen Dido. Dido is said to have refused to marry Iarbus, the black King of Morocco. This has given Jerome Dowd, Professor of Sociology at the University of Oklahoma, an opportunity to read Southern color prejudice into classical history. Says Dowd,

"The attitude of the Caucasian toward intermixture with the Negro has not changed within the historic period. As far back as 700 B.C., the fair widowed Queen, Dido of Carthage, committed suicide rather than comply with the unnatural and selfish importunities of her subjects to marry Iarbus, the swarthy monarch of Mauretania."[9]

The first objection to this is that there is no proof as to Dido's color. She might have been anything from black to white. But supposing that she was white and that her subjects were "so unnatural and selfish" as to wish her to marry a Negro, that meant the subjects had not such undying color prejudice as Dowd endows them with. If Dido and her subjects were black then would it be "unnatural" for them to wish their queen to marry a black man? Besides there are several versions why Dido killed herself, assuming that she did. According to Virgil, she committed suicide because her lover, Aeneas, deserted her.

[9] The Negro in American Life, p. 456. N. Y. 1926.

American color prejudice is also read by certain historians into the rivalry between Hanno and Mutines, Carthaginian commanders. Mutines, who appears to be Hannibal's most gifted general, was sent to supersede Hanno in Sicily.

The latter, who was very jealous of Mutines, said, "Mutinem sibi modum facere, *degenerem Afrum* imperatori Karthaginiensi, misso ab senatu populoque." (Livy, book xxv, chap. 40.)

The phrase *degenerem Afrum* (degenerate African) is generally interpreted to mean that Mutines was a mulatto and Hanno, a white man. Liddell says, "Hannibal sent over an officer named Mutin, or Mutton, who, henceforth became the soul of the war in Sicily. This man was a half-breed Carthaginian and the African blood in his veins degraded him in the eyes of pure Carthaginians as the taint of black blood degrades a man in the United States." (History of Rome, p. 330.)

Spillans and Edmonds translates it as "mongrel African."

The sources of these historians are Polybius (200 B.C.), and Livy, (59 B.C.-17 A.D.) neither of whom mention color or race. Harper's Latin Dictionary uses this passage from Livy to mean "mentally or morally degenerate, ignoble, base."

Chapter Nine

WERE THE JEWS ORIGINALLY NEGROES?

E UROPEAN painters and sculptors by their use of white models to typify Biblical characters have falsified tremendously the physiognomy of the ancient Jews. We are familiar with the scores of portraits offered to us as Christ. But do good Christians ever stop to think what he really looked like? Josephus, first century historian, described him as dark skinned and simple in appearance, in the Halosis, suppressed portion of his work.*

Solomon, too, is portrayed as a white man, though in the Songs attributed to him he speaks of himself as "black but comely." After visiting most of the leading galleries of Europe and America, the only realistic painting of an Eastern crowd that I have ever seen is "Christ and Barabbas" by Verlat in the Royal Museum of Antwerp where the mob is clamoring for Barabbas in preference to Christ. Solomon, too, is always painted white. The only picture I have ever seen of him as a Negro was in a certain luxurious palace of Cytherea in Paris.

Mention was made of the biblical theory that Negroes became black because Noah, supposedly white, cursed the sons of Ham. But the earliest Jews were in all probability, Negroes. Abraham, their ancestor, is said to have come from Chaldea and the ancient Chaldeans were black. "The Chaldees," says Higgins, "were originally Negroes." As was said, too, relics of prehistoric Negroes have been discovered in this region. It is even possible that the Jews originated, not in Asia, but in Africa. Gerald Massey has advanced considerable argument in proof of that theory.

Whatever was the original color of the Jews they lived for more than four centuries among the Negroid Egyptians. Their supposed oppressor, the Pharaoh, Mernepthah, shows marked Negroid traits.

Only seventy Jews went to Egypt, but according to the Bible, 600,000 men left it, which must have meant an additional two or three million women and children. Since the Jews were slaves their women were undoubtedly concubines of the Egyptians and must have produced mixed offspring. After more than three centuries of slavery almost every trace of the first seventy Jews must have been lost, together with their culture. Thus Jewish culture was Egyptian culture. For instance, the Egyptians did not eat pork, and still do not eat it.

To get an idea what must have happened to only those seventy Jews, think of what has happened to Negroes in the United States who came in

* See sources in "Nature Knows No Color-Line" p. 40.

hundreds of thousands over a period of centuries and not all at once as the Jews did in Egypt. The Negroes are so Americanized that were it not for their color one would forget that they ever came from Africa.

The Falashas, or Black Jews of Ethiopia, are probably very ancient. They claim lineal descent from Abraham, Isaac and Jacob, call themselves Beta-Israel (The Chosen People), and observe the passover.[1]

Tacitus (80 A.D.) says that many Romans of his time believed that the Jews originated in Ethiopia, having left there to escape oppression from Cepheus, the king. Whiston, translator of Josephus' History of the Jews, asks with regard to this: "One would wonder how Tacitus or any other heathen could suppose the African Ethiopians under Cepheus, who are known to be blacks, could be the parents of the Jews, who are known to be whites?"[2]

But, as was said, the Negro Jews in Ethiopia are actually Jews. Moreover, it is only in the white men's lands that the Jews are white, this being the result of intermixture with the whites. In the black man's land they are black. If some Romans believed that the Jews were of Ethiopian ancestry, there must certainly have been black Jews in Rome. Negroes were very well known to the Romans.

Moses himself was black. In all likelihood he was the son of Pharaoh's own daughter, which would account for his adoption and rearing for the throne. The story of his finding in the bullrushes is so identical with that told about Sargon, King of Babylon, who preceded him, that to some it seems doubtful."[3] Moreover, this finding a child in the water is an old African tradition.

When Jehovah wished to give Moses a sign, so runs the famous legend, he told him to put his hand into his bosom. The hand came out white, proving that it could not have been white before. The miracle lay in turning a black skin white, and turning it to black again. Hence the perfect logic of the Mohammedan belief that Moses was a Negro.

As Sir T. W. Arnold says: "According to Mohammedan tradition Moses was a black man as may be seen from the following passage in the Koran, 'Now draw thy hand close to thy side; it shall come forth white but unhurt'— another sign (XX, 23). 'Then he drew forth his hand and lo! it was white to the beholders. The nobles of Pharaoh said, "Verily this is an expert enchanter." VII, 105-06).' "[4]

Similarly Suyuti tells: "A Negro who pretended to the gift of prophecy was brought before al-Mamun (the Caliph) and said: 'I am Moses, the son of Imram,' and al-Mamun said to him, 'Verily, Moses the son of Imram

---

[1] Fishberg, M., The Jew, pp. 117, 147-48; 120-134. London, 1911. Nesfield, Brief View of the Caste System, para. 135. Massey, G. A., Book of the Beginnings, Vol. II, pt. 2. pp. 364-441. London, 1881.
[2] Josephus' History of the Jews. Dissertation III, p. 923. London, 1841.
[3] Jewish Encyclopedia. (See Moses).
[4] The Preaching of Islam, p. 358. London, 1913.

XXV. Falasha Jewish students of Ethiopia and their teacher, Rabbi Abraham.

drew forth his hand from his bosom white, therefore, draw forth thy hand white that I may believe thee.' "[5]

Turning to modern anthropology one finds confirming evidence. Ratzel says: "The entire Semitic and Hamitic population of Africa has...a mulatto character which extends to the Semites outside of Africa."[6] Prof. Elliott Smith in "Human History," similarly states: "Every kind of intermingling has taken place between the original groups of the Negro, Hamitic and Semitic peoples."[7]

In the Sudan, Upper Egypt, and North Africa there are Jews whose color and features are indistinguishable from Negroes. The Jews outside Africa retain, large numbers of them, their Negroid traits.

Fishberg traces the physical resemblance between the white Jews and the black ones. Speaking of the color prejudice among Jews in India he says: "The white Jews keep aloof and do not associate with their (black) co-religionists." Of the latter he says: "Such persons also have a Jewish physiognomy, which is so specific that one would be inclined to believe that they are of mixed blood, were they not so cruelly maltreated by their white co-religionists and treated as black Jews." They are kept at a respectable

[5] History of the Caliphs. (trans. H. S. Jarrett), p. 342. Calcutta, 1881.
[6] History of Mankind. Vol. II, p. 246.
[7] p. 143. London, 1934.

distance and not permitted to enter the synagogue of the whites, nor do they bury their dead in the same cemetery.

Dr. Hans Guenther in his "Rassenkunde des Judischen Volkes," does the same. His work is illustrated with portraits of Negroid Jews of Europe and elsewhere. As was already said he compares a portrait of Abraham Plattje, a Hottentot, with that of Benjamin Disraeli, Jewish Prime Minister of England.[8] The resemblance is striking. Guenther, it is said, did this

Left: Assyrian women of about 1300 B.C. A type common among Aframericans. Right: Negro bust of 1500 B.C. from Egypt. Guenther thinks it was a Jew.

to depreciate the Jew but since we do not concede that Negro ancestry is a disgrace we cannot consider that Guenther's alleged aim has been achieved.

Count Adam Gurowski of Poland, who visited the United States in 1857, said similarly, "Numbers of Jews have the greatest resemblance to the American mulattoes. Sallow carnation complexion, thick lips, crisped black hair. Of all the Jewish population scattered over the globe one-fourth dwells in Poland. I am, therefore, well acquainted with their features. On my arrival in this country (The United States) I took every light-colored mulatto for a Jew."[9]

Measurements of the skulls of Polish Jews in Whitechapel, London, revealed that about 30 per cent of them were Negroid.[10]

The Negro strain is apparent among a considerable number of American Jews. Some Jewish women go to Negro hair-dressing parlors to have their hair straightened. The Island of Jamaica has a considerable number of mulatto Jews, also.

[8] pp. 90-95, 99-115, 143-148. Munich, 1930.
[9] America and Europe, p. 177. N. Y., 1857.
[10] Man, Vols. 5-6. No. 55, p. 93.
Additional Bibliography:
    Williams, J. J. Hebrewisms of West Africa. N. Y., 1930.
    Wheless, J. Is it God's Word? N. Y., 1926.
    Wheless, J. Forgery in Christianity. N. Y., 1930.
Scribner's Maga Apr., May, June, July, 1929, for West African Jews. Additional data and sources in Rogers, J. A. Nature Knows No Color Line, pp. 122, 130, 140-142.

Chapter Ten

RACE-MIXING UNDER ISLAM

ONE fact about Islam stands glowingly forth through the centuries: Its almost total freedom from race and class prejudice; the opportunity it gave to every capable and aspiring follower, regardless of color or social status, to rise to the highest possible rank. Slaves rose to be sultans, and slave women to be favorites of the ruler, and mothers of heirs to the throne. At times the slave, himself, became a master while still enslaved and held freeborn men of wealth and power in dread of him.

Christianity, which too, was an Oriental religion, had begun with the same broadmindedness. "Of one blood," said St Paul, "God made all the races of the earth." Race distinctions were unknown in early Christianity. The first great leaders of Christianity, next to St. Paul, were all born in parts of Africa where Negro strain was abundant in the population, and were very likely Negroes themselves. This is true of St. Augustine, Tertullian, Origen, Cyprian, and Clement of Alexandria. Tertullian and St. Athanasius (296-373 A.D.), for whom the Athanasian Creed is named, are definitely said to have been Negroes. Nevertheless, Christianity was not long in developing class differences in addition to slavery and after the discovery of the New World color prejudice too.

Of What Race Was Mohamet?

Mohamet, the founder of Islam, was an Arab. What is an Arab?

The Encyclopedia Britannica (11th edition) says of Arabia's present inhabitants, "Arabia has a considerable free black population and there again by intermarriage with the whites around have filled the land with a mulatto breed of every shade till in the eastern and southern provinces especially a white skin is almost an exception. In Arabia no prejudice exists against Negro alliances; no social or political line separates the African from the Arab."

There is every reason to believe that the above picture has been true of Arabia for the past several thousand years. Arabia is but an extension of Africa where black people from the southwest, and white, or nearly white people, from the northwest met to mingle their cultures and their blood.

Mohamet, himself, was to all accounts a Negro. A contemporary of his describes him as "large-mouthed," and "bluish-coloured, with hair that was neither straight nor curly,"[1a] that is, hair that was probably frizzly like that of the "Fuzzy-Wuzzy." "Bluish," also, happens to be the precise color of certain very Negroid natives of the Sudan. Mohamet's mother was also African. His grandfather, Abd el Mottalib, is spoken of as being "very dark." He might have been a slave, "Abd" or "aabd" originally meant "slave." Therefore when Dermengham[1b] says that the Negro strain "seemed scarcely perceptible,"in Mohamet, he is evidently wrong.

Most of Mohamet's first disciples were Negro slaves. His second convert and closest and most honored friend until his death was Bilal, an Ethiopian ex-slave. Mohamet thought so highly of Bilal that he gave him precedence over himself in Paradise. Mohamet also adopted as his own son, another Negro, Zayd bin Harith, his third convert, who rose to be one of his greatest generals.[2] Later, to show his regard for Zayd, he took one of Zayd's wives, the beautiful Zainab, as his own.

One of Mohamet's earliest injunctions was, "Variety of your languages and of your complexions, verily herein are signs unto men of understanding." (Koran XXX, 21). Of course, the mere issuance of this injunction is proof that there must have been some prejudice against color. In fact, wherever differences of color exist, there are certain preferences, mostly sexual, which like anything else in creation can be expanded into a fetish over which human beings can be made to fight. Hollywood, for instance, gives the preference to blondes; and gentlemen, we are told, prefer blondes. It must be rather irritating for a brunette beauty to find herself rejected by a movie director, because her skin and hair are not whiter.

Arabia, in Mohamet's time, was, even as it now is, a mulatto land. These mulattoes considered themselves superior, but not very seriously so to both the "pure" whites and the "pure" blacks. This trait was not local, nor is it entirely of the past. Certain old mulatto families of the West Indies, West Africa, and Ethiopia still feel the same towards whites and blacks. The Arab considered a white skin inferior; perhaps one had better say he had a certain repulsion for it such as exists today nearly over all Africa and Southern Asia because of its unfamiliarity. Gobineau says that Mohamet was too near divinity "to show a white skin" to his followers. Professor Toynbee says also, "The Primitive Arabs who were the ruling element of the Umayyad Caliphate called themselves 'the swarthy people' with a connotation of racial superiority and their Persian and Turkish subjects 'the ruddy people' with a connotation of racial inferiority, that is to say, they drew the distinction that we draw between blonds and brunets but reversed the values."[3]

[1a] Margoliouth, D. S. Mohammed, p. 63. London, 1927.
[1b] Dermengham. Life of Mohamet, p. 5. London, 1930.
[2] Islamic Review. Vol. 20, p. 220. June-July, 1932.
[3] A Study of History. Vol. I, p. 226. London, 1934.

This feeling of superiority on the part of a mixed race was probably heightened by the very low culture of the Nordics of that time. Draper, writing of the eleventh century, speaks of the vastly superior social and artistic development of the swarthy Moors, who, he says, might well have looked "with supercilious contempt on the dwellings of the rulers of Germany, France, and England, which were scarce better than stables—chimneyless, windowless, and with a hole in the roof for the smoke to escape like the wigwams of certain Indians."[4]

The Zenghs, or Zends, the very black natives of Africa, who were imported in great numbers as slaves, were looked down on too, probably for the same reason. A work by Al-Jahiz, a Negro writer, whom Christopher Dawson calls "the greatest scholar and stylist of the Ninth Century,"[5] leaves little doubt of that. This book is entitled *Kitab al Sudan wa 'l-Bidan,* or "The Superiority in Glory of the Black Race Over the White," a title that speaks for itself. "White" here, be it noted, does not mean the fair whites, but dark-skinned whites and mulattoes. In parts of the East, as in Ethiopia, the fair white is called "the red man." Moreover, Jahiz in his essay includes the East Indians among the blacks—a people which many modern ethnologists claim as white.

Another writer of that time, Masudi, has written at length of these primitive blacks.[6]

The latter were treated so badly by their masters, some of whom were native-born blacks, that they rose in what was undoubtedly the greatest slave rebellion in history, including even that of Haiti. Under their leader, Al Burkhui, (The Veiled Prophet), they seized Bagdad, the capital of the world's then mightiest empire, and held it for thirteen years (870-883 A.D.). The Zenghs killed more than half a million of their oppressors, an enormous number for that day. Cutting off the heads of their masters they would toss the heads in the canals of the Tigris and let them drift down the stream to anxious relatives waiting to see who were the next.[7]

Several passages in Arabian literature also reveal a certain prejudice against the pure blacks. In the great Arabian sex classic, *Er Roud el aater fi nezaha el khater,* (The Perfumed Garden), the remarks of the Caliph when he witnesses the sexual prowess of the Negro, Al Durgham, and his careful inquiry into the cause of his powers, leave little doubt of that.[8] Also, the

---

[4] Intellectual Development of Europe, p. 348. N. Y., 1863.
[5] The Making of Europe, p. 152. N, Y., 1932.
  Hitti, P. K. History of the Arabs, p. 382. London, 1937.
[6] Les Prairies d'Or. (trans. C. Barbier de Meynard), Vol. I, pp. 163-67; Vol. III, chap. 33. Paris, 1863.
[7] Hitti, P. K. Ibid, pp. 467-68.
[8] Nefzawi. Le Jardin Parfumé. History of the Negro, Doreramus, pp. 44-72. Paris, 1927.

XXX. Types of the Anglo-Egyptian Sudan and adjacent regions, all save that in the centre are
called Hamitic by the European scientist. Central figure is an Ethiopian.

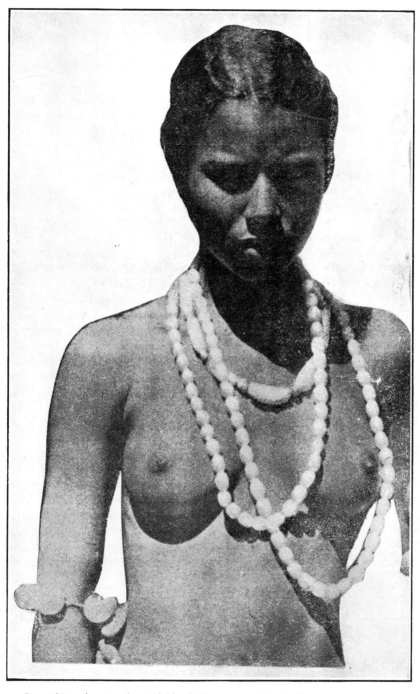

East African beauty of mixed blood. The type could also be Polynesian.

poet, An-Nami, when mocked about his gray hairs by another, who said that An-Nami had but a single black hair in his head, replied, "A dark African spouse will not remain long in the house where the second wife is white." (Note that "white" in the East, as in Brazil, is sometimes dark mulatto).

Abu Ishak, a poet, who wrote much in favor of his black slave, Yumn, also says, "The dark-skinned Yumn said to one whose colour equalled the whiteness of the eye, "Why should your face boast of its clear complexion? Do you think that by so clear a tint it gains additional merit? Were a mole of my colour on that face it would adorn it, but one of your colour on my cheek would disfigure it.' "[9]

Two of the greatest of all Oriental rulers, Antar and Kafur, both suffered from color prejudice at first. Antar, who was the son of an Ethiopian slave, was despised by the Bedouins, themselves a Negroid people, because of his blackness. Antar is the greatest chivalrous figure of the East and one of the world's great poets.[10]

Kafur, "a Negro of deep-black color with a smooth shining skin," who had been brought out of the Sudan as a slave, and who later rose to be ruler of Egypt and Syria, was at first mocked by his fellow-slaves, and called "the moon of darkness' by the celebrated poet, Al-Muttanabi.[11]

The phrase, "black but comely" which is said to be a correct translation, also shows some objection to black. Some of this feeling still exists in the East. I recall seeing once in Cairo a very black man with short woolly hair but with an almost Grecian profile. The type being unfamiliar to me, I asked my companion, a Bedouin, who was at least three-fourths Negro, himself, whether the man was an Egyptian. "No," he replied, "that's what they call a nigger." He said that his father had people like him as slaves but added quickly that they were treated very kindly.

This prejudice against unmixed white and unmixed black has long existed in Ethopia also.[12] Count Gleichen correctly said that the Ethiopian "hates a white man" and is anxious to keep him out of his country. The Amhara, who, in general, show more of the Negro than the average Aframerican, look down upon the Chankalla, or primitive black. But this is largely true only of the first generation. Numbers of leading Ethiopians show a marked Chankalla strain. The great Emperor Menelik, who was coal-black, came of this stock. His mother, Edgig-aiehou, was a Chankalla slave. In Egypt, too, these black Negroes, some of them with their tribal

[9] Ibn Khallikan. Biographical Dictionary. (trans. MacGuckin de Slane), Vol. I, pp. 32, 111. Paris, 1842-71.
[10] Hamilton, T. Antar. 4 vols. London, 1880. Also Biographie Universelle
[11] Ibn Khallikan. Biographical Dictionary (McGuckin de Slane), Vol. II, pp. 524 et seq. Paris, 1842.
[12] Ludolphus. History of Ethiopia. Book I, chap. 14. London, 1682.

markings, hold high rank in the Egyptian army. The chamberlain of the late King Fouad was a black, Sammi Bey, while the prime minister, Nahas Pasha, was a mulatto. In short, the prejudice in the East cannot be explained in terms of the American one. It is cultural rather than chromatic. The nearest thing to it, I know, is the prejudice the Northern Negro entertains for most of the Southern ones.

Color, then, was no serious bar under Islam, or in the East, from the earliest times. Several of the rulers of the Mohammedan Empire, at the height of its glory were not only mulattoes, but blacks. Such a one was Ibrahim al-Mahdi, Islam's most renowned singer, and the half-brother of Haroun Al-Raschid of Arabian Nights' fame. Ibrahim calls himself "a Negro" in his autobiography. So does his uncle and rival for the throne, Mamoun the Great. Ibrahim's mother was the daughter of a Persian king.

Ibn Khallikan, Arab historian of the thirteenth century, says of Ibrahim, "Being of dark complexion which he inherited from his mother, Shikla or Shakla, who was a Negro, he received the name of At-Thinnin—the Dragon (due to his size and the blackness of his skin)... He was proclaimed Caliph at Bagdad...under the title of Al Mubarak (The Blessed)."[13] At least two of the other caliphs, Al Muktafi and Rachid, had Negro mothers, according to Suyuti.

The renowned Kafur, ruler of Egypt, was a thick-lipped Negro slave of Chankalla birth; Haroun Al-Raschid made Khusabeb, another Negro ex-slave, ruler of Egypt.[14] Mahmud of Ghazni, greatest of the Islamic conquerors, was the son of a slave. The Mamelukes, some of whom were white slaves from the Russian Caucasus, and some of whom were Negro slaves from the Sudan, ruled Egypt for three centuries (1250-1517), and held great power when Napoleon invaded Egypt. Moslem India, also, has had many great rulers of Negro descent, one of whom was Malik Ambar,[15] a Negro ex-slave, who ruled in Bombay; and Malik Andeel, another Negro ex-slave who ruled in Bengal.[16] The Nawabs, or Nabobs, great Moslem princes of India, are originally of Ethiopian Negro stock.[17] They enjoyed great power until the beginning of the nineteenth century.

Negro Ranked First in Sexual Competence

As regards sex relations, the real index to prejudice, there was little ill-will either. Black men, some of whom were eunuchs, had sometimes great harems with women of many races. One of these latter, Sunbullu (The

13 Ibn Khallikan. Ibid, Vol. I, p. 17.
14 Sadi. Gulistan (ed. Sir Edward Arnold), pp. 80-1. N. Y., 1899.
15 See 40.
16 See 41.
17 Morie, L. J. Histoire de l'Ethiopie, Vol. II, p. 33. Paris, 1904.

XXXI. 1. Princess Tsahi, eldest daughter of Haile Selassie; 2. Lidj Yassu, Emperor, who was deposed, (note the strong resemblance to Amen-ophis III); 3. Ras Hailu, King of Godjam, once Ethiopia's richest man; 4. Haile Selassie at the age of six.

Black Hyacinth) once presented one of his choicest white wives as a gif
to the sultan. In sexual competence, which is highly admired by the Arab,
the Negro was given the first place, and given it without any apparent ill-will.
In the sex orgy described in the story of "Zorah" from "Le Jardin Parfumé"
the honors of the occasion are awarded to Mimoun, a Negro, who alone could
satisfy the nymphomanic, Mouna. Mimoun performs a rare feat of
venery, thereby winning the favours of the Princess Zorah for his master,
and Mouna as his own wife.[18]

In Arabian tales, too, the Negroes are usually reserved for · queens
and women of high degree. In the above mentioned sex classic of Sheik
Nafzawi is the "Story of the Negro, Al Durgham, and the Beauteous Lady,
Al Budoor" in which some of the leading women of the empire as the wives
of the prime minister, of the secretary of state, the state treasurer, and the
Caliph's own daughter, meet amid scenes of Oriental splendor to enjoy the
sexual embraces of lusty Negroes. Al Durgham had women "the likes of
which even the King had not in his palace." In fact, the Negro bucks about
the harems, were, by all reports, overworked, amatorily speaking. As Al
Durgham sang,

"We, Negroes, have had our fill of women
We fear not their tricks however subtle they are."

Sir Richard Burton in an English translation of this work, declares
that such scenes were not singular. He adds, "Cairene society of the 1860's
hastened to shut up a great scandal over the sexual prowess of a Negro
who had charge of a Pasha's harem . . . he had supplanted the conjugal
duties of his owner to the profound satisfaction of the lascivious ladies of
the household." The pasha, it appears, had bought the Negro for a eunuch,
but had been fooled by the slave-dealer.

Burton, in his translation of the "Arabian Nights' Entertainment," gives
several stories that are usually expurgated, as "The Story of King Shahryar
and His Brothers," "The Story of the Eunuch Buhkayt," "The Man of
Al Yemen and His Six Slave Girls," and "The Story of The Ensorcelled
Prince." In the first story, the women, who are white or near-white, and
are attendants of the queen, go into the garden, and each selects for sexual
pleasure a man of their own color, but the queen, herself, chooses a coal-
black Negro on whom she showers all her endearment. "But the Queen
who was left alone presently cried out in a loud voice, 'Here come to me,
Oh my lord Saeed,' and then sprang with a drop-leap from one of the trees
a big slobbering blackamoor with rolling eyes, which showed the whites, a
truly hideous sight. He walked boldly up to her and threw his arms around
her neck while . . ." The remainder of the story pulls no punches.

[18] pp. 281-97. Paris, 1927.

XXXII. Ethiopian types with slight amount of "White" blood. Upper left is a young man.

ln a footnote to the second story in which the master's daughter gives herself to a Negro, Burton says, "This familiarity with blackamoor slave-boys is common in the East and often ends as in the story.

"In my time no honest Hindi-Moslem would take his women-folk to Zanzibar on account of the huge attraction and enormous temptation there and thereby offered to them." (Burton, here refers to the muscular black men, wandering nude on the streets.)[19]

Napoleon on Race-Mixing in the East

When Napoleon invaded Egypt in 1798 and saw how the different colors of mankind lived in harmony under Islam, while in Christian Haiti, whites, mulattoes, and blacks were at one another's throats in a three-cornered war, he was so impressed that he tried to introduce legal race-mixing in Haiti. He said,

"These countries were inhabited by men of different colors. Polygamy is the simple way of preventing them from persecuting one another. The legislators have thought that in order that the whites be not enemies of the blacks, the blacks of the whites, the copper-colored of the one and the other, it was necessary to make them all members of the same family and struggle thus against a penchant of man to hate all that is not like him. Mohamet thought that four women were sufficient to attain this goal because each man could have one white, one black, one copper-colored, and one wife of another color...

"When one wishes to give liberty to the blacks in the colonies of America and establish a perfect equality, the legislator will authorise polygamy and permit at the same time a white wife, a black one, and a mulatto one. Then the different colors making part of the same family will be mixed in the opinion of each. Without that one would never obtain satisfactory results. The blacks would be more numerous and clever and they would hold the whites in abasement and vice versa.

"Because of the general principle of equality that polygamy has established in the East there is no difference between the individuals composing the house of the Mamelukes. A black slave that a bey had bought from an African caravan became katchef and was the equal of a fine white Mameluk, native of Circassia; there was no thought even of having it otherwise.

"Slavery has never been in the Orient what it was in Europe. The customs in this respect have remained the same as in the Holy Scriptures: the servant marries with the master. In Europe, on the contrary, whoever bore the imprint of the seal of slavery remained always in the last rank..."[20]

[19] Vol. I, pp. 1-16. 6. 71; Vol. II, p. 49; Vol. IV, pp. 245-60, 253, 278.
[20] Memoires. Vol. III, pp. 152-54, 259-76. Paris, 1904.

XXXIII. 1. Ibn Saud, King of Nejd and Hedjaz, Arabia; 2. Bedouin (Arabian) ladies; 3. Modern Egyptian of white stock.

Sudanese women, like this one, have frequently been the mothers of Oriental rulers from time immemorial. Inset: Sheikh Hafiz Wahab, son of Ibn Saud, King of Arabia, who shows Sudanese features.

In short, the Negro, was discriminated against in no phase of Mohammedan life on the ground of color alone. Islam was the greatest and freest
of all great melting pots.

And it carried race-mixing throughout the length and breadth of what
was the vastest empire the world has ever known. At the height of its
power Islam stretched from the centre of France south to the Mediterranean
and along both shores of this sea to the Levant and from thence to India,
China, and the islands of the Pacific, as well as into Asiatic Russia. The
sultans in this vast area were of all colors from blond to coal-black and wives
of all colors were to be found in their harems. White captives of both
sexes were taken from Europe and scattered over North Africa and Asia and
black captives of both sexes were carried into Europe and Asia. Differences
of color among the Mohammedans came in time to count for almost as little
as the different colors of flowers in a garden does to the flowers themselves.

A Negroid strain, more or less predominant, ran through the whole. As
Keane says, "All who accepted the Koran became merged with the conquerors
in a common Negroid population."[21]

It was this empire founded by the black Mohamet with the help of
brown, yellow and white mongrels that aroused proud Europe from the
slumber of the Dark Ages, and laid the foundations of its present culture.
It was the great Arab chemists, architects, mathematicians, physicians, and
experimental scientists to whom we are largely indebted for modern science.
Go to any part of the Mohammedan world—to India, Indo-China, Egypt,
Morocco, Spain—and you will behold art whose beauty mankind seems to
have lost the conception of. Near to the Alhambra, for instance, is a structure erected by the architects of the Emperor Charles V of Spain and Germany. Compared with the superb beauty of the Alhambra the latter, is to
say the least, crude and clumsy.

It was the Arabs, too, who gave to Europe her present system of numerals, which they, in turn, had taken from the Hindus. Match this Arabic
or Hindu numeral, against the tedious and cumbersome Roman letter-
numerals! No wonder Nietzsche raged in anger when he thought of how
the Moors who had done so much for European civilization had been driven
out like dogs by the Christians.

Race-mixing, as we thus see, has been one of the functions of empire.
Egypt, Persia, Macedonia, Rome, brought hordes of whites, browns, and
blacks and amalgamated them. All great empires seem to begin with race-
mixing, and die when they become too pure. The races that are furthest
down are the purest ones, as the Veddahs of Ceylon, the Andaman Islanders,
the Pigmies, and the Semangs. The mixed ones are the furthest up. What

[21] Man, Past and Present, p. 64. Cambridge, 1920.

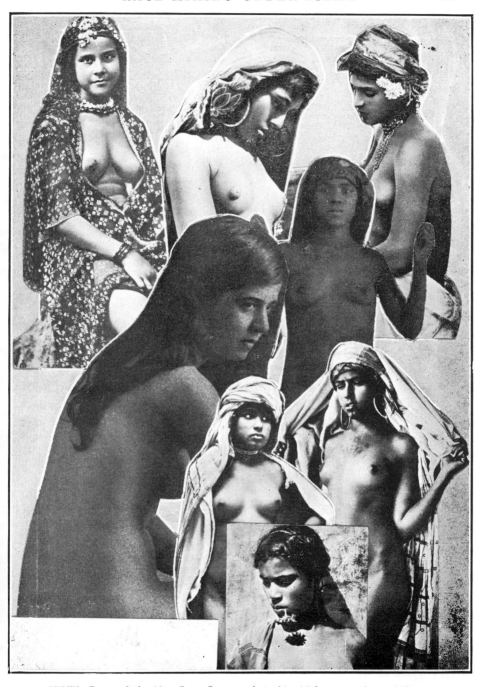

XXXIV. Types of the Near-East—Egypt and Arabia, Mulattoes and near-Whites.

land is more mixed than the United States, which is now at the top? America, as we shall show in Volume Two, is more vastly mixed than the average person imagines. The race-purists usually shut their eyes to this fact. Petrie showed how repeated Ethiopian invasions brought new life to Egypt. A pure race may be compared to standing water; a mixed race, to running water. The former soon becomes stagnant; the latter by running purifies tself. Nature knows her business. She is wiser than all in this respect.

Egypt Today

The color pattern of the Egyptian population today may be summed up as follows: In Alexandria and the Delta rather more white than black due to European immigration; at Cairo, there is also a large European population but the native population is mulatto, and shades off towards dark mulatto; at Thebes, it is predominantly dark mulatto with a large proportion of blacks; and in the Anglo-Egyptian Sudan, it is far more black than mulatto with only a sprinkling of whites, mostly Europeans. Some of these blacks haven't the broad features of the average West African black, but their hair is woolly. Some of the jet-black, woolly-haired Negroes, as the so-called Fuzzy-Wuzzies, have Grecian profiles. A Levantine strain is also apparent in certain of the population. In short, this black population s very highly mixed.

The people of Southern Persia are still largely Negroid. Some are pure Negroes, like the Bombassi. The Susians in the lower valley of the Euphrates are also strongly Negroid. In all this region of the Near East the supply of "pure" Negroes was kept up by the slave trade and the recruiting of black women for the harems, which still goes on. Negroes in this latter region also marry white women.

Chapter Eleven

RACE-MIXING UNDER ISLAM (Continued)

North Africa and Morocco

R ACE-MIXING in North Africa took a form that was almost the reverse of that of the United States. There it was the fair whites who were brought in as the slaves and concubines of mulattoes, dark-skinned whites, and blacks.

This process had gone on for probably thousands of years prior to the eighth century. From before Julius Caesar and down to the early part of the nineteenth century, the Barbary sea-rovers, who were largely Negroid, raided the ships and the coasts of Europe as far north as the British Isles.

With the invasion of Spain by the Moors in 711 A.D., the number of white captives into Africa increased. The invasion of France brought in other hordes. For four centuries, roughly from 1400 to 1800, collections were taken up in the churches of Europe for the ransom of white Christians held in African slavery.

Holland, Sweden, Denmark, Spain, and even the United States after her severance from England, had to pay tribute to these Negroid sea-rovers. White Americans were captured on the high seas and taken into the Sudan as slaves. The United States sent warships to Africa several times to free the white Americans held in bondage there, once being under Decatur in 1815.

Abbe Busnot, who was sent by Louis XIV to negotiate with Mulai Ismael, Emperor of Morocco, for the release of French captives gives a touching story of their plight and of their numbers. Pidon de St. Olon, another Frenchman who visited Morocco at this time says as regards Mulai Ismael and the French captives, "Upon that Mulai Ismael made a sign to the French slaves to approach him and all threw themselves flat on their bellies at his feet."[22] By all accounts the Africans treated their white slaves as harshly as the American colonials did the blacks. There was this exception, however, the Christians always had the alternative of embracing Islam and becoming one with the fold, a step which was highly repugnant to most of them.

J. G. Jackson, another writer of the times, says, "They (the Moors) carry the Christian captives about the Desert to the different markets to

[22] See Rogers, J. A. 100 Amazing Facts About the Negro, pp. 37, 45, 18th edition for biblio. Illin. Cathol. Review. Vol. IX, pp. 162-76. 1926-7. Asia Maga., May, June, July, 1932

sell them for they soon discover that their habits of life render them un-serviceable, or very inferior to the black slaves from Timbuctoo. After travelling three days to one market, five to another, nay sometimes, fourteen, they at length become objects of commercial speculation and the itinerant Jew traders, who wander about Wedinoon to sell their wares find means to barter them for tobacco, salt, a cloth garment, or any other thing."[23]

Frederick Moore says: "There can be no mistake about the records of history which state that thousands of Christian slaves, many of them British, were sold in the great white market at Salli. The faces of many of the people today are distinctly European. Here there seems to be less mixture of black blood than in the other towns, many of the people being white as Europeans."[24]

Jackson adds as regards this mixing, "Their complexion from frequent intermarriage or intercourse with the Sudanic race is of all shades from black to white... Whenever a blue or grey-eyed Mooress is seen, she is always suspected to be the descendant of some Christian renegade."

Adolphe Bloch has given the following precise description of the present race of the Moors and the manner in which black and white amalgamated over long centuries to form it. He says, "The race which gave birth to the Moroccans can be no other than the African Negroes because the same black type with features more or less Caucasian is found all the way to Senegal upon the right bank of the river without counting that it has been recognized in various parts of the Sahara...and from there comes black Moors who still have thick lips as a result of Negro descent and not from intermixture.

"As to the white, bronze, or dark Moors, they are no other than the near relations of black Moors with whom they form the varieties of the same race; and as one can also see among the Europeans, blondes, brunettes, and chest-nuts, in the midst of the same population so one may see Moroccans of every color in the same agglomeration without its being a question of their being real mulattoes."

This is a fact that those who talk about "Hamites" overlook. The so-called Hamite and even the Semite is nothing else but a fixed mulatto type. My own impressions of the native quarters of Moroccan cities is that but for dress and customs, the population was very much like Negro districts in the United States.

Voltaire, who lived in Mulai Ismael's day, also wrote about the white slaves of Morocco in the eleventh chapter of Candide. One of his characters is the beautiful daughter of Pope Urban X and the Princess of Palestrina, who was captured by a Moorish sea-rover," an abominable Negro" who

[23] Empire of Morocco, pp 272-281. London, 1809.
[24] Passing of Morocco, pp. 133-34. London, 1908.

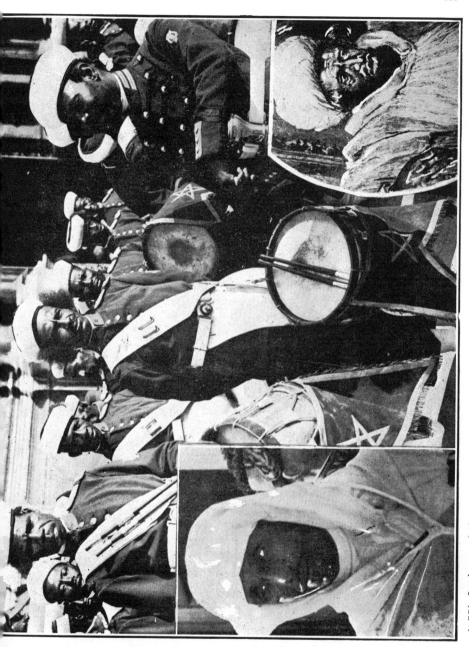

XXXV. Bandsmen of the present Sultan of Morocco. Inset (left) Glaoui Pasha, Morocco's richest man. Insert (right) the late Sultan Mul ai Youssef.

made her his mistress, and who in doing so "believed he was conferring an honour" on her.

These Moorish sea-rovers dominated the northwestern coasts of Scotland for centuries. David McRitchie tells of these corsairs, and adds, "Allan McRuari, the black-skinned Hebridean pirate of the fifteenth century, is one notable instance of these black invaders." George Hardy says, "The Merindes (Moors) profited by their maritime situation to create a powerful fleet and to undertake against the Christian countries of the Mediterranean, a savage struggle.

"From their ports left armed ships manned by men of proved bravery and maintained by communal societies. These 'corsairs' descended unexpectedly upon the coasts or isles of the Mediterranean, and they captured and sold as slaves the sailors and the passengers. A veritable terror reigned in the Mediterranean... They ravaged the coasts of Portugal, Spain, Southern France—and even went as far as Britain."[25]

George I of England in his speech from the throne, October 19, 1721, speaks of "the great number of my subjects delivered from slavery" because of a treaty with Mulai Ismael.

According to C. B. Driscoll, these sea-rovers raided Baltimore Castle in 1631, and their Negro chief, Ali Krussa, carried off Mary, daughter of Sir Fineen O'Driscoll, master of the castle.[26]

Some of these white European women were taken into the harems of the sultans, and rose to positions of great influence. One of the most noted was Shams Ed Douha (The Morning Sun) favorite wife of Abu Hassan Ali, the renowned "Black Sultan." Their joint tomb at Shella is one of the architectural gems of Morocco.[27]

Mulai Ismael, "The African Louis XIV," Morocco's most famous ruler, and the son of an unprepossessing Negro slave, had one of the largest harems of history. Abbe Busnot who visited him says that his favorite wife was a huge, coal-black woman; his second favorite, an Englishwoman, who had been captured at the age of fifteen, and the third, another Negro woman, whose son was the next Emperor.

Mulai Ismael's greatest general was a Negro, Empsael, whose favorite wife, Zoraide, was French. Bernardin de St. Pierre, author of "Paul and Virginia" uses this mixed marriage for a satire on the treatment of blacks in America, and the belief of the whites that their color makes them superior. In his play, "Empsael and Zoraide," or "The White Slaves of the Blacks of Morocco," he gives a dialogue between two of Empsael's generals as regards

[25] Les Grands Etapes de l'Histoire du Maroc, pp. 50-54. Paris, 1921.
[26] Doubloons, pp. 290-304. N. Y., 1930.
[27] Vision of Morocco, pp. 99-100. London, 1923.

the marriage of their chief to a white woman:

"Hannibal.—I don't know why our great general married a woman of that color. He must have been bewitched. Our black women are more beautiful, better formed, more gay, and yet more obedient to their husbands than white women.

"Balabon.—One must not despise Zoraide because she is white. God gave her a soul even as He did you and me.

"Hannibal.—I do not despise her for that. But how could our great general have so poor taste. One sees many whites falling in love with black women but few blacks falling in love with the white women. A black skin is natural; it is the sun that gave it and it is never effaced. A white skin on the contrary is a sick color that is preserved only in the shade. All the whites of Europe have effeminate faces."[28]

One West Indian girl, Aimee, also rose to high power in the East. Captured on the high seas in 1789, while on the way to her home in Martinique, she was sold as a slave. Later she was bought by the Sultan of Turkey and became the Sultana Valideh, or the mother of the heir to the throne.[29]

Incidentally, Mulai Ismael sent an offer of marriage to the Princess de Conti, beautiful daughter of Louis XIV, chiefly, it seems, to bind his friendship with the French king. The princess declined saying that the Moroccan ruler already had enough wives.

Morocco, in short, was the scene of an amalgamation of black and white as great as that of the southern United States but with the blacks dictating the terms. But, as was said, there was no degradation, save for those whites who refused to embrace Islam. Mulai Ismael's greatest admiral was a white man, Abdalla Ben Aicha, who captured hundreds of European ships and was later ambassador to Louis XIV.

Mulai Ismael also brought from the south across the desert hundreds of thousands of unmixed Negroes with their wives and settled them in his empire. From these, he made up his Bokhari, or pretorian guard, of 150,000 loyal blacks with which he dominated his subjects and his neighbors. These blacks were permitted no intercourse with the population. After his death, they ruled the empire for years. Mulai Ismael also had an army, a smaller one, of captive white men.

The brother of the last Sultan, who is still alive, is coal-black.

[28] Pub. by Maurice Sourneau. Caen. 1905.
[29] Morton, B. A. The Veiled Empress, p. 291. N. Y., 1923.

Algeria and Tunis

What Flournoy says of race-mixing in Morocco, namely, that a considerable portion of the population, especially the aristocracy and the royal family had Negro blood in their veins,"[30] is also true of Algeria and Tunis, but to a somewhat less extent.

Large numbers of white captives were also taken to Algiers, one of the great strongholds of the African corsairs. Both Algeria and Tunis were once under Moroccan domination.

Morgan, in his "History of Barbary and Algiers," tells of Hamida, a "mulatto," ruler of Tennez, who conquered Tunis in 1544, and who was "eloquent, of high spirits, and undaunted courage."[31] He also names other Negro rulers of North Africa. Negroes and Negroids still constitute the largest portion of the Algerian population, and especially the soldiery. The proportion is somewhat less in Tunis, but it is as great or greater in Tripoli (Libya). When the late Professor H. B. Moens showed the Bey of Tunis, photographs of American Negro girls, he said, "Why they look just like some of my people." This fact is supported by the 171 North African portraits reproduced by Bertholon and Chantre.[32]

The Byzantine Empire, Later the Turkish Empire

The Byzantine, or Eastern Roman Empire, included what is now Asiatic Turkey, European Turkey, Bulgaria, Greece, Roumania, Albania, Yugoslavia, Sicily, the tip of the Italian boot, and Sardinia, with Constantinople as its capital.

This empire was also a great melting-pot. Arabs, Greeks, Armenians, Jews, Nordics, Negroes all met and mingled. Byzantium was closely linked, culturally and commercially, with Ethiopia.[33] The Byzantine rulers took their title of Basileus[34] from Ethiopia, and led in the Christianizing of the land. Later at Byzantium's request, Abraha, emperor of Ethiopia, sent an army across the Red Sea to Yemen to the rescue of the Christians being persecuted by the Jewish ruler, Dhu Nowas. It was this step that led to the war of more than one thousand years between Islam and Christianity.[35]

Steven Runciman says of the Byzantine period, "The races of the whole Mediterranean world amalgamated...there was extraordinarily little racial

[30] British Policy Towards Morocco, p. 17. Baltimore, 1935.
[31] pp. 245. 345, 370, 384 (1728).
[32] Recherches Anthrop. dans la Berberie. Vol. II. Lyon, 1913.
[33] Frobenius. Voice of Africa (chap. on Byzantium, Vol. II). London, 1910-12.
[34] Ibid.
Diehl. C. J.'Afrique Byzantine. Paris, 1896.
[35] Harris. W. B. Yemen. pp. 317-321. Edin.. 1843.
Muir, W. Life of Mohamet. London, 1894.

XXXVI. Moroccan, Algerian and Tunisian Mulatto types.

prejudice among the Byzantines." It is true that there was a protest when Justinian II married his Negro cook to a noble Roman lady, but this was rather from class, than from racial snobbery, he says.[36]

Byzantium's greatest ruler, Nicephorus Phocas (912-969 A.D.), was a black Arab. Liudprand, bishop of Cremona, who saw him, says that he was "in color a Negro."[37] As to the southern part of the Byzantine empire as far west as Sicily, it was held for a long time by the African sea-rovers. In 904 A.D., Leo the African invaded southern Greece with 54 ships and 10,800 Negroes, and held it, until he was finally driven out by Nicephorus Phocas.[38] The Greeks' title for king is still Basileus.

In 1453 Constantinople, the capital, and the last stronghold of Christianity in the East, fell before the conquering Turks. Under the latter, Negroes also rose to positions of the highest power. Some of their most valiant generals were black. It was a gigantic Negro, Hassan, who was the first to mount the walls of Constantinople during the siege and made the breach that led to its capture. Later the Turks drove into Hungary, Switzerland, and Austria as far as the gates of Vienna, mixing the blood of the vanquished in their march. The Negroid strain apparent in a number of Hungarians and Austrians is undoubtedly due to the Turkish invasion.

The ancestry of Goethe, greatest of all German writers, has been traced to this Turkish Negroid stock. In addition there were two Mohrs—German for Negro—in his family tree.[38a] Goethe was swarthy and full-lipped, especially in his earlier portraits. As for the Bulgars, that word itself means "The Black People." A visitor to all this part of Eastern Europe cannot help but be struck by the Negroid faces of many of the inhabitants.

Negroes, principally women, were brought in large numbers from the Sudan and Ethiopia for the Turkish harems. The late Sultan Abdul Hamid liked Negroes so well that when Negro slavery in Egypt was doomed he founded a Turkish village composed entirely of "pure" Negroes from whom he reared his attendants and eunuchs.

Some of the Turkish Negroes as late as 1907 enjoyed power that was little short of royal. Others were sultans in all but name. This was because the blacks had the highest reputation for loyalty.

India

Great numbers of African Negroes also went to India either as mercenaries, slaves, or merchants under Islam. Some of them rose to be prime

---

[36] Byzantine Civilization, pp. 180-2. London, 1932.
[37] Diehl, C. Byzantine Portraits. (trans. Harold Bell), p. 215. N. Y., 1927.
[38] Schlumberger. Un Empereur Byzantin au 10ème Siècle, p. 34. Paris, 1911.
[38a] Knetsch, K. Goethes Ahnen, p. 19 and Table 12, and pp. 28-31. Leipzig, 1908.
Sommer, R. Familienforschung und Vererbungslehre, pp. 107-206, Leipzig, 1907.
Other sources on Goethe's ancestry in Nature Knows No Color-Line, p. 131.

ministers, great military and naval commanders, hereditary admirals, and in several instances, great sultans. The Nawabs, or Nabobs, are of Ethiopian ancestry. Ethiopian industry, skill, and statesmanship helped greatly in making India the rich and prosperous country which the Portuguese, and later the French and the English, found it.[39]

One of the greatest of the Negro rulers of India was Malik Ambar,[40] who dominated in Bombay and the Deccan until his death in 1628. Another was Malik Andeel[41] who ruled Bengal from 1481 to 1494. Moors from Spain and Morocco were also a power in India prior to the Europeans.

The Portuguese mixed so freely with the natives that they soon became more Indian than European. "The number of marriages between the Portuguese and Indians was enormous through India," says Campos.[42] The same was largely true of the French. When the English came in 1628, they too, having left their women behind, took freely of the native ones. Thus a vast amount of white European blood was poured into the Indian population.

Today, there are hundreds of thousands, perhaps millions, of European mixed-bloods, the Eurasians, in India and Burma. Certain Eurasian groups, as the Burghers of Ceylon, have strong castes of their own.

Cedric Dover, who has gone deeply and extensively into this subject gives an impressive list of distinguished Indians with a white strain; of noted Europeans who took Indian wives; and of Eurasians, who married white wives of the upper-class. Lord Liverpool, Prime Minister of England for fifteen years, during the struggle against Napoleon, had a Eurasian mother. In the Proceedings of the Victoria Society, already mentioned, one of the speakers on India told of "an extraordinary British genius, living today," who "has Eastern blood in his veins." (The name was not given.) Some Englishmen and women of noble family married into the families of the Nawabs, or Nabobs, who, as was said, were originally of African Negro ancestry. Dover says, "The story of such Eur-Indian alliances could be expanded into a romantic book which would illuminate the history of many aristocratic families now free from suspicions of having been touched with the tar-brush."[43]

As regards some of the more modern aspects of race-mixing in the East, particularly the white slave traffic, we shall deal with it in its proper place.

[39] Benaji, D. R. Bombay and the Sidis. London. 1932.
[40] Gribble, J. D. B. History of the Deccan. Vol. I, pp. 51, 100, 104-05, 125-6, 251-62. London, 1896. Balfour, E.; Cyclopedia of India. (See Negro Races.)
Ferishtah. Rise of the Mohammedan Power in India. Vol. IV, p. 341.
[41] Stewart, C. History of Bengal, pp. 100-108. London, 1813.
[42] History of the Portuguese in Bengal, pp. 171-2; 177-203. (alcutta, 1919.
[43] Half Caste, pp. 117-120; 178-80. London, 1937. The famous Lord Fisher, once head of the British Admiralty, had an East Indian strain.

Chapter Twelve

THE MIXING OF WHITE AND BLACK IN AFRICA
SOUTH OF THE SAHARA

SO much race-mixing has taken place in this region that it needs a volume to itself. Nearly every human type may be found in this part of Africa, some of which are very ancient. Other types have become fixed as the result of mixed-bloods breeding with themselves, and still other types have been formed since the coming of the Northern Europeans and East Indians. There are also clear evidences of Negro-Mongolian admixture in Central and South Africa, probably as the result of Chinese migration thousands of years ago. Perhaps, the Negroes themselves might have brought this strain with them from Asia.

The Hottentots, who have a Negro-Japanese aspect, and are a very ancient South African race, were so greatly mixed with the white Dutch colonists from the sixteenth century, A.D., onwards, that their mulatto off-spring went off into whole tribes as the Baastards, Griquas, Rehoboths, Bondelswarts, and Witboois. Even the Bushman and Pygmy, perhaps the most ancient races on earth, have not escaped white amalgamation. "In fact," as von Luschan says, "the natives of Africa who were considered not long ago to be a homogeneous mass now turn out to be in reality a most complicated mixture of quite different elements, the outcome of immigration at different periods and from different parts of the globe."[1]

John H. Appel declares, "Not even among the yellow races of China, nor in sun-burned India (with its mixed Aryan strains) nor in Java or the black islands of the West Indies has the mingling of bloods come so forcibly to my attention as here in Africa."[2]

The first wave of white amalgamation in the historic period was brought into Africa by Islamic traders, slavers, and missionaries, who are principally spoken of as Arabs. The latter, who were of all colors, from black to white, took no women with them. With no color prejudice to speak of they took wives from among the Africans and reared families. Though they regarded the primitive blacks as inferior they adapted themselves to the fact, and by kindly treatment tried to make good Mohammedans of them. Once these blacks entered the faith, they became equals. Mohamet, about to die,

[1] In G. Spiller. Interracial Papers, pp. 13-14. London, 1911.
[2] Africa's White Magic, p. 3. N. Y., 1928.

enjoined his followers to obey the one who had been named as his successor even though he be "a Negro slave with hair like dried grapes." Once when the great Mahdi of Allah entered a mosque and knelt beside one of his humblest followers, the man stirred frightened and uneasy. The Mahdi at once put him at ease. "We are all one before God," he said.

Later, the Africans, as the result of the absorption of Islamic culture, strengthened and increased their empires which they had founded before the coming of Islam, as the Mandingo, Mellestine, Timbuctoo, Sokoto, Bornu, and swept westwards to the Atlantic; eastwards to Lake Chad; northwards into Morocco, where uniting with lighter colored brethren of the faith, they crossed into Spain and marched northwards victorious almost to Paris, France. As late as the 1880's, the Negroes of the Sudan under the Mahdi revolted against the English and founded a large empire which they ruled with success until defeated by the high explosives of Lord Kitchener in 1896. In the harems of these Negro chiefs were women of all the well-known races.

Christianity, which prior to the rise of Islam, had dominated in North Africa, also brought in a white strain. Byzantine Christianity also took much white blood into Egypt, the Sudan, and Ethiopia. In 1442, the Portuguese also brought much of the same into Northern Ethiopia. Coming in as allies of the Copts, they remained there until expelled in 1649. The mulatto appearance of such Ethiopians as the Tigreans, Shoans, and Amharas, is perhaps more directly due to this Portuguese admixture.

The Somalis, further to the south, are probably mixed with Arab, due to Mohammedan penetration. Some are jet-black with frizzly hair, like certain East Indian peoples, while others, though as black, have straight hair and regular profiles. And here we call attention to a fact that has fooled many anthropologists, who have spoken of these peoples as Hamitic, Semitic, or what not. Mixed peoples by long mating only among themselves seem to produce a fixed type, a different "race," and develop some physical characteristic. Some retain straight hair; others straight noses. For instance, those Negroes who are mixed with Oriental whites, so-called Semitic, tend to have straight noses as certain of the Berber peoples and others of the Anglo-Egyptian Sudan as the Bischarin. A singular fact is that those Negroes who are mixed with European are inclined often to have flat noses, since the European nose is more Negroid than the Oriental one. Even in the West Indies there is a facial difference between the Latin Negro and the British one. The Negroid strain in both, however, would be apparent to anyone acquainted with the Negro type. In the United States the distinction is so loose that sometimes a black man is classed as white simply because he does not speak English.

Following Islam, the Christian traders, slavers, and missionaries—Portuguese, Spaniards, Dutch, French, English, German,—came into Africa. These whites also brought no women with them and took the native ones. The Europeans had less of the colonizing spirit than the Mohammedans; they brought their class distinctions with them, and were, on the whole, less democratic. The Portuguese came nearest to the Islamic ideal. But Islam was no saint in some other respects. It also ravaged Africa with the slave-trade, and fought to continue it after the English, who had done so much to build it up, too, tried to destroy it.

The Europeans in West Africa gave free rein to their lust and found the Negro women very willing. Barbot wrote, "They make no scruple to prostitute themselves to Europeans for a slender profit, so great is their inclination to white men; which often occasions mighty quarrels with their husbands."[3] The picture of these slave-dealers drawn by Hervey Allen in Anthony Adverse is historically true. G. F. Dow tells of a Brazilian mulatto on the West Coast who had a harem of women of all colors and invited Drake to take his pick of them.[4] White wives were even brought from Europe for the native chiefs in the hope of pinning them down to Christianity, or to get good bargains in slave-trading. The Catholic missionaries married a white sister of the Order of St. Thomas to the black king of Benin.[5] Others were married to the kings of Warri. Two Negro priests secured a white wife for King Mingo of the latter kingdom about 1683.[6] Her mulatto son, Don Antonio, inherited the kingdom, and became one of the most notorious slave-dealers of West Africa.

In time some of the Negro chiefs came to demand white wives just as they did rum, and gunpowder. Chaka, Zulu king, and one of the most formidable conquerors of all time, had two white wives, one of whom had "long red hair that covered her like a mantle."[7]

The Negro chiefs wanted white wives principally to impress their neighbors with the idea that they were now united with their white ruler "brothers" in Europe with their guns and armies. Dan Crawford, noted missionary, tells of Chief Mushidi of South Africa who asked for and received from the Portuguese a white wife hoping thereby "to link his capital with the Courts of Europe" and acquire "an awe-inspiring prestige so great that the tribes lining his trade route out to the Atlantic will not dare to molest his caravans."[8] The most celebrated offer of this kind from Africa to Europe was, however, that of Mulai Ismael, Morocco's greatest

[3] Description of the Coasts of North and South Guinea, p 34. London, 1746.
[4] Slave Ships and Slaving, pp. 234-6, 252. Salem, 1927.
[5] Stanford, P. T. Tragedy of the American Negro, pp. 19-20. Boston, 1898.
[6] Barbot. Ibid., pp. 377-78.
[7] African Monthly. Vol. II, June-Nov., 1907, p. 143.
[8] Thinking Black, pp. 183-5; 190-1. London, 1912.

XXXVIII. Unmixed Types. 1. Mangbetou Queen (Belgian Congo); 2. Zulu Belle;
3 and 4. West African Belles.

ruler, to the Princess de Conti, daughter of Louis XIV.

At least one white woman tried to emulate the white men. She was Mrs. Leybonn, an Englishwoman, and a slave-trader, who had a Negro husband and three mulatto children, one of whom married the white English consul at Lagos.[9]

Cromwell shipped 2000 white Irish to the West Coast and it may be presumed that they either died off or amalgamated with the natives. Again in 1787 when the British were about to colonize 351 Negroes who had been freed by Lord Mansfield's decision on slavery in England, the authorities, the night before the Negroes sailed, scoured the town of Portsmouth, England, for all the loose white women they could, rounded up some sixty or more, made them drunk, married them to the Negroes, and sent them off to Sierra Leone.[10]

In time mulattoes became numerous all along the West Coast. Some rose to be great chiefs; others great slave-traders. One of the most rapacious of the latter was John Ormond, better known as "Mungo John," and "Mulatto Trader."[9a]

His father was an Englishman and his mother a paramount chieftess. Educated in England, he returned to Africa in 1758 to take charge of the vast territory he had inherited from his mother One of his first acts was to raise the wholesale price of slaves from $50 to $60 a head. On the slightest pretext he would send his soldiers to raid the native villages. One of his employes was Rezin Bowie, a white Texan, and father of the hero of the Alamo.

Others of the mulattoes allied themselves with their parent blacks and became thorns in the sides of those whites who tried to seize the native lands. Some who had been reared in Europe, like the counsellors of Behanzin, gave the native chiefs advice that helped to checkmate the greed of the whites.

Today the West African mulatto has castes of his own. The oldest group are the Portuguese-Brazilians, who are the descendants of the mulattoes of slave-trading days. They live chiefly in the larger towns as Porto Novo, Cotonou, Whydah, Grand Popo, and bear such aristocratic names as da Sousa, da Silva, de Almeida, and Albuquerque. Some even have an American-Indian strain brought by their earliest mulatto ancestors from Brazil. These Portuguese-Brazilians are the aristocrats of the mulatto group. Some are wealthy and consider themselves superior to most incoming Europeans.

Another group of mulattoes are the descendants of repatriated slaves from the New World. A number of these are in Liberia. There is also the

[9] Demaison. Faidherbe, p. 273. Paris, 1932. (3 ed.)
[9a] Mayer, B. Adventures of an African Slaver, pp. 70, 78 et seq. 1928
[10] See Rogers, J. A 100 Amazing Facts About the Negro, p. 32 (18th ed.) for sources

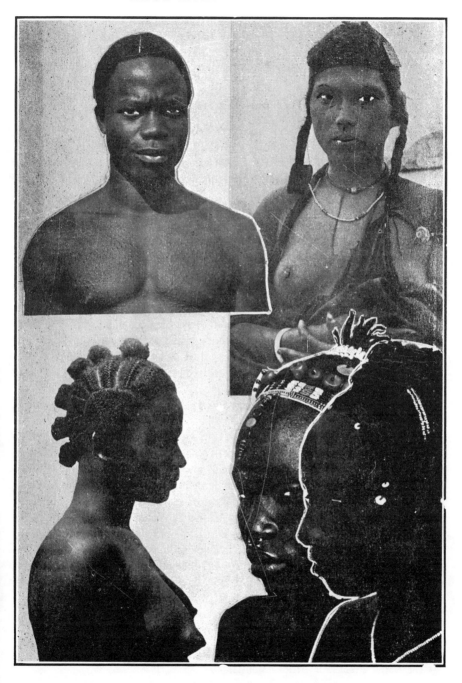

XXXVIII. West African types, mixed and unmixed.

mulatto offspring of a later English and French colonization, some members
of which marry among themselves, have their own caste, and shun the black
natives. Of this stock came General Alfred Amedee Dodds, France's leading
commander, immediately prior to the first World War.

The African Mulatto Today

Mixing still goes on freely in West Africa between Europeans, especially the French and the Belgians, and the native black women. We shall
speak later of the more intimate aspect of these unions as they occur in
Africa and Asia as well as of the relations of the white women with the
Negroes.

Some of the mulattoes are the offspring of legal marriages. As Buell
says, "There is no color bar in the French colonies. Frenchmen not only
have native mistresses but they marry native wives. They acknowledge sons
born of native women out of wedlock, take them into their homes, and send
them to France to be educated."[11]

The lot of the mulatto child is not always a happy one, especially the
one of the interior. Since he is neither black nor white he is regarded
as inferior by both black and white and drifts neglected between the two.
In the Belgian Congo and parts of French West Africa, the mulattoes are
reared apart from the blacks largely because of this.

Their status, in short, is pathetic. Albert Londres, noted French writer,
has given us the following picture:

"The other day a general whose name is celebrated wrote to the general
in command at Timbuctoo:

" 'It is now thirty-three years, but I have never ceased to think of my
time in the Soudan. Ah! my Soudan. What has become of my little hut
near Fort Bonnier? Where is my black sweetheart? And my son? He
was so handsome and lithe. He was named Robert. He is a man now.
Where is he? I must tell you that I have often asked about him, but have
never heard anything. His mother's name is Aissa...I would be very
grateful if you would send me news of him.'

"Here is another letter from another general:

" 'You will remember that in 1904 I buried in the French cemetery
of M..., near the fort, a child. On his tombstone I placed only the word
Henry. If the sand has not covered it all, would you...?'

"Robert! Henry! Andrew! Only that, no surnames.

"The mulattoes!

"The little ones suck their Negro mothers. The father may be there

11 The Native Problem in Africa. Vol. II, p. 79. N.Y., 1928.

or he may not be. He is an official, a merchant, an officer, or he may be only a passer-by. If he is there, it will not be for long. If he is away, it will probably be for all time. The child will grow up in the hut, the mother having returned to her parents. The people of the village will regard the child as a pariah, a beggar and will want to know why he continues to eat their corn.

"No fine social reasoning will influence this manner of looking at the mulatto child. The manner of looking down on him is instinctive. It is neither white nor black, hence it is nothing! The mother will marry with a Mandingo. Its little brothers by this marriage will have a race, a family, a country; they will be blacks. The mulatto will be a mulatto. He will have no name, no soil on which to place his feet as his own.

"Even the breasts that he sucks belong only half-way to him. He will pass his life seeking the other half. As children, they have never the air of being at ease.

"They are like those little play-boats one sees in fountains. As soon as the wind blows them toward the edge they are immediately pushed back into the water. No harbor for them. If they reach the center of the fountain, a stream of water plays on them. Many sink. Those who survive have lost their force.

"Nameless, these half-bloods are sons of the saints of the Catholic religion. The Republic does not let them stay in the bushes. When they are seven years old they are torn away from the maternal calabash. They are brought together in the towns, in the schools, for the half-bloods. They form a strange category; orphans with father and mother.

"While the father is in Africa he does not abandon them. Does he happen to be near the school, he stops to see them. He goes to see them even when he happens to be married to a white woman.

"One meets these mulattoes even in the best homes sitting between husband and wife. The husband in coming to Africa breaks the news gently to his wife on the boat. The French woman recognizes that it is normal, in the colonies, and as she is often intelligent, she welcomes the child during her stay.

"As soon as she has some white babies, however, the little mulatto is thrust through the door. Poor little mulattoes. The sons of their mother, who are black, are not their brothers; the sons of their father, who are white, are not their brothers. It is, perhaps, because of that; it is because they have been trying so hard to understand this, that all have such large, wide-open eyes.

"Those whose fathers have disappeared and who have nothing to do at the school are to be found in the villages. The mother has grown old. She

is only a Negro woman in the land of the blacks. The child has only a
Christian name.

"'Look,' says a passing white man, 'it is the son of so-and-so,' And
he gives the child a penny.

"If it's a girl and she is pretty, the white men all know her.

"Some are luckier. Joseph, for instance, has his father. He eats every
evening at the table with his father at Mother Vaisselle's. His father is a
buyer of cacao. Joseph is a favorite with everybody. And folks caress him
as they pass. Joseph is happy. He does not yet know that there are ships
which take away white papas to France.

"Later boys will become teachers and the girls midwives. The teacher
and the midwife will marry. The wedding is sometimes grand when the
midwife is the daughter of a governor.

"These happy endings are very rare, however. The mulatto is profoundly unhappy.

"At school they are taught that, normally, they are French. But the law
holds them down to the status of native. The law forbids them to take the
name of their father. At 20 they are conscripted into the black army. A
Negro, because he is born at Dakar, Rufisque, St. Louis or Goree, is in name
a French citizen.

"The son of General X, of the governor, or the governor-general, is,
however, only a black like the rest. If he does wrong he is judged only as a
Negro. When he gets a promotion he will be paid only like a common black.
Nine francs a day indemnity for the white elector, two and a half for the
mulatto. One hundred francs for the child of the first; ten francs for him.
Does he knock at the door of the administration? He is received as any
other Negro. If he is a Negro of Dakar, who knows how to hold a pen,
he is chased like a dog.

"The blacks have sent a deputy to Paris; the mulattoes remain in the
Niger. They are neither black nor white, French nor African; neither kinky-
haired nor straight-haired. The unhappy thing, however, is that nevertheless
they are something.

"'If one was nothing one could be happy,' said Robert, 'one would not
suffer. And yet, look here!' He showed a picture on the wall of a famous
general, cut from a magazine:

"'That's my father.'

"They have abandoned them. And they say nothing. They understand
obscurely that they are not children, but accidents, and that accidents are
always unhappy. As the same time they are sent to schools. They recite that
they are children of Frenchmen. They wear shoes, shirts and trousers. They
themselves have added spectacles. It will be necessary to keep them from

learning to read if one does not wish them to see their father's name in the newspapers.

"However, they wish to better themselves. They do not ask for the right to bear the name of their father; they know the respect due to a real white man—not son of so-and-so, but son of a Frenchman, Andrew, Henry, Jack, Robert, if you want, but French citizens."[12]

Londres added that the mulatto girls were better treated; they fetched high prices as wives or concubines; the prices ranging from $80 to $120. That of a black woman was only $20, he said.

Some Frenchmen take the black women and their mulatto children to France with them. I know of three or four instances. Several times I have seen Frenchmen with heir mulatto brood and African wives enter cafes or other public places with no one taking undue notice of them.

[12] Terre d'Ebene. pp. 66-72. Paris, 1929.

Chapter Thirteen

MISCEGENATION IN SOUTH AFRICA

SINCE about 1700, the Union of South Africa has become the chief area of the mixing of whites and blacks in Africa. When the Dutch arrived at the Cape in 1652 they brought no white women with them and took mates from among the the native ones. In 1663, there were only thirteen white women in a colony of several hundred men.

There were then three varieties of Negroes at the Cape: The Hottentots, a people of yellowish color with pepper-corn hair, who had been mixed centuries before through contact with a lighter-skinned race, or who perhaps, had lightened in color from living in a cooler climate. The second were the Bushmen, a very ancient and diminutive people with pepper-corn hair and brownish skins, perhaps the descendants of the Grimaldi. Bushmen cave drawings, as was said, are strikingly like the Grimaldi, or Aurignacian ones, in France and Spain. The third were the Bantus, tall, graceful, muscular, and with the most superb physiques. Of these three groups, the first two lived towards the south; the last, further north.

Later with the introduction of slavery, two other racial elements appeared: Negroes from Angola and Madagascar; and Negro-Mongolian-Dravidian stock from Malaysia and Southern India.

The Dutch started miscegenation with the Hottentot women; then with the African and Malay slaves; and finally with the Bantus. The Bushmen were at first too wild and untamable. Soon a mulatto brood appeared in the colony.

The white men were, on the whole, kind to these first mulattoes. They kept them and their black mothers in the same home with themselves. Marriage with the native women was forbidden but the restriction was sometimes waived. Peter van Meerhof, an early explorer, married Eva, a Hottentot girl, who had acted as interpreter for the whites. Jan van Riebeeck, the first governor, also authorized two similar marriages.[1] One of the earlier governors, Simon van der Stel, had a Negro mother of Bengalese origin.[2]

In time, the first generation of mulattoes came of age, and the white men were permitted to take wives from them. Eva's female offspring mar-

[1] Liepoldt, C. Jan van Riebeeck, pp. 152, 168. London, 1936.
[2] Walker, A. A. History of South Africa, pp. 44, 50, 76. London, 1935.
Cape Quar. Review, Vol. I, p. 13. Oct. 1881-2.

ried white men; their offspring in turn married white until the Negro strain disappeared.

Quadroons, too, became "white by law." Each generation grew whiter. Thus it is clear that the older the South African family, the more likely it is to have "Negro" blood.

As the colony prospered and life grew safer and easier, more white women arrived from Europe. The white men now had separate homes for white wife and black concubine with the result that the mulatto child who had had all along his father's companionship was set apart with his black mother. The distance widened as more white women came out until the gates were closed against the mixed-blood altogether unless he was light enough to pass for white.

Some of the mixed-bloods at the intolerable situation went off and formed tribes of their own. Later when the white man started to move northward, they became his bitter foe. One of these mulatto tribes, the Griquas, under their chief, the very able Adam Kok, resisted the whites for years, but were finally forced back into one of the most barren regions, or what is now Griqualand. Here they lived in peace for a time then their troubles started worse than ever. Their "worthless" territory proved to be one of the richest in the world. It had diamonds aplenty. Something similar happened in the case of the Indian-Negro people of Oklahoma whose almost worthless land assigned them by the government turned out to be rich in oil.

As for the greater part of the mulattoes they remained in the towns, chiefly Cape Town, where they developed a caste of their own. They strove for social recognition, and tried to get rid of the word "coloured." Even as certain Aframerican groups create confusion among themselves and the Aframerican mass by arguing over what name they should be called, what name will put them nearer the level of the white man, so the Cape Coloured argued. Their latest choice is "Eur-African." The "Eur" in it shows the European relationship. However some of the more literal whites object saying that they are the real "Eur-Africans." The whites are called Afrikanders.

But being neither white nor black, and being also generally poor and landless, the Cape Coloured, is, as a rule, despised by both whites and blacks. The blacks have, most of them, an even fiercer race pride than the whites. Were not some of their heroes as Chaka, Moshesh, Cetewayo, Khama, among the greatest in history? The mulattoes, on the other hand, take refuge in their white blood. Their attitude is strikingly like that of the poor white mountaineer in America in the case of all Negroes.

The South African whites with an eye to dividing and conquering, encourage both sides. They tell the blacks, that since they are unmixed they are superior; however, they give the mulattoes certain rights that are withheld from the blacks, such as being able to move from place to place without a pass.

The little taste of freedom has made the mulattoes look more hungrily towards the whites and away from the blacks. However, the economic and social advantages the mulattoes seek seem as far away as ever. South Africa has a Colour Bar Bill. Only white men can fill certain jobs, something like the Panama Canal Zone where there are "gold" jobs and "silver" jobs—the gold for the whites; the silver for the blacks.

Those mulattoes, who are ambitious, but not light enough "to pass" chafe at these restrictions. All that keeps such back is "the black drop" in their veins. Olive Schreiner, a humane white South African, quotes a mulatto girl as saying, "I could bite my arm when I see how black it is. My father was a white man." Sarah Millin, another white writer, depicts the tragedy of the mulattoes in her "God's Step-Children." "Terribly proud of their white blood," she says, "it is the black man that calls up the bitterness in their heart, the reflection of the shamed, betrayed, and desolate half within themselves."

Present Condition of the Mulattoes

To increase their irritation, the mulattoes see around them the poor whites—the poorest whites on earth. The white man farthest down is in Africa. The upperclass whites of South Africa, as elsewhere, control everything, and as they have set a line between white and black they give the rougher and badly paid jobs to the blacks, thus the poor whites "with the divine White skin" may not compete with the blacks even if they would. Nearly all over British Africa there is a gulf fixed between white and black that must be seen to be realized. To find the like, one must go back to Colonial days in Virginia.

Max Massot of Le Journal of Paris, says of the Cape Town mulattoes: "Among the disdainful whites, gentlemen dressed all alike in British style, noble ladies with eyebrows trimmed to a narrow line, and who would be nearly Parisian were it not for their large hats, circulate a crowd of colored people called the Cape Colored, quite distinct from the black natives and the Europeans."

He adds: "The 115,000 mulattoes furnish for the 130,000 Europeans the servants and the low, unskilled labor. They live to the right and to the left of the city, in little cubical, one-story houses, resembling dominoes carefully arranged by a child.

"The mulatto women are gay, laughing, and know how to attract attention without pretense, except when they wear the detestable large Gainsborough hat of their white mistresses, in which case they appear comic."

When, however, it is a question of being served, then the conditions are American. "I enter a bar," he says: "a mulatto is drinking there. The boss, on seeing me, gives a start. Without a word he shows me to the left of the bar of the whites between double swinging doors. I enter through politeness and pay 18 cents for a beer that I would have had in Paris for 3 cents. I have just committed a grave breach of etiquette in entering the part of the saloon reserved for the blacks, but I am happy to think that, if I were black and had entered the part reserved for 'Europeans Only,' I would not have escaped so easily.

"A Hindu Brahman, were he even a member of the King's Cabinet, is 'colored' in South Africa. He could not travel first class in that land nor drink a bock beside a white foreman."

On the street is a smart-looking colored policeman, with waxed mustache, the blue uniform and a Boer hat, balancing with cadence a white stick. M. Massot asks a white man at the bar about the policeman and learns that he occupies himself solely with the colored people.

"But suppose a white man breaks a window and steals the watches, what would the colored policeman do?"

"He would try to find a white policeman."

"But suppose there was none. Would he let the thief escape with the watches?"

"Well, what do you expect? That a Negro should put his hand on a white man?"

To enter South Africa, says the writer, there is also an inquisition as to color. For instance, one is asked, among other questions: "Are you colored, Jewish, or Asiatic?" If one answers in the negative and the truth is discovered, as, say, "in the case of a colored American, whose skin has been fraudulently bleached, or a European Jew who has become a Russian orthodox to escape the quota, it is very simple. He will be shipped back on the first boat (third-class compulsory in the case of Negroes). There are some notions which remain engraved in the brain of the white South African as they are engraved on stone.

"Jews are treated not much better and are barred entirely from entering now."

Negro Blood in the Whites

As for the whites they are in a numerical position not unlike that of the early days of the colony. They are still hopelessly outnumbered. Against their 2,000,000 souls are 6,000,000 blacks with 700,000 mulattoes in the middle. The whites are therefore as eager as they were in the old days to increase their numbers and they recruit them as they did in the past from the light-skinned Negroes. To be white in South Africa one only has "to look white."

The result is that most white South Africans have developed "a blind eye" that is amazing. Inquiry into ancestry is taboo; indeed to dig into the parentage of one who is not a European is like the sin against the Holy Ghost. South Africa is one of the richest countries on earth; it is the land of opportunity for the ambitious, but a visible smear of the tar-brush can ruin all one's chances.

As may be imagined, therefore, a large percentage of South African whites are of Negro ancestry. George Findlay, an authoritative writer, and a white man, estimates that of the 2,000,000 whites, at least 700,000 would be classed as Negroes in the United States. He says that the Negro strain in the white South African to an incoming European is evident but that the native whites with their "blind eye" cannot, or do not, choose, to see it.

Findlay gives three unmistakable signs of Negro blood in the white population. The first, he says, is the prevalence of Bantu traits in the faces of the whites. The ordinary observer, he says, "has a shrewd eye for race when he wishes to observe it and where appearances suggest Jewish, Syrian, Portuguese or other blood in most cases prove to be correct. A loud outcry that you cannot always rely on dark complexion, curly hair, and so forth usually emanates rather insincerely from those who are anxious to avoid the particular diagnosis of native blood. Habitually, however, we rely on these diagnoses of ancestry and are guided by them.

"Nothing is more remarkable than for the trend of ugliness in South Africa to take the form of flattened, rather bridgeless noses, thick lips, heavy jaws, and innumerable other Bantu traits. Now in England this is by no means the case. There the less favored visage most frequently is thin and bony in the nose; the lips are thin and prominent, incisors overhang the weak chin of a receding retrognathous jaw. To one returning to South Africa after a long period spent in England this difference is very striking. One observer on arrival travelled with a local football team and was astonished to note that every member of it had strong Negroid traits. Indeed this fact is so ordinary with us that we do not trouble to observe it, and, of course, comment is not supposed to be in good taste. With the bridge before us is perhaps unnecessary to deal with the explanations that rely on the sun, the climate, and so forth in attempting to account for thickening lips and flattening noses."

To hint as to the true ancestry of such persons is regarded as a deadly insult, "To say of a man passing as a European that he has colored blood even merely to raise the enquiry is insulting and defamatory . . . It is offensive, defamatory, or dangerous for Europeans to raise so much as an eyebrow of doubt about the ancestry of anyone classed as European." Such persons usually become "more royal than the king," and are the chief emphasizers of the color bar. "It is surprising," says Findlay," to note how frequently the discriminating slogans of 'White South Africa' and 'keeping the native in his place' flourish in the mouth of those who in their own person hardly exemplify their doctrine. Over-emphasis in these points evoke a suspicion of coloured ancestry that in most cases prove well-founded."[3]

The natives, most of whom are Bantus, are getting increasingly restless, too. Born warriors, they numbered among their ancestors some of the greatest warriors of all time, as Chaka and Cetewayo. Today they are forced into household drudgery or into the diamond mines and gold fields, where they are treated like prisoners, for a bare livelihood. No wonder some of them nourish the deepest hatred of everything white. One of them when told about the Devil by a missionary said, "To me the only real devil is a white man with blue eyes and yellow hair." A reckoning is inevitable.

In the meantime, Sex thumbs a nose at all of this and continues amalgamation in spite of law, the moral code, or the social opposition of the masses of the whites and the blacks. The great number of mulatto children being borne by the native women was one of the causes of the Zulu rebellion in 1906.

A Commission appointed by the British government to investigate this revolt said:

"The evidence teems with reference to this unpalatable subject, the cumulative effect of which cannot be disavowed or ignored . . . The Morality Act imposes severe imprisonment upon Native men going with white women, who may also be penalized, but avoids the converse, and they do think and frequently say in reference to the law with telling scorn, 'If your men may go with ours, why may not ours go with yours? One old Native in vehement language suiting gesture to word with dramatic effect asked: 'What were these white things which our girls were bringing home on their backs in such number? What did the government mean by allowing our girls to bear so many children? Did they want to breed mule drivers? In allusion to the fact that the man of mixed race invariably drive Government conveyances. Native law and practice sanction the penalizing of and the reparation from illicit intercourse among themselves."[4]

Solomon Plaatje, a leading South African writer, and a native black, who was once chairman of a Native delegation to England, says as regards race-mixing, "White and black unions are not only prevalent in Transvaal city slums (Doornfontein, Roodeport, and Maraisburg), but also in such

---

[3] Miscegenation. Pretoria. 1936.
[4] Report Natal Native Affairs Commission, 1906-07, para. 70. London, 1908.

country places as Korsten, Magatespruit, and Mara, up in the Zoutpans-bergen of the Transvaal, where white and black parents cohabit and pro-create children that are neither white nor black.

"The impression of equality is written in ineffaceable blood on the fore-heads of hundreds of thousands of half-caste children all over South Africa They are to be found in the streets in urban centres, around water-furrows in the rural areas and carried on washerwomen's backs all over the Transvaal . . .

"The same travesty of law allows a white man to cohabit with as many black or coloured women as he chooses so long as he does not marry any in Transvaal. The result is that some white men take advantage of the one-sided law to flood the country with illegitimate half-castes. I have known white men who (encouraged by this devilish law) have spent the flower of their manhood in procreating illegitimate children with coloured concubines in Transvaal and who years afterwards deserted their offspring and moved to another part of the country; where, in the evening of their days they settled down with lawful white wives and thought no more of the past."

Referring to the different manner in which the Frenchman or the Belgian treats his black concubine he adds, "The Continental libertine is more honest. For instance, the Belgian will drive side by side with his Congolese escort along the streets of Elisabethville. But the British colonial specimen of the same brood, on the other hand will leave his swarthy concubines to mind his suburban cottage after supper while he proceeds to Johannesburg to join the white man's chorus perhaps in declaiming against the employment of native labour and the presence 'in our midst of these millions of unsophisticated savages.' Having done his 'duty' in that connection he will take a seat in a suburban tramcar (which clean-living black taxpayers are not allowed to use) and return for the night to share a concupiscent bed with the black companion of his liaison."

Some of the more humane white men, says Plaatje, take the black women out of the province, marry them, and return to live with them. Of course such a marriage is not legal.

Intermarriage is legal in the two oldest colonies, Cape Colony and Natal, however. According to the South African Year Book, there were 774 mixed marriages from 1920-1928—575 of white men and black women; and 199 of Negroes and white women.[5] From 1927-1931, there were 569; and from 1933-1939, there were 305. The best known mixed marriage in South Africa was that of Harry Grey, eighth Earl of Stamford, to Martha Solomon, a Negro woman,[6] with whom he had been living in concubinage, and whom

[5] Official Year Book of the Union of South Africa, 1927-28, p. 941.
[6] Burke's Peerage, Vol. II, p. 3223. La Marquise de Fontenoy also wrote on this subject in the Chicago Tribune about 1914.

he had been persuaded to marry by the missionaries. A son was born to them but since he had been conceived out of wedlock, he did not inherit the title, nor reach the House of Lords. The second child born before Grey's death was a girl, Lady Mary, who married a white South African.

White Women and Black Men

In South Africa as in the United States, the chief objection is to the union of the black man and the white woman. In Transvaal, where the blacks are the worst exploited, the penalty for a Negro cohabiting with a white woman is eight years' imprisonment and the lash. "There is no objection," says Findlay, "to the miscegenatory action of the white men. Only the European women are restrained."

But the white women do not seem at all inclined to give the men the monopoly in miscegenation. Sir J. E. Alexander told of his great surprise in visiting a Boer farm to see several mulatto children, the offspring of the farmer's white daughter. He says, "Though the farmers affect to have a great abhorrence for any mixture of black blood, yet strange to say, I saw, at a farm-house, several dark children running about, who, I was told, were an offspring of one of the daughters of the family by a Hottentot youth. Another of the daughters of the same family married a Boer, and seven months after marriage produced a black child, which a trader, seeing, asked 'Hoe kom dat,' (How did that happen) when the husband cooly replied, 'that one day his wife was going out and was frightened by a black man whom she suddenly saw behind the door and that the child became black in consequence.' The wife was by and on hearing this she merely laughed. So both parties thought no harm."[7]

In South Africa, as in other parts of Africa, the housework is done by native men, called "boys." There are frequent liaisons between the white women and these "boys." Some women have the "boys" to bring in their "morning coffee" while they are in various stages of undress or even in their bath. A white writer in the Church Quarterly Review, July 1909, took this type of woman severely to task for spoiling the morals of the black men, to some of whom are made all manner of immoral proposals. Some of the "boys" are married and when they refuse are sometimes accused like Joseph of old by the women. Plaatje tells of one case where a mistress called the Negro boy "to come and sponge" her back while she was bathing. When he obeyed after much hesitation, she made further advances and ordered him "to sponge a good deal more than her back." Orders succeeded orders, says Plaatje, "until he was ordered to perform duties of an unmentionable

[7] Expedition of Discovery, etc., pp. 77-8. London, 1838

character." Finally the boy complained to the woman's husband, who set watch, and thus saved the boy from a later accusation of rape. "I could fill a book," says Plaatje, "on such first-hand information about the vicissitudes of houseboys."[8]

Other white women either prostitute themselves to Negroes or live with them unmarried. A vast amount of evidence on this subject was brought out in an extended investigation on South African life by the South African Native Affairs Commission. Speaking of venereal disease contracted from white prostitutes, the report said, "The Natives come to town and contract syphilis, and they go back to their kraals and spread it all over the country. We have had here quite lately as many as 62 French and German women living in the town, prostitutes, and Natives visited them night after night." By "Native" is meant the unmixed Negro.

In Natal and Cape Colony where intermarriage is legal, a situation that is the height of all that is paradoxical, exists in the case of the off-spring of white women and black men. If the child is illegitimate it is classed as "white"; if legitimate, it is as "Negro". A slave law provided that an illegitimate child took the social status of its mother. Thus, it was brought out in the testimony of the above-mentioned report that in several cases mulatto children of the same mother came to be classed "white" or "Native" depending upon whether they were born before or after the woman had married the Negro. The child born out of wedlock had all the rights and privileges of a white man; the one born in wedlock, all the disabilities of a Native. One could carry a gun, the other could not; one could buy a drink, the other could not; one could only take one wife, the other could marry as many as he pleased; one could vote, the other could not, and so on. A police inspector, in his testimony said that he knew of several cases in his town where white women were living with Negroes, one of whom had four children. He added that it was to the distinct advantage of such children to be illegitimate. "If," he said, "a Negro and white woman have been co-habiting without marriage and have had children it would involve no loss to their children. If the children were illegitimate they'd rank as Europeans but after marriage and thus being legitimatized, they'd rank as natives." When asked how it was possible for such a contradiction in law to exist, the inspector replied that when the law was passed making an illegitimate child take its mother's status no one "ever imagined that a white woman would sink so low as to associate with a Native in that way."

A law was passed inflicting a severe penalty on white women who had

---

[8] The Mote and the Beam: An Epic on Sex Relationship 'Twixt White and Black in British South Africa. Cape Town, 1921.

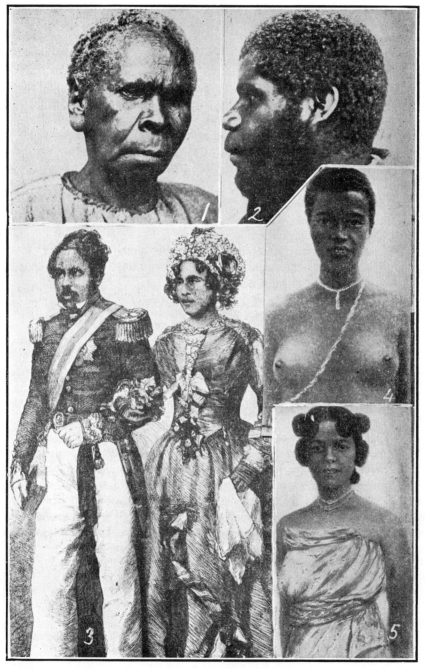

XXXIX. I and 2. Tasmanian Negroes; 3. Crown Prince and Princess of Madagascar;
4 and 5. Mixed-blood belles of Madagascar.

relations with Negroes, but the inspector said it had not been put in force as it was impossible to prevent the races from mixing.[9]

Leading South Africans Who Are Said to Be of Negro Blood

As was said, many of the oldest South African families have a Negro strain. Some of the most distinguished men who are of this stock are said to be:

The late Baron Henry de Villiers, Chief Justice of South Africa.

W. Buckner de Villiers, M.P. chief whip of the National Party (Dutch).

Hon. H. C. Hull, First Minister of Finance to the Union of South Africa.

Sir David Graf, cold storage magnate and millionaire.

The Reverend Van Heerden, one time Moderator of the Dutch Reformed Church of South Africa.

General Erasmus, a Boer commander in the South African War.

The Rex Family, Knysna, Metterkamp, Duthbys, which is descended from George IV of England, hence its name.

Race-Mixing in Portuguese Africa

In the adjoining Portuguese colony of Mozambique, the picture is quite different. The natives, it is true, are exploited as in other parts of Africa, but they are on the whole more humanely treated. Livingstone says that he found as little color prejudice in Portuguese Africa as exists "in any other country in the world." Sarah Millin, white South African writer, says similarly of Mozambique, "One may meet coloured people everywhere. They attend at Government functions, dine at the best hotels, play together, black, brown, and white in orchestras and make a sinister appearance in white families." The white South Africans, like the English on the borders of the Portuguese colony of Angola, complain of this. Sarah Millin says that the white South African conjures up something disagreeable and irritating at the word "Latin" because France and the Latin nations show so much more broadmindedness in their dealings with the blacks.[10]

[9] South African Native Affairs Commission, 1903-05. Report and Minutes of Evidence See Vol. V, p. 77, Index for Illegitimate Half-Castes; Intermarriage, and related subjects. Cape Town, 1905.
[10] The South Africans, pp. 205-219. N. Y., 1927.

The Islands of Africa

All the islands of Africa as the Madeiras, Canaries, Cape Verdes, Ascension, St. Helena, Madagascar, Comoro, Mauritius, Zanzibar, as well as the Azores, have a highly mixed population. The majority of the St. Helenians are mulattoes. At Tristan d'Acunha, where Tylor, the anthropologist, said he found the most beautiful women in the world, the population sprang from the union of white sailors and five Negro women. In Mauritius, white and black mixed freely under the French and later under the English. The famous French surgeon, Brown-Sequard, is said to have come of this mulatto stock, as well as Maurice Donnay, one of the present Forty Immortals.

Zanzibar, the land of the Zenghs, or Blacks, has a population of mostly Negroes. Madagascar has three principal types, the Hovas, who are Mongolian-Malay-Negro; the near-blacks, as the Saklavas and the Baras, or blacks; and the mulattoes, who are a mixture of the first two with Europeans.

Malta, which is European or African, as you wish, also has a highly mixed poulation. British army regulations class, or used to class, the Maltese as colored, and gave them the same lesser rate of pay as the West Indian Negro regiments.

Additional Bibliography:
Laing, G. D. Formation of the Native Races of South Africa. S. African Jour. of Science, Vol. 23, pp. 905-08. Dec. 1925.
Theal, G. M. History of South Africa, p. 16.
Poor White Problem in South Africa, Carnegie Institute Comm., 1932.
Pratt, Ambrose. The Real South Africa. London, 1913.
Fischer, E. Die Rehbother Bastards. Jena. 1913.
Evans, M. Black and White in South Africa. London, 1911.
Schreiner, Olive. Thoughts on South Africa. London, 1923.
For present day case-histories of race-mixing, see Fantham, N. B. and A. Porter, "Cases of Physical Inheritance and of Racial Admixture in South Africa," in South African Jour. of Science, Vol. 27, pp. 391-405. This work amply bears out Findlay's Miscegenation.
See also: Scientific Monthly. Feb. 1936. pp. 151-168; and Robinson, Victor G., Encyclopedia Sexualis, pp. 690-707, New York, 1936.
Also Launcelot Hogben's "Preface," in Cedric Dover's Half-Caste.
Farson, N. Behind God's Back, N. Y. 1941

Chapter Fourteen

RACE-MIXING IN AFRICA AND ASIA TODAY

Sex has always been one of the great lures of the adventurer to foreign lands. When the average male thinks of the South Seas almost his first thought is of their voluptuous women clad only in a sarong or less.

When the American fleet made its tour around the world in 1908, the theme song was, "I've a girl in Tokio." When the Fascists wanted to prime their young men for the Ethiopian adventure, they flooded Italy with pictures of nude black women. The pictures were so highly prized that some of the soldiers kept them among their cherished belongings later. I saw some of these pictures in the kits of Italian soldiers captured in Spain and placed on exhibition in Paris. The best selling novel in Italy during the Ethiopian War was Faccètta Nera, or Black Girl (literally Black Facet).

An English woman, Mary Gaunt, who travelled much in West Africa said that one of the reasons why white men like Africa is "the freedom that the absence of white women gives them." Dr. Jacobus was quoted about the French officials who return to France from Africa and marry fine girls but "cannot forget the black skin and the woolly hair of the daughters of Ham."

The average white man who goes to Africa simply runs riot among the women. The latter can usually be had for a few dollars per month, or be bought outright from their parents. Some white men keep a harem and when they leave Africa sell out to the incoming official or clerk. The more reserved ones usually have at least one woman about the house.

Felix Bryk, who is a frank and unprejudiced white writer, speaks of a type of white man who finds the black woman repugnant—at first. But this type is rare. In the larger African towns where venereal disease is rampant, due to European penetration, some white men will only lie down beside the black women just to be in contact with them.

Bryk says of the type of white man who has an aversion for black women, "These powerful whites, fond of life, who, at the end of a day's work find distraction in sport, hunting, cards and especially hard drink at first live for months, at times a year, without any sexual intercourse, since no opportunity presents itself. They are usually single and it is almost impossible to find white women. The free life under the tropic sun, which in itself loosens sensuousness, the free use of liquor, the involuntary, long-

142

lasting sexual abstinence, daily surrounded by voluptuous half-naked women, drive them towards a discharge of sexual passion.

"One day the white man with his *master-morality* finds an apparently dramatic conflict: I say apparently because he does not feel it to be such. He, the white man, the lord, the *bwana mkubwa,* must depend upon the black woman! At first it requires great self-control to ignore a prejudice that is common to his race, and share his bed with a black. A phrase that a dandy once let fall in my presence is very significant: 'I must always get pie-eyed drunk before I take a black.' "

"Nor will it surprise one in the face of such an attitude, another farmer saying, 'Sleeping with a Negress is the same as sleeping with a she-ape.' "

"Or that a third could coin this priceless sentence: 'Whoever has a Negress is degenerate."

"But these are prejudices unsupported by experience.

"Once the ice is broken, once the white man has condescended to a passing mésalliance, then he begins to drink the poisonous enchantment which the black Eve knows how to prepare only too well. He corrects the false feelings of his prejudice. Only yesterday he found it impossible to touch a black woman. I hear him exaggerating today:

"No white woman is as good !"

"There is no denying, that in the course of time, after the overcoming of his racial prejudices, he succeeds in revaluating his emotions, and a strong attraction and passion for the black woman takes possession of him."[1]

Pierre Mille, leading French writer on colonial subjects confirms this as regards the dark-skinned woman in general. He says in a review of De Renel's book, "Le Decivilisé,"

"It happens sometimes—it happens often enough—that the European who has experienced a union, marriage or concubinage with a native woman is no longer able to experience, I will not say even happiness, but conjugal peace with a woman of his own race. It can even happen that not having yet known native women, but coming newly-married from Europe, if by caprice of the senses or out of simple exotic curiosity, he has relations with one of these women, he can no longer leave them alone. This is what he finds—sometimes with remorse, with pain, and horror: *that he can no longer live with a white woman."*

It is commonly believed that such unions are only "carnal" and never end in love. For instance Dr. Jacobus, the French army surgeon recently mentioned, who spent twenty-eight years among the natives of Africa and the West Indies and studied their sex life closely, says that "the African woman does not love the white man because the latter is incapable of satis-

[1] Dark Rapture, trans. Norton, Dr. A. J., pp. 158-167. N. Y. 1939.

fying her sexually." He adds, "La Négresse est généralement d'une nature passionnée et ne s'amuse pas aux bagatelles de la porte. Je parle plus loin de l'aubergine excitante et des breuvages aphrodisiaques qu'elle fait boire a ses amants pour exciter leur ardeur; mais elle ne connait pas less raffinements. Elle accomplit l'acte charnel un peu brutalement et dans la position classique, sur le dos, l'homme entre ses cuisses . . .

"If faut a la Négresse un homme-cheval pour lui faire éprouver la sensation physiologique, et elle le trouve rarement en dehors du mâle de sa race. D'ailleurs, elle a le système nerveux bien moins richement organisé que la Blanche, ses muqueuses sont plus sèches, surtout celles des organes génitaux. Dans ces conditions, pour obtenir la sensation voluptueuse, la Négresse a besoin d'un congrès lent, que seul peut donner le Noir avec son gros pénis . . . L'amour de la Négresse pour le Blanc n'est qu'un amour de tete, qui flatte son orgueil et non son amour des sens." ("The love of the Negro woman for the white man is only a love of the head; it flatters her pride but not her senses.")

"Il résulte de cette organisation caractéristique de la femme Noire: ampleur de la vulve et du vagin coincidant avec un système nerveux peu sensible, que la Négresse ne peut pas aimer le Blanc, lequel est généralement impuissant a lui procurer la sensation voluptueuse. Elle trouve au Toubab (white man) deux irrémédiables défauts pour elle: d'abord l'exiguité de son pénis, car, a part de rares exceptions, l'Européen est un homme-lièvre par rapport au Négre, ensuite la rapidité avec laquelle il accomplit le coit. L'éjaculation du blanc a lieu avant que la Négresse ait éprouvé la moindre sensation. On ne connait pas au Sénégal l'usage de l'opium qui retarde l'éjaculation, aussi la Négresse compare-t-elle le Toubab a un coq, tandis qu'elle assimile le Négre au chien. Cette comparaison que j'ai recueillie de la bouche meme d'une vieille entremetteuse Noire, ne manque pas de verité.

"Le Nègre est bien l'homme-étalon, et rien ne saurait donner une meilleure idée (comme couleur et grosseur) de l'organe d'un nègre en érection que la verge d'un petit âne Afrique . . . Elle ne se borne pas cependant a la couleur et au volume, car la verge du Noir quoique en complète érection, est encore molle comme celle de l'âne et donne a la main qui la presse la sensation d'un tube en caoutchouc a parois épaisses, pleine de liquide. Dans l'état de flaccidité, la verge du Nègre conserve encore une grosseur et une consistance plus grande que chez l'Européen dont l'organe se ratatine et devient mou et flasque. Les dimensions moyennes du pénis m'ont paru, en général, de dix neuf a vingt centimètres sur cinq centimètres de diametre. Excepté chez les jeunes pubères rarement le pénis descend au-dessous de seize centimètres sur quatre et demi. J'ai pu prendre ces dimensions chez les Tirailleurs, ou l'on recontre des specimens de la plupart des races du Sénégal et du Haut-Niger. Il m'est arrivé souvent de trouver des pénis de vingt quatre a vingt cinq centimètres sur cinq et demi, un organe monstrueux de vingt neuf centimètres de long sur six et demi de diamètre au bourrelet circulaire de la circoncisión.

"J'estime en moyenne au triple si ce n'est plus, le temps que met le Nègre pour terminer le coit et je n'exagère pas . . . Le Noir a-t-il le pouvoir de faire durer le coit longtemps avant l'éjaculation, de la retarder meme a son gré, en ralentissant la cadence amoureuse, il peut accomplir ainsi des exploits qui rendraient fourbu un Européen . . . Il est certain qu'un Nègre bien nourri et circoncis peut besogner une femme pendant presque toute une nuit en n'éjaculant que cinq ou six fois. Je ne crois pas qu'il y ait beaucoup d'Européens capables de ce tour de force amoureux."[2]

Sir Richard Burton, another traveller, experienced in African and Asiatic ways, is of the same opinion. He says:

"Europeans . . . are contemptuously referred to as village cocks by Hindu women . . . Hence, too, while thousands of Europeans have cohabited for years and have had families by native women they are never loved by them . . . at least I have never heard of a case."

Havelock Ellis quotes this passage with approval and adds: "I have received confirmations of Burton's statements from medical correspondents in India."[2a]

The above is nevertheless not quite true. I know mixed couples in Africa who seem to be as much in love with each other as if they were both Europeans. Elisée Rèclus, the great French geographer, married a native African woman, and their love was ideal. So did "Grenfell of the Congo."[3] "Jacouba," a former French priest, who lives in Timbuctoo, married a Negro woman by whom he has thirty children.[3a] Both whites and blacks adore this couple. Their life has been a radiant light for all that region of Africa. In mixed marriages as in everything else, much depends on the personality. Bryk more truly says, "The black woman is truly capable of loving a white man. Even scenes of jealousy take place, in which, to be sure, she does not cry, but controls her modest behaviour. If she sees him casting eyes at other blacks, she may even leave him. He may go after as many white women as he likes, this does not affect her; but after no black without her consent. As to white women she says, 'Why they belong to him.' In Uganda, a black woman

[2] L'Art D'Aimer Aux Colonies, pp. 149-50. Paris, 1927. (The English translation of this work is "Untrodden Fields of Anthropology.")
[2a] Studies in the Psychology of Sex, Vol. III, p. 237. Phila. 1913.
[3] Hemmens, H. L.. George Grenfell: Pioneer in Congo, p. 74. London. 1927.
[3a] For portraits of this famous couple see, Seabrook. W. B. Jungle Ways, N. Y., 1931. (also pp. 221-34.)

when she learned that her master, a major, had taken another black and rejected her, killed herself out of love for him. I myself read a love-letter of a married Budama woman to a young Italian, which, in spite of its broken Kisuaheli, affected us very deeply, because therein we found the same *all-human* emotions and phrases that we had not expected but even denied in the Negroes."

There are even those African women who learn to be as monopolizing as the European ones. When such go to live in Europe they rapidly absorb European ways.

The white women, who, happily for them, are few in West and Central Africa, are furiously jealous too of the black woman. As Bryk observes:

'The white woman hates the black woman more than the white man hates the black man. It is no race question that brings about this unchristian feeling in her. Here the struggle is a sexual one; for life and death. She sees a rival and feels how the white man seeks and finds in the black woman that what she had thought she alone had the right to give. That 'dirty, stinking, infected' creature is now on an equal plane with her . . .

"Because of the white's conception of the blacks, it is no wonder that the white, especially the Englishman, keeps everything about the Negress secret, and has rejected the phrase *black love*. He will converse on everything, on the prices of coffee, corn and wheat, on thefts by the blacks, the way he had given a Negro a bloody chin for it . . . But the Negress, here he breaks off the conversation. This hypocrite, this champion liar, who acts so indignant, if you ask him about it . . . a black woman is already in his bed."

Some white men will even smuggle a black sweetheart into the home under the very nose of the white wife. The black girl will be dressed up as a "boy." In Africa, the housemaids are very nearly always men.

Black Men and White Women

Outside of South Africa, sex relations between black men and white women are rare for the simple reason that white women are few. Moreover, the truth, as Darwin pointed out, is that the primitive African thinks the most beautiful white woman ugly. To most Africans today a Miss America and even a Miss Universe would mean nothing at all, especially in her one-piece bathing suit. Take however, even the last runner-up in the beauty contest, dress her from head to foot in bright colours, put on a lot of bright ornaments and she'd make a hit.

With plenty of nude women about him, a nude white woman is just another nude to the average African. The white woman who goes down to the river and bathes before everybody will have no one peeping at her. They might be sorry for her because she is so white, that's all. Others of both sexes might even stop to see if white people bathe the same as black ones. But if she goes into a hut to bathe and closes the door, curiosity is immediately aroused and dozens of black eyes, male and female, young and old, will be peering at her through the cracks wondering what she is up to.

It is only recently that the moving pictures, the introduction of European dress, and the high-powered glorification of the white woman in the sexy picture magazines have begun to change this concept in the more urban centres of Africa and Asia. Mary Gaunt, an Englishwoman, who travelled alone in West Africa, said that no African male ever seemed to dream of molesting her even when she was alone with them. She said that the Africans were "very courteous" and that it seemed to her "that the farther you get from civilization the more courteous the population." Sir Harry Johnston, a leading authority on Africa, is also very precise on the subject of the African Negro's not wanting the white woman.

The simple truth is that most Africans and Asiatics shun sexual unions with white people. Such affairs do occur between native women and white men because the white man is economically and militarily stronger. But marriages between native men and white women are severely frowned on by the natives themselves. Englishwomen who marry Indians and go to India almost always get a cold reception from the men's parents and friends. When the Crown Prince of Siam married a white woman, the Siamese objected strongly. This princess is now living in France with her children. As for the Japanese, they are strongly opposed to marriage with white people. Viscount Aoki, Japanese ambassador to Germany, lost much prestige with his own people when he married a German baroness. A leading Japanese writer, Inazo Nitobe, who married a white Quakeress of Philadelphia, and took her to live in Japan, was one of the first to be mobbed in the anti-European riots in Tokio in 1935. White prostitutes in Yokohama and other Japanese sea-ports get very little, or no patronage from Japanese men, who much prefer their own yoshiwara.

The same is generally true of the Chinese. Some Chinese mandarins and a Chinese or two educated in Europe will have a white wife or a white concubine but such rarely, if ever, receive social recognition from the Chinese themselves. There was considerable protest in China when a son of a President of China who was studying in Ohio married a white girl there about 1933. After the defeat of Kolchak, anti-Bolshevik leader, more than a hundred thousand Russians, mostly women, fled into China southwards to Peiping, Tientsin, Chefoo, Tsingtao, Shanghai, Hankow, Amoy, and Canton. With no means whatever of making a living, numbers of them were forced into prostitution.[4] But they had a hard time getting even the Chinese coolie, who comes very near to being the man farthest down to take them. A Russian detective said, "At that time (1926) most Chinese would not even touch white women . . . Yes, what a shame it was! Adolescent blondes mingled in the streets with troops of hideous yellow prostitutes just to get something to eat. And the coolies refused to go to bed with them. Then they held their robes open so that the men could see that they were really women."[5]

As for the mixed-blood women, who, as a rule, are more white than colored in their ways and desire to live like Europeans, they fare little better. A League of Nations report said that probably a half of those in Indo-China were prostitutes.

The same is true of East Africa. Ingida, a talented Ethiopian painter, while studying in Paris, married a white woman and took her back to Ethiopia. His family absolutely refused to have anything to do with her. The white people there ostracised her too, and the heart-broken Ingida had to let her go back to Europe.[6] With the exception of one or two towns in French West Africa, Africa is no place for the white wife of a black man. Such a couple had better far remain in Europe.

Even illicit unions with white women are frowned on in Ethiopia. Most Ethiopians were shocked when the former Emperor, Lidj Yassu, took a white concubine. She still lives in Addis-Ababa and was pointed out to me in a derogatory way by natives. At Cardiff, Wales, one could always make the Arab and the Somali boys angry by saying that they were going to marry white women. In addition to the difference of color there was also that of religion.

A French judge who served eighteen years in West Africa told me that the cases he knew of the cohabiting of black men and white women were few even though white women were there in fairly large numbers. Such cases as occur are mostly with house-boys, and are probably largely induced by the conduct of the white husbands themselves who may be off somewhere with a black woman. Then there are some white women who have developed a desire for black just as the white men, and as Charles Royer, a French novelist relates, start with the white and finish off with the black.[7] And it is not the white man alone who tries to throw his partner off the scent. Bryk says that a Kenya boy told him that his mistress would

---

[4] Problem of Women Refugees of Russian Origin in the Far East. Bandoeng Conference, pp. 68-72, also p. 52. Series of League of Nations Publ IV. Social. 1937. IV. 10. Ibid. 11, p. 16.
[5] Quoted from Henry Champly's "The Road to Shanghai," p 200. London. 1934.
[6] Farrago, L. Abyssinia on The Eve, p. 111-2. Lond. 1935.
[7] La Maitresse Noire, pp. 80-1, Paris.

always quarrel with him in the presence of others so that they might not suspect that there was anything between them. He adds:

"Penitent black women would confess to a missionary in Nyangori about the wild doings of their·white mistresses.

"White women, as well as men, can not for long, in spite of all sincere resolutions and inbred aversions, resist the elemental love power and seductive charm of black love in this black section of the world."

Nevertheless, there is a type of African, apart from those educated in Europe, to whom the white woman is the most desirable creature in the world. These are some of the missionary boys, and the interpeters, as well as those who are studying European languages, and have other close dealings with white people. Such aspire to be white and consider a white woman a mark of high prestige. Some of them really prefer their own women—the African woman is circumcized and this makes the vagina drier—Africans say that the European women are too moist—nevertheless such boys will spend their last penny on the white prostitutes of the coast towns.

In short, liberalism in the matter of mating of black and white comes as a result of education, of sophistication, of a broadening of one's vision of humanity. The whites of Europe being more educated in the humanities than the Africans and the Asiatics are less averse to miscegenation than they. There is still a deeper reason, a psychological one, that we shall speak of in the next volume on the chapter, "Why Do White and Black Mix in Spite of Opposition in the United States."

White Slavery and Miscegenation

Still another exception in the case of the white woman are the near-whites and near-blacks of North Africa and Arabia. As was said, the North Africans had been accustomed for thousands of years to have both black and white women in their harems. The white women were captured in Europe. But the whites are too powerful for that today, so a more subtle form of seizure is resorted to, namely, white slavery.

The League of Nations, especially in its conference on the International Traffic in Women and Children, March and December, 1927, has thrown much light on the subject.

A Paris press dispatch says as regards this also, under the heading: "White Girls Slaves in Harems of Africa."

"Reports shortly to be issued will show an alarming increase in a new form of slavery in the African colonies of France.

"These reports concern the traffic in white girls for the harems of colored potentates.

"So far, it will be shown, this form of slavery has defied all effort at control, for most of the girls involved are of age and have the rights to sign their liberty away if they wish to do so.

"At first, this traffic in white girls was confined to Algeria, Tunis and Morocco, but now it is extending all over Northern Africa.

"It is stated that there is hardly a dusky vassal of France in this territory who has not a quota of white girls in his harem.

"They may be "wives" or just dancing girls, but, in either case, their position is the same—they have been bought in the open market.

"The situation is amazing—the white races which have done so much to stamp out slavery in Africa supplying slaves for the race that was formerly enslaved.

"Many of the victims, it is true, believe that when they sign their contracts they are taking up dancing engagements in the harems and palaces of the African "kings" and nobles; but, once signed up, they are no longer their own masters.

"They are fed and housed so long as their looks last, then—beggary, or worse.

"It is believed that throughout Northern Africa there are thousands of these white slaves of all European nationalities."[8]

White slavery has placed colonies of white prostitutes in almost every seaport of the Mediterranean, the African coasts, the Red Sea, the Indian Ocean and the Pacific as well as Las Palmas and Teneriffe, where they come into competition with their darker-skinned sisters for the tourists and the sailors, numbers of whom are Negroes. According to a League of Nations report, numbers of these white women were brought principally for English and American tourists.[8a]

Some of these women came on their own initiative, and for the same reason that the white men left Europe: to seek wider fields and to escape boredom. The German women must have been the pioneers for there is a saying in the East, "A Scotch engineer, a Swedish match, and a German prostitute, you'll find everywhere."

As for Arabia, black women from the Sudan and white women from the Caucasus are still being imported for the harems.[9]

[8] Feb. 2, 1935. Greensboro, N. C. News, Feb. 3, 1935.
[8a] Harris, H. W. Human Merchandise, pp. 152-69. London 1932.
[9] Forbes, Rosita. Women Called Wild, pp. 11-48. New York, 1937. Other authorities cited in Rogers, J. A., "100 Amazing Facts About the Negro," 18th ed., 41.
See also Henrik de Leeuw's "Cities of Sin," chapters on Port Said and Singapore. 1933. And Henry Champly's "White Women, Coloured Men." 1936.

Chapter Fifteen

MISCEGENATION IN SPAIN, PORTUGAL, AND ITALY

SOUTHERN Spain and Portugal are in reality Negroid lands. They are only geographically European. Napoleon was pretty nearly right when he said Africa began at the Pyrenees.

The oldest skulls found in the peninsula are Negroid. This is especially true of one of Mugem, Portugal, which is one of the earliest of the present human type yet discovered. Other Negro peoples have come in since that distant time but the original Negro type persists. As G. Young says, "It is easy to recognize not only the imported Negro type but also a type generally confused with him: the aboriginal Negroid Iberian."

Later we know not how there arose in Spain a mixed-blood people, which, as Vicuna says, was "almost Negro with frizzly hair."[1] These are very probably the Celtiberians, or Black Celts, who took civilization, such as it then existed in the West, to Britain and were found there by Julius Caesar. Tacitus describes them as "swarthy with curly hair."

The present oldest race of the peninsula are the Basques, "the mystery race of Europe," who have a language of their own and claim to be "pure." Some Basques have a certain type of Negroid face, and it is not improbable that such are the descendants of the Negro aborigines just mentioned. The Basque emblem is the swastika, which has caused them much pain since Hitler appropriated that ancient African and South Sea emblem. I have seen signs in Basque shop-windows disclaiming connection with Hitler and pointing out that the Basques used the swastika thousands of years before him.

The first colonizers of ancient Spain were the Carthaginians, who, as was said, were also Negroid. Barcelona was founded by Hamilcar Barca, father of the illustrious Hannibal.

Black peoples and white continued to pour into Spain under the Romans. But the first great wave of miscegenation came with the Moorish conquest in 711 A.D., under the leadership of a Negro slave, Tarik, who gave his name, as was said, to Gibraltar. The rulers of Spain were then the Visigoths, a white Germanic race. Tarik, after defeating the white king, Roderick, at Xeres, pushed victoriously northwards. In less than three years the Moors had seized almost the entire peninsula.

[1] Historia de Espana, p. 52.
Mendes Correa. Os Povos Primitivos da Lusitania, p. 170. Porto., 1924.

151

Other waves of African invasion followed. In 1086, came a people from Upper Senegal that was almost purely Negro. These were the Almora-vides, a religious sect. Houghton says, "The Almoravides.,.were Berbers and were largely mingled with pure Negroes."[2] Yusuf, their leader, was himself a Negro. The "Roudh-el-Kartas," a Moorish work, describes him as having "woolly hair" and being "brown" in color.[3] Yusuf's favorite concubine was a white captive, Fadh-el-Hassen (Perfection of Beauty). She was the mother of Yusuf's successor, Ali. Alphonso VI, the white Spanish king, who was often defeated by Yusuf, had, in turn, a Moorish Queen, the lovely Zayda, who was the mother of his favorite son, Sancho. It was the latter's death in battle that hastened the aged Alphonso's death. When the power of the Almoravides passed, another African people, the Almohades, swept in. Under their influence Moorish power in Spain reached its highest peak of grandeur, and reared such monuments of artistic splendor as the Alhambra and the Mosque at Cordova.

For the next eight centuries, Moors and Germans, with other incoming whites and blacks, mingled their blood in the peninsula. The Moors have left an ineffaceable mark on Spanish and Portuguese physiognomy, art, language, and music, especially the latter.

At Granada, on a mountainside facing the Alhambra are still the tunnelled-out homes of the Negro guards of the Moorish sultans with the words, "Barrancos de los Negros," (Barracks of the Negroes.) Some of the barrancos are inhabited by dark-skinned people who are said to be gypsies. The word, gypsy, comes from "Egyptian."

Towards the end of the fourteenth century Moorish power began to decline, and in 1492, the year of America's discovery, the Moors were over-whelmed by the white armies of Ferdinand and Isabella. In 1610 they were driven bag and baggage across to Africa or over the Pyrenees into France. Others went to Holland, Belgium, and Germany.

Modern Negro Strain in Spain and Portugal

In the meantime, however, another influx of Negroes into Spain had already been set in motion—an influx that was to have the most tremendous repercussion on the history of the New World and the United States in particular. This influx was the beginning of Negro slavery and the slave-trade.

The event began in a singular manner and gave no herald of its signifi-cance. In 1440 Prince Henry the Navigator sent his lieutenant, Antam Gon-

[2] Encyc. Britannica, Vol. 21, p. 128 (14th ed.) Much additional data in Nature Knows No Color-Line, pp. 55-68.
[3] Beaumier. Histoire du Maghreb. p. 190. Paris. 1860.

salves, to the coast of Guinea for a cargo of skins and oil. Getting it easier than he had expected Gonsalves started off to see the interior, where he was attacked by the natives. Seizing ten of them, including a chief and two children of noble family, he took them to Portugal.

They were very kindly treated there, and aroused considerable curiosity because of their manner and their dress. An attempt was made to convert them to Christianity but they pined for home, and on promise of a large ransom, were sent back.

In time, the Portuguese returned with the ransom, which included ten slaves, gold dust, a leathern shield, beautifully wrought, and ostrich feathers. The slaves fetched a high price. This fact, together with the gold stirred the cupidity of the Portuguese and the slave trade was on.

Another expedition to Guinea returned with two hundred and thirty Negroes and mulattoes, who also were quickly sold. In justice to Portugal, however, it must be said, that Henry III of Spain had started a slave-trade fifty years before but it had not been a success. Portugal, however, popularized it, and England made big business of it.

The West African's First Reaction to Caucasian Contact

In this day when it is the fashion to accuse the Negro of seeking inter-marriage and social equality with white people, it will be interesting to note how those first Africans acted when brought among white people for the first time. And fortunately, we have an eye-witness account, a most touching one, from a leading historian of the times, Eannes de Azurara. He says:

"What heart was that how hard, soever, which was not pierced with sorrow at seeing that company, for some had sunken cheeks and their faces bathed with tears looking at each other; others were groaning dolorously looking at the heights of the heavens, fixing their eyes upon them, crying out loudly as if they were asking succor from the Father of Nature; others struck their faces with their hands, throwing themselves on the earth; others made lamentations in song according to the customs of their country, which, although, we could not understand their language we saw corresponded to the height of their sorrow—

"But now for the increase of their grief came those who had charge of the distribution and they began to put them apart from the others to equalize the portions; wherefore, it was necessary to part children and parents, husbands and wives, and brethren from one another. Neither in the partition of friends and relations was any law kept, only each fell where the lot took him. O powerful fortune! who goest hither and thither with thy wheels compassing the things of the world as it pleaseth thee, if thou canst place before the eyes of this miserable people some knowledge of the things that are to come after them that they may receive some consolation in the midst of great sadness! and you others, who have the business of partition look with pity on such great misery and consider how can those be parted whom you cannot disunite. Who will be able to make this partition without great difficulty? for while they were placing in one part the children who saw their parents in another they sprang up perseveringly and flew to them. The mothers enclosed their children in their arms, and threw themselves with them on the ground receiving wounds with little pity for their own flesh so that their children may not be torn from them."[4]

The Portuguese, anxious to convert the captives to Christianity, treated them kindly. Their dark skins also intrigued the Portuguese. Faria y Sousa, Spanish historian of the times, says of this, "The slaves were greeted with admiration because of their color." (Entraron en el Reyno con admiracion comun causada del color de los esclavos.)

Azurara goes on to speak of the treatment of the Negroes as follows:

"Although the sorrow of these captives was for the present very great, especially after the partition was finished, and each one took his share aside (while some sold captives which they took to other districts) and although it chanced that among the prisoners the father remained in Lagos, while the mother was taken to Lisbon, and the children to another part, yet this sorrow was least felt among those who happened to remain in company. But from this time forth they began to acquire some knowledge of our country; in which they found great abundance and our men began to treat them with great favor. For as the people did not find them hardened in their belief as the other Moors; and saw how they came in unto the law of Christ with a goodwill they made no difference between them and their free servants, born in our country; but those whom they took while still young, they caused to be instructed in mechanical arts and those whom they saw fitted for managing property they set free and married to women who were natives of the land, making them a division of their property as if they had been bestowed on those who married them by the will of their own fathers and for the benefit of their own service they were bound to act in like manner. Yes and some widows of good family who bought some of these female slaves either adopted them or left them a portion of their estate by will so that in the future they married right well; treating them as entirely free. Suffice it to say that I never saw one of these slaves put in irons like the other captives, and scarcely one who did not turn Christian and was very gently treated."

A footnote to the above says that "the black men" were married to the

---

[4] Discovery and Conquest of Guinea. Vol. I, pp. 81-86. Hakluyt Soc. 1896.

XL. 1. John VI, King of Portugal; 2. His son Pedro I, Emperor of Brazil and
later King of Portugal.

Portuguese women. Another significant fact about these first slaves was that they were not all full-blooded Negroes. Azurara says, "Some were white enough, fair to look upon and well-proportioned; others were less white, like mulattoes; others again were as black as Ethiops." Considerable mixing of white and black must therefore have taken place on the Guinea Coast, prior to 1440.

For the next three centuries, the Negroes came in droves to take the place of the Moors, and the Jews who had also been expelled. Soon whole provinces of Portugal, especially the southern one of Algarve, became black. Lisbon, the capital, itself, was more black than white in the sixteenth century.[5] Amalgamation went on so freely that in time even the royal family was more Negro than white. John IV shows Negroid traits; John V, the Louis XV of Portugal, still more; while John VI, adversary of Napoleon, is recorded as being a Negro, a fact that his portrait bears out. The Duchesse d'Abrantes, wife of the French ambassador to the Court of John VI, and a leading writer of the times, says of him, "His enormous head with its Negro hair, which, moreover, was quite in harmony with his thick lips, his African nose, and the color of his skin."[6] Of John's wife, who was a daughter of Ferdinand VII of Spain, she says, "Her skin was brown and hair dry and woolly." Of the Duchess of Alafoes, a member of the Portuguese nobility, she wrote: "Her skin is brown, so very brown, that one would not take her at first sight for a European. She was a grand dame of such remarkable beauty that she could well say, "I am black but comely, Oh, ye daughters of Zion." Descendants of John VI have married into other royal houses of Europe.[6a]

The Duchess d'Abrantes says that she was struck by the Negroid appearance of the Portuguese, "their thick lips, Negroid noses, black hair, often woolly. In their bearing, their hands, and especially in their nails, one sees the Negro blood." Negro slavery was abolished in Portugal in 1773, or 330 years after the coming of the first blacks.

On my trip through Southern Portugal, I was struck by the resemblance of many of the people to the West Indian mulatto type. Some degree of race-mixing still goes on with natives from Africa and the Cape Verdes.

Negro slavery also flourished in Southern Spain. It was from Seville that the first Negro slaves to the New World were taken in 1502. Only Spanish Negroes were exported, that is, those who had come "under the influence of Christians." Seville had a large number of Negroes, who lived in what is now the Barrio Carmona. These blacks had a government of their own under a Negro Count, Juan de Vallodolid. "El Conde Negro "[7]

[5] Williams. M. W. People and Politics of Latin America, p. 100. (1930.)
[6] Memoires. pp. 150 200, 207, 224, 245, 265. Paris. 1837.
[6a] Rogers, J. A. 100 Amazing Facts About the Negro. (18th ed.), p. 38.
[7] Helps, A. Conquerors of the New World, pp. 29-30. (1848.)

XLI. Upper left: Castilian Senorita. Below: Mulatto type from Granada. Right: top and bottom, Street of El Conde Negro in the Barrio Carmona, Seville. Center: Juan de Pareja.

A streel in the quarter still bears his name.

The people of Southern Spain still show evidences of their Negro ancestry, and some of the dark-eyed senoritas remind one of those of Cuba.

Incidentally there is some American Indian strain in the Spaniards too. Thousands of Indians of both sexes were taken to Spain as slaves. Amerigo Vespuccius took 222 of them to Cadiz in 1498 and sold them there. So did Columbus and others. And, of course, people of mixed Indian, Negro, and Spanish blood from the New World also migrated to Spain.

Miscegenation Today

On my several visits to Spain I saw a fairly large number of Negroes, chiefly in Madrid, Barcelona, and Cadiz, some of whom had Spanish wives.

In Madrid an incident occurred involving a Negro musician that furnished much diversion for the press and the populace, and was written into a popular song. It happened that the proprietor of one of the leading cabarets had a much beloved wife to whom he had been married for years but who had given him no children. Finally a "blessed event" was announced and there was much wining and dining and congratulation. At last the child was born, but there was something queer. It looked like neither parent, especially in color and hair. In short, there could be no doubt that it was a mulatto.'

Atavism! explained the doctor. Either father or mother had a Moorish ancestry, more or less distant, he said. The father accepted that but the public didn't. The mother had been seen too often dancing cheek to cheek with one of the eight American Negro musicians in her husband's cabaret. The eight Negroes were fired and the child sent to a convent. Later a reconciliation was effected between husband and wife and the child taken to live with them. But one noblewoman who had a mulatto child was abandoned by her husband. A handsome Negro bull-fighter, Julio Mendoza, from Venezuela, was extremely popular with the senoritas.

Another influx of Moors, most of them unmixed Negroes, came in during the late Civil War to help Franco.

Race-Mixing in Spanish Literature

Spanish literature has been kind to the Negro, too. One of its most heroic figures is Rosambuco in Mira de Amescua's "El Negro del Mejor Amo,' to which the Enciclopedia Espanola Ilustrada devotes a whole column. Lope de Vega also wrote another Negro play, El Negro Santo. These characters like "El Valiente Negro en Flandes" are no Uncle Toms. A more recent novel, Alberto Insua's, "El Negro que Tenia El Alma Blanca, (The

Negro Who Had a White Soul), deals sympathetically with the love of a Negro—*un hombre en quien no importaba el color*—with a white girl. As for certain other pamphlets dealing with race-mixing and which must be mentioned sotto voice as "Las Gracias de la Mulata," I saw them on sale on newsstands openly in Seville, Barcelona, and elsewhere.

As regards this Negro admixture, certain writers love to point out that the downfall of Spain and Portugal was due to it. For instance, the Infanta Eulalie, a near relative of ex-King Alphonso, says:

"The Black Peril originally began in Portugal and it still continues to contaminate her as the Negroid element in Portuguese blood is invariably attended with disastrous results since the black strain dominates the feeble stock and reproduces and intensifies the vices of the Negro, allied to the more refined decadence of the Portuguese... Many Portuguese and English girls now give themselves soul and body to black men."[8]

However, the Princess, like most racists, shuts her eye to the facts of history. The truth is that for nearly two centuries after the last miscegenation began, Portugal was one of the two leading countries of the world. Indeed she was the first world power. She owned Brazil and vast possessions in India, Africa, and the Pacific. Lisbon was an intellectual centre second to none in the world, "the home of poets, historians, and philosophers." The court of John V rivalled that of Louis XIV. Besides, as was said, Portugal had been a Negroid land from the dawn of history.

What really crushed Portugal were the following: The ill-fated expedition of her king, Sebastian, in 1588 into Morocco and his defeat and death there, leaving no heir. Spain seized Portugal as a result; wars followed in which Portugal was stripped of nearly all her possessions until she defeated Spain sixty years later. In 1755, came the Lisbon earthquake, one of the world's greatest catastrophes, and finally the Napoleonic wars, which ravaged the country and brought such ruin that it has never recovered.

Moreover, some of Portugal's greatest men were of Negro ancestry. One of them Antonio Vieira, (1608-1697), was her greatest orator, her greatest prose writer, and her noblest soul. Vieira, whose grandmother, was a Negro domestic, defied the Portuguese Inquisition, which, seeing his dark skin and frizzly hair, thought it could outlaw him by proving that he was of heretical blood, that is, Moorish or Jewish. It started an investigation which revealed that Vieira came of nothing more dangerous than Negro stock. This was not considered tainted as it was Christian, and Vieira's foes were discomfited.[9] For years Vieira preached for the Pope. The

[8] Courts and Countries After the War, p. 126. London, 1925.
[9] D'Azevedo. Historia de Antonio Vieira. Vol. I, p. 9. Lisbon, 1918. (Appendix, Vol. II. has testimony of witnesses on his ancestry.)

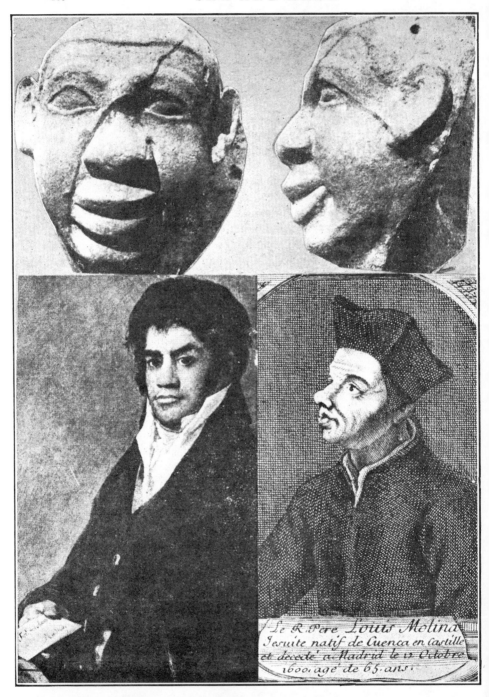

Upper: Front and profile of a Spaniard of 1500 B.C., probably the ancestral type of the Silures. or Western Britons. (Cadiz Museum). Lower left: Don **Francisco del Mazo**, a Spanish mulatto nobleman, painted by Goya. Right: Louis Molina, great Catholic reformer. (Bibliotheque Nationale, Paris.)

XLIa. Princess Dona Juana of Spain, Austria, and the Netherlands with her Negro favourite. (See Notes on the Illustrations.)

roving Queen Christina of Sweden was enamored of him. Incidentally other
Negroes have preached for the Pope in St. Peter's since, one of them being
Father Gladstone Wilson of Jamaica, West Indies, in 1939.[9a]

The racial harmony that has prevailed in Portugal ought to settle a
point so often advanced by certain Americans of both "races" who, when
told that there is no color prejudice in Europe, usually reply, "Well, if they
had the same proportion of Negroes as we, the situation would be the same."
Portugal had a higher percentage of Negroes than the South, while its
whites are of old Germanic stock.

Portuguese royalty, itself, set the example by being kind to the Negroes.
Noble Portuguese ladies had Negro favorites and pets. William Beckford,
the author of "Vathek" says as regards this, "In the stage-box I observed
the mincing Countess de Pombeiro, whose light hair and waxen complexion
was finely contrasted by the ebon hue of the two little Negro attendants,
perched in style, each side of her. It is the high ton at present in this
court to be surrounded by African implings, the more hideous, the more
prized and to bedizen them in the most expensive manner. The Queen has
set the example and the royal family vie with each other in spoiling and
caressing Donna Rose, her Majesty's black-skinned, blubber-lipped, flat-nosed
favourite."[10]

Beckford was an Englishman, and the owner of slaves in Jamaica.
J. C. Murphy, who visited Portugal in 1789 and also saw Donna Rosa was
more sympathetic. He tells of seeing her talking with the Queen, and resting
her hand upon the Queen's lap, but adds that the Queen showed her this
high honor out of sympathy for a persecuted race.[11]

Another Negro girl, Chicava, from Guinea, was adopted by the Emperor
Charles II of Spain. She entered the Convent of La Penitencia, Salamanca,
where she became an important figure in the religious life of Spain.[12]

In good Bourbon tradition, Don Carlos, pretender to the Spanish throne,
also adopted a Negro girl as his daughter. She was with him when he died
in Vienna.[12a]

Italy

The Moors also dominated parts of Italy. In 846 A.D., they laid
siege to Rome. In 878, they captured Sicily from the Normans; and in 898
defeated Otto II of Germany in South Italy. As in Spain they mixed

[9a] Samuel S. Cox. pro-slavery congressman, tells of his great amazement at seeing
a coal-black Negro preaching in fluent Latin before the Pope and a great audience in
St. Peter's. (A Buckeye Abroad, p. 133. N. Y. 1852.)
[10] Italy, Spain. and Portugal, p. 108. N. Y., 1845.
[11] Travels in Portugal in 1789-90, p. 252.
[12] Enciclopedia Univ. Illus. Vol. 53, pp. 136-37.
[12a] N. Y. World-Telegram, Sept. 29, 1936, p. 14.

ALEX.MED. FLOR.   DVX. I. LAVREN. F.

XLII. ALESSANDRO DEI MEDICI, Duke of Florence, and son-in-law of the Emperor Charles V. Alessandro's father was a pope and his mother was a Negro servant of such great beauty that she is called "The Italian Cleopatra." (Medici Palace)

their blood with that of the native Italians, who at this period had a large infusion of German blood due to the invasion of the Goths, and Vandals.

Negro slavery of the fifteenth century from Spain and Portugal also spread into Italy. The parents of St. Benedict the Moor, Catholic saint, who attained great fame during his life, came of this stock. Negro "blood" also found its way into the leading Italian families, including the most illustrious royal family of the times: the Medicis. The faces of some of

the Medici as given in "Regiae Familiae Mediceorum Etruria," are undoubtedly Negroid, especially that of Cosimo III and his son Gian Gastone,
who bears a striking resemblance to the great Negro novelist, Alexander
Dumas. Charles II of England came of this stock. G. F. Young says
of the latter, "His dark hair and swarthy complexion showed traces of the
Medici blood."[12a]

One of the Medicis, Alessandro, "The Moor," first reigning Duke of
Florence, actually had a Negro mother. The latter, who was in the service of
the Pope's aunt, was the wife of a mule-driver, but Pope Clement VII, then
Cardinal dei Medici, took her as his mistress, and was the father of Alessandro.[13] Nearly all the writers are agreed that Alessandro was a mulatto,
which moreover, is clearly indicated by his portrait by Bronzino. The Enciclopedia Italiana says, "His color, his lips, and his hair" revealed his Negro
strain. Gino Capponi, Italian historian, says that his mother was "a Moorish
or mulatto slave" (una schiva mora o mulatta) and that Alessandro had
"a dark skin, thick lips, and woolly hair." (La pelle scura, le labbra grosse e i
capello crespi.") Benevenuto Cellini, who worked for Alessandro, says,
as do several others, that everyone believed that Alessandro was the son of
the Pope.

Alessandro married Margaret, daughter of Charles V, emperor of Germany, Spain, and Austria, but had no children by her. His children by other
white women were: Julius, who became an admiral of the Order of St.
Stephen; Cosmo, who by Lucretia Cajetana, had Angelica, first wife of
Peter, Duke of Altemps and Galesio. Alessandro also had two natural
daughters, one, Julia, who was twice married, first to Francesco Cantelmo,
Duke of Popola, and secondly, to Bernardo de Medina, Baron of Ottogano;
from this latter marriage descended the princes of that line. Portia, the
other daughter, became a nun.[14] Staley reports yet another daughter who
married Francesco de Barthelemmi.

Another great Italian, who was most likely of Negro ancestry was Ludo-
vico, "The Moor," Duke of Milan, foremost member of the powerful Sforza
family. Biographie Universelle says he was called "The Moor" because of
his very swarthy skin.

Brantome tells of another love affair in high life with a Negro—"a
beautiful grand dame of Naples," who had a Negro slave, "the ugliest in
the world, her groom, her lover," whose "ugliness and odd appearance made
him beloved by her."[15]

[12a] The Medici, Vol. 2, p. 300. London, 1909. In the Barcelona Treaty Alessandro
was acknowledged as the son of the Pope—Trollope, Commonwealth of Florence. Vol. 41,
p. 287.
[13] Cotterill, H. B. Italy From Dante to Tasso, pp. 483-85. N. Y., 1919.
[14] Noble. M. Memoirs of the Medicis, p. 214. London, 1797.
[15] Oeuvres. Vol. IX, pp. 703-04. (Lalanne). Paris, 1873.
For other works on the Negro in Castilian literature see: I. Peredas Valdes, "El
Negro Rioplatense," pp. 8-9, Montevideo, 1937.

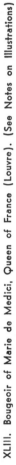

Noble Italian Ladies and Their Amours With Negro Slaves

Juvenal and Martial, early Roman writers, scored the fondness of the Roman matrons of their time for blackamoors, as was said. Masuccio, another Italian writer of the fifteenth century, is even more severe in this respect. In his stories, which throw much light on the history of the period, noble Italian ladies, who are cold and indifferent to men of their own class are infatuated with Negro slaves. In his Novellino XXII, the wife of the rich Nicolao d'Aguito of Trapani, a woman of great beauty, is so deeply in love with her husband's Moorish slave, "a young fellow, strong and robust of body but ugly beyond measure" that she would have killed her husband if the slave had said so, and finally ran away to Africa with him.

Novellino XXIV tells of a young man who was desperately in love with "a gracious and beautiful lady, the wife of one of the foremost gentlemen of the city." After trying to win her in every way, he entered the yard of her home one day, and hid behind a pile of casks, intending to enter the house and get under her bed when she went out. But she stayed at home all that day.

While he was still hiding, a Negro slave came into the yard driving a mule, loaded with wood. The lady, hearing the slave, hurried to the window and began scolding him for being so long. But the slave took no notice of her on which she came down into the yard and began "to sport with him in tender wise with her hand and she went on from one endearment to the other; the wretched lover who stood wonder-stricken and for his own sake wishful that he could have won the favour which was now being granted to the black man without any labour on his part beheld the lady go and make fast the door and then without any farther ado or demur, throw herself upon the mule's saddle which lay there and draw the horrible black fellow towards her. He without waiting at once set himself to the task and gave the wanton what she desired."

Novellino XXV deals with " a very young and beautiful woman" named Geronima, "vain beyond measure" who held captive the hearts of some of the noblest and choicest men without ever letting them taste "the supreme fruit she held in store." One nobleman set himself the task of winning "this finished artist in coquetry" but had no success. Finally he thought of reaching her through one of the Negro slaves of the family, Alfonso. He treated the latter so well that he became more attached to him than to his master. At last the nobleman asked the slave to intercede with the lady for him. The slave, greatly embarrassed, tried to dissuade him. The lady wasn't worth his notice, he said. Pressed for the reason the slave confessed that the haughty dame was already his mistress, and gave the nobleman most convincing proof.[15a]

[15a] Novellino. Trans. by W. G. Waters. London. 1895.

KLIV. I to 7 and 9 and 10, Cameos from the Bibliotheque Nationale, Paris. 8. Attic Greek Vase of the Fifth Century B.C. (See Notes on the Illustrations.)

Casanova, the world's most famous lover, had a Negro mistress.   He says," A handsome Negress who served the prettiest of my actresses to whom I showed great attention said to me one day;

" 'I can't make out how you can be so much in love with my mistress who is as white as the devil.' "

" 'Have you never loved a white man?' " I asked.

" *'Yes:'* " *said she,* "*but only because I had no Negro to whom I certainly should have given the preference.'* "

"Soon after the Negress became mine and I found out the falsity of the axiom: *Sublata Lucerna nullum discrimen inter ruinas* for even in the darkness a man would know a black woman from a white one."[16]

This observation may be more significant than it seems.   Casanova appears to have had more than a touch of the tar-brush, himself, as the most intimate descriptions of him indicate.

The Prince de Ligne who knew him very well says, "Ce serait un bel homme, s'il n'était pas si laid; il est grand, bâti en Hercule; mais un teint africain . . ." (He would have been a fine-looking man if he had not been so ugly; he was tall, built like a Hercules, but he had an African complexion . . .)"[17] Casanova's father is unknown.

Garibaldi's wife and companion in battle was a colored Brazilian woman, Anita, who was called "Coffee."   A magnificent monument was reared to her recently in Rome.   Southern Italy is still decidedly Negroid as well as parts of Albania.

Southern Italians are very much mixed.   Some Sicilians are indistinguishable from dark mulattoes.   Poincaré refused to withdraw the colored troops from the Rhine on the ground that they were no darker than large numbers of Italians.

---

[16] Memoirs.   Vol. XII, Chap. 13.   Marsan, E.   Les Femmes de Casanova, p. 18. Paris 1924.
[17] Oeuvres Choisies, p. 130.   Paris 1890.   Also the translation of this work by K. P. Wormeley, Vol. II, pp. 160 61.   Boston, 1899.

Chapter Sixteen

MISCEGENATION IN HOLLAND, BELGIUM, AUSTRIA, RUSSIA, POLAND

NEGRO strain entered Belgium and the Netherlands after the Christian era principally through the Jews who migrated there in large numbers from Spain and Portugal; and from the Spanish occupation of the Low Countries which lasted nearly three centuries (1526-1792). As was said, Spain had large numbers of Negroes in her armies, and Negro blood in her nobility. According to a seventeenth century Spanish classic, "El Valiente Negro en Flandes," by Andres de Claramonte y Corroy, a Negro ex-slave, Juan de Merida, rose to be the lieutenant-general of the Duke of Alba, the Spanish commander in Flanders.[1]

The Spaniards tinged the fair skins of the Nordics of the Netherlands, and created, according to Theophile Gautier, "a new Flemish type with brown skin and black hair, a second race which the soldiers of the Spanish Duke of Alva have sown between Brussels and Cambrai." Another writer, Bogaert Vache claims, however, that there was a black-skinned race living in the Low Countries before the Spanish invasion. He says, "There are documents which prove the existence of blacks in Flanders in the Middle Ages. I have long called attention to this fact in the Life of St. Godelieve (eleventh century) written by one of her contemporaries, Drogon, a monk of the Abbey of St. Andre-les-Bruges."[2] Margaret, Countess of Flanders, (1568) was known as "Black Meg" (Zwarte Griet). Beethoven's "blackish-brown" skin and "Negroid traits" might have come from this Spanish stock.[3] Indeed, he was called "The Black Spaniard of Bonn." His Malay strain might have come in by a Malaysian's settling in Holland. Countries as Holland, France, Belgium, England, which have colonies usually have a considerable number of their dark subjects living in the mother country.

Negroes, in fairly large numbers, are to be found in Belgian sea-ports, principally Antwerp. I saw hundreds of them there. Some of them had married Belgian wives and had children. They came principally from the Congo. Negroes are also in the Belgian army in Belgium.

Whatever the Belgian may be in Africa, he is free from color prejudice at home. In 1929, when one of the hostesses, in a Brussels night-club re-

[1] Biblioteca de autores espanoles. Vol. 43. (1857).
[2] Intermediare des Chercheurs et des Curieux. Vol. 55, p. 569.
[3] For biblio. see Rogers, J. A. 100 Amazing Racts About the Negro (18th ed). pp. 21-22.

iused to dance with a Congo merchant at the instigation of the American patrons, the proprietor threatened to discharge her the next time she did so.

The Hollanders, too, were utterly free from color prejudice. One morning in Amsterdam I came down to breakfast at my hotel to see a tall, handsome Dutchman with a coal-black West Indian wife. The other guests, at the table, about nine in number, were chatting and laughing with this mixed couple, apparently oblivious of the difference in color. When I mentioned this to the editor of one of Amsterdam's leading dailies, he added, "There are several colored officers in my regiment and the white men obey them as readily as the other officers. My fiancée had colored ancestors, too, and nobody thinks any the worse of her."

At the Hague a white cigar salesman told me with glee how some residents of the town had squelched the racial enthusiasm of certain Americans who had tried to have a Negro doctor ejected from a hotel in which he had been living for years. In Rotterdam, at the leading vaudeville house I saw what was billed as "A Black and White Act," in which an Aframerican entertainer, Harry Wellmon, danced and sang with his white partner. At one hotel I saw a Negro, who had married the daughter of the proprietor and lived as free from care and work as a pet cat. Rotterdam, like Amsterdam, had a fairly large number of Negroes.

Austria

Austria, as was said in Chapter Two, was peopled by Negroes in prehistoric times.[4] Evidences of Grimaldi culture have been found there, the most noted of which is the statuette of a Negro woman with woolly hair, enormous breasts, buttocks with large humps of fat, and elongated nymphs, all of which are characteristics of the unmixed Hottentot-Bushman race of South Africa. This statuette, the oldest known sculpture of the human form was discovered at Willendorf, hence its name the Venus of Willendorf. It is now in the Vienna Museum.

The Tatars, or Tartars, a Mongolian race, which had a Negro strain, swept through European Russia in the thirteenth century under Batu Khan, subduing the Slavic princes, and conquering the peoples of Poland, Eastern Germany, Poland, Austria, and Hungary. J. J. Marcel says, "Their frequent alliances with the Pelasgians, Semitic, and Negro races modified the primitive type of the Tartars."

Later, as has already been said, came the Turks, who went as far as the walls of Vienna after conquering parts of Russia, Poland, Hungary, and Switzerland. The most famous body of Turkish troops were the Janizaries,

[4] Histoire Universelle, Vol. I, p 55, says Austria "was inhabited by Negroes in the Paleolithic Age."

XLV. Dutch Negro woman of the 17th Century by Gerard Dou.

who were largely Negro slaves of the Sultan. It may be presumed that these soldiers made free with the women as conquerors usually do. The German invaders of Belgium in 1914 left behind progeny to fight Germans in 1940; the French soldiers on the Rhine also left children to attack France in 1940; and Americans, white and black, left thousands of children in the Philippines, some of whom later, may have been clamoring for independence.

The people of Central Europe especially the Hungarians, show to a marked degree the mixing which has happened as the result of the various invasions. Haydn, great Austrian composer, who was called "The Blackamoor" because of his very dark skin, probably came of this Turkish-Negro stock. The same has been said of Goethe.

At least one noble Austrian family of the eighteenth century, the von Feuchtersleben, had a direct Negro strain. The daughter of Angelo Solliman, a Negro from the Congo, who was a favorite of the Prince of Lichtenstein, and also of Joseph II, of Austria, married the Baron Eduard von Feuchtersleben. Their son inherited the title. Solliman, himself, also married into the nobility.[5]

Vienna was also the scene of the triumphs of the great mulatto violinist, George A. P. Bridgetower, whose father was an African Negro and his mother, Polish or German. Bridgetower was a close friend of Beethoven, accompanying the latter on the violin and interpreting his works. The two friends parted when the Countess Guiccardi, with whom Beethoven was madly in love, became too friendly with Bridgetower.

Franz Joseph II of Austria-Hungary, like Czar Nicholas II, had a number of stalwart Negro attendants at his court, splendidly dressed, and who served largely for show. These Negroes had white wives and mulatto children.

At present, Negroes are few in Central Europe. One meets from time to time, however, the child of an occasional Negro student or musician by some white mother.

In 1933, an incident occurred in Budapest that caused considerable excitement and had a play put on about it. A coal-black Cuban, who was a physician and a boxer, went into an aristocratic wave-bath with a white girl to the horror and indignation of the sixty English and American visitors and bathers. Descending on the proprietor, the English and the Americans declared that if the Negro used the bath again they'd quit. It was sixty against one and the proprietor told the Negro not to use the bath. The latter protested to the newspapers, which, together with the doctors of the town, raised such a fuss that the mayor issued an order against the discrimination. The play about the affair was entitled, "The Man They Wouldn't Let Take A Bath."

[5] Bauer, W A   Angelo Solliman: Der Hochfurstliche Mohr.   Wien, 1932.

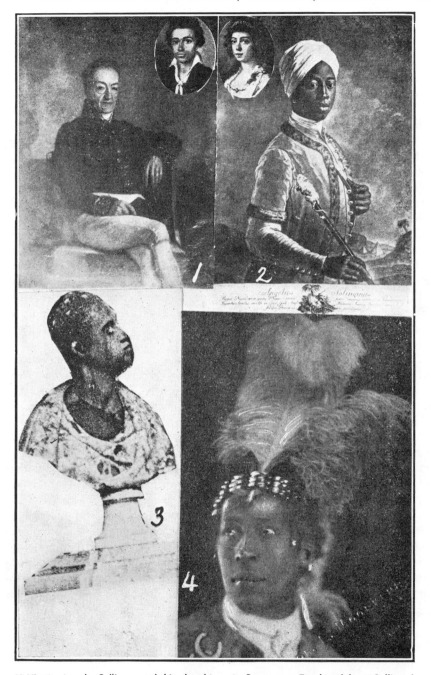

XLVI. 2. Angelo Solliman and his daughter; 1. Baron von Feuchtersleben, Solliman's son-in-law. Inset: Baron Eduard von Feuchstersleben; 4. "Rass Prince Monolulu."

European Russia and Poland

That a prehistoric Negro race also lived in Russia is highly probable. Statuettes of the Grimaldi type have been found at Gagarmo on the Upper Don. Professor Dixon in "The Racial History of Man" said that the early Negro type could be discerned in Eastern Russia as late as the Middle Ages.

Tatar and Mongolian invasions from Asia brought in considerable Negro strain, too. There is a type of Russian whose skin is white and hair is straight but whose face is distinctly Negroid as, for instance, Yermoloff, who was one of the lovers of Catherine the Great. It was probably this that caused Potemkin, Catherine's principal lover, to call Yermoloff "a white Negro." Princess Murat in her "Catherine the Great" calls him a "half-Negro,"[6] but Yermoloff's portrait shows him a white man with a strongly Negroid face. Maxim Gorki came of this stock, and Lenin, too.

From the sixteenth century onwards and perhaps earlier, hundreds of Negroes were taken into Russia as mascots, the most noted of whom was Abram Hannibal, great-grandfather of Pushkin, who rose to be general-in-chief of the Russian army under the Empress Elisabeth. Schuyler, in his "Life of Peter the Great" says, "Negroes were in esteem, as indeed they have been of recent years. Volynsky sent from Astrakan a couple to Catherine in order to ingratitate himself with her and Peter had several, one of whom was Abram or Ibrahim Hannibal."[7]

Hannibal's first wife, a Greek, bore him a white child and when accused of infidelity replied that tricking a Negro was no wrong. His second wife, Regina von Schelberg, a German noblewoman, gave him eleven children, all mulattoes. Five of these were sons, all of whom rose to distinction. Ivan, the eldest, was victor over the Turks at the battle of Navarin in 1770, and governor of the Ukraine. Another, Joseph, was a naval commander and navigator, whose daughter, Nadejda, married Count Pushkin, who belonged to one of the thirty-one leading families of Russia. She became the mother of the poet, Pushkin, whose descendants have married into the royal families of Germany, Russia, Luxembourg, Italy and England.[8]

Pushkin's daughter, Natalie, Countess of Merenberg, was married to Prince Nicholas of Nassau. Their daughter, the Countess de Torby, wed the Grand Duke Michael, brother of Nicholas II of Russia. A daughter of the latter union married George, Marquess of Milford Haven, great-great-grandson of Queen Victoria.[9] One of Pushkin's sons, General Prince Pushkin, was commander of the Russian troops in Poland in 1890. Direct de-

---

[6] p. 172. N. Y., 1928.
[7] Vol. II, p. 438. N. Y., 1884.
[8] Ruvigny. The Titled Nobility of Europe, p. 1450. London, 1914.
[9] Burke's Peerage. Vol. II, pp. 1675, 1733. London, 1936.

scendants of Pushkin still live in Russia.

Catherine the Great in her portrait by Lampi has a Negro with her. So has Peter the Great in one of his portraits. Peter III was so fond of his Negro, Narcissus, that he would make the ambassadors of great lands wait while he played with him. When he was imprisoned by Catherine he asked that Narcissus be permitted to stay with him. When T. Morris Chester, a captain of United States Volunteers, an unmixed Negro, visited Russia in 1867, the Czar invited him to a military review, during which he rode with the Emperor and later lunched with him and his family at the Winter Palace.[10]

Another African Negro, Michael Egypteos, was taught naval designing, built several warships and rose to be major-general and head of the naval dockyards at St. Petersburg. He married a Russian wife and one of his daughters married a Swedish army officer.

The late Czar, Nicholas II, had a corps of thirteen Negroes, very black, and of magnificent build and height as an exotic setting for his palace. They were dressed in gorgeous robes and jewelry. An English army officer who spent twenty-four years in Russia tells me that "their position was that of privileged servants, who after a service of twenty years received a pension of a hundred roubles a month and the title of civil servant of the third grade." They were married to Russian women and had children by them. He said that he also saw other Negroes with Russian wives, one of them, an Ethiopian, who had been bought in Africa for three roubles by a rich merchant, named Kropensky. This child, he says, was reared with all the luxury of the Russian upper class, but after the revolution became a waiter in a small cafe.

An American Negro, John Gordon, was a member of the Military Revolutionary Committee of the Bolsheviks in 1918, and later a general in the Red Army.[12]

Considerable Negro strain was brought into Russia and Poland by Polish Jews. Count Gurowski of Poland has been cited on the Negro strain in the "Polish Jew."[11]

In 1932, a case of miscegenation occurred in Posen, Poland, that was a nine days' wonder. The wife of a rich merchant of the town gave birth to a child that was unmistakably a mulatto, in fact, it was almost black. As neither parent showed the slightest sign of Negro ancestry, the doctors were intrigued. Finally, they agreed it was atavism. But one more sceptical than the rest followed up the case. He finally discovered that the woman had been spending time at Toulon in Southern France, where one or two regiments of Sengalese soldiers were stationed.

[10] Brown, W. W. The Rising Son, p. 527. (1874.)
[11] See Chapter IX of this book.
[12] World's Work, Oct. 1918. Other sources in Nature Knows No Color-Line, p. 135.

Chapter Seventeen

NEGRO-WHITE MIXING IN GERMANY

IN the matter of ancient Negro strain, Germany seems to be no different from the other countries mentioned. The famous Neanderthal skull, the oldest Negro type known, was discovered at Dusseldorf, Germany, in 1856.

There are other abundant archaeological evidences also. Professor Dixon says, "In Mecklenburg and Silesia in the south-east, it was the Proto-Negroid type which was in the majority." He also thinks that an early Negro people inhabited eastern Norway. Julius Caesar undoubtedly took Negroes in his legions to Germany. The skull of an ancient Negro was found at Cologne. Baring-Gould thinks it was that of a Christian martyr since it was pierced by a nail.[1]

The Huns, a Negro-Mongolian people, who over-ran Europe in the fourth and fifth centuries, A.D., also contributed much towards the present German stock. The Huns had swarthy skins, flat noses, and frizzly hair. Jordanes, a writer of the sixth century, who saw them, says, "They made their foes flee in horror because their swarthy aspect was fearful."[2] Of Attila, their greatest leader, who is called "The Scourge of God," Jordanes says, "He had a flat nose and a swarthy complexion showing the evidences of his origin."[3] McRitchie says, too, that certain of the Danish tribes living in northwestern Germany were "like the Moors, black." And, as was said, in the chapter on Japan, we have clear evidences of an ancient Negrito race in Northern Europe in the Laplanders.

There might even have been a considerable penetration of Egyptians into Germany as relics of the worship of Isis have been found in the Moselle region. The Jews also brought in a considerable degree of Negro strain as they did in Poland, Russia, and elsewhere. Fishberg in his book, "The Jew," shows that in spite of prejudice, German and Jew have mated pretty freely

All through the Middle Ages and well into our times, Negroes were fairly plentiful in Western Germany as servants and favorites, especially in the homes of the nobility and the rich. Most of the rulers of the little kingdoms and duchies had Negro favorites. George I took two of them with him from Hanover when he left to take the English throne. Negro favorites and mascots were common in Prussia. The kings of Prussia had

[1] Lives of the Saints. Vol. X, p. 331.
[2] Gothic History of Jordannes, trans. C. C. Mierow, p. 54. Princeton, 1915.
[3] Ibid, p. 102.

XLVII. Detail from Rubens' Bacchanale. (Berlin Museum)

several of them, whose statuettes are in the gallery of the Moors in the Royal Park at San Souci. One of the latter, William Anthony Amo, rose to be state counsellor in Berlin. William I of Germany had a coal-black Negro at his court, the celebrated musician, Brindis de Sala, whom he made a baron. Brindis de Sala, who was court violinist, had previously scored resounding triumphs in Paris, Milan, and other cities. He married a German woman of high rank.[4] William I was most kind to Ira Aldridge, great Aframerican Shakespearean actor. He gave Aldridge one of the only four medals for distinction in the arts and sciences he ever conferred on anyone—the other three being Liszt, Humboldt, and Spontini. The Duke of Saxony knighted Aldridge, while other German rulers gave him command performances. Aldridge's wife was the Countess Amanda Pauline Brandt. William I also adopted a Negro given him by the explorer, Rohlfs, as his son, and made him an officer in the German army, and a member of his suite.[4a]

The ex-Kaiser Wilhelm II was also very kind to Negroes. The band-master of his favorite regiment was a Negro, born in the royal palace, Sabac El Cher. The parents of the latter had been brought from the Sudan by Prince Albrecht, the Kaiser's uncle. Sabac El Cher was a musical prodigy. Two of Kaiser Wilhelm's bodyguard at San Souci were Cameroon Negroes, one of whom, Hari Mambo, I have met. Wilhelm II also had a stately American Negro, named Wilson, as the drum-major of one of his regiments at Konigsberg. Wilson married a German woman, and had children who were living in Saxony. Once when German troops were leaving for Africa, Wilhelm II exhorted them in person to be kind to the Negroes.

Monuments to Negroes may also be seen in parts of Germany. The great Catholic Saint of Germany, St. Mauritius, or Maurice (from Moor) is depicted as a coal black Negro of purest type. He is shown with the German eagle on his head by Hans Baldung and has a massive statue to him in the Magdeburg Cathedral by Walter Greischel. He is also patron of the city of Cobourg; and has his portrait in the Alte Pinokathek of Munich and elsewhere. On the principal bridge over the Spree near the Cathedral of Berlin on the north centre of the bridge is (or was) a statue of a Negro.

In the Berlin Museum is Rubens' "Bacchanale," which has two Negroes in it. One of the latter is clasping the nude body of Rubens' own wife and has his cheek close to hers. On his face and hers is a look that cannot be misinterpreted. Another white woman, wearing a coronet, is also shown leaning affectionately on this Negro.

When Germany had her African and Asiatic colonies, she treated those natives, who for one reason or another came to settle in Germany, very kindly. When she lost the colonies, however, she lost interest in the blacks.

[4] Encicl. Univ. Illustrada. (Brindis de Sala, Claudius.)
[4a] See Rogers, J. A. 100 Amazing Facts, etc., p. 45 for sources.

XLVIII. Cameroon Negro residents of Berlin in 1931. Inset: Cameroon native dancer in Berlin.

I am convinced that if she hadn't lost the colonies, the Nazis wouldn't have started anti-Negro agitation. The latter was largely strategy to win American support.

Negroes on the Rhine

In this matter of race-mixing on the Rhine, the important question was what did the German masses and the German women themselves think about the colored troops, especially those women, who, of their own will, became the mothers of several thousand mulattoes.

Maximilian Harden who was then Germany's most influential journalist said frankly that the Negroes were very far from being unwelcome to the German women. "Unfortunately," he said, "we have seen the aberration of the female every time when Hagenbeck has shown us tribes of natives. Everywhere the German women followed the black and yellow men, pestering them with love letters. They were not repelled by their smell. On the contrary, they found it a special stimulus."[5]

Other writers reported similarly. J. Ellis Barker ("Colored French Troops in Germany") said, "I was told that not only girls of the lower classes but even ladies belonging to the upper and middle classes, both married and single, were running after the French soldiers, and the colored men seemed to have a particular attraction for them... I saw German girls whose dress and fluent French indicated they belonged to the upper class make love to the colored soldiers and their advances bordered only too often upon the indecent."[6]

General Henry T. Allen, American commander on the Rhine, said in his report to the Secretary of State (July 2, 1920), "German women of loose character have openly made advances to the colored soldiers as evidenced by the numerous love-letters now on file in the official records and which have been sent by German women to colored French soldiers. Several cases have occurred of marriages of German women with French Negro soldiers. One German girl of a first-class burgher family, her father a very high city functionary of a prominent city in the Rhinelands, recently procured a passport to join her (Negro) fiance in Marseilles. Other Negro soldiers have had French wives here and the color line is not regarded either by the French or the German as we regard it in America to keep the white race pure

"At Ludwigshafen, when the Seventh Tirailleurs left for Frankfort. patrols had to be sent out to drive away the German women from the barracks where they were kissing the colored troops through the window gratings...

"I was told that the German police and the French authorities in the

---

[5] Quoted from Die Zukunft in Current History. July, 1921. New York.
[6] Current History. July, 1921. New York.

Brigitte Helm

Joé Alex

XLIX. A study in Black and White from Pre-Hitler Berlin.

occupied districts found it very difficult to prevent the German women from
pestering and pursuing the colored troops. In many cases the colored soldiers
themselves complained to their officers about the shameless advances made
to them by German women and, frequently, a military guard had to be called
to keep women from entering the barracks by the window."[7]

Lilli Jannasch said similarly:

"Many white women find something alluring in entering into close relations with blacks. This we have been able to verify when members of Negro
tribes were placed on exhibition in Germany. At the time of the Industrial
Exhibition in Berlin, for example, it repeatedly happened that Negroes on
exhibition disappeared for several days, and it was town talk that women
of good society had been entertaining the Negroes. Similar things have
happened in cities in all parts of Germany, especially in Hamburg."[7a]

A writer in Intermediare des Chercheurs et des Curieux also gives
his own experiences on this matter. "Our good Africans," he says, "have
violated only those German virgins who wished to be violated. Furthermore,
I have noticed in the different countries of the world I have visited that a
difference of race acts as a stimulus... Twenty-five years ago at Copenhagen
the male element of a Negro village exhibited in the famous public garden
of Tivoli obtained such a great success with the young girls of the town that
when the troop was leaving Denmark, I saw with my own eyes a pretty large
number of these blond Ophelias accompany them to the station with all the
marks of the most profound desolation at parting from the black Othellos
of whom they had been the casual Desdemonas."[8]

At the Hagenbeck Zoo in Hamburg in 1929 there was an African village
with some thirty or forty natives, mostly men. It was enclosed with wire
netting which I thought peculiar. But later when I saw the great interest
of the women, and remembered what had been said about how society women
had inveigled away previous blacks, I fancied I saw the reason for the fence.
One handsome, finely built girl in particular seemed so fascinated that I
engaged her in conversation on which she admitted with that frankness characteristic of the German that she found black men very appealing. The pre-
Hitler German was very frank about sex. Magazines, like Licht Land, with
photographs of men and women quite nude, on the front cover, were hung
up on the news-stands. Hitler, according to his former chum, Rauschning,
had pictures of this type—men and women with nothing concealed—in his
bedroom.

Pierre Mille, noted French writer, has given in Le Journal of Paris,
the following true love story between a German woman and a Senegalese
soldier, which might help to throw some light on similar romances:

7 Current History. Ibid.
7a Quoted in Crisis Maga. March 1921, p. 222.
8 Vol. 85, pp. 951-2.

1, 2, 3. An Aframerican in Germany, his German wife and child and the latter's aunts and **grand-parents**; 4. Popular figure of the Latin Quarter, Paris, a Cameroon Negro. who had a German wife and three grown sons; 5. Sabac El Cher.

" Mahmady n'Diaye, Deserter'

"Deserters are very rare among the Senegalese sharpshooters, who incidentally are not recruited in Senegal alone but in all of our black African colonies. These brave soldiers know only 'duty' and 'orders,' and have never failed to obey either. Yet some years ago I met an ex-sergeant of Senegalese sharpshooters, named Mahmady n'Diaye, dressed in a magnificent livery, who was the valet at the famous hotel Adlon in Berlin. But that he was a deserter was not entirely his fault, as you'll see.

"In 1920 his battalion occupied the city of Mainz in the Rhineland. The commandant of this battalion was named Desgrieux... One morning as Desgrieux was signing papers his orderly, who was naturally also a Senegalese, entered, saluted, and said:

" 'Major, there is a white lady who wishes to speak with you.

" 'Who is she, and what does she want?'

" 'I do not know, sir. She is German. I don't understand that kind of monkey talk. She doesn't speak French. She talks like a savage.'

"A German woman. The major, disturbed in his daily routine, was troubled. What did she want? Was she going to complain of one of those cases of 'rape' of which the German papers were speaking so vociferously, although up to now not a single one had been proved. If it were so, good God, what trouble it was going to cause. And in his own battalion, too. If the man was guilty he was going to have him shot. To the orderly he snapped: 'Show her in.'

"The woman entered. She bore a child in her arms and from its color it was evident, alas, what had taken place between her and one of our brave defenders from the banks of the Niger and the Volta. Looking at the woman the major noted that she was not only good-looking but was well-dressed.

" 'You have a complaint to make?' he demanded.

" 'Sir,' she replied in that tone of profound respect with which officers of superior rank are addressed in Germany. 'I came for permission...'

" 'What do you say? What permission?'

" 'Permission for my marriage with Sergeant Mahmady n'Diaye, the father of my child. My father strongly wishes it, my mother strongly wishes it, and I desire it also.'

" 'Very good.' Then the major said to himself: 'It is clear then that it is this animal of a Mahmady who doesn't wish it. Good soldier. Excellent sergeant. Twelve years of service, about to obtain French naturalization even at the price of giving up his own personal status, and in consequence renouncing his Mohammedan faith. But in spite of all this if he doesn't marry this girl I am going to give him fifteen days in prison and have the general increase it to two months.'

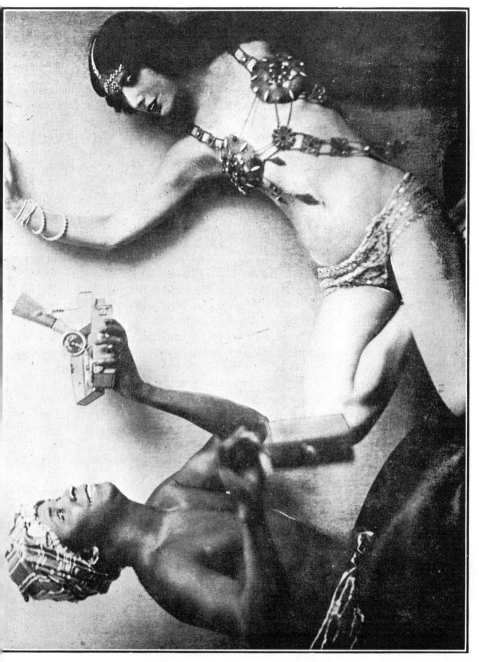

LI. A Pre-Hitler German advertisement.

"To the orderly he said 'Bring Mahmady here at once.'

" 'So,' said the major when Mahmady arrived, 'You do not wish to marry this girl. You're a bad soldier and a bad father. What sort of man are you? Have you no affection for your son?'

" 'Me?' demanded Mahmady in surprise. 'You say, sir, that I do not wish to marry her. Why I want to right away. I am French, and I want her to be French, and my son, too. He is a little black, it is true, but that won't matter.'

"To the major it was clear that all were agreed on the marriage, 'Well,' said he, 'why do you come to bother me? Get out all of you, and get married whenever you will.' Then he suddenly remembered that permission for such a marriage must come from headquarters. So this explained why this couple, hoping to have a rapid and favorable response, had appealed to him.

"And he was not mistaken. Eight days later he received the following reply from headquarters: 'Because of the circumstances and the propaganda being waged in Germany as well as in other lands against the black troops in the Rhineland with regard to the feminine population—although this propaganda has no foundation whatever—it is necessary to exercise the greatest care in giving a permission to marry. This matter will have to be taken up in Paris. The demand of the sergeant, and his fiancee, together with that of their parents, must accompany the application.'

"It developed that Mahmady had no parents living, and that those of the German woman demanded nothing better than to have this Senegalese as a son-in-law. Major Desgrieux, therefore, sending for the couple, told them that he hoped for a happy solution to their problem in a short time.

"But they waited for a long time. Then when the child grew until it could babble both French and German there at last came the following reply:

" 'The desire expressed by Sergeant Mahmady n'Diaye, medaille militaire (high French decoration for valor) and that of Miss X.... of German nationality, raises a grave question of international law. Can a native of one of our colonies marry a German woman? The Minister of War does not wish to accept the advice of his own legal counsels. He has taken up the matter with the League of the Rights of Man, itself, so as to have every guarantee of independence and to protect himself. The unanimous opinion of the legal counsels is that a Frenchman has a perfect right to marry a German woman even as a French woman has a perfect right to marry a German, as well as a Frenchwoman to marry a Negro. But there is a doubt when it is a question of a native from our colonies who is only a French subject, and is not naturalised, or is not French by virtue of law. It appears, therefore, that it is preferable in order not to cause any international dispute, that the request of Sergeant Mahmady and Miss X.... be denied.'

"Major Desgrieux laid the missive on his desk, feeling that Mahmady was going to make an awful fuss. And he did, whilst Miss X.... and her parents added to the flow of the Rhine with their tears. Moreover, Mahmady, this old soldier so faithful to discipline and to the sobriety imposed on him by Islam began to drink abominably, after which he cursed to the seventh generation the children of Mme. Piblique, Queen of France, those of the major, his colonel, his general, and of Marshal Foch himself, relegating them all to that part of his body least worthy of consideration. In consequence he was reduced to corporal and condemned to two months in prison, which he served.

"But on the day after he was not at roll-call. Without consulting the Minister of War or the League of the Rights of Man he had simply slipped into that part of Germany not occupied by the French, where without delay he married Miss X....

"And this is how I met him at the Hotel Adlon dressed in a uniform more gorgeous than that he would have worn had he continued in the noble corps of Senegalese sharpshooters. He was a naturalised German and was the proud father of three children, dark-skinned, it is true, but very legally Germans."

The foregoing, however, is not all of the picture. Some Negro soldiers did attack the German women, as Dr. Magnus Hirschfield, reports in his Sexual History of the World War.[8a]

What Is the Real Feeling of the German Towards Negroes Now?

In Hamburg and other German sea-ports are several dozens of Negro sailors married to German women and who have children for them. In Berlin also there was a small colony of Cameroon Negroes, mostly males, who had white wives, and German-born children. One British West Indian student had a son by a German woman, and since neither of them was able to support him, he was handed over to the state. That boy, now fourteen, is probably goose-stepping in some labor battalion.

On my several visits to Germany, during which I went fairly well over the country, I saw not the slightest sign of color prejudice except from Americans. I spoke to German audiences, including one high school, whose principal was a Jew, and they were shocked to hear of the treatment of the Negro in the United States. In fact on my first visit to Berlin in 1927 the first Negro I saw was a woman who was walking arm in arm with a white man on Friedrichstrasse. Later in the dance-halls, I saw Cameroon Negroes dancing with German girls. In 1929, when I entered a Berlin cafe, patronized by the more respectable folk, my companion, a Negro, selected the prettiest girl in the place, a Saxon blonde, smooth skinned and rosy-faced, whom he

[8a] pp. 367-8. N. Y 1937.

had never met before, and engaged her in conversation. She responded the most amiably in the world and later they danced. At one bathing beach where men and women had adopted the Russian and the Japanese habit and bathed together quite nude, I saw several Negroes in the altogether, too. Some Berlin Negroes I knew were married to girls of good family, and their mulatto children were received as one of the family by the grandparents.

Anti-Negro propaganda hadn't much effect on the older Germans. It is as difficult to imbue a people with color prejudice, especially when there are no Negroes around as it is to rid them of it when once it has been taught them by an older generation. Apart from Hitler, himself, the Negroes at the 1936 Olympics at Berlin were very well treated by the German people. Negro ministers who met at a convention in Berlin about the same year reported most excellent treatment so much so that when they came back and said so they were scolded by Communists. It was easier in Hitler Berlin for a Negro to get service in a hotel or restaurant than in Washington. It is true that Nazis did pull a Negro minister from Africa out of a Lutheran pulpit while he was preaching to a white German congregation, but in 1938, when Adolph Hodge, a Negro school-teacher, who conducts an annual tour abroad, wrote Hitler saying that he was bringing a party of colored folk to Germany and asking him how they would be treated, he received a letter from the Berlin Tourist Bureau saying that they would be received with the same courtesy as all other visitors to Germany. The writer took pains to add that the story of the ill-treatment of Negro athletes at the Olympic was a falsehood, which it really was, according to the Negroes themselves. Had Hitler occasion to reverse himself on Negroes as he did for a time on Communism, it would have been easy.

German Men and Negro Women

I spoke of the German women and their attitude towards the Negro man, what of the German man and the Negro woman?

When I said in the American Mercury[9] that I had found the Germans very fond of Negro women, and how when I once entered the famous Hofbrauhaus at Munich with two colored women, the Germans crowded around, kissing the women's hands, and even trying to kiss their lips, too, the New York correspondent of the Die Zukunft of Frankfurt branded it as an infamous lie. Nevertheless it had happened, and moreover, I was not surprised. For years I lived in a mountain district in the Island of Jamaica,

[9] May, 1930. For mixture of German women and Negroes during and after World War II, see Nature Knows No Color-Line, pp. 112-135.

that had been settled by Germans about fifty years before, and almost the entire black population had been amalgamated by them. Every German I knew had one or more black concubines. One of them in particular had so many children and grandchildren named after him that it was a standing joke that he was the father of the village. Mulattoes with names as Sauerlinder, Swaby, Meyer, Brandt, were common. Some of these mulattoes married white German women, and at least one unmixed Negro had a German wife. The white Germans, as I knew them, had much less color prejudice for the blacks than their mulatto offspring.

Rear-Admiral Shufeldt, U.S.N., says: "In conversation with a very intelligent German gentleman the other day, a man of fine education, intelligence and family connection in Germany where he was born, he informed me that he very much preferred congress with a fine, good-looking black Negress than with any white woman he had ever known, and from all accounts he had not been backward in such matters."[10]

It is my impression that the Germans and the Scandinavians are fonder of miscegenation than any other portion of the white race. Thus Nazi blasts against race-mixing in France is not without its irony. Conspicuous among these attacks was one in the Illustrierte Beobachter of Berlin, which declared that it was not German guns, airplanes, and poison gas that is France's danger, but the Negro.

The article is copiously filled with "horror" pictures showing how the French whites of both sexes associate on intimate terms with the Negro. Some of the typical sub-titles are: "An everyday picture in Paris—nigger dancers with white women. French newspapers filled with lying atrocity stories about Germany would do well to worry about atrocity-ridden France." A dance hall billboard showing a Negro dancing with a white woman is entitled: "The Betrayal of the White Race." A picture of white and colored students of the Sorbonne together is headed: "France sacrifices the future mothers of its children to racial death." A Jewish-looking man is shown cheek to cheek with a black woman with: "The Jew as usual prepares the way for decay." It is indignant that a Negro woman should be called a "French woman," and declares that France would do well to learn from the United States where Negroes are kept "in their place" and are lynched when they try to get out of it.

It continues: "A certain French tabloid paper lately started a crusade against Germany and her inner political relations based upon clumsily forged material. The aim was to stimulate hatred and the war spirit against Germany. But our today's pictures taken in Paris show that France is endangered from quite a different side. The French press, in its own interests

10 The Negro: A Menace to American Civilization, p. 86. N. Y., 1907.

would do better to study German methods for race-preserving and profit by it.

"The French Army Chief, Gen. Weygand, wanted to import 5000 Negroes from Africa to France, hoping thereby to stop further decrease in the French birthrate, which makes it difficult for France to get enough recruits for her army. But Marshal Lyautey, Governor General of Morocco, opposed this project declaring that the Negroes would give in to alcohol and Communism, and that France should bring the Negroes only when needed as in the last war. Lyautey—the lone voice in the desert—is no doubt well acquainted with the manners and character of the "niggers." In the summer of 1916 black heads suddenly rose before us from the trenches and we had to stand for it in 1921 when France sent colored troops into the Rhineland and the Ruhr—black foremen for white people. Whoever looks about France now is grieved to see how all the blood barriers between white and black are falling.

"France is the first civilized country to have a Negro Cabinet Minister. Negro lawyers, who are French citizens, defend white people in the courts. The famous Sorbonne has a Negro professor. Colored students, who are trying to get some knowledge in their black "nigger" heads abound in the Latin Quarter. Along the Boulevard St. Michel may be seen these black students looking as if they had stepped out of a London tailor's. They go about in expensive limousines. A few days ago they may have been in loin cloths in their native land. Now they are strutting like the conquerors of Paris—and I hesitate to say it—white women and girls are turning to look at them with longing eyes.

"The danger is much greater than is imagined. But France shuts her eyes to it. She pretends not to see these bastards in the streets of Paris, the Rue Pigalle, Rue Fontaine and the quarters of the Arabs and Kabyles around the Place d'Italie. You never know who are fathers of these bastards, a Frenchman, a Negro, or an Arab. In Montmarte you'll find a number of white dance halls—each of which wants to be as Negro-like as possible— and carrying the tax stamp of the City of Paris. Negroes looking like gorillas are dancing with white women who are clingingly lovingly to them. Thus what is the worst crime against race is made into a business.

"In America a distinct line is drawn between white and black. America would gladly send all her Negroes back to Africa. She attempted that with Liberia. Is this race question no problem for France? Or has France already solved it in the most dangerous, most shameful way? This should wake up the white race here and elsewhere to the consequences. This race-question is more important than that of national differences. It is the sacred right of Germany to deal with the race question in its own country. We have not only France with its 40,000,000 people facing us but a powerful country from the Mediterranean to the Congo inhabited by 100,000,000 French people of the white and black race."[11]

In spite of the frothings of this writer, the sole difference one can see between the conduct of the French with the Negroes and that of the Germans with them in the matter of race-mixing is that France has the greater number of Negroes, and therefore more miscegenation.

La Depeche Coloniale, white Paris daily, said as regards the law making it illegal for Germans to marry Negroes and Jews:

"The German people, as everyone knows, consider themselves as God's own people. In their eyes, men of color are not human beings and as such merit no consideration. They have never been able to understand why our black sharpshooters should be treated as men. The cruelties of a Peters or a Jesko von Prittkamer in South-East Africa, or the Cameroons, without speaking of the methodical extermination of the Herreros, have forever fixed the opinion of the world on the attitude of the Germans towards black people.

"Before the war a Negro was not permitted in the German ranks... Besides the noise that the German press has made about the so-called 'Black Shame' is well-known. Indeed, one also knows only too well the keen curiosity of the German women in everything that concerns Negroes, and we recall very clearly what we personally saw of the suggestive scenes between these German women and Negroes in Berlin, Leipzig, Hamburg and other cities.

"Recently even black boys seem to be enjoying special favor in certain high Prussian quarters, as one may see by reading the advertisements. Here, for instance, is one that was just published:

" 'Handsome young Negro wanted as page in a Chateau des Masures belonging to a count. Good salary.' But whilst these handsome young Negroes are being sought to serve in the homes of German countesses, the German Parliament is occupying itself with a law that is truly monstrous— a project that emanates from the National Socialists of Hitler and the Nationalists of Hugenberg.

"This idea of race superiority still thrives in Germany, and it was indeed a fortunate day for the black race when the treaty of Versailles took its members out of the clutches of these dangerous beings."

An earlier Reichstag had refused to pass a similar bill. In 1912, when the Nazis of that day tried to make it illegal for Germans in the African colonies to marry Negroes, they were defeated by a vote of 203 to 133.[12]

[11] December 9, 1933.
[2] African Times and Orient Review. Feb.-March, 1913, p. 241.

I ha,e done very little research on the intimate side of the life of the
Negro favorites in the German kingdoms, but I was reliably told that there
were several scandals in high life, including cases of homosexuality. One
German princess, whose descendants are counted among the greatest of the
great, socially, was distinctly Negroid while her parents showed not the
slightest evidences of Negro strain.

Denmark

Johann Dietz in his "Autobiography" (1655-1738) tells of an instance
of intermarriage in Denmark. He says, "I was greatly amazed when we
came at night to a great noble's house, where we found a coal-black, finely-
dressed woman and three tawny-yellow children. Everything was magnificent. I should never have dreamed that this was the wife of my Master
Gansberger... He had married this lady, his wife, at the King's Court,
she being of Moorish origin."[13]

Sweden

The present royal family of Sweden is descended from Jean Baptiste
Bernadotte, who came from the south of France, and was of Moorish ancestry, and was swarthy and had woolly hair. Sir D. P. Barton says, "Jean
Baptiste Bernadotte, son of a lawyer of Pau, with a dash of Moorish blood
in his Gascon veins."[14]

As regards the preceding Swedish dynasty there was a great scandal,
incidentally involving miscegenation. The one most immediately concerned
was Gustavus IV, Adolphus, the king.

Gustavus IV was said to have been illegitimate. What gave strongest
credence to the story was that its most active propagandist was his own
grandmother, Louise Ulric of Prussia, sister of Frederic the Great. This
Queen-dowager declared that her son, Gustavus III, had committed a fraud
in saying that he was a father.

Gustavus III, like his cousins, the Great Frederick, and Henry of
Prussia, was impotent. General Suremain, who held a confidential post
in the palace of Gustavus III, and was tutor to Gustavus IV, is among
those who confirm the story of the king's sexual inability.

Gustavus III had been married for eleven years and had not yet con-
summated his marriage, making the Queen very unhappy. In this she was
like her contemporary, Marie Antoinette, whose husband Louis XVI of
France neglected her for seven years until her brother, Joseph II, Emperor
of Austria, interfered.

---

[13] Translation by Bernard Miall, p. 162. N. Y., 1923.
[14] For details see Rogers, J. A. 100 Amazing Facts About the Negro (18th ed.),
pp. 38-9.

LII. 1. Count Munck von Fulkila; 2. Gustavus IV. Adolphus, King of Sweden; 3. Gustavus III.; 4. Queen Sophia of Sweden. (See Notes on the Illustrations).

The ministers of Gustavus III were demanding an heir, declaring that the stability of the kingdom depended on it. At last after a stormy session of the Cabinet the king promised them one.

Gustavus was a great man. Nature had liberally endowed him with gifts. He was an able general; one of the greatest monarchs of his time; one of the leading poets in his realm, and highly developed artistically. But in procreative ability he was nil. How then to keep his promise?

There seemed but one way. To get a proxy.

Gustavus III, it is said, thought of his most intimate friend (with an accent on the "intimate," it is alleged), Major Adolph Frederick Munck, thirty, of Finnish-Swedish ancestry, and with a Negro strain inherited from his maternal grandmother. This African descent was visible in his frizzly hair, dark skin, full lips, and the length between nose and lips.

The evening after he had given his promise to his ministers Gustavus III, it is said, requested Munck's aid. Munck, already in love with the Queen, readily agreed. Conducting him to the Queen, "he told the confused and blushing woman, of his dilemma, exposed to her the service he had demanded of his friend, and came out shutting the door after him and leaving them there."

When the king's mother learnt that Queen Sophia was with child she at once suspected a trick. She saw the throne passing from the Vasa dynasty to one not of that house, with her second son, the Duke of Sudermann, heir apparent to the throne, excluded. She agitated openly and exposed her son's inability.

Count Munck emphatically denied the charge. He swore that the prospective heir was the king's son; that he, himself, had led the king, six nights in succession into the Queen's bedroom, once picking him up bodily and locking him in, and that finally the king had performed his conjugal duties. It seems, however, that little credence was given to his story. General Suremain, who, as was said, knew the royal family very intimately, clearly intimates that he believes that the child was not the king's.

Years later Munck retracted his statement. After the death of Gustavus III in 1792 he became virtual ruler of Sweden, but his rival, the Duke of Sudermann, succeeded in having him exiled. Later he threatened to tell all unless a pension was granted him.

Petiet, quoting from documents in the French National Archives, on instructions that had been sent at that time to the French Government, says: "Everybody in Sweden is convinced that Gustavus IV is the son of Baron de Munck, former favorite of Gustavus III, and this belief goes back to the time when the queen was in child with him, everybody considering the king as incapable of having children." A foot-note to the above reads:

"In 1796 Baron de Munck then an exile in Italy imperatively demanded a pension declaring that he held in his possession documents on which the wearing of the crown by Gustavus IV depended. This letter has contributed not a little towards confirming the belief that he was the father of the young king." Finally Munck declared that he was, and told the story openly.

But what did more than anything else to give credit to the story is that Gustavus IV, (in contrast to his mother, and Gustavus III, who were quite Nordic in appearance), had the dark skin, full lips, and prognathous features of Munck. His Negroid features were so evident that he was called "The Moor."

Another fact that aroused suspicion was that soon after the alleged fraud, Munck rose rapidly from one high post to the next until he was second only to the King. From a major he became Court Chamberlain; the governor of Stockholm; governor of the provinces of Upsala and Svartsjo; governor of the royal.chateau of Drottingholm, and Haga; president of the Chamber of Control and Grand Master of Ceremonies; Chevalier of the Order of Seraphims, and Field Marshal.

Because he was generally believed to be illegitimate the young king's life was a most wretched one. On March 29, 1809, at the age of thirty-one he abdicated due largely to political difficulties. He had hoped to save the throne for his son, but because of the belief regarding his ancestry, supported, it is said, by his mother's confession, Parliament declared the throne forfeited to him and his family forever.[15]

[15] An unusually well-informed writer on mixed marriages and the Negro strain in certain distinguished Europeans, who signs himself "Ex-Attaché," says in a copyrighted article in the New York Tribune, Sunday, April 17, 1910 (IV,3) :

"Gustavus IV, the last sovereign but one of the Vasa dynasty in Sweden used to go by the name of 'The Moor.' When he was born his grandmother, the old Queen Dowager, Louise of Sweden, sister of Frederick the Great of Prussia openly proclaimed that he was not the offspring of the King but of Baron Munck von Fulkila, one of the handsomest men of the court of Stockholm, a fervent admirer of the young Danish-born Queen and who was himself the grandson of a Moorish lady of high rank. . ."

According to this writer, the present Queen of Sweden is a descendant of Gustavus IV, while a Swedish royal prince married a descendant of Munck. He says, "The present Queen of Sweden as well as the reigning Duke of Baden are great-grandchildren of this King Gustavus IV, surnamed the Moor, and it may be of interest to add that the now reigning King of Sweden's sailor brother, Prince Oscar, renounced his rights of succession to wed Ebba Munck von Fulkila, a lineal descendant of that handsome Baron Munck von Fulkila."

This writer also mentions that the founder of the present Swedish dynasty, Bernadotte, was colored.

On the alleged illegitimacy of Gustavus IV, see:
Suremain. Mémoires, pp. 15-17. Paris, 1903.
Léuzon le Duc, L. Les Couronnes Sanglantes, pp. 129-150. Paris, 1886.
Beskow, Baron de. Gustavus III. Stockholm, 1868.
Bain, R. N. Gustave III. Vol. I, pp. 238-51. London, 1894.
Dumas, Alex. Mes Mémoires. Chap. 52. Paris, 1863.

Chapter Eighteen

THE MIXING OF WHITES AND BLACKS IN THE BRITISH ISLES

WERE the first Britons, Negroes? There is considerable evidence that they might have been. Grimaldi relics have been dug up in England.[1] Very ancient huts, strikingly like those of Africa and the South Seas have been unearthed at Glastonbury. Ring money of the kind used by the Negroes of the Sudan to pay tribute to the Pharaohs, and which is still being hammered out by African goldsmiths, has also been found.[2] Blue beads of 1500 to 1200 B.C., that are common in the Egyptian ruins, have been found in considerable number in the Stonehenge district.[3]

African relics of other kinds have been discovered. C. van Riet Lowe says, "Implements recovered from the oldest and most classic terraces of the Somme and the Thames are indistinguishable in contour and shape from those of the Vaal and Caledon valleys in the Orange Free State or from the Bushman's and Eerste Rivers in the Cape. Our conviction that the cultures presented in the Old Stone Age of Europe and South Africa, and for that matter, of the western half of the Old World generally, are most closely interrelated, grows steadily. We believe that from some common centre, most probably in Africa, prehistoric folk carried their cultures to practically all corners of the Old World, and that the problem of the prehistoric in Western Europe and South Africa particularly, form part of a closely interwoven whole."[4]

As regards color, Tacitus, Roman historian of 80 A.D. distinctly mentions "the dark complexion and the unusually curly hair" of the Silures, or Black Celts, who occupied England together with a fair-skinned, fair-haired people. He believed that these Black Celts had migrated there originally from Spain. Professor Elliott Smith also finds that "The populations which occupied Northeast Africa, the whole Mediterranean littoral, the Iberian Peninsula, Western France, and the British Isles before the coming of copper, were linked together by the closest bonds of affinity."

An immense amount of data on the Negro in ancient Britain has been unearthed principally by three British archaeologists: Gerald Massey, poet

---

[1] Bulleid, A. and Gray H. The Glastonbury Lake Village, Vol. II, p. 405. London, 1917.
[2] Wilson, D. Archaeology of Scotland, p. 309. Edinburgh, 1851.
[3] New York Times Magazine, Nov. 1, 1936, p. 22.
[4] South Africa in the Stone Age. Illustrated London News, 606. April 29, 1933.

ana Egyptologist; Godfrey Higgins, who traced religious origins; and David McRitchie, who worked from folk-lore.

Massey devotes most of Volume One of his work, "A Book of the Beginnings" to "Egyptian Origins in the British Isles." He thinks that Stonehenge, the most famous ancient monument in England, was built by a Negro architect, named Morien, (that is Mor, or Moor, from the ancient Egyptian). He says, "Now as a Negro is still known as Morien in English, may not this indicate that Morien belonged to the black race, the Kushite builders?"

Higgins, an earlier writer, says these Negro builders were Buddhists— and originated in India. The earliest Buddhas are all woolly-haired, flat-nosed, and thick-lipped. He says, "A great nation called the Celtae, of whom the Druids were the priests, spread themselves almost over the earth and are to be traced in their gigantic monuments from India to the extremity of Britain. Who can these have been but the early individuals of the black nation of whom we are treating I know not; and in my opinion I am not singular. The learned Maurice says, "Cushites, that is, Celts, built the great temples in India and Britain and excavated the caves of the former." And the learned mathematician, Ruben Burrow, has no hesitation in pronouncing Stonehenge to be a temple of the black, curly-headed Buddha."[5]

Massey says, as regards this, "It is certain that the Black Buddha of India was imaged in the Negroid type. In the black Negro God, whether called Buddha or Sut-Nahsi we have a datum. They carry their color in the proof of their origin. The people who first fashioned and worshipped the divine image in the Negroid mold of humanity must, according to all knowledge of human nature, have been Negroes themselves. For blackness is not merely mystical, the features and hair of Buddha belong to the black race and Nahsi is the Negro name. The genetrix represented as the Dea Multimammia, the Diana of Ephesus, is found as a black figure, nor is the hue mystical only, for the features are Negroid as were those of the black Isis in Egypt."[6]

With regard to the worship of this Negro goddess in Britain, D. A. MacKenzie, "Ancient Man in Britain," says, "In Scotland, a black goddess (the Nigra Dea) in Adamnan's Life of Columbia is associated with Loch Lorchy." The celebrated Black Virgin of Chartres, France, is said to have been brought there from Britain.

McRitchie in his "Ancient and Modern Britons" deals with a later date. He mentions the dominance of the Moors in Scotland as late as the time of the Saxon kings. He says, "So late as the tenth century three of these

5 Anacalypsis, Vol. I, p. 59. London, 1927.
6 A Book of The Beginnings, Vol. I, pp. 18, 218. London, 1881.

provinces (of Scotland) were wholly black and the supreme ruler of these became for a time the paramount king of Transmarine Scotland...

"We see one of the black people—the Moors of the Romans—in the person of a king of Alban of the tenth century. History knows him as Kenneth, sometimes as Dubh and as Niger...

"We know as a historical fact that a Niger Vel Dubh has lived and reigned over certain black divisions of our islands—and probably white divisions also—and that a race known as the 'sons of the Black' succeeded him in history." These Negroes, he adds, were bred out just as a Negro finally disappears by mating with whites only, so "that no ethnologist could detect the presence of other blood." "And," he adds, "yet in both cases, the male descendants would bear the surname first given to their remote ancestors—a surname signifying 'the black man.' "[7]

McRitchie continues, "You may see faces of a distinctly Mongolian and even of a Negroid cast in families whose pedigree may be traced for many generations without disclosing the slightest hint of extra-British blood . . .

"So far as complexion goes there can be no doubt as to the presence of a vast infusion of 'colored' blood. There are, of course, no living Britons who are as black as Negroes, but some are as dark as mulattoes and many darker than Chinese. To regard ourselves in the mass as a 'white people' except in a comparative degree, is quite a mistake."

McRitchie gives the names of several of these Negro families whose names are famous in English history, and American history, too. One of these is the celebrated Douglas, one of the ancestors of the present royal family of Britain. J. A. Ringrose says of the founder of this family, "About the year 770 in the reign of Salvathius, King of the Scots, Donald Bane of the Western Isles having invaded Scotland and routed the royal army, a man of rank and figure came seasonably with his followers to the king's assistance. He renewed the battle and obtained a complete victory over the invader. The King being anxious to see the man who had done him such signal service, he was pointed out to him by his colour, or complexion in Gaelic language—sholto-du-glash—'behold the black or swarthy-coloured man' from which he obtained the name Sholto the Douglas."[8]

McRitchie points out further that the best proof of the Negro origin of some of these noble British families are "the thick-lipped Moors" on their coat-of-arms. Some of these families are still named Moore. Berry's Encyclopedia Heraldica says, "Moor's head is the heraldic term for the head of a black or Negro man."

---

[7] Ancient and Modern Britons, Vol. I, pp. 21, 121, 131; Vol. II, pp. 17, 20, 87, 102, 107, 112, 113, 127, 188-9, 297, 322, 328-9, 360, 392. London, 1884.
[8] Heraldry, pp. 68-9. London, 1913.

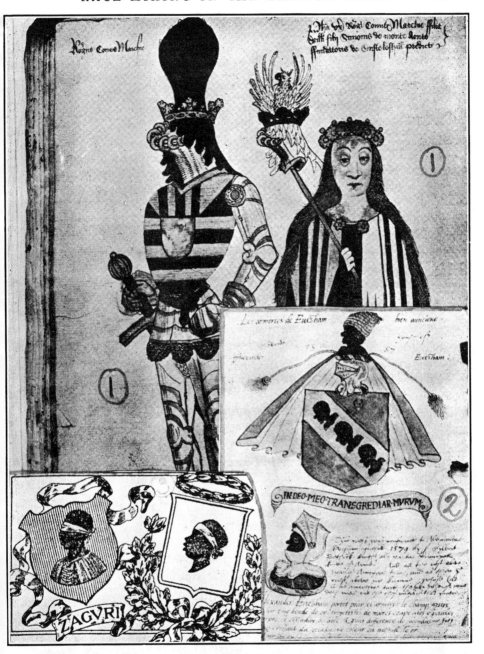

LIIIa. (1) Negro Norman knight with his lady. (2) Arms of the noble Evesham Family. (3) Arms of the Noble Zaguri family of Italy. (See Notes on the Illustrations.)

Grandmaison believes that the "Moor's head" originated in the Crusades and also in memory of certain arms against the Moors of Europe,[9] but McRitchie says that this does not sufficiently explain it since there were black peoples domiciled in Scotland, where, moreover, some of the bearers of the insignia of the Moor's heads are named Moore.

Among the latter are the Rt. Hon. William Ponsonby Moore, Earl of Drogheda; Moore of Hancox; and Moore of Moore Lodge. Others are the Earl of Annesley, and Morrison-Bell of Otterburn.[10]

According to "Burke's Peerage," the coat-of-arms of the Marquess of Londonderry consists of "a Moor wreathed about the temples, arg. and az., holding in his exterior hand a shield of the last garnished or, charged with the sun in splendor, gold. Bearers of similar coats-of-arms are the Earl of Newburgh; Viscount Valentia, whose family is related to Annesley and whose arms bear a Moorish prince in armor; and Baron Whitburgh.

The Scots, in their earliest chronicles, claim descent from the Egyptians and the Greeks, says R. Holinshed in "Scottish Chronicle." Skeane, referring to John of Fordun, who wrote the first formal history of Scotland in the Fourth Century A.D., says, "The leading features of the early history of Scotland as told by Fordun in his five books are these: The Scots derived their origin from Gaythelos, son of Neolus, king of Greece, who went to Egypt in the days of Moses, where he married Scota, daughter of Pharaoh, king of Egypt, and led the Scots from thence to Spain. From this country several colonies went to Ireland."[11]

MacRitchie says: "That the Egyptians should have colonized Italy, Iberia, the Islands of the Oestrymnides and the British Islands before the days of Julius Caesar and that all of these should have originally called themselves Rom, Rome, or Romani (from the Cophtic word for "a man"), this is a theory supported by a considerable number of facts."

Negroes were well received at the Scottish court. McRitchie says, "In 1501 one of the king's minstrels was 'Peter the Moryen,' or Moor . . . In 1504 two blackamoor girls arrived and were educated at the court where they waited on the Queen. They were baptised, Elen and Margaret. In June 1507 a tournament was held in honor of the Queen's black lady, Elen Moore, which was conducted with great splendour." Queen Elizabeth had at least one Negro favorite, according to Welsford.

---

[9] Dictionnaire Heraldique. Vol. I, p. 55 London, 1884.
[10] Fox-Davies, A. C. Armorial Families, p. 328, pl. 29 (1). Vol. I, pp. 121; 261. Edinburgh, 1895. Burke's Peerage, Vol. II, pp. 1711; 1522; 1773; 2375; 2479. London, 1936.
[11] Preface and Chronicles of the Picts and Scots. London, 1867.
Nature Knows No Color-Line, pp. 69-108, has additional data and hundreds of coats-of-arms with Negroes.

Britain's More Recent Negro Strain

Still another Negro strain came into the people of Britain with the introduction of Negro slavery, the precise date of which is in doubt. Beckwith fixes it at 1440,[12] or about the same time it began in Portugal. Hakluyt sets it at 1553, or eleven years before Shakespeare was born. What is certain is it continued until 1772 when it was abolished by order of Lord Chief Justice Mansfield. In any case, Negro slavery lasted in England for not less than two centuries.

During this time, hundreds of thousands of blacks were brought into British ports. Numbers of them were transshipped from the great slave-ports of Liverpool and Bristol to the Americas, but many remained. "There were fairly large numbers of slaves in England," says Klingberg, "and buying and selling and transporting of Negroes went on there."[13] The slave auction rooms may still be seen in Bristol and Liverpool.

In 1731, there were enough Negroes in London alone to evoke the passing of a jim-crow law. The Lord Mayor and Aldermen of that city decreed that no Negroes should be taught trades,[14] the reason for which was evident. Nevertheless, it was an English Negro who invented the first fine needle.[15]

In 1764, the number of Negro slaves in London alone was estimated at 20,000.[16] These together with the free Negroes and mulattoes must have constituted a fairly large proportion of the population. The number must have been even higher in Bristol and Liverpool. Black bandsmen were common in the British army. A fairly large number of Negroes were in the British navy, too, one of whom won the Victoria Cross; and another, a woman in male disguise, who served for years with distinction.

In the reign of the Georges, Negro and mulatto slaves and servants were common in the homes of the nobility and the rich. Royalty, itself, set the fashion. George I had two Mohammedan Negroes[17] of whom he was very fond. They attended to his personal needs, and dressed him, much to the discontent of certain dukes, whose prerogative dressing the King was. George IV showed high favor to at least three Negroes, Prince Saunders of Boston, Mass., Bridgetower, the great violinist; and the Chevalier de St. Georges, celebrated French swordsman.

Negroes appear several times in the drawings of Hogarth. In "The Four Times of the Day (Noon)" one of them is seen kissing a very beautiful

---

[12] Black Roadways, p. 3. Chapel Hill, 1929.
[13] Anti-Slavery Movement in England, p. 35. Yale University Press, 1926.
[14] Notes and Queries. Vol. 161, p. 272.
[15] Fuller, T. Worthies of England, Vol. II, p. 334. London, 1840.
[16] Gentleman's Maga. (1764). Vol. 34, p. 493.
[17] Thackeray's Works, Vol. 23, p. 30. London, 1885. (The Four Georges.)

white girl, his hands on her breasts. In the Rake's Progress a Negro girl
appears among the white prostitutes. She may have been Harriott, one
of the most notorious creatures of that time.

The mixing of whites and blacks went on apace. Shakespeare devoted
two of his plays to it: Titus Andronicus and Othello. In the Merchant of
Venice he mentions Negroes twice, once of a Negro woman who is with
child by a white man ("I shall answer that better to the commonwealth than
you can the getting up of the Negro's belly; the Moor is with child by you,
Launcelot."); and of a Moorish prince who seeks the hand of the heroine,
Portia.

In the "Two Gentlemen of Verona" he uses the old English proverb,
"A black man's a jewel in a fair woman's eyes" as follows:

"Thu.   ...my face is black
"Pro.   But pearls are fair, and the old saying is: Black
        men are pearls in beauteous ladies' eyes."

Certain critics maintain that "black" here means character but Shakespeare says "face is black." It is very likely that Shakespeare, himself,
had a Negro sweetheart named Lucy Negro.[17a] In Sonnet 127 he praises
"black beauty" and in 144 speaks of "a woman coloured ill." There were
tens of thousands of Negroes in England in his day. In the picture of the
tournament given by Henry VIII to Catherine of Aragon one of the trumpe-
teers is a Negro. The blacks were called blackamoors (black as a Moor)
and the mulattoes, tawny Moors.

Dr. Samuel Johnson had a Negro servant and favorite, Francis Barber,
to whom he left all his property, who was very popular with the women.
Johnson said of him, "Frank has carried the empire of Cupid further than
most men."[18]

Another black Don Juan of this period was Soubise, son of a Negro
slave of St. Kitts, West Indies, who was adopted by the rich Duchess of
Queensberry. Soubise was one of the most accomplished swordsmen and
riders of the times, and a violinist of distinction. According to Henry
Angelo, he became "one of the most conspicuous dandies of London. He
frequented the Opera, sported a fine horse and groom in Hyde Park, became a member of fashionable clubs and generally cut a figure."

Garrick and Sheridan, famous actors, gave him lessons in elocution,
and were especially pleased with his unassuming ways. For his host of
feminine admirers, he wrote gay sonnets set to his own music. Gainsborough
made a sketch of him, and Zoffany painted a life-size portrait.[19]

[17a] See Sex and Race, Vol. 2, p. 326.
[18] Hill, G. B. Johnsonian Miscellany, Vol. I, p. 291. Oxford, 1897.
[19] Reminiscences of Henry Angelo, Vol. I, pp. 446-52. London, 1828.

LIII. I. Coat of Arms of the Earl of Drogheda, Ireland; 2. Jacob Capitein; 3. Gustavus Vasa.

What Became of the English Negro Slaves?

Negroes, as was said, were imported into Britain for centuries, what became of them and their descendants? Absorbed into the white population, evidently, as they had been in Portugal. Probably not more than 351 were ever shipped back to Africa. They were returned in 1787 with their white wives. And before leaving Portsmouth, the authorities scoured the city for all the loose white women they could find, and seizing sixty-two of them married them to the Negroes while drunk and shipped them off too.

After the emancipation, Negroes continued to arrive in the British Isles in fairly large numbers, principally as sailors and servants. One of the latter, Andrew Bogle, was the key figure in the Tichborne Case, one of the most celebrated lawsuits in the annals of imposture.[20]

The largest Negro district was, and still is, at Cardiff, whose Negro residents now number about 8,000. The married women of this settlement are all whites or mulattoes born there. The husbands are blacks. In Europe, race-mixing takes a form the reverse of Africa. In the latter, it is the white man and the black woman; in the former, the black man and the white woman.

The richest Negro I met in Cardiff was a West African, a former seaman. He owned several houses, lived in a beautifully furnished home, had one of the finest race-horses in England, and owns a prize Alsatian dog, but could neither read nor write. His five mulatto daughters are well educated and used to spend their holidays on the Riviera. Manchester, Liverpool, Edinburgh, and London also have a considerable number of Negroes and their mulatto children born in England. The most famous of the latter was Coleridge-Taylor, one of England's greatest musicians. His father was a Negro doctor of unmixed ancestry and his mother white. The celebrated poet, Robert Browning, also was of Negro ancestry, according to Frederick J. Furnivall, head of the Browning Society.[21]

The first world war brought tens of thousands of Negroes to England as sailors, soldiers, and workers in the munition plants. No sooner was the war over, however, than the Negroes found themselves most unwelcome. In 1919, race riots swept English cities as London, Liverpool, Cardiff, Manchester, and Hull, precisely as they did American States that year. Bottomley's John Bull took the lead in attacking the blacks. In 1929, I saw a book of English newspaper clippings on the Negro; no Southern, or Ku Klux papers could have been worse.

[20] Kenealy, M. E. Tichborne Tragedy. London, 1913.
[21] Browning Society Papers. Feb. 28. 1890. Vol. III, pp. 31, 36.

LIV. English mulattoes, Negro father, white mother. Upper: Miss Ira Aldridge. Rev. Thomas B. Freeman. Lower: Samuel Coleridge-Taylor and Miss Betty Rowland, dancer.

Royal Ancestry and the Negro

"Negro" blood has penetrated even into the royal family, as was said. Colonel W. H. Turton traced the ancestry of Elizabeth, daughter of Edward IV of England, and the mother of Henry VIII, and found, in only 7000 of her ancestors, several Moorish kings, an Arab born in Mecca, a Moorish ex-slave, named Mujahid, and Leon, a Jew,[22] all people known for their Negroid ancestry The earlier Moorish kings were nearly all Negroes or dark mulattoes. As Flournoy says, "A considerable portion of the Moroccan population, especially the aristocracy and the royal family had Negro blood in their veins."

The portrait of Queen Charlotte Sophia, consort of George III, by Ramsay clearly shows a Negro strain. Horace Walpole, who saw her, wrote of her, "nostrils spreading too wide; mouth has the same fault." (See frontispiece.)

Miscegenation, however, has never been palatable to the English. Shakespeare reveals this when he makes Portia say after the Prince of Morocco loses her by choosing the wrong casket," Let all of his complexion choose me so."

The celebrated boxer, Bill Richmond, a native of Staten Island, who was taken to England by the Duke of Northumberland after the Revolutionary War in America, and who taught boxing to Lord Byron, suffered a good deal from color prejudice, together with his white wife.

Objection to intermarriage does not hold as strongly against the light mulatto as against the black man. And even in the black man's case, it would not be so much minded if he took only the older and plainer women as England has a vast surplus of women. But as it happens the blacks usually get the young and pretty ones. When the average Englishman sees this, it makes him feel that his civilization is on the way out.

The following excerpts from English writers, the first of which dates from 1889, will reveal some of this sentiment.

London Press: "To anyone who has spent some years in Africa, the familiarity which exists between certain white women visiting the Kaffir kraal at Earl's Court Exhibition and the blacks on show there, is a peculiarly revolting spectacle. From the hour this 'savage' side-show is opened until late at night, the kraal is besieged by crowds of females who hustle each other in their rivalry to obtain personal association with the Matabele and other colored men on view.

"Some of these women use all their arts of fascination to please these

---

[22] The Heiress of the Plantagents, pp. 44-54. Notes 78, 83, 97, 98, 99, 126.

sons of the African wilderness. But lately we saw a European girl detach flowers from her bosom to adorn the person of these niggers and we have seen grown women not only shake hands with them but stroke their limbs admiringly. Nothing is left undone by certain misled English females to gratify the vanity of these miscellaneous African natives in whose delightful manners and customs this show is presumed to instruct us. The Kaffir Exhibition at Earl's Court has in fact degenerated into an exhibition of white women visitors, and a very disgusting exhibition it is.

"These raw, hulking and untamed men-animals are being unwillingly and utterly corrupted by unseemly attention from English girls."[23]

Raymond Blathwayt: "Some years ago we used to have large bodies of natives sent from Africa either on military service or in some travelling show, and it was a revelation of horror and disgust to behold the manner in which English women would flock to see these men, whilst to watch them fawning upon these black creatures and fondling and embracing them, as I have seen dozens of times, was a scandal and a disgrace to English womanhood...

"How then it is possible to maintain as the one stern creed in the policy of the Empire the eternal supremacy of the white over black?"[24]

Stephen Black: "For many years white colonials had shuddered at witnessing repulsive Ethiopians intimately, almost maritally consorting with beautiful British girls in streets, in restaurants, in theatres, in night clubs, lodging houses and hotels. There was no concealment of the affectionate attitude of a certain type of white female toward the brown, black and yellow male."[25]

The reason why Negro troops were barred from the coronation of George V was, I understand, the great attention showered on the Negro troops by the white women of all classes at the coronation of his father, Edward VII. One Negro athlete of herculean build and strength who won the heavy-shot put of the British Army, beating the white champion by six feet, was an especial favorite. Necessity, however, forced the Empire to bring over Negro troops during the World War, when they received the same attention from the white women as on the first occasion.

In 1925, much the same thing happened at the Wembley Exhibition. I talked with several of the Africans on exhibition there in an African village, great, strong, muscular fellows and I learnt that they were not permitted to go alone into London or anywhere else. The fear was that some of the English women would "capture" them. At the coronation of

[23] Quoted by Count Roscaud in "Human Gorilla," p. 223.
[24] Tit-Bits, July 21, 1917. London.
[25] The English Review, Oct. 1919. London.

George VI, I saw the same as regards the Negro and the Indian soldiers. The latter were encamped on the grounds of Hampton Court Palace, well outside London.

In 1930 when Paul Robeson played Othello with a white actress, Peggy Ashcroft, there was considerable agitation, pro and con, because he had to kiss her on the lips. Hannen Swaffer, noted English columnist, said,

"Now that 'Othello' is drawing near—it is due at the Savoy on May 19— I feel I must stem the protest that is being made against Paul Robeson playing the Moor.

" 'Why do you say in the "Daily Express" that you expect Robeson to play Othello with distinction?' demands Mrs. M. Truburn, from Brighton. 'I should think Robeson modest enough to be wholly surprised at being asked. Othello was a Moor, a prince of blacks. Robeson is an Ethiopian.

" 'Salvini was a perfect aristocrat of a Moor. Can Robeson feel as Salvini felt the part? Never in the world! Salvini *was* Shakespeare. Although Robeson will be England's modern effort, the soul of the Moor aristocrat cannot be put into a man of Robeson's boyhood.

" 'I come from Boston. We are not against Negroes, but we do not like them near us.'

"Racial Prejudice

"I noticed today that you speak of the coloured question as if you wonder at the prejudice some people hold against the coloured races,' writes a woman called Newton—I cannot decipher the Christian name—from Elgin avenue.

" 'Is it not an entirely personal outlook?

" 'I am a fairly tolerant woman, believing in live-and-let-live, but I have invariably a feeling of nausea when in contact with a man or woman of the coloured race. I was watching "Blackbirds" from a box at the Pavilion, and how I managed to keep smiling I don't know. There was no reason, for the show was clean and decent.

" 'I believe coloured people often have the same feelings where we are concerned.

" 'How, in that case, can two great races of different colours amalgamate happily?

" 'I cannot stomach the idea of a coloured man playing opposite to a woman of my own race, and feel sure there are many who will share my views, though I bow to the fact that Paul Robeson is a great artist.'

"Give 'Colour' a Chance!

"No such feelings seem to have been aroused when, sixty-five years ago, Dame Madge Kendal played Desdemona to the Othello of Ira Aldridge, a Negro Shakespearean tragedian. Dame Madge survived it."

The protest against Robeson was led by white Americans, who are largely responsible for most of the color prejudice in England. It was the American slave-holders resident in England who brought about the revival of Negro slavery in England in 1739 after it had been abolished by Chief Justice Holt in 1707.

Another writer in the London Daily Express expressed himself on race-mixing as follows:

There is in London's underworld a shabby little coffee-house where white and black people resort after the public-houses have closed. It has one room the size of a dining-room in an ordinary suburban villa. The coffee bar adjoins it—a place of bath-room proportions. A long table runs along the window with a bench behind it; there are two other tables, benches round the walls, and some stray chairs.

There were three Negroes and a white woman present when I entered. I sat down, ordered coffee from the obsequious proprietor, himself a Negro, and waited.

I have seen films of the American underworld; I know something about the "poor white" district of Chicago; but I had never imagined that a place of this blatant variety existed in the center of London. Gradually it filled up with white women and Negroes and mulattoes. I was again an object of suspicion, but it was an aloof suspicion, a defiant suspicion. There was bravado in their attitude towards me, finely tinged with something akin to contempt—the attitude of the lover in "Tess of the D'Urbervilles" to Tess' husband—for I was of one race with these women, and these women had betrayed their race.

A girl came in alone, saw a vacant chair at my table, and asked if she might sit down there. I said she might, and offered her a cup of coffee. She accepted my hospitality. We began to talk.

"I've never seen anything like this," I said, after a few preliminary remarks about the weather.

"Haven't you?" she replied. "Well, I suppose it would strike a stranger as curious. You're not round this part much, are you?"

"Not much. But you know a lot of these men, don't you?"

She nodded. "Oh, yes, I know most of 'em."

"Tell me," I said, "do you like colored men? I mean, it has always seem to me...strange that a white girl should—"

"My boy's a colored man," she said simply.

A group of Negroes was gathered round the long table, talking loudly. The laughter was hearty. Capacious mouths showed incredible expanses of teeth. Others broke from their conversations to dance spasmodically to their own singing. "And how!" was a frequent expression, uttered with ecstatical emphasis.

The proprietor pushed his way through the mass, announcing musically that he was "funny that w-a-a-y," and shouting for orders. He got a few A white woman in a fur coat came in and greeted a Negro familiarly; he was the variety known as a "spade"—that is to say, coal-black, as black as the ace of spades—and every crooked wrinkle in human mentality seemed remodelled in his face.

The door burst open suddenly, and three girls, talking at the top of their voices, surged in. They all made for the one dingy mirror, and began briskly to powder their noses. I had seen two of them previously that evening patrolling Shaftesbury avenue. Then a colored girl appeared, and was hailed shrilly with "Hullo, black woman!" by her white sisters.

"O-o-o-y!" she bellowed—a deep contralto—"This is a fine joint for a lady to come into. Look at your ceiling: it's a dirty ceiling! it's a nasty ceiling. George!"—this was roared at the proprietor— "Georgie boy, your dirty ceiling was wanting a washing." She began to dance, swaying and snapping her fingers. She paused to ask the world if any one wasn't going to buy her a drink. A white girl, wearing a beret and a waterproof, replied that there was just five minutes before "they closed." They disappeared at full speed; and a little later returned, an ill-assorted brace of bedraggled Bacchantes, living for the hour, grinning at life.

"Have all these girls got colored boys?" I asked my acquaintance.

"All of 'em," she replied. "My boy's out of town just now. Just a minute: I'll show you his photo. There it is."

I looked at the postcard she had fished from her bag, and saw a tall, practically full-blooded Negro. "I don't like 'spades,'" she remarked casually. "They're too black."

There was a trace of provincial accent in her speech, and she informed me that she was born in the eastern counties. She was twenty-three. Was she happy? Oh, yes, she was happy enough. She hadn't much to worry about. She was successful in her profession.

"Of course, I make my living out of white men mostly," she said, "but I wouldn't go with a white boy permanent. They're a lot of rotters, I think. Now a colored man always treats you well. He'll never let you go hungry. Naturally, I send my boy money for expenses —did I tell you he's on tour with a theatrical company—and, when he comes back to me I share with him what I've got

"I hate that table!" she said abruptly

"Why?"

"Why?" Because that's where they gamble. I gave my boy three pounds last time, and he came back with nothing. It's just luck, of course. One time I gave him ten shillings, and he came in with seven pounds. He gave me a dress out of that."

He gave her a dress.

"And in the morning I found a razor on his pillow—you know, not the safety kind, the old sort. He'd been ready for a fight, I suppose. Lots of 'em carry razors—these girls, too. Me? No. I'm not that sort. But, do you know, there was a proper dust-up in here just before Christmas. There were bottles and glasses flying, and out came the razors, and three colored men got their faces slashed.

"Two white girls started it," she added calmly; "they were jealous over a colored man. George here chucked 'em out, but not before some one got hurt. The girls had their razors, and they were just mad. I was giving a hand behind the bar, and I saw it all. Coo! What a mess."

She nudged me. "Look: there's one of the men." A vast Negro strolled into the tiny bar. His right cheek bore a strip of sticking plaster from ear to chin. He glanced at me, and glanced away rapidly.

I got up to go and heard, from the dusky party round the long table which the girl hated, the murmured words, "I'll say we'd be a lotta fools to start a game with a policeman sitting in de corner. Kid, you jest collect yourself."

So that was my assumed occupation. I wished the girl good-night. 'It will be," she said: "we're all going on to a colored party soon. So long: see you sometime."

An elderly woman—an elderly, plump Englishwoman, carrying a straw bag, and wearing, of all things in the world, a black bonnet—brushed by me at the door. I fancied I had caught a glimpse of respectability, but this woman was followed by a white girl—obviously her daughter.

I came out under the sky. Thank God for the fresh air!

* * * *

It was fortunate perhaps for this writer's sanity that he did not happen to be in one of these Shaftesbury Avenue Clubs one night I was there. I saw a Negro give a white girl an awful beating. He struck her down to the floor and kicked her about the body as she lay there. Each time she got up, he knocked her down again, belaboring her most unmercifully. I was strongly tempted to protest but I remembered that Havelock Ellis said that a certain type of English and Irish women love to be beaten by their men. English law permits, or used to permit, a husband to beat his wife with a stick no thicker than his little finger.

No one in the cafe made any attempt to stop the man, nor any of the white people who stood in the street looking in. The woman, I also thought, could have run away, but she remained there stubbornly taking the punishment. She never even attempted to strike back. Finally the man walked out and she rose and ran after him, and took his arm. A man at my table laughed aloud, and said for the benefit of all in Rabelaisan language that the two of them would have a sweeter time than ever now. It was a clear case of masochism with an exhibitionist setting.

In some cases, the Negroes seemed to have little to recommend them save the novelty of color, yet some of the women hung to them with dog-like devotion. I have seen three Englishwomen with the initials of their Negro lovers tattooed on their bodies.

In 1936, Inspector Benton told Justice Whiteley in the Old Bailey, "lots of girls, especially from the country, go to the cafes frequented by colored men, and once they associate with a colored man, it is difficult to get them away. They won't have anything to do with white men." When the judge asked whether many of these men "were in the West End," the most fashionable part of London, the inspector said there were "hundreds. They gather in cafes frequented by the rich, and seem to do no honest work."

It was extremely difficult for a Negro to get any kind of work in England and it was a common thing to hear a British Negro say, "If it weren't for the Englishwomen we wouldn't be able to stay here." Some Negroes were pimps, others white-slave agents; others peddled drugs. There seemed to be no other way for them to live. Most unemployed Negroes could not get on the dole. The lot of the poor Negro in England as I knew it as late as 1937 was one of the toughest in the world. One need only say that the lot of the poor white man was very tough and that the Negro's lot fell below his.

Negroes would be put out of jobs they had held for years just to make places for white men. One man, who had a wife and five children, and had been a cook for a chain of restaurants at a good salary, was finally forced out, although he was much liked by the management. Numbers of the Negroes in England lived not on muscle power, or brain power, but on sex power; and when that failed with the women, they sold themselves to male homosexuals. I deal with this in the chapter on Race and Homosexuality in Vol. 3. This sort of thing did not exist in Paris where the Negroes had an equal, or nearly equal, chance with the white man of getting work.

Several of the women told me that their husband's color and hair, and difference of race served as a special attraction, a constant refresher against the monotony of the married relation.

One well-educated Negro who had a great bush of woolly hair said that he made it grow like that as it was a special attraction for the women. "They love to run their fingers through it," he said. "It gives them an electric thrill." His wife had a mulatto child of which she was extraordinarily proud, though she .rarely took him out, as crowds would follow her. Her husband was one of the most publicized men in the British Isles. This marriage went on the rocks, however, because the second child was born a pure Nordic. When this man's friends twitted him about it, he said that the difference in color of the children could be easily explained. "The black one was born at night," he said, "and the white one in the day."

All in all I saw much miscegenation in England and the sole general difference I noted between the mixed and the unmixed couples was that the former were usually on the defensive. The mixed couples like the unmixed ones had the same air of solid British self-respect and respectability. Some of the mixed couples had adapted themselves to the situation however. As Agatha Pemba said,

"The writer once asked a gentle refined woman with three children of various shades of color, all with woolly hair, how she could have brought herself to marry a black man, and what sort of future she expected for the children, and this was her answer: 'They make good husbands these men. They are so thankful to us women for marrying them that they treat us like queens; they give us plenty of money; they don't drink; they are good to the children; the pay is regular while they are away, and they always come back to us. There's many a woman with a white husband worse off. The children? Well, there are such a lot of them now that nobody seems to think much about it; they don't mind them in the schools. They won't hurt.' That apparently was the prevailing attitude in these Welsh ports."[26]

Truth to tell, the English Negroes kept their bearing pretty well. Their mulatto children looked healthy and on Sundays were well-dressed according to their class. In Cardiff, for instance, the only wrecks I saw in the Negro neighborhood, were white men.[27]

"Negro" Scandal in Royal Circles

In 1932, London society was rocked by a scandal involving Lady Louis Mountbatten, wife of a great-grandson of Queen Victoria and cousin of George V. Lady Mountbatten, who used to have Negro entertainers for her parties, was accused by a leading newspaper, "The People" of having had improper relations with a Negro. Under the heading: *"Society Shaken by Terrible Scandal,"* it said:

"I am able to reveal today the sequel to a scandal which has shaken

[26] Spectator, July 3, 1926. London.
[27] The American Negro in Europe. American Mercury, May 1930.

Society to the very depths. It concerns one of the leading hostesses of the country, a woman highly connected and immensely rich. Her associations with a colored man became so marked that they were the talk of the West End. Then one day the couple were caught in compromising circumstances. The sequel is that the society woman has been given the hint to clear out of England for a couple of years to let the affair blow over and the hint was from a quarter which cannot be ignored."

No names were mentioned in the article, and this made tongues wag the faster. White society immediately named the leading American singer; the Negroes, a handsome, fascinating West Indian, who entertained for royalty and the elite.

Lady Mountbatten faced the scandal boldly. She brought suit against the newspaper, and the case came up before Lord Chief Justice Scrutten July 7, 1932. Her counsel declared "that there was not one single syllable of truth in the horrible allegations, nor was there the faintest ground on which the rumors could be brought into existence. The publication had caused Lady Louis Mountbatten and those closely connected with her unspeakable anguish of mind.

"She had been informed by friends of the identity of the coloured man supposed to be referred. to in the article. She had never even met him, and had never anything to do with him in any shape or form. When that fact was remembered there were no words in which counsel could characterize the infamy of such a publication."

Lord Louis Mountbatten supported his wife. He said on the stand, "The whole thing is a preposterous story." The editor of the paper, made profoundest apologies and was severely lectured by the Court.[28]

"Black Man and White Ladyship"

Tongues wagged, too, in the case of Miss Nancy Cunard when she arrived from the Continent with her Negro friend, a well-known entertainer. Miss Cunard, who is editor and part author of a voluminous work, entitled "Negro," is the daughter of Lady Maud Cunard, American-born heiress, and a member of Edward VIII's set, replied in print. She wrote a pamphlet, "Black Man and White Ladyship" in which she attacked her mother; Lady Asquith, wife of the Prime Minister; Sir Thomas Beecham, noted conductor, and George Moore. author, with considerable satire. "I have a Negro friend," she said, "a very close Negro friend (and a great many other Negro friends in France, England, and America). Nothing extraordinary in that. I have a mother—whom we will at once call: Her Ladyship... I sedulously avoid her social circle both in France and in

[28] London Times, July 8, 1932, p. 3

England. My Negro friend has been in London with me five or six times. So far so good But a few days before our going to London last year, what follows had just taken place and I was unaware of it until our arrival. At a large lunch party in Her Ladyship's house things are set rocking by one of those bombs that throughout her 'career' Margot Asquith, Lady Oxford, has been wont to hurl. No one could fail to wish he had been at that lunch to see the effect of Lady Oxford's entry: "Hello Maud, what is it now— drink, drugs, or niggers?" (A variant is that by some remark her Ladyship had annoyed the other Ladyship, who thus triumphantly retaliated.) The house is a seemly one in Grosvenor Square and what takes place is far from 'drink, drugs, or niggers.' There is confusion. A dreadful confusion between Her Ladyship and myself. For I am known to have a great Negro friend—the drink and the drugs do not apply. Half of social London is immediately telephoned to: 'Is it true my daughter knows a Negro?' etc., etc.

"It appears that Sir Thomas Beecham, in the light of 'the family friend' was then moved sufficiently to pen me a letter, in the best Trollope style, in which he pointed out that, as the only one qualified to advise, it would, at that juncture, be a grave mistake to come to England with a gentlemen of American-African extraction whose career, he believed, it was my desire to advance, as, while friendships between races were viewed with tolerance on the continent, by some, it was...in other words it was a very different pair of shoes in England especially as viewed by the Popular Press! This letter... was announced by telegram 'strongly advising' me not to come to London until I got it adding that the subject was unmentionable by wire! I was packing my trunk and laid the telegram on top—time will show. We took the four o'clock train.

"What happened in London?

"Some detectives called, the police looked in, the telephone rang incessantly at our hotel. The patron (so he said) received a mysterious message that he himself would be imprisoned 'undt de other vil be kilt.' Madame wept: 'Not even a black man, why, he's only brown.' Her Ladyship did not go so far as to step round herself. The Popular Press was unmoved This lasted about a month and I used to get news of it daily, enough to fill a dossier on the hysteria caused by a difference of pigmentation... I am told that Sir Thomas Beecham says I ought to be tarred and feathered."

Still another case that made London society gasp was the elopement of a Negro on the dole at four dollars a week with the daughter of a millionaire attorney.[28a] The girl on leaving her home made the mistake of telling her solicitor, who promptly warned her father. The latter appeared

[28a] Empire News, about June 13, 1921.

NOTED MULATTOES OF THE OLD WORLD

LV. 1. General Ivan Hannibal; 2. Paul Belloni DuChaillu; 3. Alexander Dumas, the younger;
4. Robert Browning; 5. Marie Dumas, daughter of Alexander Dumas, the elder.

just before they were married and had the girl arrested as a lunatic. A long trial followed. The girl was found sane. But her father, who died soon after, cut her off to the tune of $4,000,000. However, she had inherited several hundred thousand dollars from her mother and with this she and her husband lived in a sumptuous apartment in the West End. They had two sturdy boys with ruddy brown skin and thick frizzly hair, who were very popular with the neighbors in the building and the strollers in the park where their parents took them daily. I lived with this couple for months and saw no prejudice against them or their children. This girl's rich friend also married a Negro, who ran through her money. Another, the daughter of a rich farmer, eloped with a Negro. I heard of several similar cases.

A more recent mixed marriage was that of Lady Heath, noted English aviatrix, to George A. R. Williams of St. Lucia, West Indies. They were married in Kentucky, too!

Another instance of race-mixing in aristocratic circles which was common talk among the Negroes but didn't seem to make much of a ripple among the whites was that of a titled lady with an enormously rich husband. She maintained for a while a Negro actor in high style, thereby incurring, it is said, the jealousy of another Negro with whom she was friendly. The latter finally ousted the first.

In 1934, there was a resounding divorce suit in the case of a very popular vaudeville entertainer, an Aframerican, who had won the affections of a rich woman away from her husband. The Negro singer also had a wife in America. Still another scandal involved a leading Negro specialist, who had married the daughter of a titled Englishman.

One case that bordered on the fantastic was that of Dr. James Barry (1795-1865), a British army general. General Barry was a woman. A former nurse, she studied medicine, and finding her sex a handicap disguised herself as a man, joined the army medical corps and rose to be inspector-general. She once fought a duel, too. Her sole confidante was her Negro attendant, Black John.[29]

Strange to say that in spite of prejudice, a black man is considered good luck at least by a certain portion of the English people. I have seen more than once at the race track, a white man or woman touch a black man before making a bet as in America one touches a hunchback. Some English people carry black beans as Americans carry a rabbit's foot. In 1925 and later, Negroes, chiefly Africans, used to clean up a tidy sum all over the British Isles selling black charms of various sorts. I have seen several of them at the great Sunday morning market at Whitechapel. The best known tipster

[29] Hargreaves, R. Women-At-Arms, pp. 175-190. London, 1930.

OTHER CELEBRATED MULATTOES

LVI. 1. Pushkin; 2. Ambroise Vollard; 3. Murat, King of Naples; 4. Maurice Donnay, one of the Forty Immortals.

in England is a black West Indian who dresses fantastically in feathers and colored garb, and calls himself Rass Prince Monolulu. He receives more publicity than many leading Englishmen. On Sundays he can be seen in Hyde Park surrounded by an enormous crowd which he keeps in roars of laughter. The Tatler, June 5, 1929, carried a two-page colored picture of him surrounded by the racing magnates of England. A privileged character, he button-holes even the King. His slogan at the race-track is:

Black for luck,

White for pluck.

Black physicians are also popular. Some of them are honor graduates of Glasgow and Edinburgh but their chief efficacy to the public is their color which is believed to have something of the witch-doctor in it. One African, whom I knew very well, was a privileged character in the pubs of the West End from which other Negroes were barred. He was an expert in the treatment of gonorrhea and each Sunday morning would make the rounds of the pubs to keep in touch with his clients. Once I went with him and left him fatigued after he had been into seven of them.

As in the colonies where black and colored are classified separately, the English at home make a difference between a lighter-colored mulatto and a black. The former may go almost anywhere, and women who object to blacks sometimes do not mind mulattoes. One girl, who was taken by her friend for the first time to a Negro club, and who said her mother and her friends would cut her if they knew she had come to such a place asked to be introduced to a light-colored man there. She said to him, "You're the only white man in the place." Of course there are many who wouldn't go with mulattoes, if they knew them to be such.

Finally, it may be said that the English are, on the whole, not unkind to Negroes. And they respect intelligence, ability, and integrity when it appears under a black skin very much more than Americans. But for the competition for jobs, which is severe—England has suffered from unemployment for centuries—I am convinced that the Englishman in England would be much kindlier to Negroes.

*For instance, in 1950 I saw much less color prejudice in England. There was a shortage of labor and Negroes found ready employment.

Additional data on Negro slavery in England will be found in "Notes and Queries," 2 Ser., Vol. VI, p. 267; Vol. VII, p. 153; 3 Ser., Vol. I, p. 348; Vol. II, p. 345; also Claridge, W. W., "History of the Gold Coast and Ashanti," Vol. I, p. 256, London, 1915; McCarthy, Justin, "The First Georges," Vol. I, p. 77.

Additional Bibliography on Ancient Britain: Lockyer, Sir N., "Stonehenge," pp. 233-64, London, 1906; MacIntosh, J., "History of Civilization," in Scotland, Vol. I, p. 43, London, 1892; Stone, G., "Wales: Her Origins," pp. 1-35, London, 1915.

Mackenzie, D. A., "Ancient Man in Britain," pp. 49, 104, 105, 218, London, 1922.

See also "Nature Knows No Color-Line" Chapter Nine for much additional research, and for race mixture, as result of World War II.

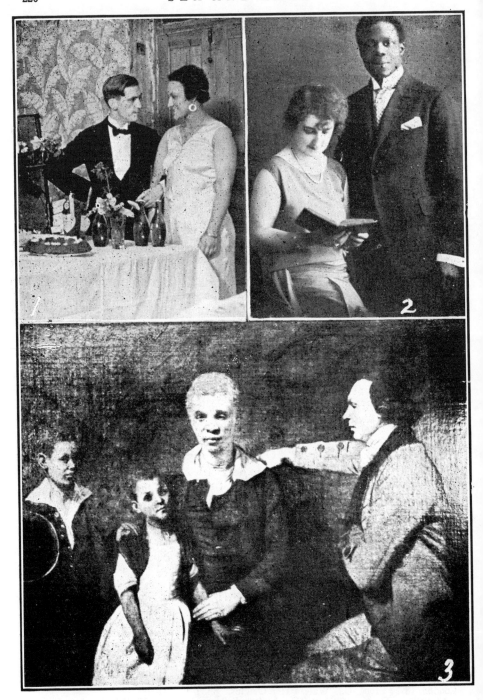

MIXED COUPLES
LVII. I. Emil Faller, Haile Selassie's Belgian chef and his mulatto Ethiopian wife; 2. The late
Prince Behanzin of Dahomey and the Princess Behanzin; 3. Englishman with
his Albino Negro wife and their mulatto children.

Chapter Nineteen

MISCEGENATION IN FRANCE

NEXT to Spain and Portugal, France has had the most miscegenation. The first known inhabitants of France were, as was said, the Grimaldi. In the third century, B.C., Hannibal and his Africans penetrated into France as far as Tarascon. In the eighth century, A.D., the Moors swept through it as far as Tours, a hundred and forty miles from Paris, from where they were driven back by Charles Martel. In 1610, came another invasion of Moors, a peaceful one, when over a million of them, who had been expelled from Spain settled in southern France at the invitation of Henry IV. The result is that the French in the region nearest Spain, especially the Auvergnats, are Negroid. "There is a strong Negroid cast to many Auvergnese," says John Gunther.

Bertrand Du Guesclin (1320-1380), greatest of the earlier heroes of France, was of this Moorish stock. He claimed descent from an African king. Cuvelier,[1] a contemporary of his, speaks of him as "black" and "flat-nosed." R. Vercel says he "was pug-nosed, thick-lipped, and dark, above all dark, as dark as the face of Aiquin, his legendary ancestor."[2] The Annales of Bretagne says that the fact that Du Guesclin had an African ancestor "will seem strange to modern readers. To be descended from a Saracen king, who might have been a Negro, does not flatter our vanity. We are all imbued with the theories of race. But these theories are recent. They are barely a century old."[3]

Another illustrious figure who claimed Moorish origin was Murat, King of Naples, brother-in-law of Napoleon, and the greatest cavalry leader of the nineteenth century. Masson says, "It was believed that he was a descendant of one of those Moors who came with Abdel-Rahman to the succor of the Duke of Aquitaine."[4] Murat was distinctly Negroid in features, dark, with thick lips, and frizzly hair. The Duchess D'Abrantes, who knew him well, said, "There is a great deal of the Negro in his face. His nose, it is true, is not flat, but his lips are thick. This nose, though straight, lacks distinction, and gives him, together with the rest of his features, at least the appearance of a mixed blood." (Il avait une figure dans laquelle on retrouvait

[1] Chronique de Bertrand DuGuesclin, line 55. Paris, 1921.
[2] Bertrand of Brittany, p. 4. N. Y., 1934.
[3] Vols. 15-16, p. 292. (1899-1901.)
[4] Cavaliers de Napoleon, p. 289. Paris, 1921.

beaucoup de nègre," etc., etc.)[5] One of Murat's sons married a grand-niece of George Washington.

Still another celebrated royal figure, who came from this region was Bernadotte, founder of the present Swedish royal family. Bernadotte, who was one of Napoleon's great marshals had a dark skin and woolly hair, though the rest of his features were Caucasian.

Still another noted Auvergnat is Pierre Laval, ex-Premier of France. Laval is distinctly Negroid. When he came to America to confer with President Hoover in 1932, several American newspapers, including the New York Sun, mentioned this. Collier's Weekly said, "He is so dark that his complexion has recalled the old legend that there is a strain of Moorish blood in the Auvergnats."[6] John Gunther mentions the same.

Racial amalgamation between the Moorish and the Jewish refugees from Spain in 1610 with the French was not accomplished easily. The French complained that the Moors and the Jews smelt bad.[7] But that seemed rather to have been a case of rival odors because the French, as most people of that time, smelt none too sweet themselves. The burning of incense in churches originated in order to drown the effluvia of the worshippers, it is said. Perfume was used in the palaces of the English kings to keep down the body odors. The Good Queen Bess certainly wasn't the sweet-smelling Queen Bess as she rarely ever had a bath. Henry IV of France—Le Vert Galant (The Always Gallant) smelt so badly that Mme. de Verneuil remarked that it "was good for him he was king, or no one would have been able to support him." The same was true of Louis XIV. Meunier says that "he inherited this from his grandfather along with the throne."[8] Dr. Fagan declared that the great Louis was so odorous that "he frightened away from his court a number of great lords who lacked nothing at being perfect courtiers save of always being on their nose." It was reported of the Moorish children, however, that when washed they had less of the alleged African odor.

Still other Moors were brought into France and held as slaves in the centuries of war between the Christian powers and the Barbary corsairs. Louis XIV liked the Moorish sailors so well that he refused to exchange them for the Frenchmen held by Mulai Ismael, in spite of the heart-rending letters sent by the Moorish captives to their king.

Other Negroes of even purer ancestry came in numbers to France with the slave-trade that began in Portugal in 1442. Nantes was the great French slave-trading port, and corresponded to Liverpool in England. Negro slaves

5 See Rogers, J. A.   100 Amazing Facts About the Negro, p. 38, (18th ed.), for biblio
6 Collier's Weekly, Oct. 31, 1931, p. 36.
7 Michel, F. Les Races Maudites, p. 25, et seq. Paris, 1847.
8 Les Gaieties de Science, pp. 108, 301. Paris, 188

were held in southwestern France; and later, the slave masters of the French West India colonies brought Negroes in such numbers that mulatto foundlings became a serious problem in Paris.

Louis XV, hoping to stop this, ordered all Negroes deported from France. Anisson du Perron, in a news summary of the times, says, "An order from the king has instructed all the Negroes, male and female, to retire into the possessions of their masters in America; those who are free will be shipped to Cayenne. The cause of this expulsion is the desire, too marked, of the white men for the Negro women, and of the white women for the Negro men. There is so much of this mixing that there are nearly 1,500 mulatto foundlings. It is this which has awakened the attention of the government, which is afraid that the French nation will lose the whiteness, beauty, and purity of blood."[9]

Previous to that, March, 1685, a law had been passed forbidding the marriage of whites and blacks in France. The slave-holders of Haiti who lived in France took care to see that the Black Code of the colonies was introduced there too. The prohibition of the marriage of whites and blacks lasted at least until 1820.[10] When Josephine wished one of her black servants to marry a white woman, Napoleon had to issue a decree to that effect. It is not known whether this prohibition against intermarriage included the mulattoes. It probably did not, because Napoleon in his private orders to General Leclerc said that the marriage of whites and mulattoes in Haiti should be encouraged but that between whites and blacks should be sternly prohibited.

The order for the expulsion of the Negroes was probably not carried out because in the succeeding reign there were enough Negroes in France to form a regiment or two. Murat had a full regiment of them,[11] and kept up the supply by recruitment from Greeks and Neapolitans "who were of the same color."

Napoleon had twelve Negro generals in his army in France, one of whom was the renowned General Alexander Dumas, commander of his cavalry till 1798, and father of the great novelist. There were also hundreds of Negro officers, who, after Napoleon had re-introduced slavery in Haiti turned against him and were used as "a fifth column" by Massena. Considerable prejudice rose against the Negroes in France as a result, and in 1799 there was talk of deporting them all. They were accused of being too rich, and driving around in elegant carriages with white footmen and servants. "There

9 Anisson du Perron. Nouvelles a la Main. pub. by Vte. de Grouchy, p. 29. Paris, 1898.
10 Bull. et Mem. Soc. D'Anthrop. de Paris, Vol. I, Nov. 18, 1886, p. 661.
11 Chesney, A. G. Negro Soldiers in Murat's Army. New Service Maga. Vol. 169, pp. 198-202. London, 1913.

will soon be no other than mulattoes in France" was the cry.[12]

But the race-mixing went on. Negro women were brought in large numbers from Egypt for the brothels.[13] Negroes of all sorts also continued to arrive from the colonies. Some of them, French-born, attained great influence, among them the two Dumas and Victor Sejour, a New Orleans Negro, who was a very popular playwright, and the secretary of Napoleon III. Another Negro, Vries, "The Black Doctor" of Surinam, won great notoriety after a leading maker of musical instruments, named Saxe, announced that Vries had cured him of cancer. Vries convinced even Velpeau, the foremost physician of the times, who assigned him to the care of cancer patients in La Charité Hospital. But Vries turned out to be a quack and wound up in prison despite his array of legal talent and host of influential friends. A mural was painted in the hospital entitled, "The Triumph of Esculapius," showing Velpeau chasing the Black Doctor through the hospital with a whip

The number of Negroes who have come to France from the French West Indies, and East, West, and North Africa since is considerable. Most of the men have white wives. There is also a fairly large number of mulatto children, the offspring of Senegalese soldiers, who are, or were, stationed in such places as Toulon, Marseilles, Perpignan, Paris, and Verdun, with no black women about. Louise Faure-Favier, a French aviatrix, has written a fine novel praising the children of these unions.

As regards my own observations on race-mixing in France, they are extensive. I once lived sometimes for more than a year at a time in the Latin Quarter of Paris, which is not only the centre of French university life, but is also cosmopolitan. Students of the Sorbonne and visitors from nearly all parts of the globe filled its hotels, restaurants, and cafes.

It was a common sight to see white and colored students arm in arm on the Boulevard St. Michel or in the nearby Jardin de Luxembourg. White students strolled with colored girls, most of whom were from the West Indies, and Negro students with white girl students, some of whom were rich men's daughters. There was an affair of one of the latter with a colored American student that received much mention in the European papers. She was the daughter of Dr. Edouard von Greiner, retired Hungarian cabinet minister. When her parents learned that she was in love with a Negro, they took her back to Budapest but she attempted suicide, at least she was reported as having attempted it, on which her parents sent a wire to the Negro student to come to Budapest where he married the girl.

Mixed couples, other than students, were often to be seen in the Quarter.

---

[12] Aulard, A. Paris sous le Consulat. Vol. I, p. 341; Vol. II, pp. 49, 79, 789-90; ''ol. III, p. 393. Paris.
[13] Block, Iwan. Sexual Life of Our Times, p. 614.

"The Dancing Lesson," painted by Mathieu Le Nain, French artist, about 1650. There was Negro slavery in France at the time. But note, even then the Negro was treated as an equal. In this charming scene, the dance mistress has her hand on the Negro's shoulder.

Left: Bishop Moussa of Paris (1811). Right: Dr. Carlos Tavares, physician to the late King Carlos of Portugal.

As for the popular Paris dance-halls as the Bal du Moulin Rouge, the Coliseum, the Bal Bullier, and the Bal Negre, mixed couples were always much in evidence. Paris is a cosmopolitan city, thus all the mixed couples were not French but included many European peoples, and some white Americans.

In the leading music-halls white artistes danced with female Negro partners such as Josephine Baker and Ruth Bayton; and Senegalese dancers as Habib Benglia and Feral Benga with white female partners. Everywhere I went in France from Strasbourg to Marseilles and from Havre to Lyon I found the same freedom in race relations. Even in some of the most exclusive artistic and literary circles I saw mixed couples and the same absence of color prejudice.

With the exception of Portugal, no other European country has been kindlier to Negroes than France. This does not mean that France is entirely free from color prejudice. There are Frenchwomen who have an instant dislike for a black skin. This was most easily seen in the bordels where some of the girls firmly refused to go with a black man though they would with a mulatto. This prejudice increased after the war due to American influence and black sailors who used to go into certain bordels in Havre were refused by all the girls. In the later 1930's some of the most popular of such places in Paris treated the black men very coldly. While they did not prevent their entering, they pretended not to see them. In my opinion the Nordics—Germans, Flemish, Danes and Scandinavians—as well as the Russians are more instinctively attracted towards blacks than the French or the Italians. Maupassant in one of his most touching stories, "Boitelle," tells how a Frenchman's parents absolutely refused to give him permission to marry a Negro girl because she was "too black." With the French, however, equal treatment of the black is a cardinal principle of their democracy and has been for more than a century. The chief prejudice against the blacks in France was that shown by white Americans and mulattoes from the colonies.

The number of colored men who have reached high positions in France exceeds every other country save Brazil. There have been six Cabinet Ministers,[14] one of whom Heredia, was Minister of Public Works in 1887, and one Minister of Justice, Lemery, 1934.[14a] There has also been one prefect of a department, equivalent to a governor of a state in the United States, Hector Simoneau; and one head of the Army Medical Corps, Surgeon-General Jean St. H. Dumas; as well as two admirals, Amiot and Porthuan.

[14] See Rogers, J. A. 100 Amazing Facts About the Negro, p. 29, 18th ed. for data.

[14a] Lemery was named Minister of Colonies by Petain in 1940, but Hitler had him thrown out.

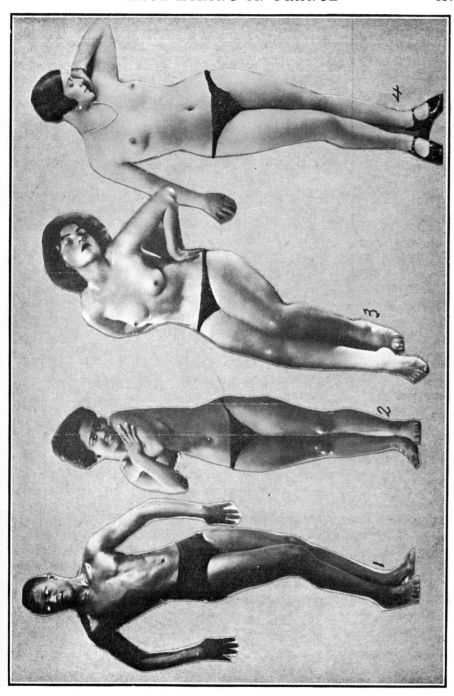

LVIII. France—Two unmixed and two mixed types, and all of fine physique. I Senegalese; 2. Mulatto; 3. Octoroon; 4. Caucasian.

The French Attitude Towards Race-Mixing as Given Mainly by French Writers

Count Gleichen-Russwurm: "The strong attraction which the black races exercise upon the European women is strongly reflected in an order sent out by General Leclerc to the effect that whatever their rank French women who associated with Negroes would be sent home."[15] (The order was handed to Leclerc by Napoleon, who added that the marriage of whites and mulattoes should be permitted but that between whites and blacks strictly barred. By all accounts Leclerc's wife, sister of Napoleon, was the first to violate it.)

Dr. Jacobus X, says: "I have known a good many officers and officials who have returned to France from Africa, married to charming young women, who miss the black skin and the woolly hair of the daughters of Ham."[16]

Carolyn Wilson, writing from Paris during the war of 1914:

"Across the aisle at one of the big reserved tables sits a blacker-than-the-ace-of-spades Senegalese. Nearly every woman in the house is breaking her neck to see him and smile at him and, recently, he held a little reception of seven of the most wonderfully gowned, swelte women, in the room, who wished to inquire if he had been wounded or réformé.

"It is simply amazing and to an American revolting to a degree to see the attention these men receive. At the Comédie Francaise, two in a box were the object of all opera glasses, women threw them flowers, and the entire audience went into such shrieks of laughter over the remark of one of them that it was necessary for M. Mounet to stop speaking."[17]

Charles N. Wheeler, speaking of the reception accorded Negro American soldiers in France:

"In one respect France is the paradise of the black man. The social line is not drawn here as at home, owing to the fact that the French women share their admiration with the dark-skinned French troops from the colonies."[18]

Joseph Hemard, writing in Le Sourire of Paris, says, "It is scarcely a few moons ago that the amateurs of exotic love, the curious ones, les raffinés, les petits vicieux, considered the possession, even though brief and paid for, of a Negro woman, as the crowning glory of a career of debauchery. In this contact with a black skin there was something especially passionate. In the maisons de societé where the Negro woman figured on the program

[15] The World Lure, p. 243. N. Y., 1927.
[16] L'Art D'Aimer Aux Colonies, p. 154. Paris, 1927
[17] Chicago Tribune, Jan. 24, 1915.
[18] Chicago Tribune, Nov. 15, 1918.

and many of these houses did not have such women—the customer who had the happiness of getting one, had the impression for several instants, at least, of being a sort of Sardanapalus, an Oriental sultan, gorging himself, so to speak, with rare voluptuousness, and preparing a future of palpitating souvenirs at the remembrance of these wild orgies. How many pharmacists of the provinces, how many retired lieutenant-governors, conservators d'hypothèques lost at the bottom of distant cantons have recalled with ecstasy moments of their gay youth when they were simple students in the Latin Quarter, where on an evening of joyous love, they had the happiness of tasting the pleasures of Venus in the arms of a Negro woman.

"Among the young men, it was then a sort of glory, as radiant as it was rare for those who could get one. The Negro woman was almost a mystery; the first question one often asked a friend returned from the colonies was of his loves with Negro women, and the fact of his having had a Negro mistress, conferred on such a one an enviable notoriety."

Times have changed, however, said the writer. The black woman is no longer a mystery. She now walks the street like her white sister and "her chief client is the white American, who as soon as he arrives in Paris throws off the inhibitions forced on him in his native land, runs hither and thither, drinks alcohol, and takes the Negro woman to his arms. No longer afraid of losing caste, he lowers himself eagerly.

"The American's most serious competitor in this respect is the German who scolds us for having enlisted Negroes in our army but avidly seeks the Negro women enlisted in the battalions of Cytherea."[19]

Apropos of this a native of Arkansas, who had visited Europe for the first time told the Negro chauffeur who was showing him Paris to take him first of all to a Negro woman. This, after he had come four thousand miles!

Certain American white women also enjoy the freedom of being away from the U.S.A. and go with Negroes to dance-halls and elsewhere. Some who go to the houses of men for women as told by Maryse Choisy in her "Un Mois Chez Les Filles," ask for Negro men. I knew two or three American and West Indian Negroes who made a living this way. Again certain rich Americans stage orgies between white girls and Negroes. One such affair staged in high Oriental style became the talk of Montmarte. The white girls came from a well-known troupe of American singers and dancers and the blacks were Aframericans. One of the latter, a stalwart six-footer, was one of the figures of Montmarte. One of the girls objected to him at first but yielded under the large sum offered. Of course, there are Harlemites who will tell you it isn't necessary to go to Paris to see affairs of this sort.

Blanche Vogt, a prominent French writer, when asked by a reporter

[19] May 28, 1931.

for L'Intransigeant, Paris daily, whether she would marry a Negro replied, "No, because I am already married and I don't wish to go to prison."

"But if you were single?"

"Oh, well, in that case, why should I not trust my happiness to a colored man?

"Do white men make such excellent husbands?

"It is understood that if I were to marry a colored man I'd take some precautions. My colored fiance would have to court me for a long time. I would submit him to long and exacting tests—such tests at which white men usually fail. For example, I would tell him that my dot (sum of money which a French woman brings to her husband at marriage) was lost in the recent crash of the Gazette de Franc; that I love pearls and dainties, as well as idleness, and music, a house in the country and children. Instead of playing the comedy of sweetness, I would so act as to make him mistrust my character like a savage mare.

"In short, all that the white fiances consider as very vexatious I would apply to my colored fiance. If he passed these tests I would place my pale hand in his colored one and let him conduct me to the altar in spite of all else.

"An old school-mate of mine married some five years ago, a fine mulatto. She has already four fine children. She is president of the club of Happily Married Women.

"One day while joking with her I said:

" 'Have you ever thought of going around with another man, sometimes.'

" 'No,' she replied, 'there are some white men who stand for that sort of thing but my husband if he knew—is capable of tearing the nails from my toes one by one.' "

A coal-black and very handsome Negro dentist, who used to cut a figure at Deauville was pestered by women who wanted him to examine their even perfectly sound teeth.

"Would You Marry a Colored Man?"

Eve, a woman's illustrated daily of Paris, held a symposium on inter-marriage and a contest with four prizes to its feminine readers for the best letter on: "Would You Marry A Colored Man?"[20]

Three questions were asked. The first was what was thought of American treatment of the Negro; the second was what was one's opinion of mixed marriages, and the third read: "Do you think that a man distantly descended from a Negro, and who shows no physical characteristics of one, could be loved and even wedded by a white woman, if he is tender, agreeable, and faithful?"

20. February 20—March 29, 1920.

Questions were sent to members of the Academy, playwrights, authors, publicists and others. The following are excerpts from their replies:

Mme. Rachilde, writer: "The kultur, the socialization and the peculations of all sorts, warlike as well as humanitarian (of civilization), have shown me during the past five years what it is capable of producing, hence, I claim the right to prefer the natural savage to the artificial one—without counting the fact that he is better for purposes of reproduction."

Henry Barbusse, author and editor: "One cannot approve, in principle, a union between persons of different races. The persons, themselves, must be the sole judge."

Pierre Mille, author and traveler: "If France had the same number of Negroes as the United States, the French would be forced to do as the North Americans. Besides, that would make us kindlier to the Jew."

Romain Coolus, dramatist: "The marriage of a black man and a white woman does not shock me. There is no difference in the music of love... and love like the wind blows where it will."

Charles Henry Hirsch, lawyer: "It is not without irony that you ask whether a man distantly descended from a Negro could be loved and even wedded by a white woman. There are white women who would marry a real ape if he had enough money and could procure the civil status of a man. We saw between 1914 and 1918, thousands and thousands of white women love blacks, perfectly black, of pure black blood, whom they might have loved less if their lips had been thinner and their skins fairer...

"At the bottom of love is curiosity. It can captivate the wisest white woman and deliver her to a Negro for reasons that the heart knows not of."

Marcel Boulanger, author: "I declare to you that I can find no reason whatever for persecuting a Negro. If a woman had just deceived me with a Negro I would not be able to keep myself from laughing. That's my nature."

Roland Dorgelès, author: "I disapprove the union of a white man and a mulatto. The white woman would not be lowering herself but the pair would be guilty of stupidity. It is true, however, that folly is a symptom of love."

Charles Richet, Prof. of the Faculty of Medicine and Nobel Prize winner: "A white woman should by no means marry a Negro. Even if the signs of his ethnic inferiority is little apparent, they will appear in the children... All mixture of race is detestable. Alexander Dumas was an exception."

Maurice de Waleffe, journalist: "I believe that the marriage between races, slightly different, helps to neutralize defects and purify the blood... But only within the limits of the white race... In café au lait we have a softening of the coffée, but not of the milk."

Hugues Delorme, poet, answered in poetry of which this is a free translation of the first two verses:

> "If a quadroon presents himself
> Well-made and of good manners
> The white woman who refused him
> Would reveal herself as stupidly proud.
>
> But yesterday, the blacks, marvelous soldiers
> Showed themselves free from fear and sans reproach
> Therefore to choose a black is better far
> Than to have as husband a Boche."

De la Fouchardière, columnist: "The white woman alone is in a position to appreciate the pleasure she may find in a Negro lover. I have seen too many blondes in love with worthless blond men to object to a Desdemona or a Titania loving a Negro, a fine Negro of Senegal or the Congo. As to marriage between them I do not hesitate to answer that there is nothing better."

J. H. Rosny, Sr., of the Academy Goncourt: "I am hardly in favor of marriage between blacks and whites and whites and mulattoes."

Abel Faivre, cartoonist: "What valid reason can be given against the marriage of a white woman and a mulatto? Has not Nature shown in the most peremptory manner that color counts for nothing in the affair."

Pierre Benoit, of the French Academy: "Mixed marriages do not seem monstrous to me, at all. If I were a woman I would much prefer an amiable mulatto to President Wilson, who it seems to me must not be droll in intimacy."

Jean Finot, editor and scientist: "All radical measures taken with the aim of preventing marriages between whites and blacks, or what is more grave, whites and mulattoes, become a crying injustice . . .

"To soften the hatreds and implacable fears it is necessary to remember that one of the first phases of civilization, that of ancient Egypt was of Negro origin, and that the mulattoes have everywhere proved that they are not inferior to whites."

Victor Marguerite, author: "Quite funny your question coming after a time when we have been seeing so many unexpected unions of whites, yellows, and blacks...the example of America, that of North America, especially, has it not proved over-abundantly, the virtue of a marriage where the blood of the different races are mixed?"

André de Lorde, dramatist: "The eyes, the odor, the touch of the Negro place between him and us a barrier that all the fine laws of the world and the most eloquent pleading cannot overthrow."

Max and Alex Fischer, authors: "Can a Negro be loved by a white woman? Yes, why not? And in any case in the dark."

Madeleine Lemaire: "Why should not a white woman love a colored man if he is handsome and intelligent? Have we not the example of Alexander Dumas, fils, who was one of the most remarkable, charming, and best loved men of his time?"

Others in favor of were Fernard Grech, M. Grosclaude, Victor Snell, Rene Benjamin, Reynaldo Hahn, Dr. Maurice de Fleury. Opposed were Andre de Fouquieres and Gabriel de Lautrec.

Of the thirty-three distinguished French persons asked: nineteen were in favor; eight opposed, one was neutral; and five did not answer the last question.

* * * *

Prize Winning Letters

In the contest there were 2040 answers. Of this 1060 women said they would not marry a Negro, and 980 said they would.

Paul Reboux, author of "Romulus Coucou," who conducted the contest said in his summary, that many of the women who opposed said they were not opposed to intermarriage for others, but for themselves, only. All in all, he said the proportion of opinion on both sides was about "fifty per cent," adding that if the contest had been held in America "perhaps not a single woman would have said, Yes."

Among those who objected, he said, were those who were deterred by thought of the color of the offspring, as well as by physiological repugnance based on the interior color of the hand. the shape of the nose, and the lips; as well as what their neighbors would think. The last-named, he said, would not have minded marrying a Negro in the tropics but not at home.

Those in favor said that they thought mulatto babies very beautiful and that Negroes being "great athletes" would have robust children; that so far as the charge of "natural savagery was concerned a Negro was worth more than a drunken man, apache, or rogue; that Negroes made the best husbands in the world, and that marrying one was a good act and gave a white woman the advantage of saying that she perceived the good qualities in a Negro where others could not."

The winners of the first and second prizes were both married to Negroes. The winner of the third, Baroness de G.⌃.... was opposed. She said: "Marry a colored man? No, my dear Eve, I never would. I will even add a white woman ought not to marry a colored man. She has not the right: the black race is incontestably inferior to ours..."

She went on to say that Europe will regret its benevolence on the color question, and will change its idea some day, but that she thought it quite likely that a white woman could love a Negro, since some of them are endowed "with the most remarkable intelligence, and a delicate and generous soul. Since it often happens that a woman falls in love with one of her own kind with a very black soul, it is difficult to see why she should not be capable, sometimes, of loving a black man with a white soul."

The winner of the fourth prize a girl of eleven gave the following response. It is interesting because it reflects the psychology of those untouched by any form of color propaganda.

"I do not know whether I'd find it agreeable with a Negro before me at breakfast. In any case I would not like him to eat without white gloves on because I would always have the impression that his hands were dirty, and that he would soil the napkin and the table-cloth. Apart from that if I loved him I do not see why I could not be happy with him. I could very easily wipe my cheeks after he had kissed me."

The following was the prize-winning essay.

"When I married a mulatto, that is to say, a colored man, I was warned by my friends. Be careful, you're likely to have a little Negro.

"The prophecy came true. At the moment of his arrival in this world my little Jack was a peculiar color—a little grayish. And then he grew darker. Now he is the color of a whitish-brown bread crust. He is four years old and a superb child—a little golden Hercules with strong limbs and harmonious features. He has large eyes with pupils of jade, with whites, bluish like spilt milk, and long, curved lashes which give them the appearance of being larger and more caressing.

"At birth his father, who is consideration itself, was worried at seeing Jack, growing darker day by day. He feared its affect on me, the loss of my love. But from the moment this little being held his dear mouth towards me, to live from me, he became my very own, and I live entirely for him by that mysterious joy of mother-love...

"I love him for all the inquietudes he has caused me, for all the sacrifices I have made, and all the joys I have had in watching him grow. Certainly he does not look like the other children. I confess it. But those who object will certainly have to reckon with me.

"Such are the confessions of a blonde Frenchwoman who married a colored man. I can, therefore, only approve such unions. The worst menace that of a dark colored child I have experienced and I regret it in no way."

The Second Prize

"Yes, I believe that a white woman can marry a colored man. I believe it because I have experienced it. May I risk a confession? When this gentleman with a black skin began to court me I experienced at first a bit of gaiety, somewhat mocking. I asked myself this question: How ought a Negro to conduct himself in a situation in which white men have sometimes shown themselves either pitiably clumsy, or excessively passionate? Then I had the obsession to learn whether the soles of his feet were as fair as his palm. Again, it gives a woman a thrill to be seen in public with a black man, arousing as it does the curiosity and the vague jealousy of the other women who see her. In short when this man asked me to say, 'Yes,' I did not say 'No.'

"I have never regretted this step. My husband is a good worker, and is sober, faithful, and very attentive. He is inclined to be poetic and of an extreme goodness. Sometimes his laughter rings with pleasure like that of a child. He has all the fine feelings of a truly cultured man, and is gentleness itself.

"We have a child, brown in color, tanned just as if he had returned daily from a vacation by the sea-shore, and with eyes blue like mine. All three of us are happy, and although I am white I ask nothing else than to continue being so."

Marcus Garvey and His Theory of Segregation

As regards the attitude of the intellectual radicals towards race relations I once had an excellent opportunity for getting a close-up on the same. In Paris, there is, or was, a circle known as the Club du Faubourg, whose members included some of the leading writers and thinkers of France. The utmost freedom of speech was permitted and ofttimes there was so much excitement that I left with a headache.

In October, 1928, Marcus Garvey, great Back-to-Africa leader, was announced as the principal speaker. A vast crowd turned out to hear him, of which about thirty were Negroes. The theatre was packed only as French theatres are permitted to be.

Garvey started off with an excoriation of the white race for its treatment of the blacks, and of white America in particular. This latter brought several interruptions from white Americans present.

Garvey went on to say that the only solution of the race problem was segregation. Whites should keep to themselves and blacks to themselves. "God," he said, "had made people of opposite colors and He intended them to stay that way." That remark brought much laughter, especially when some one gravely complimented him on knowing what was in the mind of God Almighty.

Undaunted, Garvey went on to denounce race-mixing. Race-mixing, he declared, was the great obstacle to Negro progress. "The only Negroes

LIX. Pictures illustrative of the absence of color prejudice in the white European.
(See Notes on the Illustrations).

LX. "UNE NOIRE VAUT DEUX BLANCS." (One Black Woman is Worth Two White Men) is the title of this drawing.

who want to remain in America," he shouted, "are those who are in favor of miscegenation."

There was another howl of disapproval when this was translated. One woman shouted, "Il n'est pas beau." (He is not a nice man).

The next speaker was a white Frenchman, Captain Desmond Hugon. of. the French merchant marine. Hugon had lived many years in Africa and was as full of venom for the Negro as Hitler. No sooner had he uttered the first few words than Marcus Garvey was forgotten. Hugon had probably been invited because of his extreme views.

Pulling out a script that was big enough to make a book, Hugon sailed into the Negroes. They were hopelessly inferior and incapable, he said, and had been so since the dawn of history. "Look at the United States," he said, "there are thirteen millions of them there and yet with all of the vast opportunities offered by America there isn't even a single Negro lawyer, doctor, or engineer."

As for opposition to interracial marriage, he was even more fierce than Garvey. It is the death of the white race, he said. It ruins French prestige in the colonies. It gave the blacks cocky ideas and made them difficult to handle in Africa. African Negroes who have lived in France, he declared, took back with them photographs of white women, show them to their friends and say, "This is the white woman who blacked my shoes." (In France it is a custom for a wife to shine her husband's shoes.)

Hugon never got very far with his harangue. Shouts came at him from all parts of the hall. Some of the more excitable Negroes challenged him to a fight. From then on he had as much chance to get in a word, even sideways, as a Jew at a German-American Bund meeting, or an advocate of racial intermarriage at a Ku Klux rally. The chairman pounded his gavel, and clashed his cymbals, and appealed to the audience in vain. Hugon had to quit.

For the next hour or so he had to listen to a denunciation of himself by speaker after speaker. Rene Maran, author of "Batoula" and Goncourt prize winner, turned on him angrily, "You say that I said in Batoula that the most contemptible creature in Africa is a white man. Yes, I said it, and when I did I had in mind white men like you. In France the Negro must court the white women to get her, but in Africa the white man takes the black woman by force from her husband and punishes and kills the husband, too."

Some Notable Cases of Intermixture in France

Ismeria, a Negro woman from the Sudan, was married to Robert d'Eppes, son of William II of France. She bore him a son, Jean, who was a companion of St. Louis, king of France in the Crusades. In a chart of 1236, Jean is designated as the "son of the Negro woman." Ismeria, herself, was a famous figure, and at her death was made a Black Madonna. While in the Sudan, she had saved the Christian knights there from death. So great was her fame that a town sprang up near her shrine, and pilgrims from all parts of France came to pay homage to her, with rich presents. Among them were Joan of Arc, Louis XI, and Francis I. She is known as Notre Dame de Liesse.[21]

Anselme d'Isalguier, a nobleman of Toulouse, married Casais, a Negro princess of Gao, in 1405. Their lovely mulatto daughter, Martha, was the belle of Toulouse, while their descendants married into some of the leading families of the city.[21a]

Francis, Duke of Vendome, commander-in-chief of the armies of France, and relative of the King, who was courted by the most beautiful women of the kingdom, left them all, including his wife, for a Moorish woman, according to Brantome. This was about 1560 when "Maure" (Moor) was used for Negro.[22]

Francis I of France had a Negro mistress.[23] The first mistress of Louis XIV was a Negro woman.[24] Louis, Queen, Maria Theresa of Spain, had a mulatto daughter, Louise-Marie, by a Negro dwarf, named Nabo. Louis XV is reported to have had a Negro son who claimed the throne of France."[5] His mother might have been Mademoiselle St. Hilaire, a lovely West Indian, who was one of Louis' many mistresses. The beautiful Countess Du Barry, favorite of Louis XV, had an extraordinarily spoilt Negro favorite, Zamor, whom she was accused of having seduced. At her trial, which led to her execution, he was one of the principal witnesses against her. Madame de Sevigne reports that the Countess de Coetlogen had a Negro child "black as the devil."[26] According to Du Barry, the Count d'Artois, son of Louis XVI, and later king of France, had a Negro girl, a rich and dazzlingly beautiful West Indian, Isabeau, as his mistress. The Chevalier de St. Georges, a Negro of Guadaloupe, most noted swordsman and violinist of the reign of Louis XVI, had many titled mistresses, among them Madame de Montesson, Duchess of Orleans, and sister-in-law of the King; the Marquise de Montal-

[21] Calixte, R. P. Les Plus Illustres Captifs. Vol. I, pp. 93-101. Paris, 1892.
 Drochon. Les Pelèrinages Français, pp. 67-94. Paris, 1900.
[21a] La Roncière, C. de., La Decouverte de l'Afrique au Moyen Age. Vol. III, pp 2-13, Le Caire. 1927.
[22] Brantome. Oeuvres. Vol. VI, p. 123. Paris, 1875. Lalanne.
[23] Hackett, F Francis I, p. 319. N. Y., 1935.
[24] Michelet, J. Oeuvres Complètes. Vol. XII, p. 37. Paris, 189—.
[25] Intermediare des Chercheurs, etc. Vol. 56, p. 160. Paris, 1907.
[26] Rogers. Ibid., p. 30.

embert; and others. [27] Pauline, Napoleon's favorite sister, had several **Negro lovers**, among them the Negro, Thomas, who used to bathe her, and General Dumas, father of the great novelist.   She is also said to have had several Negro lovers while in Haiti, among them Christophe, Petion, and Toussaint L'Overture.   Barras, head of the French Directory, who gave Napoleon his opportunity, strongly hints that the Empress Josephine also had love affairs with Negroes.   The Countess de Beauharnais, who was related to Napoleon by marriage, married a **Haitian Negro**, named Castaing.   Placide, son of Toussaint L'Ouverture, **married Marie**-Josephine, daughter of Joseph, Marquise de la Caze, former **officer of** the Court of Louis XVI.[28]   Marshal Junot had a Negro son, named **Othello,**[29] by a woman in Egypt of whom Napoleon was fond.   Baudelaire **had** his Negro sweetheart and inspirer, Jeanne Duval. General Faidherbe, empire-builder, is said to have had an African wife.[30] Elisee Reclus, noted geographer, married a Negro woman and had several mulatto daughters by her.[31] ꞌPaul LaFargue, Cuban mulatto, and writer on economics, married the daughter of Karl Marx.[32]

Among the most prominent mixed marriages in the 1900's were those of the late Blaise Diagne, noted Senegalese and Cabinet Minister, whose mulatto son, Raoul, is one of the leading football players of France and an officer in the medical corps; Gratien Candace, West Indian of unmixed Negro ancestry, Cabinet Minister, and head of the budget for the French Navy; General Henri Barbe, head of the Commissary for the Colonies; Naval Captain Mortenol, commander of the Air Defenses of Paris in the first World War; Rene Maran, author of "Batoula" and winner of the Goncourt Prize; Benglia, Senegalese dancer and motion picture star; and Josephine Baker, Aframerican dancer and favorite of the Paris music-halls who was married to an Italian count, and later to a rich French manufacturer.

Amongst the most noted mulattoes and quadroons born in France or in French possessions in the Old World were Dumas, pere; Dumas, fils; Paul du Chaillu, explorer; Paul Gaugin, painter; Ambroise Vollard, millionaire art collector, and discoverer of Cezanne, Renoir, Picasso and other painters; Colette, France's best known woman writer;[33] and Maurice Donnay, member of the French Academy, who is also popularly said to be colored, and looks it.   Cezanne, himself, is said to have been colored.

[27] Beauvoir, Roger de. Chevalier de St Georges, 2v. Paris, 1857.
    Capon, G. Les petites maison galantes de Paris, p. 14. Paris, 1902.
[28] Steward, T. G. Haitian Revolution, p. 219. N. Y., 1914.
[29] Napoleon I. Memoirs of. Universal Classic Library, Vol. I, p. 252. London, 1901.
[30] Durham, F. A. Lone Star of Liberia, p. 17.
[31] Reclus, E. Correspondance, Vol. I, p. 184. Paris, 1911.
[32] Enciclopedia Univ. Ilus. (see La Fargue, P.).
[33] Durtain, Luc. Diversions Afrique. M. Durtain also personally told me that Colette, herself, had told him so.

Chapter Twenty

ISABEAU, BLACK VENUS OF THE REIGN OF LOUIS XV

I SABEAU, a West Indian mulatto girl, created a considerable stir in France during the reign of Louis XV with her beauty, wealth and taste in dress, which combined the refinements of France with the exotic charms of the Indies.

Among those who fell under her spell was the Comte d'Artois, later King of France. Mme. du Barry, favorite of Louis XV, devotes a whole chapter to the beautiful creole in her memoirs. "She was," say du Barry, "a Venus, a black Venus that all Paris ended by admiring· For the sake of the white Venuses, I should not have spoken of her if my life had not become entangled with hers in an odious scandal . . .

"Isabeau was proclaimed a charming creature, and more than one grand personage of the Court, more than one financier placed his heart and his purse at her feet. Rare and magnificent adornments; great luxury; jewels and precious stones; a natural taste in dress; an accent, piquant because of it strangeness; numerous servants; great sums of money to spend, helped to decide the success of Isabeau. Whenever she came to Versailles to see the king at dinner, there was a great crowd to see her. When she saw the Count d'Artois, then at the height of his handsomeness and elegance, she could not repress her admiration, and said aloud that she would willingly give a thousand louis to obtain the honor of an intimate conversation with him.

"Nothing that is said at court is lost. Isabeau's words were conveyed to His Royal Highness. It was not in this manner that the prince would have consented to an increase in his revenues, but, hearing of this new, naive homage, he laughed a great deal and was flattered. He had seen this beautiful Negro woman only in passing. In order to see her more closely, he invited her one evening to Bagatelle, it is said. As for me, the desire to chat with her came differently . . .

" 'Have you seen Isabeau?' the wife of the Marshal de Mirepoix asked me.

" 'Have you met anywhere the beautiful Negress?' the Baron de Sugère demanded.

"I replied, 'No,' and showed surprise· My curiosity excited, I wrote to Celine.

" 'Have you seen Isabeau?'

" 'Yes, indeed,' she replied, 'she is a fine hunter, who has come to hunt in our territory. In truth, if the men are so carried away with these inky skins, we white women have nothing left to do but dye ours.'

" 'I wish to see her.'

" 'I will gladly bring her here, but let her continue to enjoy for a while longer the happiness of her visit to Bagatelle.'

" 'Then it is true?'

" 'Well, what else did you expect,' replied Celine impatiently, 'It is said that the prince in parting said: *Oui noir, mais pas si diable.*'

"I understand the anger of Celine without sympathizing with it too much ... (The following week, Isabeau, who ought to have come with Celine, visited Luciennes (chateau of du Barry) alone.)

"She was dressed in Asiatic magnificence. Her short dress of damask stitched with gold and with golden fringes, permitted a glimpse of her stockings the color of fire and shoes of red satin ornamented with buckles of diamonds. She wore also a sash of very fine linen remarkable for its richness and beauty; a shawl of white wool spun in gold, and ornamented with a golden fringe. This is called a Cashmere shawl. Because of its extraordinary fineness, it did not spoil the lines of her figure. This shawl was a marvel of adornment and I was eager to have one like it. Lace of gold trimmed the top of Isabeau's robe; a silken handkerchief of the Indies with brilliant and striking colors, arranged with a piquant originality that pleased me so much, served as head-dress. I will say nothing of the necklaces, bracelets, pendants, and the agrafes of a thousand jewels that she wore. All represented an enormous sum.

"I can assure you, that except for her color, that African woman was charming. Imagine her: tall, supple, but voluptuous, with a walk that was elegance itself. Her well-shaped eyes were alive; her mouth admirably formed; her skin was something between satin and velvet; and the most beautiful ears that one could see. Indeed, I must admit that she merited her reputation."

These two most beautiful women of France, the one black, the other white, embraced each other and became fast friends.

Isabeau, according to du Barry, was born in Africa, and had been sold into slavery in Haiti with her mother. She had had three different masters, the last of which freed her, and left her a large fortune. Several white Haitians were madly in love with her and wished to give her other fortunes, but she loved a Negro, named Plato, who had been given to her by one of her white lovers.

Du Barry. Mémoires, Chap. CXXVI. Paris 1851. (Lamothe-Langon, E.L.)

Zamor, Negro Favorite of the Lovely Countess Du Barry

Louis Zamor, an unmixed Negro from Bengal, India, enjoyed considerable power in France under Louis XV. He was the favorite of Countess Du Barry, who was in turn the favorite of the King, and the power behind the throne. Zamor was in charge of the private affairs of Du Barry and was governor of her chateau, Les Luciennes, to which post he had been appointed by the King. Zamor was extraordinarily spoilt and took liberties even with the King. His influence was so great that when the Chancellor of France once tried to see Du Barry to get her support on a matter he wished to place before the King, he first had to pay court to Zamor. Emile Cantrel wrote of Zamor, "He was an ugly savage, spoilt, capricious, uneducated, but superb with his colored plumes, bracelets, necklaces, and ear-rings... To win Du Barry's favor, one had to win Zamor's first." Du Barry used to kiss and fondle Zamor to the extent that it was charged at her trial that she had spoilt the morals of this Negro—"one of the people." Zamor, either because he had been won over by the revolutionists, or to save his own neck, gave damaging testimony against Du Barry, revealing many of her secrets and the hiding-place of her jewels. Du Barry was guillotined.[1]

Another favorite of French royalty was Scipio Africanus, who was bought when young by the Duchess of Orleans, who saw him on sale together with a Newfoundland dog. Reared as a member of the royal family, he ate at the same table with the royal children and rode pick-a-back on the Duke's son, later King of France.

When he reached manhood, Scipio lived in high style but he fell into disfavor with his royal benefactors, and went over to the republicans, who made him a captain in their army. He was killed at the battle of Novi.[2]

Pauline Bonaparte and Her Negro Lovers

Most of the writers of Napoleon's time are agreed that Pauline, Princess Borghese, Napoleon's eldest sister, and the leading beauty of the times, had affairs with several Negroes. Among those named are General Dumas, father of the great novelist; Christophe, emperor of Haiti; Petion, the first president of Haiti; and Thomas, her stalwart personal attendant.

Pauline, according to Pasquier, made no effort to conceal the intimate details of her life. She didn't seem to care what people thought.

Barras, head of the Directory, who was largely responsible for Napoleon's early rise, said, "Her illness was ascribed to excesses of licentiousness com-

---

[1] Cantrel, Nouvelles à la main sur la Comtesse Du Barry, p. 221. Paris, 1861. Houssaye, A. Gazette d'un Curieux, p. 145. Vatel, C., Histoire du Mme. Du Barry, pp. 358-368. Paris, 1883. Goncourt, E. and J., La Du Barry, p. 115. Paris, 1932. Also Du Barry's own memoirs.

[2] Child, L. M. The Oasis. pp. 132-144, Boston, 1834. (Trans. from the French.)

mitted by her not only in Europe and in San Domingo, with the white men composing the army, but with the Negroes, as she had been desirous of instituting a comparison."

Lewis Goldsmith says: "Pauline reserved a strong dose of love for Petion and Christophe." H. Almeras also discussed her alleged love affairs with Negroes in Haiti.

Alexander Dumas says of her and his father, General Dumas, "The princess' (Pauline) white and pink cheeks brushed against my father's dusky one, making his skin look darker and hers more white."

Duke de Pasquier, Napoleon's chancellor, said: "She had, like Josephine, a lusty Negro to lift her into her bath." When teased about her Negro, Paul, she is said to have replied: "A Negro is not a man."

Alvaro Retana, citing writers of Napoleon's time on the private life of Napoleon, Pauline, and others, tells at some length of Pauline's amours with Thomas, who used to bathe her. He says, "Pauline, skipping as lightly as a kitten, headed for the pink-coloured marble bath, in shape like a piscina and which was sunken under the paraphernalia of the shower apparatus. And on her entering the bathroom, Adelaide closed the door, leaving the Emperor's sister in the power of the Negro, Thomas, who received his mistress with profuse courtesies.

"The ebony statue, marvelous specimen of his race, by virtue of the symmetry of his features and the irreproachable plasticity of his gigantic figure, appeared with no apparel save an abbreviated pair of leathern drawers."

Retana goes on realistically for three pages and a half to tell how the Negro obtains "complete possession of her," in the water. Pauline was undoubtedly a nymphomaniac. Her doctor warned her of her excesses in vain.

"Pauline," says Pasquier, "was perhaps the most beautiful woman of her time. Perhaps no woman has so excelled in the making use of her charms since the days of the wife of Emperor Claudius."

She married General Leclerc for his money. When someone wished her a happy honeymoon, she replied, "What! a honeymoon with that ass! Is such a thing possible?" Pauline died with a mirror in her hand, believing herself beautiful till the last.

Barras. Memoirs. Trans. C. E. Roche. Vol. 4, p. 220. N. Y., 1896.
Dumas. Mes Memoires. Vol. I, pp. 219-221. Paris, 1863.
Blangini, F., Souvenirs, pp. 140-42. Paris, 1834.
Goldsmith, L. Histoire Secrete du Cabinet de Napoleon, p. 184. Paris, 1814.
Almeras, H. Une Amoureuse, p. 106.
Retana, A. E. Espejo de Pauline Bonaparte, pp. 32-35, et seq. Madrid, 1922.
(This writer gives a bibliography of little known books on the private life of the Bonapartes. His accounts of Pauline and the Negro, Thomas, are far too frank to be quoted here.)

The Empress Josephine also had a Negro to bathe her, and it was commonly said that she had Negro lovers. Barras, the real ruler of France immediately before Napoleon, said of her: "It was even said that the infidelities of the Creole had overstepped the bounds of propriety and that, rising superior to the prejudice existing against a dark skin, had intercourse with Negroes." (Memoirs, Vol. II, p. 64.) Once when the Empress was accused of misconduct with one of the Negroes who bathed her, she had him married to one of her attendants. Josephine was born of white parents in Martinique. She was to all appearances white. There seems to be no proof, whatever, that she was of Negro ancestry as is so commonly said.

Countess de Beauharnais, sister-in-law of Josephine, married a Negro named Castaing, a native of San Domingo. Castaing's father was a member of the Convention, and had aided Mme. de Beauharnais in recovering her property. Pasquier says that this man was a mulatto, but Garnot and Masson, historians, say he was an unmixed Negro.

Pasquier, Duc de. Memoirs. Vol. I, p. 128. N. Y., 1893.
Abrantes, Duchesse de. Memoires, Vol. II, p. 367.
Intermediare des Chercheurs, etc., Vol. 58, p. 582. Paris, 1908.

Chapter Twenty-one

THE BLACK NUN—DAUGHTER OF MARIE THERESA, QUEEN OF FRANCE

IN Titus Andronicus, Shakespeare depicts a Roman empress who had an illegitimate mulatto child. Here is a true story of a Queen of France, who had one.

The affair was hushed up at the time, of course, but enough of it leaked out to make a first-class scandal. In later years it was expanded into several romantic versions. Here, however, is the story stripped of romance as told by G. Le Notre of the French Academy.

Several years after the death of Marie-Theresa, says Le Notre, when Louis XIV had married secretly his favorite, Madame de Maintenon, a peasant, who said he was a blacksmith, appeared at the gates of Versailles and asked to see the King. The guards bade him begone but he insisted so hard that they took him to Marshal Duras, chief of the palace.

Duras, seeing the shifty looks and loutish manner of the peasant felt sure that he was an impostor, but bade him tell his story.

The man refused at first but finally stammered out a tale of a spirit he had seen, and of a message it had given him to give the King. Duras drove him away with a warning to keep his mouth shut.

A few days later, however, the King sent for Duras, and to the latter's astonishment ordered that the peasant be found and brought before him forthwith.

This was done, and the peasant told his story to the King, who at the first words turned pale and shook all over. The story was that on a certain date he was going home through the woods when he saw a very bright light. As he came nearer, he discovered that it was a woman who had on bright garments and whose face shone like the sun. This spirit, he said, revealed itself as the dead Queen, and bade him give the King a message.

Louis XIV, who was very superstitious, continued to tremble. The man concluded, "And, sire, the Queen's spirit has appeared to me again. Both times it has given me the same message. It says you must make your second marriage public."

At that a lightning change came over the King. From being frightened, he grew very angry, and lifting his stick, struck at the man. It was a trick, court intrigue, he felt. The supposed vision of this peasant was a dream he, himself, had had. Someone hearing him tell it, had told it to this peasant

246

LXI. Upper: Princess Rogotsky with her Negro favorite. Lower: Duchess of Portsmouth, favorite of Charles II of England, with her Negro favorite.

and sent him here with it, hoping to trick him into announcing his secret marriage.

The peasant dropped to his knees and insisted he was telling the truth. "Sire," he said, "the Queen told me that if you didn't believe me to tell you she had sent me *in the name of the Negro woman of Moret.*"

Again, the King turned pale. He bade the peasant never to mention the story to anyone and to make sure that he never would sent him off to solitary confinement in the Bastille.

The preface to this strange incident, says Le Notre, went back twenty years before when the Grand Admiral of France arrived from Dahomey bringing with him a dwarf which the King of that country had sent as a present for the Queen.

The Queen, pleased with the little black, dressed him in silken robes, ornamented with precious stones, costly bracelets and arm-bands, and a magnificent turban for which Madame de Maintenon gave him an aigrette of rubies, pearls, and diamonds.

Soon other ladies of the kingdom, following the Queen's example got little Negroes too, to carry their trains and to show off the whiteness of their skins. This explains, says Le Notre, why Mignard and other painters of the time included Negroes in their canvases. "It was the mode, and became a veritable frenzy among the fashionable which lasted until a misadventure befell the Queen."

When the Queen was about to become a mother again, she became strangely restless, and kept repeating:

"I no longer recognize myself. I experience strange disgusts and caprices such as never happened before. If I were to do as I wanted to, I would be cutting somersaults on the carpet, like my little Negro, and eating green fruits and living birds like him."

"Ah, Madame," replied the King, "you make me shiver. Forget your foolish fancies or you will have a child, bizarre and unnatural."

The King was only too right. When the child was born, it had a dark brown, African tint. The King recoiled in horror at the sight of it, and stamped about in rage. The Queen swore she was innocent. The doctors to pacify the King, told him it was atavism, a throw-back. The King seemed about to believe this when someone unfortunately mentioned the Queen's dwarf, Nabo. "Why," said one doctor, "the color of the child might have been caused by the black man's looking at the Queen."

"A look!" exploded the King. "It must have been a very penetrating look." The King demanded the dwarf brought before him. "He is dead, Your Majesty," said someone. The dwarf had been spirited away some time before.

LXII. I. Louis Zamor; 2. Louise-Marie, the Black Nun; 3. Maria Theresa, Queen of France.

The King was for having the child strangled as the fruit of adultery, and threatened the impeachment of the Queen, and the punishment of all her Spanish attendants. When he had stormed about until he was exhausted, the Queen's confessor took him aside, and assured him of the Queen's innocence. The mother, he said, had been bewitched. Evil spirits had caused the baby's color. One of the doctors assured him that it could be made white by an application of antimony. The King, somewhat calmed, decided to spare its life, but said that it could not be kept in the palace. Accordingly it was sent to a convent and a notice was inserted in the Gazette de France that it had been born dead.

A first-hand account of the birth is given by the King's own cousin, Mademoiselle de Montpensier. She says:

"The Dauphin told me of the trouble they had with the illness of the Queen and the crowds that were there when the King arrived; how the Bishop of Gardes, his first almoner, now Bishop of Langres, almost fainted with sorrow because the Prince and everybody laughed; that the Queen had been angry, and that the royal infant that had just been born, resembled a little Negro dwarf that M. de Beaufort had brought her from foreign lands—a little Negro that the Queen always had with her, and who was well-built for his kind of dwarf and Negro; that the child would not live and that I should not mention it to the Queen. When the Queen was a little better I went every day to the Louvre to see her. She told me that everyone had laughed at seeing the child, and the great pain their laughter had caused her."

The child lived. The King went once to the Convent of Moret to make sure that she was really alive. But she was kept a prisoner and pined for freedom and restoration to what she believed was her rank. One day, when the Dauphin (heir to the throne) was hunting in a nearby forest, and she heard who it was, she burst into tears and said from behind the bars of her cell: "It is my brother."

The Duke of St Simon, statesman, and one of the leading figures of the King's Court, said:

"Speaking of the secrets of the King, it is necessary to make amends for something else I had forgotten. Everyone was astonished at Fontainebleau this year, to see that hardly had the princess arrived than Mme. de Maintenon took her to the little convent of Moret, where there were likely to be no amusements or persons of her acquaintance. She returned there several times, which awoke curiosity and rumors—Mme. Maintenon went often to Fontainebleau and finally one got accustomed to seeing her go there.

"In the convent was a professed nun, a Negro woman, unknown to everyone and who never showed herself to anyone. Bontemps, first valet to the King and governor of Versailles, to whom I have spoken and to whom the domestic secrets are known, had placed her there quite young after paying a large sum, and a regular pension. He took great care that everything that could add to her comfort was provided. The late Queen went often to Fontainebleau to see her, and after her, Mme. de Maintenon.

"The Dauphin went there several times, and the princess and the children, and all asked for this Negro woman and treated her with kindness. She was receiving more marks of distinction than the best known or the most distinguished person there.

"It is said that she was the daughter of the King and the Queen, that her color had caused her to be hidden there, and after her disappearance, to be published that the Queen had had a miscarriage. Many of the people of the court believe this. But whatever it be, it remains a mystery."

Voltaire believed that the Black Nun was the daughter of the King by a Negro woman. Speaking of the King's children, he said, "It is believed, and with good reason, that the Nun in the convent of Moret is his daughter. She was very dark, almost black, and resembled the King. The King gave her a dot of 20,000 crowns and placed her in the convent. The belief that she was of royal birth gave her a pride of which the Mother Superior complained."

Voltaire adds that he visited the convent himself and saw her. He was accompanied by M. Caumartin, treasurer of France, who, he explains, "had a right to visit the convent."

But, says Le Notre, if the Black Nun had been the illegitimate daughter of the King by a black woman, would the Queen and her children have shown so much affectionate interest in her? "Would the Queen, Marie-Theresa, the Dauphin, the Duke and the Duchess of Bourgoyne, have shown the same attachment to her? Besides, the King had other adulterine children. Furthermore, she bore the name of both the King and Queen: Louise-Marie," he says.

Touchard LaFosse, who wrote an intimate account of the reign of Louis XIV, says, "Let us record here what is generally believed about the birth of this child. Duquesne had given to the Queen a young Negro, named Nabo, who was very pleasing in his manners, and amused Her Majesty in the solitude in which most of her time was passed. When this African learned to speak French, his chatter was funny, naive, and full of vivacity; he finished, it is said, by pleasing the Queen so much that all her virtue could not protect her from yielding to a weakness that the finest gentleman in Christendom would have solicited in vain.

"Nabo died suddenly, and soon afterwards, Her Majesty gave birth to a girl so black that Dr. Felix thought it his duty to say that it had been born dead. The black child was sent to the nuns of Moret, who reared it in ignorance of its origin . . .

"How much of this story is true, I cannot say exactly, but it is positive that a young Negro lived near to the Queen; that a black girl-child was sent to Moret at the same time the Queen had a child; and that every year, Bontems, (the King's confidante), took her a large sum in gold and a necklace of coral."

The Queen was much more to be pitied than blamed. Being quite plain, she was neglected by the King. The Duchess of Orleans, the King's sister-in-law, said of her:

"Her teeth were very ugly, being black and broken. It was said that this was caused by her constant eating of chocolate. She also frequently ate garlic, and was short and fat, and her skin was very white."

"No woman in the kingdom," says Des Grieux, "had more to complain about than Marie-Theresa. She was married to a despot whose egotism went as far as cruelty . . No man was admitted to her company and she was forced to enclose within herself the ardors of her imagination and control the fire of her Spanish temperament, whilst around her lords and ladies of the court whirled in an atmosphere of voluptuousness . . . A single servant had the privileges of coming into the Queen's room before she was out of bed; a young Negro, very short in height, but otherwise well-built. The consequence of this familiarity was that Marie-Theresa had a mulatto child."

Grave says: "The little Negro of Marie-Theresa is well-known . . . Receiving little attention from the Grand Monarch, she consoled herself with Nabo."

Victor Hugo asked: "What is the use of being a Queen if one cannot permit one's self to be treated familiarly by a Negro?"

According to Beaujoint, the Black Nun was honored "as one of those Black Madonnas attributed to St. Luke, which performs miracles and attracts pilgrims. There is no Black Madonna that is not miraculous. The color compels it."

She figured in one of the most romantic love stories of later days. It is said that the King's nephew, the Duke of Chartres, fell violently in love with her on a visit to the convent, and spirited her away. When, however, the King refused to give his consent to the marriage, the Duke was forced to return her to the convent, where she remained until her death.

Her picture hangs in the art gallery of the Library of St. Genevieve in the Latin Quarter of Paris. It represents a black woman with bright eyes, a prominent nose, thick lips and a long chin. The lower part of the face is unmistakably Negroid. Specimens of her handwriting are preserved.

The original documents about her disappeared as mysteriously as her supposed father, Nabo. All that remains at the Library is the original cover.

which bears the title: "Documents concerning The Princess Louise-Marie, daughter of Louis XIV and Marie-Theresa."

Le Notre, G., "La Religieuse Noire"; Le Monde Illustré, 12 Fevrier, 1898.
Beaujoint, J., "Alcoves de Reine", p. 431, Paris, 1879.
La Chatre, M., "Histoire de Papes", etc., Vol. 9-10, Paris, 1842-43.
Des Grieux, "L'Amour dans tous les Temps", Vol. I, p. 1432, Paris, 1888.
Lacroix, P., "Oeuvres Illustrés de Bibliophile Jacob-La Folle d'Orlèans, Vol. III, Paris, 1851-52.
Montpensier, Mlle. de, "Memoires", 1664 (Tome V, p. 118-119, Paris, 1728.)
"Intermediare des Chercheurs et des Curieux, Vol. 60, pp. 684, 917, Paris, 1909.
Blumenbach, "Anthropological Treatises, p. 111. London, 1865.
St. Simon, "Memoires", Vol. I, p. 258, years 1697-81.
Touchard La Fosse, "Oeil de Boeuf," Tome II, pp. 192-193, Paris.
Boinet, Amedée, "Catalogue des Oeuvres d'Art Bibliothèque St. Genevieve", Paris.
Voltaire. Siècle de Louis XIV, Vol. II. p. 186. Paris, 1784.
NOTE: That laughter in the Queen's chamber was possible during the birth of the Black Nun may be explained by the fact that as late as 1856, Queens of France gave birth publicly so that their subjects could see that another child wasn't being foisted on them. Should the child be born suddenly, the navel-string would have to remain uncut until the crowd could be summoned. When Marie Antoinette had her first child the crowd of peasants in the room was so great that she fainted from suffocation. Madame de Campan reports, "Two savoyards got up on the furniture in order to see over everybody's head." (Memoires sur la Vie de Marie Antoinette, pp. 158-58, Paris, 1876. Intermediare des Chercheurs et des Curieux, Vol. 41, p. 761, 899.)

See Chapter Eight, "Nature Knows No Color-Line" for additional research and for race mixture as a result of the second world war.

most used — 50 centimes
Postage Stamp for France's
Colonial Exposition, Paris,
1931. It was in the issues
and 1½ francs.

Chapter Twenty-two

BAUDELAIRE AND JEANNE DUVAL

TO find a love story as touching as that of Charles Baudelaire and Jeanne Duval, one must go to grand opera. It is as full of pity as Manon or Camille with the exception that it was real.

Baudelaire is France's greatest modern poet. No writer of any century is more original, or possessed greater genius. He was also an art, music and literary critic of the finest sensitivity. Innumerable are the writers and artists to whom he gave a new understanding of life.

Unlike most genuises, he began in comfortable circumstances. His father was of the wealthy upper class and was tutor to the children of the Duke of Choiseul-Praslin, and later secretary of the French Senate. His mother came from a rich English family. His father died when he was six years old and his mother married a general, who was later ambassador to Britain.

Baudelaire was unusually handsome and dressed in the height of fashion. Scintillating and gay he dashed off witty verses with ease. His views on art, music, and literature were listened to with respect in the most brilliant salons, and he had withal an air of disdain that made people look up to him.

His disdain was most evident in his dealings with women. Refined and beautiful women in his own circle sighed for him in vain. "Women," he would say, "are natural, therefore abominable." Again, "Women should be barred from churches. What kind of conversation could a woman have with God?"

Once when a beautiful and cultured woman of his own class and race yielded to him too easily, and wrote asking him not to think badly of her, he replied: "You see, ma belle cherie, I have odious prejudices against women. In short, I have no faith. You have a beautiful soul, but after all, it is a feminine soul . . . A few days ago you were a divinity, which is so agreeable, so fine, so inviolable. But now you are only a woman to me."

But this scorner of women was to meet his match. Jeanne Duval was a nobody. She was only a black girl from Haiti, with no training, no education, no money. But she had charm—an exotic, elusive charm. When she walked she held her head in a way that made people turn to look at her.

One evening when Baudelaire was twenty-one he had dinner at a friend's house and finding it too early to go home took a walk.

Coming to a wretched little theatre with glaring posters, he stopped to look. The play advertised was "Le Systeme de Mon Oncle" (My Uncle's Plan). The title struck him as nonsensical. He was sure he would be bored. But he bought a ticket and went in.

The play was all he had imagined it and worse. But though strongly tempted to leave he sat there. Then something really happened. A tall, brown-skinned girl came on the stage. She was dressed as a maid but she carried herself like a queen. And her voice, too, was queenly, impelling,

LXIII. Charles Baudelaire and Jeanne Duval. (Sketch of latter by Baudelaire)

aloof, yet strangely musical. She spoke only three words, "Madame est servie" (Dinner is served), and left.

The poet in Baudelaire was electrified. He sat there dazed waiting for her to re-appear. But she did not.

He must see her again. It seemed to him as if worlds, eternities had been overturned. The only thing that seemed to matter in his life, hence-forth, was "this deity brown as the nights." Memories of the tropics surged back to him. He had visited India and Madagascar and their dark-skinned inhabitants had bewitched him. On his return he had told his friends a story—pure fiction—of how, in Africa, while lodging with a family to which his parents had sent him, he had gone off to the mountains with a tall Negro girl and of the strange dishes they had cooked while hundreds of nude little Negroes danced around.

Baudelaire waited until the end of the play, then he called an usher and heard to his dismay that the three words she had spoken constituted her entire part, and that she had left the theatre immediately after.

All the next day, he could think of nothing else but her. That night he was at the theatre again with a bouquet of roses and a note begging her to receive him at the stage-door the following evening.

Let us look a little more closely at the woman who had disturbed so profoundly this aristocratic dreamer. She was tall and supple with well-moulded hips. Her well-developed breasts rose firm and apart from an almost flat chest; she had a straight little nose; and a mane of thick, black, unruly hair. Of books she knew little but she was a past mistress of the art of feminine seductiveness. She knew men. By all accounts she had been supplementing her slender salary at the theatre by following the oldest profession in the world.

Nadar, a friend of Baudelaire, says of her, "A tall, too tall girl, taller by a head than any other girl in the play. There was nothing extraordinary about her except that she was a Negro, a real Negro, at least, incontestably a mulatto, the white in her not being enough to subdue the copper in her face, her neck, and her hands.

"She was rather pretty besides, with a special beauty . . . for the subtle and refined. Under the thick and mischievous masses of black, almost woolly hair, appeared two eyes, very black and 'large as sighs;' a delicate little nose with nostrils exquisitely carved; a mouth that was Egyptiac, although West Indian—a mouth like that of the Goddess Isis—admirably furnished with full lips of good design."

Banville, another of Baudelaire's friends says, "A colored girl, very tall, who carried her brown head superbly and with unconscious grace—a head crowned with hair strongly crisped; in whose regal stride, full of a certain ferocious grace, there was at once something of the divine and the animal."

Jeanne Duval was astonished when she saw Baudelaire. He was so respectful, so courteous, so unlike the men she knew. She was even more amazed when he addressed her as if she were a grand dame. Puzzled, she thought he was making fun of her. She saw his fashionable clothes, his well-cared hands, and his air of wealth. She needed money and accepted his invitation to supper.

From then on they met frequently. She, the born coquette, pretended indifference. She knew instinctively that she could hold him in no other way. Intellectually deficient she said little and became an attentive listener. It is even likely that she was by nature passive.

At last he insisted that she leave the theatre and belong entirely to him. He installed her in a fine apartment and gave her a blonde maid. He himself lived in a fashionable hotel nearby but passed most of the time with her, spending money freely on her and taking her to deluxe restaurants and places of amusement.

He loved Jeanne with all a poet's passion; but his woman-hating instincts were still very much alive and at times he hated her as strongly as he loved her. In all great loves, there is an element of hate. Moreover, Baudelaire was contradictory in everything. At times he was hard and perverse and impossible to get along with; at other times, he was most tender, sympathetic, and indulgent. He adored beauty, yet he revelled in the gutter. A devout Christian, he glorified Cain, the murderer. It took a clever woman to hold such a combination of saint and devil.

Jeanne's race and type of beauty magnetized him more and more. And she was always harder, more indifferent, more disdainful than he. If she loved him, which she probably did in her own way, she rarely showed it. Once she made him feel that she had been won, she knew all would be lost. He says himself that he loved her best when she fled from him. Maupassant says that in love there is always a conqueror and a conquered. Jeanne knew this by instinct.

She made him suffer and it fired his genius. Hitherto it had been spent in aimless dandyism; now it burst into bright, magnificent flame. Baudelaire calls her his "inspiration," nevertheless, his biographers are almost unanimous in their wholesale denunciation of her. They say that she was "lazy," "crapulous," and devoid of spirit, talent, and charm. But she was his ideal.

Where others saw laziness, he saw the languidity of the tropics. Her indolence conjured up for him visions of palm-trees, of somnolent Asia and languorous Africa, of delightful oases where one could dream among unbounded wastes of sand. She was the ground that sucked up the wine of souvenirs; her eyes reflected beautiful minerals where the angel inviolate mingles with the antique Sphinx; the mirroring of her dark skin made him think of the scintillating beauty of the stars, for a sight of which he would have "changed his humanity and betrayed his God."

The poet suffers in order that humanity may benefit. He is like the dog, faithful friend of man, tortured on the vivisection table. Jeanne's apparent indifference, and the cause she gave him, real and fancied, for jealousy, increased his tortures. One moment he is full of hate and loathing for her; the next he is in ecstacies—"floating on the perfume of her presence as the souls of others float on music." She was at once his torture and his delight.

The real torture began when his money was gone, all squandered. The story of their love, especially from this time onwards, is harrowing. Contrasted with the tranquil, well-ordered, respectable love of proper folk, it is sordid and terrible—he, suffering from an incurable social disease contracted at the age of twenty; she, a heavy drinker, stricken with paralysis; he, burdened with debt, and resorting to opium; she, clamoring for money, to pay their debts; he, leaving her, only to return again as the gambler to his game, the drunkard to his bottle.

There were, however, moments of exquisite joy, "when he loved to gaze at leisure over her beautiful form," or "to lay drowsily in the shadow of her beautiful breasts." She wrote down his poems as they came to him. Some of them were written about her and then named.

In one of his moments of great despair he wrote his mother, "Jeanne has become an obstacle to my happiness . . . In the past she had some qualities but she has lost them. I shall never see her again. Let her do what she will. Go to hell if she wants to . . ."

Yet when they drifted apart again, he wrote, believing that this was the end, "My liaison of fourteen years with Jeanne is broken. I did all that was humanly possible to prevent the rupture. This tearing apart, this struggle has lasted fifteen days. Jeanne replied imperturbably that nothing can be done with my character and that anyhow, I shall see myself some day thanking her for the resolution. There you see the gross bourgeois wisdom of women. For myself, I know that no matter what luck, pleasure, money, or fame, Fate may hold in store for me, I shall always miss this woman. I had placed in her all my hopes like a gambler; she was my only recreation, my only pleasure, my only chum, and in spite of all the inner agitation of our stormy union, the idea of an irreparable break had never entered clearly into my mind. Even now, though I am calm, I surprise myself thinking, when I see some fine object, a lovely landscape, or anything agreeable, why isn't she here to admire it with me . . . the shock was so violent . . . not to mention a kind of obscure veil before my eyes and an eternal singing in my ears. When I saw that the break was irreparable, I was seized with indescribable fury . . . for ten days I could not sleep. I vomited, and had to hide myself because I was crying all the time."

They made up again, however, and five years later he was still with her, giving her money when he had any.

But harassed by debt, and gnawed by disease and inner agitation, he sank lower and lower, his life, once full of promise as an all too beautiful morning, ebbing sadly away. Towards the last, propped up in bed, he pitifully mumbled Latin verses while his friends played Wagner for him.

And Jeanne, how did she end? No one knows. Most likely in a pauper's grave. Nadar said that he saw her three years after his death on the street on crutches.

Of her real history, the most enthusiastic Baudelaireans know little. Baudelaire's mother destroyed all her letters after his death. "If Jeanne had only loved my son," said the mother weeping, "I would have gladly taken her to my heart. But in all her letters I saw not a single word of love, only demands for money."

Baudelaire's mother and all his friends of both sexes, with one exception resented her hold on him. Prejudice of class and race have influenced biographers. Yet, Jeanne Duval must have been remarkable to have inspired so great a poet. How else could those marvelous verses, crystalized out of the ferment she produced, could ever have been written?

There are values of life—and tremendous ones too—that proper folk never dream of. Beautiful and beneficial thoughts do rise at times from the depths of human debasement. Who can appreciate good that has not tasted deeply of evil?

Of "Fleurs du Mal," Baudelaire's masterpiece, Arthur Symons, his English translator, says: "That masterpiece has rarely, if ever, been equalled, has rarely, if ever, been surpassed." The finest poems of that beautiful work were inspired by Jeanne and are about her. Baudelaire's work will live as long as the French language lives, and as long as his name lives, so will hers.

Poems to Jeanne

Baudelaire's most ecstatic poem to Jeanne is "Chanson d'Apres-midi" (Afternoon Song). In this he calls her his "terrible passion," and says how "over her skin, perfume hovers as from an incense burner," how "under her satin slippers and silken hose, he places his great joy, his genius, his whole destiny," and how "her soul cures his joy by its light and color."

The most denunciatory one is "The Vampire." "Be thou forever and ever accursed . . ."

The following are two poems to her translated by Arthur Symons:

Sed Non Satiata

Bizarre Deity, dark as infernal nights,
Whose perfume mixes with musk Arabian
Work of some Obi, Faustus, that learned man
Sorceress of ebony thighs, child of midnights,
I prefer to all things, opium and the nights,

Thy mouth's elixir, strange as a Pavane;
When towards thee my desires in caravan
Pass, thine eyes assuage mine appetites.
By those black eyes, vent-holes of thy soul's shame.
Oh pitiless Demon, pour on me less flame;
I am not the Styx to embrace thee nine times, nay . . .

Parfum Exotique

When with eyes closed as in an opium dream
I breathe the odor of thy passionate breast
I see in vision hell's infernal stream
And the sunset fires that have no instant's rest
An idle island where the unnatural scheme
Of Nature is by savorous fruits oppressed
And where men's bodies are their women's guest
And women's bodies are not what they seem . . .

Thee I adore as the vault of night's pure madness
O silent and taciturn, O thou source of pure sadness
I love thee more, O fair, when thou fliest from me
And when thou seemest, night's sister, the slyest from me,
Before league upon league the Sea's insanity
Shall sever us from the immense light's vanity.

I advance to the attack, I climb to the assaults whose storms are
As it were beside a corpse where a crowd of worms are
And I cherish thee, O beast implacable and cruel
Because thou art more wonderful than a jewel!

Mauclair, C., "La Vie Amoureuse de Baudelaire", Paris.
Crepet, E., "Charles Baudelaire", p. 52-56, Paris, 1906.
Praz, M., The Romantic Agony, p. 44.

ADDITIONAL NOTES ON RACE-MIXING IN
EUROPEAN LITERATURE

François Beroalde de Verville (1558-1612), in "Le Moyen de Parvenir," mentions a married woman, who, at sight of a gay and gallant young Negro, desired him so greatly that she had a stomach-ache, which could not be cured until "qu'elle avoit le fit coucher sur elle." She found him all that she hoped—plus chaud qu'un Français. As a result she had a black baby. The husband received the blame, being told that he had had intercourse with her near his writing desk and the ink there had had an effect on the child's color. "Vraiment, vous avez bien besogné. Je m'en doutais bien! voilá il est chu de l'encre dedans si que vous avez fait un enfant noir comme un Maure." (pp. 159-160, Paris, 1841.)

In La Maitresse Noire, Louis-Charles Royer, contrasts the white wife, Yvonne, with the black mistress, Mouk, as follows, "La dure lumière accablait la blanche; sa peau semblait comme éteinte. Sur la chair de la noire, les rayons de l'astre jouaient ainsi que sur un cuivre poli." (pp. 215-16, Paris, 1928.)

On page 81, Yvonne calls in her house-boy Gorko, after the white lover has left the house. She has just assured the white man that the Negro loves her like a dog and wouldn't harm her, "I say he loves me as a dog," she repeats. She regards the black as inferior but she desires him just the same, and strokes his hand. "Elle sentait sous sa paume la chair du male noir, ferme et lisse comme du cuir de Russie. Elle s'approcha, a le frôler, regardant le duel de leurs peaux contraire . . .

"Brusquement, elle colla ses seins contre le torse dur, détourna sa bouche du sombre visage qui se penchait. offrant son corps."

Claire Goll's novel Le Negre Jupiter Enlève Europa (The Negro, Jupiter Carries Off Europe), deals with the love affair and marriage of a rich and sensitive African wih a Swedish girl. The hero of the story is supposed to be Prince Behanzin of Dahomey.

Louise Faure-Favier's Blanche et Noir deals principally with the union of Senegalese and Frenchwomen. She asserts strongly the alleged superiority of the mulatto offspring to the native French. The book is a strong argument for race-mixing.

Anatole France. in "Balthasar" makes the black king a favorite with the white women. The Queen of Sheba, who is depicted as white, is in love with him, and is jealous of the black queen of Ethiopia.

Maupassant's Boitelle dealing with the love of a white man for a black girl was already mentioned. See also Raymond Escholier's Mahmadou-Fofana, which is the story of a Senegalese soldier in the last war.

D. H. Lawrence in Lady Chatterley's Lover (unexpurgated edition) makes Connie's lover say, "I was really getting bitter. I thought there was no sex left; never a woman who'd really 'c . . e' naturally with a man: except black women. and somehow, well, we're white men: and they're a bit like mud." (p. 240, Odyssey Press ed. Hamburg.)

"White Women, Colored Men," by Henry Champly, is a strange combination of fact, fancy, and befuddlement. The writer finds that a white skin is "really ugly," but he calls it "Divine," and tries to do for a white epidermis what Hitler does for the Aryan. The world's grandest prize, he says, is the white woman, and he predicts a war between the men of the darker races and the white man for the possession of the white woman. Long & Co. London. 1936.

NOTES ON RACE-MIXING

Dr. Magnus Hirschfeld, writing on the flood of sexual irregularities let loose by the first world war in all the European capitals, tells of certain secret clubs maintained for Russian princesses, French noblewomen, rich war-widows, and over-sexed women with plenty of money. He says, "Wild female sex-hyenas found, in these secret clubs ample opportunity to draw near to attractive representatives of the black race, both soldiers and civilians, for a number of shrewd *entrepreneurs* in this entertainment business had soon realized the attraction that Negroes could exert upon these irresponsible and rampant females. As a matter of fact, when these blacks were enlisted they were inveigled into service partially by the promise of white meat waiting for them in Europe, where, they were informed, white women were very fond of their dark skin. The motive is said to have influenced many to join the ranks." Sexual History of the World War, p. 216, N. Y., 1937.

(In this connection see what was said of the sex lure to foreign lands on page 142 of this book.)

✳ ✳ ✳ ✳ ✳

Hans Habe, a member of the French Foreign Legion, who fought in France, in June 1940, tells of the atrocious treatment of the colored soldiers captured by the Nazis. He says:

"The Germans' hatred of the colored people seemed deeply rooted. I was soon to understand why. Dozens of current German periodicals, pamphlets, and newspapers portrayed the Negroes as cannibals and fed German soldiers with false statistics and pseudo-scientific data. One special issue of the *Racial-political Institute* explained that more than 21 per cent—that is, almost a quarter—of the French population was 'tainted' with Negro blood. . . . But the purpose of the propaganda was clear. As the Germans knew the French army would send the well-trained and relatively well-equipped colonial troops to the front lines, they tried to convince the German soldiers that if they did not kill the Negroes they risked having their throats cut. Unfortunate black prisoners told me that the Germans fought them much more bitterly than they did us. . . ."

"Intermarriage between whites and blacks or half-breeds and whites is forbidden. According to the Nuremburg racial laws, sexual intercourse between members of the two races is subject to sanctions including the death penalty." (The Nation, March 1, 1941).

APPENDIX TO CHAPTERS IV AND V

Did the Negro Originate in Africa or Asia? Further Opinions from Various Writers on the Mixed Nature of the Peoples of Asia and Africa

H. J. Peake says, "It is just possible that the development of the black skin and the woolly hair took place in New Guinea and Melanesia out of the dark-skinned frizzly-haired people that at first occupied all the region between South India and the East Indies." ("Early Steps in Human Progress," p. 23, London, 1933.)

According to Dorsey: "Wherever the Indian Ocean touches land it finds dark-skinned people with strong developed jaws, relatively long arms, and frizzly hair. Call that the Indian Ocean or the Negroid division of the human race." ("Why We Behave Like Human Beings," p. 44, New York, 1926.)

Sir H. H. Johnston goes into the matter deeply, approaching it from a variety of angles.

"Where did the Negro sub-species arise?" he asks. "In what part of the Old World did he specialize from the basal type of Homo sapiens, from the Australoid group, the outcome of early Homo primigenius? Possibly in Southern Europe, more probably in India. . . . This Negroid type (the Grimaldi) would seem judging from skulls and skeletal remains, to have penetrated northwestwards as far as Brittany, and quite possibly to Britain and Ireland. Eastwards it is traceable to Switzerland and Italy, coming down through the neolithic to the historical period and fusing with the northern races. In modern times and at the present day it is obvious that there is an old Negritic element in the population of North Africa, Spain, France, Ireland, and West Britain, Italy, Sardinia, Sicily and the countries bordering on the Eastern Mediterranean, not entirely to be accounted for by the historical slave trade.

"Yet the ancient Negroid elements in these European populations seem to possess slightly more affinity with Asiatic Negroes or with those of Northeastern Africa than with the typical African Negroes or Bushmen of today.

"In spite of these very interesting discoveries in the Grimaldi caverns, the deductions to be drawn from the rest of our limited knowledge point rather to India as the original birthplace of the Negro sub-species. . . .

"Assuming, then, that the Negro sub-species was originated in the Indian Peninsula, we can, in imagination, see this type of dark-skinned, spiral-haired, flat-nosed man turning eastwards as well as westwards, invading Burma and the Malay Peninsula and Archipelago on the heels of the retreating Australoids and securing as their exclusive home the Andaman Islands. (They were probably exterminated in the Nicobars by the Mongolians that followed them.) To this day dwarf Negro people survive in the Far East—the Samang in the forest of the Malay Peninsula and the Aeta in the Philippines. There are traces of the passage of a Negroid people through Sumatra and Borneo, in the island of Timor, and markedly so in New Guinea, though here they have mingled with the Australoid and produced the well-marked Papuan race. The existing population of the Solomon Islands, of New Ireland, and of the New Hebrides, are much more Negro-like in physical characteristics; in fact, most nearly akin to the African Negro of all the Asiatic or Australasian peoples. Asiatic Negroes also seem to have entered Australia from New Guinea and to have passed down the eastern part of that continent till they reached the then peninsula of Tasmania, not, of course, without mingling with the Australoids. There is a Negroid (Melanesian) element in Fiji, and as far west as the Hawaii Archipelago and among the Maoris of New Zealand; in much less degree also, in Burma, Annam, Hainan, Formosa, the Riu-Kiu Islands, and Southern Japan. . . ." ("The Negro in the New World," pp. 24-27. London, 1910.)

In another discussion he says: "The Asiatic Negro spread—we can hardly explain how, unless the land connections of those days were more extended—through Eastern

Australia to Tasmania and from the Solomon Islands to New Caledonia and even to New Zealand to Fiji and Hawaii. The Negroid element in Burma and Annam is therefore easily to be explained by supposing that in ancient times Southern Asia had a Negro population ranging from the Persian Gulf to Indo-China and the Malay Archipelago." ("Who are the Backward Peoples," p. 15, London, 1920.)

The Negro strain in the Polynesian is discussed in his book "The Black Man's Part in the War" (p. 11), which also contains a good summary of the Negro strain in the peoples of Africa and Asia.

E. Balfour says: "Ethnologists are of the opinion that Africa has had an important influence in the colonization of Southern Asia, of India, and of the Easter Islands in times prior to authentic history or tradition. The marked African features of some of the people in the extreme south of the Peninsula of India, the Negro and Negrito races of the Andamans and Great Nicobar, the Semang, Bila, and Jakun of the Malay Peninsula, and the Negrito and Negro, Papuan and Malagasi races of the islands of the Indian Archipelago, Australia, and Polynesia indicate the extent which characterizes their colonization . . . the spiral-haired Negro race seems to have preceded the lank-haired brown race . . . When we consider the position of India between the two great Negro provinces, that on the west being still mainly Negro, even in most of its improved races, and that on the east preserving the ancient Negro basis in points so near India as the Andamans and Kedah, it becomes highly probable that the African element in the population of the Peninsula has been transmitted from an archaic period before the Semitic, Turanian, and Iranian races entered India and when the Indian Ocean had Negro tribes along its northern as well as its eastern and western shores . . . Perhaps all the original population of Southern Arabia, and even of the Semitic lands, generally was once African." ("Negro Races" in "Cyclopedia of India," Vol. II. pp. 1073-80.)

J. P. Widney says: "They (the Negroes) once occupied a much wider territory and wielded a vastly greater influence upon earth than they do now. They are found chiefly in Africa, yet traces of them are to be found through the islands of Malayasia, remnants, no doubt of that more numerous black population which seems to have occupied tropical Asia before the days of the Semites, the Mongols, and the Brahminic Aryan. Back in the centuries which are scarcely historic, where history gives only vague hintings, are traces of a widespread, primitive civilization, crude, imperfect, garish, barbaric, yet ruling the world from its seats of power in the valley of the Ganges, the Euphrates, and the Nile, and it was of the black races. The first Babylon seems to have been of a Negroid race. The earliest Egyptian civilisation seems to have been Negroid. It was in the days before the Semite was known in either land. The black seems to have built up a great empire, such as it was, by the waters of the Ganges, before Mongol or Aryan. Way down under the mud and slime of the beginnings . . . is the Negroid contribution to the fair superstructure of modern civilisation." ("Race Life of the Aryans," Vol. II, pp. 238-39, 241, New York, 1907.)

This Indo-Negro civilization probably spread as far as South Africa, where there are ruins of an ancient civilization, believed by some to be the land of Ophir, from where Solomon got his gold.

Some writers who do not wish to give the Negro credit declare that the ruins are "Semitic" whatever that means. But G. Caton Thompson says, "It is inconceivable to me, now that I have studied the ruins, how the theory of Semitic or civilised origin could ever have been formulated. Every detail . . . appears to be typically Bantu." ("Antiquity," Vol. III, p. 433, 1929.) Also see Ordt, J. F. "Origin of the Bantu," Cape Town, 1907.

APPENDIX TO CHAPTERS I TO IX—PART I

Black Gods and Messiahs

Since Man makes his gods in his own image, a study of the earliest gods and messiahs offers considerable proof of the earliest human race, its evolution into a mulatto type, and lastly, its change to the present white type.

The earliest gods and messiahs on all the continents were black. Research has yielded an impressive amount of material on the subject. It will be seen, too, that the messiahs, some of whom lived many centuries before Christ, had lives which so closely parallel that of Christ that it seems most likely that the story of the latter was adapted from them. Moreover, the word, Christ, comes from the Indian, Krishna or Chrishna, which means "The Black One."

The Buddhas

The Cambridge Encyclopedia summarizes the lives of the earliest Messiahs preceding Jesus of Nazareth, as follows:

"India B.C. 1366... This is the 'First Buddha' of the Hindu Pantheon and there are many indications that the date is more or less correct though the mythos evidently belongs to Ies Christna. This Messiah was foretold by prophets; he was the son of the Holy Spirit and the Virgin, Maia; he was born in the village or town of Rajagriha; was recognised and worshipped by the Magi and by kings; the messianic star stood over the place of his nativity; a brilliant nimbus of light surrounded the holy infant's head; his complexion was black; his hair woolly; he was prematurely wise and as he grew up his doctrines embodied in the Puranas were promulgated by ten disciples. Though he came to reform mankind and save the world he was himself persecuted by the reigning king, who caused him to be crucified at the age of thirty-three years. To judge the dead, Buddha descended to the nether-world, where he remained three days and nights. Then he arose and ascended bodily to heaven. His sacraments were the eucharist and baptism; his epigraphic symbols were the cross and the swastika..." (pp. 106-107.)

"Egypt B.C. 1350... Osiris was sun-rayed; his complexion was black and his hair was woolly. He was included in a slaughter of the innocents ordered by Typhon from which he, of course, escaped. His legitimacy was proved by numerous miracles; some of his doctrines appear in the Book of the Dead; the number of his disciples was ten; he was crucified on the vernal equinox; he descended to hell where he remained three days and nights to judge the dead and rose again and ascended bodily to heaven." (pp. 107-108.) See also Diodorus Siculus on Osiris.

"India B.C. 1332... Birth of Ies Christna, the ninth incarnation of Iesnu or Vishnu. This Christna like the Christ of Europe, who came nearly fourteen centuries later had a heavenly father (Brahma) and an earthly one (Josa); his mother was Maryamma; the Messianic star appeared at his birth; he was born among cow-herds; he was recognised by the three wise men; and his father was called on to pay taxes. Christna's head shone with a divine effulgence; his complexion was black and his hair woolly. His doctrines caused his betrayal and death; he partook of the last supper with his ten disciples and was condemned to death by Kansa and crucified at Kusinara upon a tree in the thirty-third year; the sun was eclipsed; the earth shook and ghosts walked." (pp. 110-111.)

"Japan B.C. 1000... Era of Buddha...as in most other images he is represented with woolly hair—a pecularity that enables this divinity to be traced under all disguises of name and caprices of art." pp. 126-127.)

"India B.C. 721... Era of the Nativity of Buddha, son of Maya... Buddha was born among shepherds to the accompaniment of flowers, music, and perfumes. He was recognised as the Expected One by the seers or Magi; his head was rayed; his complexion was black and his hair was woolly." (p. 137.)

"China B.C. 667 . . . Era of Lao-kuin or Lao-tsze . . . Lao-tsze was a divine incarnation in a human form! He was 'born of a virgin black in complexion and as beautiful as jasper.'" (p. 142.)   Also Thornton: "History of China, Vol. I. 134-37.

"Mexico A.D. 722. .   Quetzalcoatl...was recognised as the Messiah by seers and astrologers; his head was rayed; his complexion was black; his hair was woolly; he performed numerous miracles; he fasted forty days; he was tempted by the Evil One; he resisted, was persecuted and eventually crucified on the vernal equinox."

"Bacchus.. (according to Ovid, Pausanius, and Anacreon)...his complexion was black and his hair woolly..." (p. 117.)   Cambridge Encyc., p. 198, New York, 1899.

Higgins cites several ancient Greek writers on the black color of the Greek gods. (Anacalypsis, Vol. I, pp. 311-12, London, 1836.)

With regard to the Negro origin of the earliest gods, T. A. Buckley in "Great Cities of the Ancient World" similarly says:

"The personifications of the Buddha of India are three; the past, the present, and the future; they are generally represented half-naked with woolly heads in a sitting posture."

T. Inman describes the ancient gods as of Negro origin, declaring, "From the woolly texture of the hair, I am inclined to assign to the Buddha of India; the Fuhi of China; the Sommonacom of the Siamese; the Xaha of the Japanese and the Quetzalcoatl of the Mexicans, the same and indeed an African, or rather Nubian, origin." ("Ancient Pagan and Modern Symbolism," 2 ed., N. Y., 1875.)

Godfrey Higgins says: "The religion of Buddha of India is well-known to have been very ancient. In the most ancient temples scattered throughout Asia where his worship is yet continued, he is found black as jet with the flat face, thick lips and curly hair of the Negro. Several statues of his may be met in the Museum of the East India Company. There are exemplars of him brooding on the face of the deep upon a coiled serpent. To what time must we allot this Negro? He will have been proved prior to the god, Christna (Krishna). He must have been prior to or contemporaneous with the black empire supposed by Sir William Jones to have existed at Sidon. The religion of the Negro God is found in the ruins of his temples and other circumstances to have been spread over an immense extent of country, even to the remotest parts of Britain and to have been professed by devotees inconceivably numerous " (Anacalypsis, Vol. I. p. 52, London. 1836, or New York, 1927.)

Praising Buddhist art of early times as Negro, Higgins says: "In consequence of the prejudice (for it is really prejudice against the Negro; or I ought rather to say against the possibility of a Negro being learned and scientific arising from an acquaintance with the present Negro character) I admit with *great difficulty* the theory of all the early astronomical knowledge of the Chaldees having been acquired or invented by his race and that the Chaldees were originally Negroes. But this prejudice wears away when I go to the precursors of the Brahmins, the Buddhists, and when I reflect upon the skill in the Fine Arts which they must have possessed when they executed the most beautiful and most ancient sculptures in the museum of the India House and the knowledge of astronomy shown in their cycles of stone. That the Buddhists were Negroes the icons of their God clearly prove." (Vol. I, p. 364.)

"We have found the black complexion or something relating to it whenever we have approached the origin of nations. The Alma Mater, the Goddess Multimammia, the founders of the oracles; the Memnon or first idols were always black." (Vol. I, p. 286.)

"In my search for the origin of the Ancient Druids I continually found, at last, that my labours terminated with something black. Thus the oracles of Dodona and of Apollo at Delphi were founded by Black Doves. Doves are not often, I believe, never black. Osiris and his Bull were black; all the Gods and Goddesses of Greece were black, at least this was the case with Jupiter, Bacchus, Hercules, Apollo, Ammon. The Goddess Venus. Isis, Hecati, Juno, Metis, Ceres, Cybele were black in the Campdoglio at Rome." (p. 332.)

"I think the different eras of Buddhism may be observed in its monuments. Its first era is shown by Buddha as a Negro." (p. 524.)

Higgins is of the opinion that the Buddhist Negroes were the first colonists of Britain Similarly. of Africa: "This irruption of Negroes, of the countrymen of the flat-faced Buddha from Upper India were, perhaps, the first people who settled and inhabited Africa, built and made the colossal bust of Memnon." "The Celtic Druids," p. 162. London, 1829.)

XXVI. 1. Negro head from Ancient Egypt, showing woolly hair like that of the Buddhas'; 2. Chinese Buddha; 3. Japanese Buddha; 4. Indian Buddha; 5. Javanese Buddha; 6. Siamese Buddha; 7. Indian Buddha.

For a fine collection of these woolly-haired Buddhas see the Buddhas of the Tang Period, A.D. 618-906, and those of the Ming Period (1348-1643), in the Field Museum of Chicago; also those in the Guimet Museum, Paris.

There is a tendency to deny that the ancient Buddhas were Negroes despite the fact that they are portrayed with Negroid hair and features. We are told that the curls on the heads of the Buddhas were originally snails that settled on the scalp to protect it from the burning sun. But is not the ethnological explanation less miraculous? Negro peoples lived and still live in India.

If the curls on the Buddhas are snails then the locks of ancient Negroes executed by Egyptian and Grecian artists, and even those on the Negro on the statue of Abraham Lincoln in the New York Public Library, must also be snails. All look alike.

The hair of certain later Buddhas—Indian, Chinese, Japanese, and Indo-Chinese—has evolved into a cap-like covering, which indeed, is often mistaken for a head-covering of some sort. On closer scrutiny this supposed head-covering will be seen to retain the woolly curls.

In this connection, F. Wilford says. "It is certain that very ancient statutes of Gods in India have crisp hair and the features of Negroes. Some have caps or tiaras with curls depending over their foreheads according to the precise meaning of the epithet, Cutila-laca. Others, indeed, seem to have their locks curled by art and braided above in a thick knot; but I have seen many idols on which the woolly appearance of the hair was so well presented as to preclude all doubt; and we naturally suppose that they were made by the Cutila-Cesas when they prevailed in this country. The Brahmans ascribe these idols to the Buddhas, and nothing hurts them more than to say that any of their own Gods had the figure of Habashis or Negroes; and even the hair of the Buddha himself for whom they have no small degree of respect, they consider as twisted in braids, like that of some modern Sannyasis. But this will not account for the thick lips and flat noses of those ancient images; nor can it be reasonably doubted that a race of Negroes formerly had power and preeminence in India. In several parts of India the mountaineers still have resemblance to Negroes in their countenance and hair which is curled and has a tendency to wool." ("Asiatick Researches," Vol. III, London, 1799.)

Black Gods of the New World

Black gods and messiahs were worshipped in the New World before Columbus. Africa and America, were in all probability once joined. Geologically, botanically, and zoologically they were very closely related. Camels, tigers, elephants have all been found.

There are evidences that all three "races"—the Negro, the Caucasian, and the Mongolian—occupied the New World thousands of years before Columbus, probably in the order named. They blended later to produce the so-called Indian, who, according to the region in which he lived, showed predominance in one of these three stocks.

With regard to the Negroes, C. C. Marquez says: "In the corresponding description already given may be noted that in the statutes (Fig. 13 & 14) which appear to be very ancient and are portrayed with singular attributes, are faithfully reproduced the characteristics of the Negro type. It is significant that this is not unique in America but that this Negro type is also seen in the most ancient Mexican sculptures, such as the great diorite head of Hueyapan and in the gigantic axe of Vera Cruz, which bear a striking resemblance to the statutes already mentioned."

Asking whether this signified that America in the remotest epochs was occupied by a Negro race, he adds. "This hypothesis is supported by the fact that the conquistadores found dispersed all over the New World small tribes which from the first were considered Negroes. In this respect, it may be noted that Vasco Nunez de Balboa on his expedition in search of the Southern Sea, encountered with great surprise, according to Gomara, that the Cuarecas of Panama had Negro slaves, which they were said to have obtained in remote lands.

"Further. the Negroes figure frequently in the most remote traditions of some American pueblos. Certain tribes of Darien say that when their ancestors arrived for the first time in that region it was inhabited by small black men who soon afterwards, retired in the forests while the Paejas and Tapalisas of the Cuna Cunas declare that their

XXVII. Buddhas 1 and 2 Javanese and Indian Buddha with woolly hair in cap design;
3. Mixed blood Buddha with frizzly hair.

origin goes back to a man and two woman, one Indian and the other Negro, who lived on the banks of the Tataruma.

"It is to this race that doubtlessly belongs the ancient skeletons of very distinct structure of two of the Red American races which have been found in various places from Bolivia to Mexico. Worthy of attention in this respect are two skulls, markedly prognathous, of low forehead, prominent cheek bones, and strong superciliary arches found in the mountains of Sumapaz by the distinguished Prof. Juan de Dios Carrasquilla, which in everything reminds one of the old Cro-Magnon.

"It is likely then, we repeat, that long ago the 'youthful' America was also a Negro continent and that the Otomies of Mexico; the Caracols of Haiti; the Argualos of Cutara; the Aravos of the Orinoco; the Porcijis and the Matayas of Brazil; the Manabis of Quito; the Chuanas of Darien; and the Albinos of Panama, are the remains of the aboriginal Negro race out of which developed later, what is known as the Red or American race.

"In this case, the two statues of which we have spoken, as well as its resemblances, the Mexican ones, are but relics of the original inhabitants left by the invaders who later inhabited the continent.

"Perhaps some day the dense mist that hides the remote past of the New World will be dissipated and there will be unfolded by Science brilliant and unknown horizons veiled today by darkness as profound as it is mysterious." ("Estudios Arquelogicos y Etnograficos, Vol I, pp. 270-73, Madrid, 1920.)

According to N. Leon:

"The oldest inhabitants of Mexico, according to some were Negroes, and according to others, the Otomies. The existence of Negroes and of giants is commonly believed by nearly all the races of our soil and in their various languages they had words to designate them. Several archaeological objects found in various localities demonstrate their existence, the most notable of which is the colossal granite head of Hueyapan, Vera Cruz, and an axe of the same located near the city. In Teotihuacan abound little heads of the Ethiopian type and paintings of Negroes. In Michoacan and Oaxaca the same have also been found. The almost total extinction of the Negroes during the time of the Spanish conquest and the memories of them in the most ancient traditions induce us to believe that the Negroes were the first inhabitants of Mexico." ("Historia-General de Mexico," p. 14, Mexico, 1919.)

Riva-Palacio says, "It is indisputable that in very ancient times before the existence of the Otomies the Negro race occupied our territory (Mexico) when the two continents were joined. This race brought its own religious cults and ideals." ("Mexico a traves de los siglos." Vol. I, pp. 63-67. Mexico, 1887.) He adds, "The Mexicans recall a Negro god, Ixtlilton, which means black-faced." (p. 163.)

According to the Cambridge Encyclopedia. Quetzalcoatl, the Mexican Messiah, was also black and woolly-haired; and woolly-haired, according to Buckley. "The Mexican god, Quetzalcoatl. is clearly Osiris of Egypt and Ciuacoatl is Isis." (Clavering, R. Current History Magazine, Jan., 1934.)

According to A. Hyatt Verril, an authority on the Central American Indian, a god, "The Black Christ," existed in ancient Central America as in ancient Europe. He says: "In the little church at Esquipultas, Guatemala, is the image of the Black Christ to which thousands of Indians journey annually from all parts of Central America and even from Mexico and South America. The spot has become a shrine, a Mecca for the Indians and for hundreds, even thousands of miles they travel to the obscure Guatemalan village carrying with them all their possessions in order to have them sanctified at the famous church. To all outward intents and purposes they are Christians making a pilgrimage to a Christian Church in order to worship before a figure of Christ. No doubt many of them are sincere in believing this to be the case. But as a matter of fact the underlying cause, the real urge that leads them to the spot is the ineradicable faith in their ancient gods and religion. The very fact that the image is black has a symbolic significance Moreover among many of the Indians ,the Black Christ is referred to in private as Ekchuah." ("Old Civilisations of the New World," p. 145, Indianapolis, 1929.) The same author says (p. 103) that "Ekchuah, the black god, was the special deity of merchants and cacao planters." (Aso see: Weiner, Chapt. on "The Mandingo Elements in Mexico," Vol. III.)

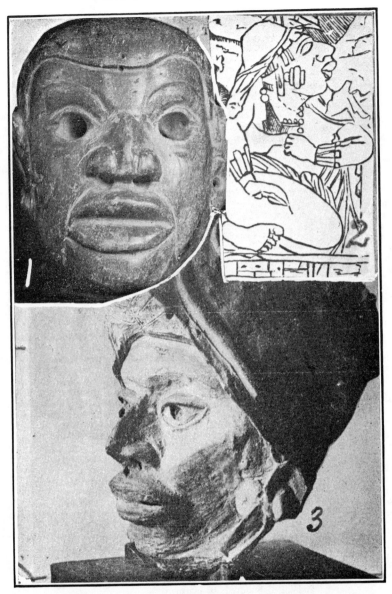

XXVIII. I. Prehistoric stone mask from Honduras, Central America; 2. Negro figure from Palenque, Ancient Mexico; 3. The Mexican Messiah Quetzalcoatl. (See Notes on the Illustrations)

272 SEX AND RACE

The Negro in America Before Columbus

The American Museum of Natural History in New York City contains several early idols. In the Central American division is a group of ancient Costa Rican divinities which are Negroid. one of them, the largest, being strikingly so. The National Archaeological Museum of Madrid (American Indian section) contains several such also. Commenting on this type of art, A. Le Plongeon says, "Besides the sculptures of long-bearded men seen by the explorer at Chichen Itza, there were tall figures of people with small heads, thick lips. and curly short hair or wool, regarded as Negroes." ("Maya Archaeology, p. 62.) In another volume he refers to "the mural paintings at Chichen Itza with strongly marked African features." "Vestiges of the Maya," New York, 1881.)

Prof. Leo Weiner of Harvard University says: "The presence of Negroes with their trading masters before Columbus is proved by the representation of Negroes in American sculpture and design; by the occurrence of a black nation at Darien early in the 16th Century. but more specifically by Columbus' emphatic reference to Negro traders from Guinea, who trafficked in gold alloy, guanin, of precisely the same composition and bearing the same name, is frequently referred to by early writers in Africa.

"There were several foci from which the Negro traders spread in the two Americas. The eastern part of South America where the Caraibs are mentioned seems to have been reached by them from the West Indies. Another stream. possibly from the same focus; radiated to the north along roads marked by the presence of mounds and reached as far as Canada. The chief cultural influence was exerted by a Negro colony in Mexico, most likely from Teotihuacan and Textla. which may have been instrumental in establishing the city of Mexico. From here their influence pervaded the neighboring tribes and ultimately. directly or indirectly, reached Peru.

"That the Negro civilization was carried chiefly by the trader is proved by Columbus' special reference but also by the presence of the African merchant...

"The identity of the spiritual civilizations, down to the remotest details in the Sudan and in Mexico and elsewhere in America, leads to the assumption that other cultural elements, identical in both continents and frequently bearing the same name are of African origin." ("Africa and the Discovery of America," Vol. III, pp. 365, 369. Philadelphia, 1920-1922.)

G. Cauvet advances the theory that the Berbers of North Africa, a Negroid people, crossed to America before Columbus. ("Les Berbères en Amerique," Alger, 1930.)

"The blacks of California" are mentioned by Topinard among "the most celebrated recently extinct races of America." (Anthropologie," p. 438, Paris, 1876.)

Columbus' Journal of the Third Voyage states: "He wanted to find out what the Indians of Hispaniola had told him that there had come to it from the south and southeast Negro peoples who brought those spear points, made of a metal which they call guanin." (p. 6.)

Peter Martyr, friend and historian of Columbus. speaking of Negroes living in Central America, said: "These were the first Negroes seen in the Indies."

According to the same Peter Martyr, Vasco Nunez de Balboa saw aboriginal Negroes in Panama in 1513: "There is a region not past two days journey distant from Quarepa in which they found only black Moors and these exceedingly fierce and cruel They suppose that in times past, certain black Moors sailed thither out of Ethiopia to rob and that by shipwreck or some other chance they were driven to these mountains the inhabitants of Quarepa lie in continual war and debate with these black men." ("The First Book of the Third Decade," translated by Richard Eden, p. 139, Birmingham, 1885.) The blacks must have been quite numerous for Balboa relates that they fought the king of Quarepa and killed hundreds of his men.

Colonel A. Braghine says that he saw in a collection in Ecuador a statuette of a Negro that is at least "20,000 years old." He adds, "Hitherto the ethnologists imagined that Negroes appeared in the New World only during our own epoch when they were imported as slaves. . . Some statues of the Indian gods in Central America possess typical Negro features and certain prehistoric monuments there undoubtedly represent Negroes . " (The Shadow of Atlantis. pp. 40-42, N. Y., 1940.)

In 1940, the National Geographic Society and the Smithsonian Institution found on the western border of the State of Tabasco, Mexico, five mammoth heads, eight feet high, each weighing about twenty tons. A photograph of one of them published in the New York Post of March 26. 1940, shows marked Negro features and a close resemblance to the colossal head of Hueyapan already referred to.

The Philippines also have a famous Black Christ but it may have been brought from Europe.

* * * *

For additional references on the pre-Columbian Negro see:

Sex and Race, Vol. 3, pp. 322-27. With pictures.
Churchward, J., "The Children of Mu," pp. 23, 80, 98-102, New York, 1931.
Dixon. R. B., "Racial History of Man," pp. 400-401, 409, 441, 449, et seq.
Hooton, E. A.. "Up From the Ape," pp. 577, 582, New York, 1931.

PART II

THE BLACK MADONNA AND THE BLACK CHRIST

Excerpts from Various Writers

Professor Churchward holds that the African pigmies and the Negroes were the real originators of the Christian religion. He says;

"The mystery of the resurrection, which was originally instituted by these Totemic Nilotic Negroes, may be seen still performed symbolically by the Arunta Tribes Every native has to pass through certain ceremonies before he is admitted to the secrets of the tribe. The first takes place at about the age of twelve years; the final and most impressive one is not passed through until the native has reached the age of thirty years. These two initiations thus correspond to, or represent the origin of those mysteries of the double Horus, or Jesus at twelve years of age; the child, Horus, or Jesus, makes his transformation into the adult in his baptism or other kindred mysteries. Horus, or Christ as the man of thirty years is initiated into the final mysteries of the resurrection.

"The doctrine of soul-making at puberty originated among the Nilotic Negroes as did many of the other Egyptian mysteries." ("Origin and Evolution of Religion," pp. 1-25, London, 1924.)

Sir Arthur Evans points to the great antiquity of the worship of the Mother and the Child, declaring: "The worship of a Mother Goddess predominated in later (prehistoric) times generally associated with a divine child—a worship which later survived in a classical guise influenced all later religion." (Report Brit. Assn. for the Adv. of Science, 1916, p. 19.)

Godfrey Higgins, who visited the cathedrals of Europe before the destruction of most of the Black Madonnas during the anti-religious period of the French Revolution says:

"No person who has considered well the character of the temples in India and Egypt can help being convinced of the identity of their character and of their being the product of the same race of people; and this race evidently Ethiopian. The worship of the Mother and Child is seen in all parts of the Egyptian religion. It prevails everywhere. It is the worship of Isis and the infant Orus or Osiris. It is the religious rite which was so often prohibited at Rome but which prevailed in spite of all opposition, as we find from the remaining ruins of its temples. It was perhaps from this country, Egypt, that the worship of the black Virgin and Child came into Italy and where it still prevails. It was the worship of the mother of God, Jesus, the Saviour; Bacchus in Greece; Adonis in Syria; Cristna in India; coming into Italy through the medium of the two Ethiopias, she was, as, the Ethiopians were. black, and such she still remains.

"The worship of the Virgin and the Child which we find in all Romish countries was nothing more than a remnant of the worship of Isis and the God, Horus—the Virgin of the celestial sphere to whom the epithet, 'virgin,' though a mother was without absurdity applied." (Anacalypsis, Vol. I, p. 316.)

Further: "The name of Christ may be fairly derived from Cristna and the traits of similarity in the lives of Cristna and Jesus have been pointed out, will probably compel the reader to believe that the black God of Italy was called in some way or other from the black God of India, or both from some common source.

"In all the Romish countries of Europe, in France, Italy, Germany, etc., the God, Christ, as well as his Mother are described in the old pictures to be black. The infant God in the arms of his black mother, his eyes and drapery white, is, himself, perfectly black. If the reader doubts my word he may go to the Cathedral at Moulins— to the famous Chapel of the Virgin of Loretto, to the Church of the Annunciata; the Church of St. Lazaro, or the Church of St. Stephen at Genoa; to St Francisco at Pisa; to the Church at Brixen in the Tyrol, and that at Padua; to the Church of St. Theodore at Munich, in the last two of which the whiteness of the eyes and teeth and the studied redness of the lips are observable; to a church and to the Cathedral at Augsburg, where are a Black Virgin and Child as large as life; to the Borghese Chapel, Maria Maggiore: to the Pantheon; to a small Chapel of St. Peter's on the right hand side on entering near the door; and, in fact to almost innumerable other churches in countries professing the Romish religion.

"There is scarcely an old church in Italy where some remains of the worship of the Black Virgin and Child are not to be met with. Very often the black figures have given way to white ones and in these cases the black ones, as being held sacred, were put in retired places in the churches, but were not destroyed, and are yet to be found there.

"In many cases the images were painted all over and look like bronze; but pictures in great numbers are to be seen, where the whites of the eyes and teeth, and the lips a little tinged with red, like the black figures in the Museum of the India Company, show that there is no imitation of bronze.

"In many instances these images and pictures, not all one color, of very dark brown, are so dark as to look like black.

"They are generally esteemed by the rabble with the most profound veneration. The toes are often white, the brown or black paint being kissed away by the devotees, and the white wood left...

"When the circumstances have been named to the Romish priests they have endeavored to disguise the fact by pretending that the child had become black by the smoke of the candles; but it was black where the smoke of the candle never came; and besides how came the candles not to blacken the white teeth and the shirt, and how came they to redden the lips? The Mother is, the author believes, always black when the child is. Their real blackness is not to be questioned for a moment."

As regards the statement that the color of the Black Virgins is due to smoke from burning candles, it may be said further that this does not account for the Negroid faces of some of these Virgins, and also for those paintings in which the Madonna is shown as black and Negroid. The Cardiff Museum has one such painting and there is also one in the Chateau of Azay-le-Rideau. At Sales (Cantal) a tapestry shows the figures of the Holy family black, save that of the Infant Jesus. On a church window at L'Oise, a Virgin with a black face is holding a rose-colored Christ.

Higgins continues, "If the author had wished to invent a circumstance to corroborate the assertion that the Romish Christ of Europe is the Christna of India how could he have desired anything more striking than the fact of the Black Virgin and Child being so common in the Romish countries of Europe? A Black Virgin and Child among the white Germans, Swiss, French, and Italians!!" ("Anacalypsis," Vol. II, pp. 137-139.)

Elsewhere in the same work Higgins says:

"I believe that the Christ whose black icon I saw in Italy...came to Italy...even before the foundation of the Rome of Romulus." (Vol. I, p, 264.)

"The first black Buddhist people... coming to Italy and bringing the Black God and his Mother along with them. And they not only brought the Black God and his Mother but they brought his house, the house at Loretto." (Vol. I, p. 264.)

Higgins tells of visiting the house at Loretto where the Black Virgin was enshrined with Negro Sybils. "Nothing of this kind is more striking than the Pagan Sybils seen in many places particularly surrounding the Casa Santa at Loretto, the most sacred of all the shrines of the black God, where, in the affected poverty of a cottage and amidst gold and diamonds, without measure, or number, I saw him enthroned." (Vol. I, p. 57.) Two centuries earlier the noted traveller, Lithgow, wrote of this Virgin, and of his "musing on the blackness of her face." (Travels, p. 30, Leith, 1814.)

A Black Madonna held in highest esteem by Catholics today is that at Alt-Otting. Hundreds of thousands of pilgrims visit her shrine annually.

C. W. King says: "The Black Virgins so highly venerated in certain French cathedrals during the long night of the Middle Ages, proved when at last examined by anti-quarian eyes to be basalt statues of the Egyptian Goddess, which having merely changed the name continued to receive more than pristine adoration." ("Gnostics and their Remains," p. 173, 2d ed., London, 1887.)

Even as late as the time of the prophet Daniel, the most ancient of the gods was visualized as a Negro. In speaking of this deity, Daniel said: "I beheld till the thrones were cast down and the Ancient of Days did sit whose garment was white as snow and the hair of his head like *the pure wool.*" (Chapt. VII, 9.) The translation is correct. In speaking of woolly hair, it is evident that Daniel was not thinking of a white, or Caucasian, God.

A coin of Justinian II in the British Museum, shows Christ with the same tightly curled hair· as that of the earlier Buddhas. The Cambridge Encyclopedia says: "Whatever the fact, this coin places beyond doubt the belief that Jesus Christ was a Negro."

Writing about the Black Virgins in Malta, J. H. Matthews says that he has seen "the Holy Child—represented as a real Negro. It is on a worm-eaten panel which some time in the 15th Century was cut into a Gothic shape. In this case the original black faces have been subjected to a little touch-up to introduce a European flesh-tint. The Child's head is distinctly Negro with woolly hair." (Notes and Queries, 9 ser. III, p. 377.) J. S. Matthews writing on the same subject says that the Christ of the ancient Church of St. Paul at Citta Vecchia is "completely Negro." (Intermediare, etc., Vol. 40, p. 129.)

A German correspondent, resident in New York City, wrote me as regards the Black Virgin of her native land, Bavaria, saying that for years she has been trying to tell Americans that Christ and the Virgin Mary were black but that they would not believe her, "I. myself, was born in a strictly Catholic country in South Germany," she says, "and in our churches the biggest reference is given to Santa Maria as Mother of God, and we have statues of the Madonna as well as pictures, which are original sculptures or paintings on wood and stone, dating as far back as 800 to 1,000 years and more.

"The faces of these images are black and of Negroid type, particularly the Madonnas of Constuchan in Tolers and the Mother of God statue in Alt-Olting in Bavaria near Munich, which was brought from Palestine more than 1,000 years ago by Ritter von Heiligers Lande.

"These two Madonnas particularly are held in the highest esteem in Catholic countries and hundreds of thousands of pilgrims go to these places to do homage to the Mother of Christ every year and wonderful healings of all kinds of illnesses are reported to the public. Every Catholic knows that Santa Maria was an Acthiopian (Ethiopian)."

Gerald Massey says, "The black Jesus is a well-known form of the child-Christ worshipped on the continent (Europe) where the black Bambino was the pet image of the Italian church as popular as Crishna, the Black Christ of India; and unless the divine son was incarnated in black flesh, the type of the black child must have survived from the black Iu, the black Kak or Jack, the black Sut Nahsi, the Negro image of the earliest God   And finally the black Jesus of the Christian cult, the son of the Virgin Mother in the Romish Church." ("Ancient Egypt," pp. 301, 346.)   Nahsi. or Nehsi, was the ancient Egyptian for "Negro."

The Ancient Christ of India

John M. Robertson says: "The name of Krishna means "the black one" and he thus in the first place comes into line with the black deities of other faiths, notably the Osiris of Egypt to say nothing of the black manifestations of Greek deities and of Jesus Christ." ("Christ and Krishna," p. 16, London, 1898.)

Robertson holds that the blackness is symbolic of night, *i.e.*, "the nightly or hidden one." But is not color of the skin an easier explanation since millions of Negroes live or lived in India, and that the Buddhas are shown black and with woolly hair? Take an analagous instance. If a few thousands of years from now statues of a white Christ are discovered among the blacks in Africa would one say that the whiteness was symbolical of dawn? Or would one say that a white people once invaded that region? If the white statutes are attributed to white people, why strain an explanation in the case of the black one?

T. W. Doane says "The Egyptian Isis was also worshipped in Italy many centuries before the Christian era and all images of her with the Infant, Horus, in her arms have been adopted as we shall presently see by the Christians even though they represent her and the child as *black* as an Ethiopian in the same manner as we have seen that Devaki and Chrishna were represented." ("Bible Myths," Chapt. XVIII, New York, 1883.)

Conyers Middleton· "The mention of Loretto puts me in mind of the surprise that I was in at the first sight of the Holy Image for it is as black as a Negro. But I soon recollected that this very circumstance of its complexion made it resemble the more exactly the old idols of Paganism." ("Letters from Rome," p. 84.)

Bonwick says: "We may be surprised that as Europe has Black Madonnas, Egypt had Black images and pictures of Isis. At the same time it is odd that the Virgin Mary copies most honored should not only be Black, but have a decided Isis cast of features." ("Egyptian Beliefs," p. 141, London, 1878.) And elsewhere he states: "The Black Osiris, with a decided Ethiopian appearance was a mystery as was the Black Isis." ("The Rosicrucians," p. 134.)

Didorus Siculus· "This Osiris was Mizraim, the son of Ham." (Book I, chapt. 2.)

H. J. D. Astley says: "We have seen Isis and Horus, Cybele and Attis, Astarte and Merodach, everywhere the Great Mother of all the gods and of life, and her Son which we find enshrined at length in the Virgin and Child of Christianity." ("Biblical Anthropology," p. 128, London, 1929.)

"She (the Church) utilised the gods by making their festivals the days of commemoration of the Christian saints or even took them over bodily and adopted them so that Isis and Horus became the Virgin Mother· and her son, and so n." (Ibid., p. 221.)

It should be noted that Isis, pattern of wifehood and motherhood, was the first Madonna; Cleopatra and her son. Caesarion, were also worshipped at Rome as Isis and Horus.

H. Guichenne says: "Each year for the Chandeleur, the clergy of the Abbey of St. Victor exposes for the veneration of the faithful, dressed in a mantle of white moire, the head surmounted with a crown of flowers, a statue with a black face that is called the Black Virgin   Black Virgins are not rare in France. There are those of Dijon, Beaune. Tournus, Le Puy, Rocamadour, St. Denis, Chartres   " ("La Vierge Noire de L'Abbaye de St. Victor Lez Marseilles," p. 4 et seq.)

In an original wood-cut of 1523 the Black Virgin is shown with flat nose and thick lips, as is also Christ, while the other two figures have decided Caucasian features. The Virgin has long hair. Of this Joseph Breck says: "The Virgin's long hair is a pure invention." An earlier wood-cut (1500) shows her even more Negro-like. ("A Souvenir of the Black Virgin of Le Puy, Metrop, Museum Studies, Vol. I, 1928-29, pp. 155-58.)

Joseph H. Ledit. S. J. Professor of Russian History, Oriental University, Rome. contributes an article on the various Black Virgins in "The Chronicle," St. Louis, Mo., (1932), and quotes St. Francis:

"Our Lady shows Herself as a familiar Virgin, kind to all who come before Her She is a sister to the Black Virgins of Moulins, of Dijon, of Bourg, of Liesse, of Rocamadour, of Chartres, and it seems that the Virgins of this color, who are older than our white Madonnas, are more our grandmothers than our mothers. We trust more in their fond weakness towards us, and we feel that they will be more indulgent, readier

to forgive, and we prefer to tell our pranks to them..."
L'Illustration, Paris, March 19, 1932, in an article by Ulysse Rouchon on Le Puy and its Black Virgin gives a list of the emperors, kings and popes, who used to worship at the altar of the Black Virgin, attracted by her miraculous fame.
This Virgin was destroyed during the Revolution but was restored in 1842 in the presence of 150,000 pilgrims. This was the case with many others. As Ledit says: "Many of these statues are quite recent. Destroyed at the time of the French Revolution, or yet some other occasion, they have been re-made, but the ancient color was preciously preserved. Is there not a symbolism beneath all this? You will often hear quoted the words of the Canticle: "I am black but beautiful," and again, "Do not consider me, that I am brown, because the sun hath altered my color."

Negro Gods in the Caucasus

Edouard Schure thinks that at one time "the black race dominated on the globe" with "cyclopean cities" in Upper Egypt, the Caucasus, and Central Asia. This black race. he says, was finally driven out from Europe by the whites, its impress having disappeared due to the immense period of time that has elapsed. Two relics of black domination have remained, he says: the fear of the dragon, and the depicting of the devil as black. This was caused, he says, by "the blacks painting their devil white out of contempt for the whites," and the whites making their devil black in return. ("Les Grands Inities," 113th Edition, p. 6, Paris, 1931.) Schure holds that the true type of Negro was represented by the Nubian.
As late as the 16th century the Abyssinians used to depict the devil as white, and Christ, black. M. Russell quotes Antonius Fernandez, a Catholic priest, as follows: "They paint Christ, the Blessed Virgin and other saints in black form and devils and wicked men in white. So they paint Christ and his apostles at the Maundy black and Judas white; Christ in his passion black, and Annas, Caiphas, Pilate, Herod and the Jews white; Michael black and the devil white." ('Nubia and Abyssinia," p. 275, New York, 1833.)
According to at least two distinguished authorities. Bryant and Massey, even the name by which the white race is known—Caucasian—is Ethiopian. having come from "Caer Cush Aur." Bryant's Ancient Mythology, Vol. III, p. 158 (1807). Massey says "Even the word, Caucasian, tells of an origin in the Kaf or Kaffir. Philosophy will support ethnology in deriving from Africa..." A Book of the Beginnings. Vol. I. p. 18.

History of Black Virgin Marys

Quotations from various sources throwing a light on the history of several Black Madonnas follow:
"Why are the majority of the virgins that are revered in the celebrated pilgrimages, black? At Boulogne-sur-mer the sailors carry a Black Virgin in the procession. At Clermont in Auvergne, the Black Virgin is revered as also at Einsiendeln, Switzerland, near Zurich, to which thousands of pilgrims—Swiss, Bavarians, Alsatians—go to pay her homage. The famous Virgin of Oropa in the Piedmont is still a Negress, as well as the not less legendary one of Montserrat in Catalonia. which receives 60,000 visitors a year. I have been able to trace the history of this one to the year 718 A.D. and it was always black. Tradition says that St. Luke who personally knew the mother of Christ, carved with his own hand the majority of these Black Virgins. It is highly interesting to know, therefore, if the mother of Christ was not a Negro woman, how it happens that she is black in France, Switzerland, Italy, and Spain?" ("Romain Rolland, Intermediare des chercheurs et des curieux," Vol. 34, p. 193, Paris.)
The Black Virgin of the Hospice of Espalion is called "La Negrette." Another writer adds that the Black Virgin of Notre Dame of Hal, near Brussels, Belgium is a shrine for a large number of pilgrims. She is credited with having performed many miracles, one of which was saving the cathedral by catching 33 cannon-balls in the folds of her robe. The cannon-balls are on display. This same writer also names the Black Virgin of the Church of St. John the Baptist in Grund, Luxemburg. (Ibid., Vol. 33, p. 633.)
"In Russia, the image of Notre Dame of Kazan is a Black Virgin. The Miraculous Virgin of Czenstochowa, Poland, is of the same color. I believe that is due to its very ancient Byzantine origin." (Ibid., Vol. 34, p. 640.)

"The Black Virgin of Chatillon-sur-seine was thrown into the fire by the revolutionists in Oct. 1793. Grenoble also has its black Virgins. In Perigord there is a Notre Dame the Black:" (Ibid., Vol. 35, p. 65, 66, 67.)

"In Normandy two Black Virgins have been the object of a veneration that goes back to the earliest times of our national history and attracts each year at Notre Dame de Deliverance, near Lion-sur-mer and at Notre Dame de Graces, near Honfleur, innumerable pilgrims, especially sailors." (Ibid., Vol. 35, p. 169.)

"The Virgin of Notre Dame de Liesse (Aisne) is one of the oldest of France, and the pilgrimage to her dates back to the 13th century with its legend of Ismery, the girl of the Egyptian Sudan which was transported by the Virgin with three cavaliers of Effies, Marchaux de Coney from the borders of the Nile to the little village of Ile-de-France where was actually built the sanctuary of the Black Virgin, another Mary of the Egyptians." (Ibid., Vol. 35, p. 300.)

Anatole France says, "In the little church of Mende (Loziere) above a fountain in a little chapel, or rather, a little altar, closed by a window, is a Black Virgin, which appears to be of the Middle Ages. The statue of Puy de Dome which was broken during the Revolution was no other than an Isis of basalt holding her son Horus, on her knees.

"I have always had a very great liking for and curiosity towards the Black Virgins, which are very ancient. They wear mantles that resemble window-shades, and are open and short. The reason they are sitting is that they dress as if though they were standing. the effect being a touching contempt for the human form. The Greeks also had their black idols." (Intermediare des Chercheurs, etc., Vol. 40, p. 293.) See also "Pierre Noziere," by Anatole France.

"There are numerous Black Virgins; they are really black: some of them are even Negresses and not merely painted wood." (Ibid., Vol. 60, p. 653, 1909.)

Huysmans in "La Cathedrale," describes the Virgin as "a Negress," and Christ as a little Negro. (p. 31.)

Georges Sand says, "A divinity of ancient Egypt, brought. it was said, from Palestine by St. Louis, is the idol that the Revolution has broken after centuries of veneration. A new Black Virgin has been inaugurated but it is said she performs less miracles than the old. Happily there has been preserved in the treasure of the Cathedral the waxes which the angels bore when they descended from heaven to place them with their own hands on the altar the figure of Isis." "Le Marquis de Villemer.")

With regard to Notre Dame de Liesse of Soissons, a Negro Virgin, she was a native African, who was brought to France, and whose exemplary life caused her later to be identified with the Madonna. The story is that she was Ismeria or Ismery. that she came from the Sudan, married Robert D'Eppes, son of William II of France. and bore him a son named Jean, who was the companion of St. Louis, king of France. during the Crusades. In a chart of 1236, he is designated under the name "Son of the Negress." So great was her fame that a town sprang up near the place of her burial, and pilgrims from all parts of France came to pay their homage. Among them were Joan of Arc; Louis XI. and Francis I. Very rich gifts were brought to her shrine. and it appears that she received much more homage than the Madonna herself. (Drochon, J. E. B., "Pelèrinages Français," Paris, 1890.)

Black Virgins abound, or abounded in Russia. The Eastern Church has two types of Virgins; one frankly African with Ethiopian or Galla features; the other Byzantine with a copper complexion and classic Greek features. The preferential worship of this Black Deity by the Slavs goes back to the dimmest antiquity. (Fraser, "The Golden Bough." (Vol. 9, p. 92, London, 1914.) Additional references to the Black Madonnas of Russia, as well as those of the British Isles, and elsewhere, are contained in "Notes and Queries," (9, Ser. II, 367, 397, 449, 475, 537. IV, 77, 135, 177, 315.)

Naturally these are objections to this theory. The Rev. Canon Brugiere puts forth the opinion that the Black Virgins are the result of a too literal interpretation of the passage · "I am black but beautiful."

He says: "We believe that the desire of the artist was to recall the passage, "I am black but beautiful, Oh daughters of Jerusalem; it is especially in a spiritual and a mystic sense that one attributes this black color to the Holy Virgin.

"Here are the principal reasons given by the commentaries cited: Although beautiful by the plenitude of grace, the Virgin Mary is black being a daughter of Adam, who

Black Madonna from Nuria, Spain. She is called "The Queen of the Pyrenees."

Left: "The Vision of Isaiah," reproduced from a Fifth Century A.D. Greek manuscript in the Bibliotheque Nationale, Paris. The great Jewish prophet is clearly portrayed not as a white man, but as an African. The figure beside him is undoubtedly white. Right: A priest of Isis from Ancient Rome with a sistrum. Not unlike a modern Coptic priest, who carries the same instrument.

had sinned and by his sin soiled all his posterity. But Mary is exempt from the common law and only has the appearance of being soiled.

"The Virgin Mary, said Rupert the Benedictine (1125 A.D.) appeared black when Joseph wished to send her away in secret, believing that she had become a mother after the common law but in reality she was beautiful because she had conceived by the operation of the Holy Spirit.

"The Holy Virgin appeared black when witnessing the crucifixion of her Son. She was at the foot of the cross, disfigured and as blackened by the excess of sorrow.

"It is, therefore, quite natural that these Biblical souvenirs suggested the idea to the artist to paint the Virgin brown and even black." (Bull. Soc. Hist. et Arch. de Perigord, Vol. 24, p. 80, 1897.)

This is highly fantastic. It is an attempt to explain away fact by allegory and theological hocus-pocus. Moreover, Isis and her son, Horus, with Osiris, her husband, (which constitutes the Holy Trinity), were worshipped in Europe centuries before the Christian era. The first historical contact of Italy with Egypt was about 1400 B.C. Later came the Phoenicians who were also worshippers of the Black Goddess and who traded as far to the northwest as Britain.

In 58 B.C., the Roman Senate ordered the statues of Isis in the Capitol to be destroyed. But in 48 B.C. her worship returned with accelerated vigor when Cleopatra came to Rome as the wife of Julius Caesar. After the battle of Actium in which Cleopatra and Antony were defeated Isis was again ordered banished. Agrippa's efforts to enforce this order caused riots at Rome, and served but to increase the zeal of the Egyptian missionaries. The persecution continued until the time of Tiberius; but the Black Virgin came back into power under Caligula. Suetonius tells of Egyptians and Ethiopians at Rome playing a scene in which Isis is represented. Under Nero the power of the Black Virgin and her son increased, and the Emperor Domitian in escaping from the Capitol wore the robe of a priest of Isis. Isis was especially adored by the women, and it was the custom of her devotees to break the ice of the Tiber and go into bathe for which they were mocked by Juvenal in his Sixth Satire.

The mystical religion of Isis with its beautiful liturgies and ceremonies; its rich ornaments; its sacred emblems; its initiations, together with the sorrows of Isis for her crucified son, Osiris, affected deeply all those who had been struck by similar misfortunes, says Plutarch. At the same time her holy life offered a lesson of piety and encouragement for all, especially women.

The worship of Isis, as the Black Virgin, lasted centuries after the introduction of Christianity. As late as 394 A.D. her processions still marched through the streets of Rome. Isis is made to say by Apuleius, African philosopher and romancer (125 A.D.):

"The Phrygians call me Pessinus, the Mother of the Gods; the Athenians call me Cecropian Minerva; in Cyprus, I am Paphian Venus; I am Diana Dictynna to the archers of Crete; Stygian Proserina to the Sicilians at Eleusis, I am the ancient Ceres; to some I am Juno, to others, Hecate. It is only the Ethiopians and the Arians, illumined by the dawning light of the sun, and Egypt powerful in her ancient lore, who honor me with the rites that are really mine, and call me by my true name, the Queen, Isis." The Arians were a religious sect of Africa.

The worship of Isis spread through the remainder of Europe and into Asiatic Russia. Ancient statuettes of her have been found in Northern France, in the Rhineland, and on the Moselle. Her temples were in all that region, as well as in Britain. She is believed to have had a temple in Paris, and another nearby, at Melun. By certain archaeologists the word "Paris," is supposed to be a corruption of "Bari-Isis," becoming through Roman pronunciation "Parisii," the name of the tribe that inhabited the site on which Paris now stands. The boat in the coat-of-arms of the city of Paris is supposed to be the bark of the Negro goddess. Isis was the goddess of navigation, as will be seen later on. According to De Breuil, a statue of Isis existed in the Abbey of St. Germain-des-Prés, Paris, as late as 1514, when it was ordered broken by Cardinal Briconnet.

Isis, says Encyclopedia Britannica, was worshipped in Egypt, Greece, Rome, Gaul, almost all the remainder of Europe, and England.· (See Isis.)

Larousse Universal Dictionary says: "One of the most ancient of the divinities of Egypt, she formed with Osiris, at the same time her son and husband, a mythical trinity in which is to be found the Holy Trinity of the Christian religion. Isis was the force of life itself which gathered all the scattered forces of life from death and decay, warmed them in her bosom, and perpetually gave them new life."

When the Christians came into power after the edict of Constantine they were power-less against the great hold of the Black Madonna on the people so they ended by compounding her religion with theirs, changing her name to Mary. It is significant, too, that the mother of Buddha, was Maryamma, indicating another source of Christianity as well.

According to Madame Blavatsky: "It was none other than Cyril, Bishop of Alex-andria, who openly embraced the cause of Isis and anthropomorphized her into Mary, Mother of God. ("Isis Unveiled," Vol. II, p. 41.)

Grant Showerman says of the transformation of the Pagan religions of Rome into the Christian one:

"What was true of pagan literature was true of other arts. It was especially true of painting. So far were the Roman Christians from resisting the seductions of pagan form that their painting not only shows the same characteristics and the same changes period by period; but it borrows pagan motives and pagan figures. The Good Shepherd in the Catacombs is not the bearded Christ of later time but a smooth-shaven and shapely figure of pagan art.

"Christian civilization was indebted to paganism not only for arts but culture in general. The new religion, itself, was not unmixed with the old. In both doctrines and ceremonial, it came to have much in common with the pagan religion. The resemblance between the doctrines of Christianity and those of the oriental religions especially was striking." (Eternal Rome, pp. 321-26. New Haven, 1924.)

St. Augustine himself says:

"What is now called the Christian religion has existed among the ancients and was not absent from the beginning of the human race until Christ came in the flesh from which time the true religion which existed already began to be called Christian." (Retract. I, 13.)

Conclusive proof that the Black Madonna is Isis is contained in the fact that Isis was the goddess of navigation. The greatest feast of the cult of Isis was that of the Ship. On a great number of the coins of Asia, Isis is represented standing on a galley, holding a 'veil inflated by the wind.

In the romance of Apuleius there is a long description of the ceremonies held at Kenchrees, the port of Corinth. This feast marked the end of the bad season and was the signal for navigation to begin again.

To this day in several sea-ports of Europe, sailors hold these ceremonies, and as their patron saint they carry a Black Virgin called Mary exactly as their fellows of two thousand years ago carried a Black Virgin called Isis in their processions.

Today, the majority of the Black Madonnas have Caucasian features. · The reason is that nearly all the original ones were destroyed by fire or by mobs during revolts against the church. When re-erected they were made black, but with the facial type of the predominant population. During the French Revolution and the Napoleonic Wars there was a general destruction of Black Madonnas in Europe, two notable instances occurring at Montserrat, Spain, and at Le Puy, France. The former is the patron saint of Catalonia; the latter, the principal Madonna of France.

Two of the oldest black Madonnas of Europe are those of Loretto, Italy, and of Nuria, Spain. The first is said to be the original of all the Black Virgins. It was destroyed by fire about 1930 and was restored by Pope Pius XI, who, according to Father Ledit, ordered "the color preserved." The Black Virgin of Nuria, which is called "The Queen of the Pyrenees" is distinctly Negro.

Thus, from this mass of evidence, we have undoubted proof that it was the Negro, who originated not only religion, but Christianity as well. The fact is significant, because no matter what some may think about religion, it was the source from which came all our learning, art, science, and culture in general.

Note: Once when I said that the original Christ was black, a Jewish girl said I was taking away even Christ from the Jews. Most German, English, American, and Latin-American Jews do not like mention of a Negro ,strain in their ·people. Anti-Semitic writers constantly refer to the Negro Semitic writers frequently use this to belittle them.

For instance, Louis F. Céline, in his violently anti-Semitic novel, "Bagatelles Pour Un Massacre," harps on the Negroid characteristic of the Jew. He says, "The single defense, the sole recourse of the white man against robotism, and certainly against war, and a return to the days of the cave-man, is to return to his own emotional rhythm. The circumcised Jew is on the way to castrate the Aryan of his natural emotional rhythm. The Negro Jew is about to tumble the Aryans into Communism and robot art, to give them an objectivist mentality that will make them perfect slaves for Jews. The Jew is only a Negro, after all. There is no such thing as a Semitic race. It is an invention of the freemasons. The Jew is a cross between the Negro and the barbarous Asiatic." (pp. 191-2, Paris, 1927.)

On the other hand, several American whites have declared that one is no friend of the Negro to class him with the Jew.

The Christ idea has evolved racially just like the human race itself. Once, it was black, now it is white. So far as we know, it was originally East Indian. In a world without its Goebbels, Mosleys, and Lindbergs the question of what race was Christ would be a ,mattter of purely ethnological curiosity.

Bibliography

The material on the worship of Isis in Europe is vast. Some of the principal works in addition to those given are:

Lafaye, C., "Divinitiés d'Alexandrie hors D'Egypte," Paris, 1884.
Lievre; A. P., "Isis et la Magie, etc.," Poitiers, 1898.
Ruby, J., "Christus," Paris, 1912.
Schaafhausen, "Ueber den Roemischen Isis Dienst am Rhein," in Jahrb. d. ver. v., Alterthsfr. im Rheinl. No. 25.
Arnoldi, Richard, "Roemischer Isis-cult an der Mosel," Ibid., p. 87.
Burel, J., "Isis et Isiaques sous l'Empire Romain," Paris, 1911.
Guimet, E., "Les Isiaques de la Gaule," Paris, 1916.—This work contains illustrations of statues of a Negro Isis found in France and other Egyptian relics.
Rusch, A., "De Serapide et Iside in Graecia," Berlin, 1906.
Weigall, A., "Paganism in our Christianity," London, 1928. (List of Virgin Births, pp. 42-46. Isis into Virgin Mary, p. 208.)
For hundreds of additional references: See Isis in Dict. des Antiqu. Grecques et Romaines, Vol. 3, pt. 1, Paris, 1900.
Misc.:
For the cross as an ancient symbol of worship in the Old and New World see:
"The Cross"—Chapt. I. The Cross before the Christian Era and in Prehistoric Times," by Seymour, W. W., New York, 1898.
Higgins, G., "The Celtic Druids," pp. 126-131.
Massey, G., "Man in Search of His Soul," London, 1897.
"The Historical and Mythical Christ," London, 1921.
On prehistoric mother-goddesses, see Childe, V. G., "Dawn of Civilization" (consult index of same), New York, 1925.

Rogers, J. A. Nature Knows No Color-Line, pp. 29, 30, 40, 41. 1952.

NOTES AND REFERENCES TO THE NEGRO UNDER ISLAM

According to Mohammedan tradition, Mohamet s mother was African. Dan Crawford, noted African missionary, says:
"Bound to the African by the two great bonds of polygamy and slavery, he (the Arab) is a witness, not at all poisoned by prejudice, albeit he so long bought the Negro as a two-legged animal. Take and try these six nuts our Arab asks us to crack. I. Was not the Prophet descended from an African woman? II. Were there not many mighty Negroes like Wanshi whose exploits as 'Liberators ar·· celebrated in secular poetry? . . ." ("Back to the Long Grass," pp. 333-34, N.Y., 1922.)
Mohamet's mother died when he was an infant. He was reared by a Negro slave woman, Barakat. (Washington Irving, "Life of Mohamet," p. 19.)

* * * *

Professor Toynbee says, "The White Muslims have demonstrated their freedom from race-feeling by the most convincing of all proofs: they have given their daughters to the Black Muslims in marriage.
"I had the opportunity to observe this Muslim freedom from race-feeling when I was an undergraduate at Oxford. At that time there were two Egyptian Muslim undergraduates in my college, one a grandee, the other a man of the same social class as the rest of us. Physically the other was a pure specimen of the Mediterranean Race. To look at him you would not have told that he was not a Sicilian or a Catalan or a Provençal. On the other hand, the young Egyptian grandee had a Negro strain in him that was not merely unmistakable but obtrusive. If this young 'man had been brought up in England or a fortiori in the United States he would have been made to feel his Negro strain as a crushing misfortune which would have permanently oppressed his spirits and undermined his self-confidence. Having been brought up in Egypt he arrived at Oxford quite un-race-conscious. From his bearing it was evident that he felt himself distinguished from other people not at all by his Negro traits but by his noble descent. . How deeply outraged the grandee would have become if he had realized how his Negro traits were regarded by his English and American undergraduates." (A Study of History. Vol. I, pp. 226-27. 1934.)
Sir T. W. Arnold, "The Preaching of Islam," says, "The converted Negro at once takes an equal place in the brotherhood of believers, neither his color nor his race nor any associations of the past standing in his way.
"The following story, also handed down to us from the golden period of Abbasid dynasty is interesting as evidence of Muhammadan feeling toward the Negro. Ibrahim, a brother of Harun al Raschid, and the son of a Negress, had proclaimed himself Caliph at Bagdad, but was defeated and forgiven by al-Mamun, who was reigning (A.D. 819). He thus describes his interview with the Caliph. 'Al-Mamun said to me on my going to see him after having obtained pardon, Is it thou who art the Negro Khalifah?' to which I replied, 'Commander of the Faithful, I am he whom thou has deigned to pardon and it has been said by the slave of the Banu'l-Hashas, when men extol their worth the slave of the family of Hashas can supply by his verses the defect of birth and fortune. Though I be a slave, my soul through its noble nature is free, though my body be dark my mind is fair.' To this Al-Mamum replied, 'Uncle, a jest of mine has put you in a serious mood." He then repeated these verses, 'Blackness of skin cannot degrade an ingenious mind or lessen the worth of the scholar and the wit. Let darkness claim the color of your body, I claim as mine your fair and candid soul.'" pp. 258-59.) Ibrahim, as was said, was Islam's most famous singer, and a son of the Caliph, Al-Mahdi.
"Islam," says Mohammed Syed Ameer Ali, "recognises no distinction of race or colour, black or white, citizens or soldiers, rulers or subjects; they are perfectly equal not in theory only but in practice. On the field or in the guest chamber; in the tent or in the palace; in the mosque or in the market; they mix without reserve and without contempt. The first Muezzin of Islam, a devoted adherent and esteemed disciple, was a Negro slave. To the white Christian, his black fellow-religionist may be his equal in the

kingdom of heaven but not in the reign of Christianity." ("Life and Teaching of Mohammed, p. 372, London, 1891.)
"In Islam the slave of today is the grand vizier of tomorrow. He may marry without
discredit his master's daughter and become the head of the family. Slaves have ruled
kingdoms and founded dynasties. The father of Mahmud of Ghazni was a slave."
(Ibid. 376.) "Khutbudden, the first king of Delhi, and the true founder, therefore,
of the Mussulman empire in India, was a slave" (p. 375.) The marriage of the slave
to the master's daughter is not accepted, however, in all parts of Islam. · Alois Musil
reports that among the Rwala Bedouins only the sons and daughters of white black-
smiths may marry slaves, and tells of one white male slave who eloped with a free-born
girl and how the girl was killed by her own brother. ("Manners and Customs of the
Rwala Bedouins," pp. 278, 137, 138, 139.)
    Race-mixing is common in Mecca. E. Rutter says: "In complexion they (the
Meccans) range from coal-black to sallow white, these two extremes being accounted
for by the custom of keeping African and Circassian concubines. The son of a slave
woman by a free man is himself a free man and enjoys the same family rights of
inheritance and so forth as does his legal half-brother whose mother is a free woman
and the legal wife of his father. A Meccan who has a fair-skinned wife usually prefers
to take as his concubine the blackest slave-woman he can find in the market provided
she be comely as well as black." ("Holy Cities of Arabia," Vol. II, p. 74, London, 1928.)
    According to W. G. Palgrave: "Negroes can without any difficulty give their sons
and daughters to the middle or lower class of Arab families and thus arises a new
generation of mixed race   Like their progenitors they do not readily take their place
among the nobles or upper ten thousand, however, they may end by doing even this in
process of time; and I, have myself, while in Arabia, been honoured by the intimacy
of more than one handsome 'Green-man' (mulatto) with a silver-hilted sword at his
side and a rich dress on his dusky skin but denominated Sheik, or Emeer, and humbly
sued by Arabs of the purest Ishmaelitish or Kahtanic stock." "All of this," he adds,
was not by Act of Parliament but by individual will and feeling." ("Central and Eastern
Arabia," Vol. I, 1866, New York.)
    Another authority, J. S. Burchardt, states: "The mixture of the races in Djidda,
port of Mecca, is an effect of the pilgrimage during which rich merchants visit the
Hedjaz with large stock of goods. During this period they cohabit, according to the
custom of the country, with some Abyssinian slaves whom they soon marry; finding
themselves at last with a family they are induced to settle in the country." ("Travels
in Arabia," Vol. I, p. 28, London, 1829.)
    "If an Abyssinian slave gives birth to a child the master generally marries her,"
Burchardt tells, "or, if he fails to do so, is censured by the community. Many Mekkawys
(Meccans) have no other than Abyssinian wives, finding the Arabians more expensive.—
The mixture of Abyssinian blood has no doubt given to the Mekkawys that yellow tinge
of the skin . . . The Mekkawys make no distinction whatever between sons born of
Abyssinian slaves and those of free Arabian women." (Ibid., pp. 341-42.)

                    *   *   *   *

    The ruler of Djidda, Burchardt says, was "a black ex-slave," (p. 911) while that of
Mecca and other parts of Arabia, was the son of a merchant and an Abyssinian slave.
This Negro monarch had white women slaves in his harem. (p. 429.)

                    *   *   *   *

    "Children of slave women, white or black, in Egypt become legitimate." (Descrip-
tion de l'Egypte, Tome II, Pte. II, Paris, 1823—researches made by Napoleon's Expedition to Egypt.)
    "A reason why color is no handicap to him (the Negro) is that the freeman also
rears black children from his black concubine." (Hurgronje, C. S., "Mekka," pp. 12-15,
London, 1931.)
    In 1763 the ruler of Yemen was a Negro, and Niebuhr, who saw him, says: "Imam el
Mansor left several sons, the eldest of whom Ali, had naturally the best right to succeed
him. However, a son named Abbas, who had been born to El Mansor by a Negress
slave, seized the throne through the connivance of his slave-mother with the governors
of the provinces and the troops, and he was proclaimed sultan with the title of El Mahdi."
Mahdi was Negro-like in features, says Niebuhr, who describes his brothers as being

"as black as ebony, flat-nosed, and thick-lipped." ("Travels in Arabia," p. 103, London, 1811.)

* * * *

Nedjeh, a Negro slave of Sultan Marjan, ruled Arabia and founded a dynasty that furnished eight rulers (1021-1158 A.D.) (Lane-Poole, "Mohammedan Dynasties," pp. 92-93.)

The Negro in Turkey

* * * *

Mme. Halideh Edib, Turkey's leading authoress, and former Minister of Education, says on recent race-relations in Turkey:

"For the Ottoman Turks there was no race question—no inferior race. The fact that most of the colored men came as slaves was no impediment to their rise. For a great many prime ministers-viziers were slaves as boys and became great rulers. Being a slave did not affect a man's status. We have had very famous black Eunuchs (white ones, too), who occupied the position of Kizlar-Agha, that is, chief of the harem. But their activities were by no means restricted to the harem. Some of them really ruled Turkey—making or unmaking grand viziers, deposing sultans, heading great revolutions. For good or for evil, men of African descent have played very great parts in Turkish history. Further, quite a number of them were patrons of art and literature, they themselves being very well educated. It would be possible, though it would mean a great deal of time, to make a list of them and of their activities from the Turkish Annals.

"In my own time I have seen a considerable number of coloured officers in the Turkish Army of all grades. They have commanded white soldiers, and have been known as good and brave men. In the "Turkish Ordeal," you will see (early chapters of my story of the Nationalist Movement 1918-1923) Uncle Marsoud, a major in the Turkish Army, who was one of the earliest heroes of our revolution, and who was the most beloved by the Turkish peasantry.

"The two greatest coloured figures in the history of Islam are: 1. Bilal-i-Habesh (Bilal of Ethiopia). He was Mohammed's liberated slave and closest friend. The Prophet liberated all his slaves and they were all well-known figures in the early Islamic history. But Bilal stands out in greatest relief. Apart from his services in the cause of Islam, it was through him that the Moslems decided to use the *human voice* instead of *bells* to call the Moslems to prayer. He had evidently a marvellous voice and was the first who called for prayers in Islam.

"2. Tarik-bin-Ziad. He also was a slave and became a great general in Islam and was the conqueror of Spain as the commander of the Moorish Army which invaded Spain. Jebel-u-Tarik (the mount of Tarik) that is Gibraltar, is named after him. One of the greatest Turkish classics is called "Tarik-bin-Ziad" and has him as its hero. It was written by Abdul-Hak-Hamid, our greatest poet (alive though 84) and equals any tragedy of Corneille. I do hope that some time the biographies of these great figures will be written in English." (Letter to J. A. Rogers, Dec. 15, 1933.)

* * * *

The Turkish commander who lost Austria for Turkey in 1683 was a Negro, Kara Mustapha, son-in-law of the Sultan. (Eversley, Turkish Empire, p. 175.)

To the Turks, "Negro" and "Arab" were largely synonymous. For the Negro as "Arab" see F. W. Hasluck, "Christianity and Islam" (Vol. II, pp. 730-735.) This writer lists Negroes who distinguished themselves in Turkey.

Lord Eversley, in his book, "The Turkish Empire," tells of the ascendancy of another Negro. He says, "Mahmoud (the sultan) fell completely under the influence of the Kislar Agha, the chief of eunuchs of the harem, Bashir by name, who acted as his secretary. Bashir had been an Abyssinian slave and was bought for 30 piastres. Little is known of the personality of this man save that from behind the curtain of the harem he practically exercised supreme power for nearly thirty years and died at a very advanced age, leaving a fortune of more than 30,000,000 piastres and immense quantities of valuables. These included more than 800 watches set with precious stones, which, it must be presumed, were the gifts of applicants for appointments. Bashir made and unmade Grand Viziers at will and if anyone of them complained of Bashir's interference with his duties that was the more reason for his instant dismissal. In Mahmoud's reign of twenty-four years there were sixteen Grand Viziers. In any case it must be admitted that the success of Mahmoud's reign, such as it was, and the continuity of policy, were mainly due to this aged eunuch." (p. 205, London, 1907.)

For an account of another powerful black eunuch named Sunbullu, or the Black Hyacinth, see Lamartine's "History of Turkey," p. 282, N. Y., 1875. The story of still another is contained in the same volume, pp. 311, 318. Further references: A. W. Hidden, "The Ottoman Dynasty, pp. 86-87, N. Y., 1912; Salaberry, "Histoire de L'Empire Ottoman" III, pp. 200-321.

The position of these Negroes is further told in Lane-Poole's "Story of Turkey," according to which: "The black eunuchs, who were all Africans, numbered about 200 and were the special guard of the Imperial Harem. Their chief... had the rank of a pasha of three tails, and administered the Holy City and the imperial mosques, from which he derived an enormous income. He wore a white robe trimmed with sable, and a cylindrical head-dress of white muslin twenty-five inches high." (p. 288, London, 1883.)

Dr. D. A. Zambaco who lived in Turkey under Abdul Hamid says," The ex-Sultan Abdul Hamid had nearly 200 eunuchs in his service. Their chief named Kizlar Aghassi— Lord of the Girls or Dar-el-Saadet-el-Cherifa (Agha of the Noble House of Felicity), had the title of His Highness, like the Imperial Princes and the prime minister. He occupied at the Imperial Court, a very high rank on ceremonial occasions immediately after the prime minister, and sometimes even before him

"This great personage was loaded with honors and decorations and he possessed great medals with plaques and diamonds. Immediately after him two mussahis (other eunuchs) who lived constantly in the closest intimacy with the sovereign who confided to them all the most delicate ones concerning himself and the state and demanded their advice." "Les Eunuques," p. 43, Paris, 1911.

Dr. Zambaco says that the uglier and the blacker the eunuch the greater favor he sometimes enjoyed as certain masters feared having a "too good-looking eunuch" among the girls.

R. Millant, in "L'Esclavage in Turquie," says that Hafiz Beheram, the head eunuch, was more powerful in 1877, than the Grand Vizier, or Prime Minister.

Two black eunuchs, Djevher Aghassi and Nadir Agha, were founders of the Mohammedan League, which tried to uphold the power of Abdul Hamid in 1907. Speaking of the 543 principal members of this party, that had been arrested by the Young Turks. Sir Edwin Pears said: "Seventeen were journalists and the remainder military men and hodjas. The most brilliant of them all, intellectually, was Nadir Agha, who in the tenth year of his age, was bought by the Sultan from a slave merchant in Egypt for one hundred and fifty francs and had developed during the last few years, into Abdul Hamid's most trusted adviser." ("Fall of Abdul Hamid," p. 55, London, 1910.)

Djevher was hanged on Galata Bridge by the Young Turks, but Nadir Agha saved his own life by revealing the hiding-place of millions in gold and jewels concealed by Abdul Hamid.

* * * *

Hassan of Oulubad, a Sudanese soldier, was the hero of the capture of Constantinople by the Turks in 1453. The Sultan had promised a handsome reward to the first who should gain a position on the wall of the beleaguered city.

Hassan, who was of gigantic stature, was the first. Gripping his shield in his left hand and fighting his way with his right, he was able to make his way to the top of the broken wall, where he was followed by thirty companions. The Greeks killed eighteen of them, but Hassan held the enemy off long enough for others to scale the wall and climb over. Hassan was killed in the struggle, but his initiative led to the capture of the city. (Georgius Pharantzes, p. 285; Hasluck, "Christianity and Islam," p. 730, Oxford, 1929.)

NOTES ON THE ILLUSTRATIONS

As regards the pictures in this book, I would like to say that those that have been used to illustrate the historical side could have been several times as many. On the other hand, those representing the more modern anthropological side are not all that I would like them to have been.

It would have been possible for me to get any number of the latter, however, and excellent ones, too, while I was in the many lands I visited. I could easily have taken photos of mixed couples in all walks of life, as well as of European, African, and Asiatic mixed bloods. On the subject of Germany, which is important just now, I could have had many good ones of the children born to German women by Senegalese fathers, and others, but, alas, I had not thought of writing a book along these lines, then.

The fact is this book was projected and started in June, 1940, or only two months before it went to the printers. Of course, I had been gathering material along this line for thirty years. The result is that with the war on, I had to fall back on such pictures in my collection as would fit nearest the thought I wished to express. Therefore it will be necessary to ask the reader's indulgence.

THE JACKET OF THE BOOK

In this panorama of Old World faces appear all types from kings and dictators to untouchables. Rulers of Europe, Asia, and Africa; primitive and civilized peoples of all races; popes, comedians, artists, queens of the stage, writers, all go towards symbolizing what has gone into the physical make-up of even the proudest of the proud in every race and class (see page 14 of this book).

PLATE I.

Charlotte Sophia, German-born consort of George III, had the broad nostrils and heavy lips "of the blond Negroid type" mentioned by Brunold Springer on page 11 of this book. Horace Walpole, who saw her wrote: "Nostrils spreading too wide. Mouth has the same fault." (National Biog. Vol. IV, p. 123). It would have been possible to reproduce several pictures of Negroes who resemble this English queen. I have one of a little Negro musician, whose features, especially the mouth, is strikingly like hers.

This blond Negroid type is not uncommon even in Nordic Europe. As was seen, whites and blacks have been mixing all over Europe from the dimmest antiquity. I recall one blonde I saw in a Paris cafe, with very fair skin and light hair, who was so Negroid in appearance, especially the nose and the mouth, that a French person who was with me, exclaimed, "Voila, une Negresse blanche."

It happened that this girl was waiting for some Negro friends of mine, and I made her acquaintance. She was born in Holland of a Dutch father and a Negro mother. She was tall, very well built and like most Europeans with a Negro strain was rather proud of it, and preferred the company of Negroes.

I hold that white people who show Negroid features had a Negro ancestor, more or less distant. When we see a lighter complexioned Negro with lips and nose rather after the Caucasian mold, we do not hesitate to say that he has "white" blood. It is a poor rule that doesn't work both ways. One's ancestry does not just come out of the air.

For a copy of this portrait of Queen Charlotte see Greenwood, A. D., Hanoverian Queens of England, Vol. II, frontispiece, London, 1909. My copy comes from the National Portrait Gallery, London.

II. and III.

This portrait of Beethoven was sketched from life by Letronne and engraved by Hofel. It was done in charcoal, and thus helps to give some idea of Beethoven's real complexion.

The color of an engraving does not necessarily correspond to the subject's real color, though many seem to think so. A white man can be made to look black, and a black man, white, in a picture. A dark tint, however, will bring out Negroid features, if there are any, as they do in this picture of Beethoven—a reason, perhaps, why this one is often reproduced in a shade much lighter than the original.

Beethoven was described by one who knew him as "blackish-brown" in color. As for his features they have been so Nordicized that as Thayer remarks the dark-skinned ill-favored little man that was Beethoven would not recognize himself if he were to return.

Every bit of evidence available from those who knew Beethoven indicate that he was of Negro ancestry. And Beethoven is not the only great German of Negro blood that we could name.

As regards the portrait of Clarence Cameron White, it shows him somewhat lighter than he is. Mr. White is about three-eighths Negro. But it will be seen that he appears less Negroid than Beethoven, whom he resembles somewhat.

For a facsimile of this portrait of Beethoven, shading and all, see Paul Bekker's Beethoven, p. 80 (pt. 2), Berlin, 1911. For a picture of his life-mask at the age of 42, and more data on his Negro ancestry see Sex and Race, Vol. 3, pp. 206-09.

IV.

See page 14 of this book on what was said of Disraeli's Negroid features by the German, Hans Guenther. Here we find the staid, reliable and old established Illustrated London News saying the same thing. When an Englishman and a German agree on a fact like this, it would be interesting to know what the Ku Klux minded ones can say? Also what of those Negroes who can only find inspiration in worshipping at the shrine of white heroes? Some of these Negroes even resent having it pointed out that this or that great man they had worshipped as white was really of Negro ancestry. Such will call writers who do this falsifiers. I have several times been attacked in print and on the platform. In 1919 when I was writing sketches of great Negroes as General Dumas, Antar, Kafur, Bilal, an Aframerican who was studying in Germany wrote to the leading Negro newspaper in America saying that I was talking all fable. His German professors had never told him of these things, ergo, they couldn't possibly be true.

The professional Nordic and his henchmen in the universities and elsewhere, are adept at raking into their fold every great man regardless of race, and claiming that he was Caucasian, the object being to prove that Negroes are incapable of outstanding accomplishment and thus only fit for labor battalions and the rougher and the badly paid jobs.

This matter, as I see it, is of great importance, if we are to have any real democracy in America, any real appreciation of minority groups. We have proof of its importance in the fact that the professional Nordic will go out of the way to say of some Negroid-looking group or individual that there is "no Negro blood, whatever" in them. Fascism runs true to the tactics of the slave-dealer. Its first step is to declare that the contemplated victims are of low mental and moral calibre and as such deserve no better fate.

In a really civilized world it wouldn't matter a hoot what race this or that great man was but with the spokesman of a certain type of humanity, asserting, louder and still louder, that their type is the only one that has ever done anything worthwhile and will ever do it, it becomes necessary to point out the truth even though it falls on prejudiced white ears or on incredulous and apathetic Negro ones.

V.

The two first figures in the upper row are prehistoric European carvings, the Woman of Laussel and the Willendorf Venus. The third is a modern Hottentot-Bushman woman showing the "apron" or elongated nymphs. Note that the prehistoric carvings show the same detail, thus adding a link to the theory that the Grimaldis of Europe were Negroes.

The Bushwomen-Hottentots are noted also for the peculiar shape and size of their buttocks, the term for which is steatopygy. Note the resemblance in this respect between the modern Hottentot woman (center) and the Grimaldi woman (lower right), as well as the huge breasts of both.

The figures to the lower left are reconstructions of Grimaldis by Dr. Alfred Rutot and are in the Belgian Academy. The man is holding the Willendorf Venus. (For article and more illustrations of modern Hottentots see E. A. Hooton, Harvard-African Studies II. Varia Africana II.

VI.

This Negro soldier is a detail from a high-relief from the excavations of Osuna, Spain, and is in the Louvre. He might have been a Roman. A figure beside him (not shown here) is clearly a white man. (2) Ancient Negro skull from Mugem, Portugal. (3) Skull of a West Indian Negro who may be yet alive as X-rayed by Prof. H. B. Moens. Note the similarity that exists between the two although the former lived thousands of years ago. (See H. B. Moens' Towards Perfect Man.) (4) This animated scene, said to be the world's oldest picture of a battle, comes from the caverns of Morella la Vella, Castellon, Spain. (See Obermaier, H., Fossil Man in Spain, p. 250, New Haven, 1924). As was said European cave-art bears a striking resemblance to African one. (5) Here is another proof of Negro penetration over the world in prehistoric times. These are finger-prints left tens of thousands of years ago by nomads in the caves of France, Spain, Arabia, Palestine, India, Mexico, California, and elsewhere. Note that some of the fingers are amputated, a religious rite that was observed not so long ago by the Bushman of South Africa, and is said to be even now by the Australian Bushman. (See W. J. Sollas, "Ancient Hunters," p. 412, N. Y., 1924.)

VIII.

Right: Nathaniel Guy of Washington, D. C., former school-teacher and actor. Mr. Guy, who is dark-skinned, and a Negro, was once barred from a musical recital in Washington, D. C., given by his son, who is lighter in color, and was believed to be white. In most white colleges and centres of learning in Europe and America, Mr. Guy's type would be labelled "Semitic" and there would be positive denial that he has any "Negro" blood. Left: Mrs. Fred Summers of Chicago, who bears a resemblance to more than one queen on the Egyptian monuments. Certain Egyptologists like Professors Reisner and Junker would call her type, Hamitic, and deny that there was any Negro strain in her. If they saw her in real life, and in America, they would immediately realize their error. So we are sure, too, had they seen most of the Pharaohs in real life, perhaps. Mr. Guy bears a striking resemblance to Sir Johnston Forbes-Robertson, noted English actor. See the latter's picture in the London Sphere, Nov. 13, 1937, p. 259.

IX.

1. Statuette of Egyptian woman (broken) of the 18th Century B.C. in the Ashmolean Museum, Oxford. An unusually good representation of an unmixed Negro type. Fatness was, and still is, a sign of affluence in Africa. In many parts of that continent young girls are sent to fattening-farms for months before marriage. Some return veritable balloons of fat—much fatter than this type.

2. Pharaoh of the First Dynasty about 4500 B.C. (after Petrie). Note the Negro Bushman features. (3) White woman bearing sacrifice (Louvre). This is one of the best representations of the Nordic type from Ancient Egypt extant. 4. A black slave and a white slave waiting upon a lady at a party, according to Sir J. G. Wilkinson. 5. Shenapt, wife of Taharka, ruler of Ethiopia, Egypt, Syria, and Palestine. Taharka was an unmixed Negro (see XVI, lower left. Shenapt seems to be almost white. 6. Saite Pharaoh (Torino Museum). Note the same kind of nose and mouth on the modern, woolly-haired, Ethiopian noblewoman to his right.

X.

1. Ra-Kheper, a general of the Ptolemys (Boston Museum). 2. Eshmunuzar II (Louvre) see page 60 of this book. 3. Ra-hotep and his white wife, Princess Nefert

(Cairo Museum) see page 52. 4. A Negro princess of the Cheops family (Boston Museum). Cheops was the builder of the Great Pyramid. 5. Bust of Negro male from the Louvre, very life-like and modern in appearance. 6. Negro noblewoman from the British Museum. 7. Egyptian lady from the Metropolitan Museum of Art.

XI.

Upper left: The high priestess, Tui, Second Theban Empire. (Louvre). Note the extreme beauty of the robe about the thighs and legs. Since these people were Negroes, it is evident that much of this beautiful work was done by Negroes, too. Upper centre: Amenhotep, chief architect of Amenhotep III. (Cairo Museum). Note his rather American Indian features. 3. Egyptian lady. (Metropolitan Museum of Art). Note the beauty of the lines and the form showing through the robe. Centre: Mouth of Queen Nefertiti. She was an Ethiopian. Distinctly Negro. Lower left: Taharka or Tirhaquah of the Bible (Metropolitan Museum of Art). See page 56 of this book. For his wife see IX, 5. Lower centre: Ramases II. Ramases shows little of the Negro strain. His mummy is white and his hair straight. Lower right: Another Pharaoh (British Museum).

XII.

1. Dagon, the Fish-God, whose temple Samson was said to have pulled down. (In Enciclo. Univ. Illus.). 2. Phoenician God. (Louvre). 3. Amen-ophis IV, better known as Akhenaton (Louvre). 4. Head of ancient Egyptian god, probably of the First Dynasty. 5. Osiris, one of the greatest of all the gods of Egypt. The last two are from the Metropolitan Museum of Art.

XVII.

Upper left. Usertsen I of the XIth Dynasty (British Museum). Pure African type. Note the look of majesty and tremendous power on his face. Upper right. Mernepthah. Said to be the Pharaoh of the Exodus. Note his full Negroid mouth. (Metropolitan Museum of Art.) Centre, left.—Nubian official (British Museum). Right.— Hyskos or Shepherd King, one of an Asiatic dynasty that ruled Egypt. Below.—Negro busts from Tanis, Egypt.

XVIII.

1. East Indian girl from Sir Rabindranath Tagore's musical circle. (Reproduced from Atlantis Magazine, Berlin. July-Dec. 1930, p. 672). 2. West African girl. 3. Ivory figure of girl from Ancient Egypt. Man, No. 107, 1901). 4. Dravidian man (Risley's People of India.) Note the Negroid features in all the types, ancient as well as modern, Asiatic and African.

XVIIIa. Upper row, left to right: Maharajah of Nepaul; Maharajkum Arani Karamjit Singh; Maharajah of Kapurthala. Lower, left to right: Rajah of Khallikote; Sir Jagadis Chunder Bose—one of the world's greatest scientists, discovered the identical nature of physiological reactions in plants and animals; Sir Alladi Krishnaswami Ayyar, Advocate-General of Madras; and Sir Muhammad Zafrullah Khan, who represented India at the coronation of George VI.

Lower group, left to right: Sultan of Pahang; Sultan of Trengganu; His Highness, the Yang di Pertuan of Negri Sembilan, all of the Malay States; and the Sultan of Zanzibar.

I have seen some of these personages, and the Negroid strain in them was evident. The Maharajah of Kapurthala, one of the most important of the Indian Princes, when in a sack suit, looks like an Aframerican professional man. I was once present at a reception given in his honor in Paris.

XIX.

1. Andaman Islanders, or Mincopies. These tiny Negro people who live off the coast of India, are one of the purest and oldest races on earth. The Hitler Aryan

or the Southern Ku Kluxer are veritable mongrels and newcomers in comparison with them. They have remained unmixed for thousands of years, which is more than the proudest German or Ku Kluxer can truthfully say. The last pure Aryans died three thousand years ago. And they weren't white even then. 2. Mongolian Negro of real old African stock from Central Africa. Note the slant eye like that of the true Mongolian, No. 3. Thus it will be seen that the slant eye is not alone a characteristic of the Mongolian, and adds proof to the theory that the Mongols were of Negro ancestry. For more of these Negro Mongolians see pictures in Man, plate M, December 1924 and February 1925. 4. Laplander Girl of Northern Europe, with European eyes, and Negroid cheek bones, nose and mouth. The Laplanders were probably Negritos, who were changed to their present type by environment and diet.

XX.

1. Siamese girl, not unlike Aframerican types I have seen. 2. Ex-King Prajadhipok, now resident in England, clearly shows his Negro ancestry. The Semangs, a very ancient race, still live in the south of Siam, which has been rechristened Thailand. 3. This Indo-Chinese soldier could easily be mistaken for a Senegalese. 4. An unmixed Negro type from the South Seas. 5. A Japanese belle—upper part of the face Caucasian; lower part, Negro.

XXI.

This very charming young woman of Tahiti, a South Sea Island belonging to France, could well have been an Aframerican or West Indian mulatto. Note the extraordinary loveliness of the arms and the bosom (Toutes Les Races. Editions Nilsson. Paris). Popular writers on the South Sea and movie-films call this type Caucasian, probably the better to sell their wares.

XXII.

1, 2, 3. Greek coins of the Fifth Century B.C., representing Helios, Sun Deity. Effigies are clearly Negro. 4. Coins of Delphos, founder of the great Delphic Oracle. 5. These two coins have faces that are decidedly Negro, and are intended to represent Athena, one of the greater of the Olympian deities, pre-eminent as a civic goddess, wise in the industries of peace and great in those of war. Athens was named after her. 6. These five other Greek coins all have the effigies of Negroes, according to Ernest Babélon, noted numismatist and archaeologist. For reproductions of the above-mentioned coins see Babélon, E. Traité des Monnaies Grecques et Romaines, Part I, (1) p. 496; Part II, (1) p. 1614; Part II (2) pp. 462-67 (CXIV); and CXLVII, (p.1015. Paris, 1907. 7. Coins of Hannibal of Carthage, see page 85 of this book. Below.—A gold coin of Justinian II, Byzantine Emperor, with the effigies of Christ and Justinian. Note the pepper-corn hair of Christ (right) and the straight one of Justinian (British Museum). The Cambridge Encyc. Co. says that this coin places beyond a doubt "the fact that Jesus Christ was a Negro."

The principal work extant on the Negro in ancient Greece and Rome is by Grace Beardsley and is published by Johns Hopkins University in its Archaeological Studies No. 4. However, Mrs. Beardsley has not done justice to her subject, and most certainly not to her excellent bibliography. She seemed a bit too eager, perhaps unconsciously, to project Southern traditions into the days of Homer, Cicero, and Caesar. Had her Southern training and her Southern publishers anything to do with this?

For her, the Negro in Greece and Rome were hardly better than slaves. Moreover, she speaks with rather too much positiveness on a period most of whose history has been lost.

It is clear that Mrs. Beardsley never consulted such works as Jacob Bryant's Analysis of Ancient Mythology: Higgins' Anacalypsis; Massey's Book of the Beginnings: nor Francis Pulzsky's able criticism of ancient iconography in Nott and Gliddons' Indigenous Races of Mankind, pp. 87-202, Philadelphia, 1857.

The coins of Hannibal, as was shown, bear the effigy of a full-blooded Negro. Beardsley, so far as I could see, makes no mention of Hannibal.

Pulzsky proves that the present accepted portrait of Hannibal is a fake. It was "not a portrait," he says, "but the ideal representation of a hero" from the silver coins of Dernes of Phoenicia (p. 93). As regards Negroes in the higher social life of Rome, which Mrs. Beardsley ignores, he says, "We know likewise several Roman cameos which represent Negroes with all the refined elegance of the imperial epoch." He gives one such portrait. (pp. 190-91).

The omissions of Mrs. Beardsley are too many to be cited here. Though she is an instructor in Latin it is clear that she did no research on the world, Niger (niger, nigra, nigrum) from which Negro comes. Had she done so she would have discovered that it is a very ancient African word, which was in all probability, brought into the Latin by the Negroes themselves, and which, though having at first nothing at all to do with color, came to be adopted as a surname just as "white" and "black," old Anglo-Saxon words found their way into the English language. In those days one's surname came from one's physical traits or one's occupation. In short, Niger, was incorporated into Latin just as taboo, boomerang, tomahawk, were into English. (For bibliography see 100 Amazing Facts About the Negro, 18th ed., p. 44.)

Another very important fact she omitted is one given by one of the authors in her bibliography, C. T. Seltman, who points out that in ancient times the Negro was used "a prophylactic," that is a charm against the evil eye. (Two Heads of Negresses, American Jour. of Archaeol., Vol. 24, 1920). Seltman cites in proof the researches of A. J. B. Wace (British School of Athens Jour., Vol. X, pp. 103-114, 1903-04), who shows how the phallus of the Negro was used as a charm, together with a certain sign which is still made in the Near East. To quote, "The phallus was, as is well-known, a most potent charm against the evil eye and Jahn gives many illustrations of this Goethe grotesque which is not a humpback but a misshapen Negro with a large *membrum* who is also making with his right hand one of the best known signs against the evil eye." (p. 110).

Might not this explain one of the reasons why the Negro was so popular in the royal courts of Europe and with the high nobility? Oh yes, much, very much can be read between the lines.

As was said, the Negro is still considered a sign of good luck in England (see page 219). And even in America, too. In Harlem, it is a common saying that when white people come adventuring into the Negro neighborhoods on a Saturday night and seek a Negro amour they come "to change their luck."

Necklaces in the form of the male organ of generation were worn publicly by even ladies of rank in Ancient Rome as the exhibits in the Museum of Naples show. It was even used as designs for candelabras and other household ornaments. I have a collection of such pictures from Naples and Pompeii. At Pompeii I saw phalluses chipped even into the pavement and protruding over doorways. As for lewd drawings they abounded in certain sections. Some of these drawings represented Negroes cohabiting with white women. One matron of Ancient Rome who gave birth to a mulatto child and was sued for divorce by her husband won by declaring that it was the husband's fault. She said that the husband had a fresco in his room showing a Negro in the act with a white woman and that at the moment of conception her eyes fell on the drawing, hence the mulatto child. (Dr. O. A. Wall, "Sex and Sex Worship," p. 564. 1932.)

I call attention to these facts here because they will be important links in my theory of race-mixing later on, and of why black and white have always mixed, even against the greatest opposition. We shall ignore the prudes. Life flows on continuous like a river; thus there are important connecting tissues between life as lived a hundred thousand years ago and now. Man has not changed physically at least in all that period.

To give one instance. Seltman in the above-mentioned article, cites a case of jealousy from Greek mythology that was not uncommon in Colonial America. This is the story of Lamia, a beautiful Negro princess, symbolic of Africa, who was beloved by Zeus, greatest of the Greek gods, and because of this was turned into a hideous monster by is wife, Hera.

Seltman says, "Mythology tells us of Lamia, a daughter of the royal house of Libya, the black princess of whom Zeus was enamored, and whom Hera, in her jealousy, caused her to devour her own children and then turning her into a hideous creature." (Ibid, p. 15.)

A Greek vase of the period shows a Negro woman on one side and a white man on the other, who are said by some archaeologists to be Lamia and Zeus.

Hera, according to the story, handed Lamia over the satyrs to be tortured. A Greek vase of the Fifth Century B.C. represents the scene. The satyrs have Lamia bound to a stake, and are pulling away her breasts and scorching her genitals. (See Archaeologisches Institut des Deutchen Reiches Jahrbuch (Mitt. Athenische) Vol. 16, Plate IX, 1891.

A decorative bronze of the period shows a Negro woman, said to be Lamia, in a happier pose. She is depicted as a queen with monkeys, guinea-hens, and other animals about her. (See A. P. Bienkowski's De Simulacrum Barbarum Gentium Apud Romanos. Fig. 85, p. 87. Cracoviae. 1900.)

Just one more notable omission of Mrs. Beardsley's: Bronze weights with the busts of Negroes have been found in lands once dominated by Rome. Wace says, "Bronze weights in the form of Negro busts are fairly common throughout the Roman world." What does this mean? An Aryan writer will probably say it means the Negro was sold as a slave. But all peoples were then sold as slaves. In any case, I have seen British bronze weights with the effigy of Queen Victoria, especially in the postal service.

In a word, Mrs. Beardsley falls short of the splendid possibilities of her subject. We are nevertheless indebted to her for what she has done so far.

XXIII.

1. Back hair of the Greek god, Apollo, whose rites were founded by a woolly-haired Negro, Delphos (see plate XXII. 4: and page 80 of this book). Note the same pepper-corn hair on the head of Christ on the coin (bottom of plate XXII). Likewise of the Buddhas (plates XXVI and XXVII). This bears out the assertion made in the appendix, "Black Gods and Messiahs" that the earliest deities were woolly-haired Negroes, and that the pepper-corn hair was a sign of divinity. I believe further that even as some Negroes now straighten their hair in imitation of white people, that white people started curling their hair in imitation of Negroes. Perhaps the whites even did so as a religious rite. White women in the civilized lands still curl their hair as a relic of the time when the Negroes were the ruling power. Negroid races are the only ones with naturally curling hair.

2. One of the Ptolemys, and an ancestor of Cleopatra (Louvre). Note the Negroid mouth, and the curly hair, which is the same as No. 4.

3. Portrait of a Graeco-Egyptian lady with long, curling hair and Negro face.

4. Ancient Greek bust, said to be Memnon. This is one of the most vigorous specimens of Greek art. (Berlin Museum). For some splendid reproductions of this remarkable head in its various aspects see Schrader, H., Über den Marmorkopf eines Negers in den Königlichen Museum. Programm Zumm Winckelmannfesten No. 60. Berlin, 1900.

5. This Libyan sibyl from the Cathedral of Sienna is the kind mentioned on page 275 of this book. It shows the influence that Negro female gods, the greatest of which was Isis, had on the early Christian religion in Rome.

XXIV.

Jean Paul Laurens (1838-1921), celebrated historical painter, of France, and a close student of Roman history, gave this Negro lad as his conception of the young Roman Emperor, Honorius. The latter, as a boy, succeeded his father, Theodosius the Great, in 395 A.D. For Negro strain in the Roman emperors see page 86 of this book.

XXV.

Falasha (Jewish) boys with their teacher, Rabbi Abraham, in Ethiopia. For pictures of other Ethiopian Jews see plate XXXII (centre, left.)

XXVI. and XXVII.

See appendix on the Buddhas, pages 264-267 of this book. Note the wooly hair and the Negroid appearance of all save XXVI, 6; and XXVIII, 3. The hair of the latter serves to show that what seems to be a cap in some cases is really hair so convention-ized. XXVI, 4, is from the British Museum. It is a woolly-haired, life-sized Buddha, coal-black, and one of the finest statues ever made by the hand of man. The lines flow in the most perfect harmony imaginable. The Buddhas on plate XXVII are in the Metropolitan Museum of Art, New York, and are reproduced through its courtesy.

XXVIII.

1. Green stone mask from Honduras, Central America. (American Museum of Natural History). 2. Negro figure from ancient Mexican monument (Ignatius Don-nelly's Atlantis). 3. Head of Quetzalcoatl, greatest of the ancient Mexican messiahs. Note the curved noses, broad nostrils, and the very large lips of all three. What better proof is needed that the Negro lived in America long before Columbus than this? See 100 Amazing Facts About the Negro for other pictures. This head of Quetzalcoatl is in the Museum of the Trocadèro, Paris.

XXIX

The majority of the Black Madonnas were of this Negroid type prior to their destruction by vandals during the French Revolution. When they were reconstructed they were still made black but with Caucasian features. See pages 272-282 of this book.

XXXIII.

This powerful Arabian King is described by all who have seen him as a swarthy and stalwart mulatto. His son, Emir Saud, is also a mulatto. For his and other pictures see Atlantis Magazine of Berlin, July to December, 1930, pp. 523, 526.

XXXIX.

These were the two last surviving Negroes of Tasmania. The aborigines were ex-terminated by the English settlers who poured strichnine in their water-holes. The treat-ment of the Australian and the Tasmanian blacks constitutes one of the most ghastly chapters in the history of white colonization. 3. Madagascar was seized by the French in 1895. But they did so only after ten years of war with the natives who had developed a high state of culture. The Malagasy Queen, Rañavalona III, was exiled to, Algeria, and a French governor installed.

XLI.

This snapshot of the street of El Conde Negro (The Negro Count) was made by the author but the lamp was in the way. For other relics of the Negroes of Seville see picture of the Negrito parade on the cover of the 100 Amazing Facts About The Negro. It looks like a Ku Klux parade but the Negrito order antedates the Klan by four centuries. Their parade was a religious one. See also paintings by Sebastian Gomez, in pictures of the Cathedral of Seville and Los Venerables. Sebastian Gomez, better known as El Molato, a Negro, was one of the best known pupils of Murillo.

Juan de Pareja (centre, right) was a pupil of Velasquez. Two of his paintings are in the Hispanic Museum of New York. Others are in El Prado, Madrid.

As regards the beautiful senorita (upper left) many strains, Negro and Caucasian, have gone into her physical heritage.

XLIa. These Negro favorites were something more than mere pets. They were treated like royalty. They bore the royal names and surname, and married into the nobility. One of these Negroes, Don Alfonso Carlos de Bourbon, adopted son of Charles III of Spain, was an architect. (Villa, J. M. Locos, enanos, negros, y ninos palaciegos, siglos XVI y XVII, p. 30. Mexico, 1939.) The portrait is by Antonio Moro.

XLII.

This portrait of Duke Alessandro by Bronzino is one of several of him extant. In the Museum of the Marquis de Cerralbo in Madrid I saw one by Andrea del Sarto that I had not hitherto heard of. The Duke's effigy also appears on dies made by Benvenuto Cellini, whose patron Alessandro was. Other portraits of Alessandro, notably one of his coronation, together with other sources on his Negro strain in his short biography in my "World's Great Men of Color," Vol. 1.

XLIII.

Portion of a magnificent candle-holder in the Louvre which was presented by the City of Venice to Marie de Medici on her marriage to Henry IV of France in 1600. In the centre is the head of a Negro woman, jet-black, super-imposed on the head of a white queen. Surrounding the Negro woman are other kings and queens, among them Alphonso II. In the lowest right, are Marie de Medici, herself, and Henry IV. This Negro woman, from her high position on this jewel is believed to be Anna, Negro mistress of Pope Clement VII, and mother of Alessandro dei Medici. (See the 100 Amazing Facts about the Negro, 18th ed., p. 31.) For a picture of the whole of this extraordinarily beautiful jewel see: Babèlon, E., Histoire de la Gravure sur Gemmes en France. Fig. 46, p. 124. Paris, 1902.)

XLIV.

All of these items, save 8, are cameos in the Bibliothèque Nationale, Paris. 1, 3 and 5 are Negro kings, or more correctly, representations of Balthasar, one of the Three Wise Men. 4 and 6 are Negro women. 10 is a full-blooded Negro woman and bears the inscription: "E per tal—variar—natura—e bela (Even in human varieties like this Nature is beautiful). 2 and 9 are heads of Negroes and white women together. This putting of the heads of Negro men and white women together was very common and goes back to the most ancient times as No. 8, which is a Greek vase of the 5th Century B.C. will show. Even earlier than that is an Etruscan vase of a similar type in the British Museum, a picture of which is in Nott and Gliddons' (ibid, plate IX).

The Negroes who served as models for these cameos were the favorites at the courts of European rulers. Babélon says, "One may be astonished in this last series at the great number of portraits of Negro men and women—the same remark has often been made on the subject of painting on seeing the frequency of Negroes in the pictures of the Italian Renaissance. It was not exclusively because of artistic taste not for pure love of contrast that the artists showed such prediliction for Negro types. The kings of the 15th and 16th centuries had the habit of keeping Negroes beside them even as they kept jesters . . . King René had several of these Negroes in his suite. Sometimes they served as interpreters. The Negro favorite of this king was named Falcon. King René also had a Negro woman favorite, named Cresselle. Some of the Negroes on the gems with crowns were one of the Three Wise Men. Other Negroes were crowned by the monarchs in fun at feasts." (Camées antiques et modernes, Introd. LXXV, Paris, 1897). A. Lécoy de la Marche. Le Roi Renè, Vol. II, p. 151, Paris, 1875, mentions the Negro favorite, Falcon, and also Cresselle.

The number of such jewels, mostly of Italian make, with the heads of Negroes, is great. C. W. King, an authority on jewels, thought they were made in such numbers to "commemorate the renowned black concubine of Clement VII. mother of Alessandro dei Medici."

XLV.

This picture hangs in the Provincial Museum of Hanover, Germany. The Negro, as was said, was also a prime favorite at the courts of the rulers of Northern Europe. Any number of such portraits are in the galleries of Holland, Germany, and Belgium.

XLVI.

1 and 2 are from the Lichtenstein Museum, Vienna. 3. One of the favorites of the German kings in the royal park at San Souci, Potsdam. (See page 178). I am

LXIII. (See page 301)

indebted to Mr. Hilyard Robert Robinson, architect of Washington, D. C., for this picture, who took it while in Germany. 4. The celebrated Rass Prince Monolulu, who, in reality is a West Indian, named McKay. He lived in Germany, married a German wife, and won great popularity there, but was interned as a British subject during the first World War. After he was freed he went back to England where he now lives.

XLVII.

This picture together with XLIV, XLIX, L, LI, LIX and LX are intended to show the lack of color prejudice among Europeans, at least the pre-Hitler ones.

XLVIII.

One of these young men is an architect; another (centre, seated) is Herr Brody, a movie actor of distinction. I have a picture of Brody surrounded by a swarm of admiring German women but it is from a newspaper and was too faint to be reproduced. The other persons are professionals of one kind or another. I met them all in Berlin in 1929. The dancer is Lerm Merze and was billed as Neger-Häuptling Sope. The most popular vaudeville artist in Berlin in 1929 was a coal-black Aframerican girl of six, named Little Esther. I saw her play to vast, applauding crowds in Berlin and elsewhere. One of Hitler's first acts on coming to power was to drive all the Negro musicians and entertainers from Germany. They were making the Germans laugh and thus probably preventing them from reaching that murderous grimness necessary for a Hitler war.

XLIX.

Joé Alex is a native of Guadeloupe, West Indies, a movie actor, and one of the dancers of the Bals de l'Opèra, Paris. This pose and others with Brigitte Helm and himself were produced by UFA, Germany's leading moving picture concern. The latter is now the chief propaganda organ of Goebbels. Joé Alex has appeared in several films with German and French actresses.

L.

1. The mother of this Negro child, as will be seen, comes from a good German family (3), which makes no hesitation in recognizing the child. The father's name is Sidney Garner. He is an American and was the manager of Little Esther, the six-year old Negro dancer mentioned in XLVIII. 5. Sabac El Cher was born in the palace of Kaiser Wilhelm II., as was said, and was one of the many Negroes in favor in high German circles prior to the war of 1914.

LII.

1. Count Munck. 2. Gustavus IV. Note the resemblance between these two, and the total lack of resemblance between Gustavus IV and his reputed father, Gustavus III. Gustavus IV's face is decidedly Negroid. So is Munck's. Note his curved Negroid (Moorish) nose, like the noses on plate XXVIII. The hair of Gustavus IV is woolly, also. Munck wears a wig. All of the portraits of Gustavus IV save one in which he wears a beard, show his Negroid features. This is especially true of one of him on horseback by Lafrensen the Younger and now in the private collection of Baron Ramel. There is no doubt in my mind that Gustavus IV had "Negro" blood. His supposed father, Gustavus III, is of pure Nordic type; so is his mother. This portrait of Gustavus IV is in C. H. Trolle's Overste Gustafsson, p. 105, Stockholm, 1923.

LIII.

The fact that this Moorish prince is on the coat-of-arms of a noble Irish family, whose surname is also Moore, is significant. Negroes appear not only in the coat-of-arms of noble European families but in those of cities as Coburg, Germany; Arras, France; and others in Italy and Corsica.

2. Jacob Capitein, who was born in Africa and sold as a slave when seven years old, became one of the leading divines of Holland in the 1700's. He wrote several books on religion. 3. Gustavus Vasa, writer, naturalist, physician and poet. Born in Africa in 1745, he was sold as a slave in Barbados. Winning his freedom, he settled

in England where he became a leading anti-slavery agitator and won the favor of the Prince of Wales, later George IV. His mulatto son, born in England, became librarian for Sir Joseph Banks, noted naturalist.

One of Hogarth's pictures that I omitted to mention in the text is entitled "An Unpleasant Discovery," and shows the friends of an English dandy discovering that he has a coal-black woman in his luxurious bed. This picture is omitted from most editions of Hogarth. A copy appears in Iwan Bloch's Sex Life in England, page 400.

Thomas Rowlandson's (1756-1827), "Dairy-Maid's Delight," showing a love-bout between a Negro and a white girl, is usually censored, too.

LIIIa. Norman blood is considered the highest in English ancestry and Negro one, the lowest. Here, however, is a Norman knight with pronounced Negro features.

His lady, with her family bearings on which is a cockatoo, looks like a mulatto.

No. 2 are the arms of Evesham, which has several Negro heads, one of which is a Moor, and another, an English knight. All are from the heraldic collection of Sir Thomas Wriothesley, Garter King-of-arms, (1504-1534).

3. The Zaguri family is of Moorish ancestry (Casanova de Seingalt Carteggi. Casanoviani, Vol. II, p. vi. Naples, 1918.)

LIV.

Upper left: Miss Ira Aldridge, daughter of the famous tragedian of that name, by his second wife, an Englishwoman. Miss Aldridge, whose pen name is Montagu Ring, is one of London's best known composers. She was a pupil of Jenny Lind. Thomas B. Freeman was a noted missionary. (See Walker. F. D. Thomas Birch Freeman. London, 1929.)

Lower left: Coleridge-Taylor; and right, Miss Betty Rowland, whose Aframerican father won much success in Europe as a juggler and vaudeville artiste.

LV.

For General Ivan Hannibal see page 174 of this book. 2. DuChaillu. For his Negro ancestry see Edward Clodd's Memories, p. 71, London, 1916. For Browning see p. 204 of this book. This picture of Marie Dumas is from the Bibliothèque Nationale, Paris.

LVI.

This rarely given picture of Pushkin is by Somov, and may be seen in the Pushkin Centenary Number of the Revue de Moscou, January 1, 1937. There can be no doubt of his ancestry here. Paul Carus is among those who denied that Pushkin was of Negro blood.

3. For Murat, King of Naples, see page 221 of this book. Note the same kind of hair and mouth as Pushkin. 2. The late Ambroise Vollard: As regards this millionaire art collector, I discovered that he was a Negro in a rather singular manner. Seeing his portrait in the New York Evening Telegram (Nov. 21, 1936) and feeling sure that he was of Negro ancestry I clipped it and put it away. Four years later while speaking of him to Arthur Schomburg, historian, he said that Vollard, who is a native of Reunion, East Africa, did have a Negro strain.

4. Maurice Donnay, who is a member of the French Academy and one of France's wittiest playwrights, is popularly said to be of Negro ancestry, and looks it too. I first learnt of this through the son of a colonel in the French Army. While the latter was looking over the pictures in my "World's Greatest Men and Women of African Descent," he said to me, "Do you know who is colored, too, and doesn't care who knows it? Maurice Donnay." He said also that his father and Donnay were good friends.

Several others, among them Professor Cenac-Thaly of the Lycée Michelet, told me the same thing. Donnay was born in France, but his parents are said to have come from Réunion, off the East African coast. Another member of the French Academy who was said to be colored, but who used to deny it indignantly was José Maria

Heredia, who was born in Cuba. There is this great difference between the mixed blood who was born in the colonies and the one born in Europe. The former hastens to deny it, if he can; the latter is most eager to acknowledge it, as did Pushkin, and Dumas. For more on Heredia, see World's Great Men of Color, Vol. 1, p. xvii.

LVII.

2. Prince Behanzin's father was the last King of Dahomey. His territory was seized by France, and he, himself, exiled to Martinique. Prince Behanzin was educated in France and grew up there. 3. This portrait is from the Royal College of Physicians and Surgeons, London. The mother was albino but the children were mulattoes of normal color.

LVIII.

1. The celebrated Senegalese dancer, Feral Benga, star of the Casino de Paris and the Folies Bergere. This picture gives only a faint idea of his superb physique.

LIX. and LX.

These pictures are intended to give, as was said, an idea of the lack of "color" sensitiveness in the Continental European. Upper left (LVIII) is the picture on the front cover of Retana's El Espejo de Pauline Bonaparte. I saw it openly displayed in the leading bookshops of Madrid. It represents the Negro, Thomas, bathing Pauline. My copy was crushed hence the scratched markings on Thomas' face.

Upper left is a front cover of the famous La Vie Parisienne. It was hung up on newsstands on the streets and gave many a Parisian a good laugh. I have several others of the same, one of them showing some French girls in a railway carriage returning from the Riviera. In the compartment with them is a jet-black Negro, and the girls are rather envious of him because they with all their pains have been able to acquire only a light coat of tan at the beach, while he has a deep coat of it merely as a gift from nature.

A picture that I thought best not to reproduce in a book for English and American readers was one from a recent number of illustrations of Voltaire's Candide, Chapter XI, in which a Negro sea-rover captures the Pope's daughter and makes her his mistress. This picture, which is of the finest artistry, was nevertheless on display in the window of the leading book-shop of the Boulevard St Michel, Paris, which was how I happened to know about it. But all Americans would not be offended at it. At least one refined American white woman, on seeing it, told me that the picture in question was the best in the collection, which is saying a great deal, from artistic and other reasons, perhaps.

Lower left speaks for itself—not an uncommon sight in America, too. Lower right is from the Moscow Art Gallery and I am indebted to Mr. James H. Hubert of the New York Urban League who brought it for me from Russia. This copy gives no idea, whatever, of the great beauty of the original.

LX appeared in the 1931 Colonial Exposition Number of Le Sourire, and gives the artist's idea of how black women should be treated. The elder man brings her jewels; the younger offers her flowers and kisses her hand. The European does not take the black woman into "dark and dirty alleys" (to quote from the Jeffersoniad) but into society and the leading places of entertainment -at least they did as late as 1939 B.H. (Before Hitler).

There is official recognition of the black woman, too, as this reproduction of a postage stamp shows. It was got out for the International Colonial Exposition of 1931, which was attended by 30,000,000 persons, and appeared on the two most popular issues, that is, fifty centimes, and a franc and half. (See page 302.)

LXI.

These two pictures are from the National Portrait Gallery, London.

LXII.

1. The portrait of Zamor is from the Carnavalet Museum, Paris, and is by Van Loo.

LXIII.

The story around these pictures furnishes another illustration of the underhand tactics of the Nazis in putting their propaganda across.

The scene is a popular West Indian cabaret in Paris where colored and white met to dance, dine, sing, and generally enjoy themselves. Coming to this night club, the Nazi newspaperman asked guests and entertainers to pose, which they readily did in the spirit of merriment and goodwill. The Nazi writer himself arranged the poses, after which he took the pictures to Berlin and used them in a terrific blast against the Negroes (see page 189-191 of this book).

The white man on the left who is cheek to cheek with a colored girl is not a Jew at all, but, of course, the Nazis had to have a Jew in it.

It was not necessary even for this Nazi to see colored and white dancing together to strike at the Negroes. One picture has two well-fed, well-dressed Negroes, who are shown to be very black. Underneath them is the title, *"Frankreich in Gefahr."* (France in Danger.)

One liberal German writer to whom I showed the article and the pictures said that the Nazis had done it, hoping to alienate English and American sympathy from France by showing her in favor of race-mixing.

Of course there are those Negroes who will object to seeing colored and white in the above-shown poses. These Ku Klux conditioned Negroes would probably feel less uncomfortable if they saw the blacks in the picture shown as servants rather than as equals, which is precisely what the Nazis and the Ku Kluxers would prefer, too.

However, it seems to me rather an expression of racial harmony of which we wish to heaven, there was more.

I knew several instances of Negro women being supported in high luxury by white Europeans. One of these was an Aframerican girl, very beautiful, who was the mistress of a French oil magnate. He gave her a Hispano-Suiza, jewels, and furs, and kept her in a sumptuous apartment on the Champs-Elysees, in which she entertained her Aframerican friends. I visited her several times.

The Paris newspapers also carried an account of a romance between her and a European ruler. This girl, who was an actress, had been in Spain, and from the description everyone said it was Alphonso.

Still another Aframerican girl in Paris, a singer, was kept in high style by a Swedish count. She had an apartment decorated in modern style on the Boulevard St. Germain in which she often received her Aframerican friends.

*   *   *   *

For additional pictures see the 100 Amazing Facts About the Negro; The Real Facts About Ethiopia; and World's Greatest Men and Woman of African Descent. Still others will appear in the large edition of this latter book which will be published soon.

*   *   *   *

The facts of race-mixing as presented in this book have been gathered from a vast variety of sources. Only the most reliable ones have been chosen. In addition are the author's own observations in Africa, America, and Europe. Errors will naturally creep in, but the facts, we are convinced, especially those coming from the centuries when color prejudice was not yet born, will more than preserve the integrity of the thought that the mixing of white and black is a fundamental law of nature.

The bibliography given is but a small part of the works consulted. Quotations, with their sources, have been given freely for the benefit of those who do not have access to large libraries.

Note: Page 240: Count d'Artois was brother, not son of Louis XVI. For source of Negro strain in Colette see also Sex and Race, Vol 3, p. viii.

COMMENTS ON THE WORKS OF J. A. ROGERS

Dr. W. E. B. DuBois: "No man living has revealed so many important facts about the Negro as Rogers."

In the Supreme Court of the United States, October Term, 1949, No. 25, in the printed Brief Amicus Curiae on Behalf of the Civil Rights Committee of the National Bar Association, which dealt with jim-crow seating on the dining cars and which ended in victory, "Sex and Race" was cited as an authority that the color-line in America had no scientific foundation. More than a page of the brief was devoted to supporting quotations from "Sex and Race." (pp. 18-19.)

H. L. Mencken, world-famed author, and dean of American letters: "Immensely entertaining and even more instructive. There is something new on almost every page, and you present it with the utmost effectiveness . . . a very competent job."

Carl Murphy, editor, Baltimore Afro-American: "As enthusiastic as a sixteen-year old is J. A. Rogers . . . His Sex and Race, was so hot he had to print it himself . . . Rogers is an authority on mixed families and backs it up with years of study in the libraries of Europe and America.

"I read Sex and Race several times a year, for, until he came along, I never knew that such world figures as Hannibal, Queen Nefertiti of Egypt, Gustavus IV of Sweden, Robert Browning (the poet), the wife of Garibaldi (the Italian patriot), and Disraeli (English Prime Minister) if they lived in America could be jim-crowed because of their colored ancestors.

"Nowhere else in contemporary literature is told the story of the Black Virgin Marys worshipped in many shrines in Europe.

"I'm waiting for Rogers' new book . . . He has infected me with his enthusiasm."

George S. Schuyler, "Rogers has spared no pains in getting the facts and the pictures, and spared no expense in bringing out a book that is typographically above par. It ought to have a big sale and certainly deserves it.

"For thirty years J. A. Rogers has given prodigally of his time, money and energy to get the truth about miscegenation. He has ransacked the libraries of the Americas, Europe and North Africa to find the facts that many people would prefer to keep hidden. He has done more than any writer I know to smash the myth about race and race purity. He has entered where more timorous writers have feared to tread. He has received no scholarships or subsidies from the various white funds and foundations. He has financed all his research, travels and publishing. We are all tremendously indebted to him and he deserves our support in the way he would best like to have it—by buying Sex and Race."

Prime Minister Nnamdi Azikiwe of Eastern Nigeria: "You are among those who inspired me to take a very keen interest in the study of the African in history."

Rose Wilder Lane, noted author, "Who's Who in America," says of "World's Great Men of Color": An omnivorous reader such as I am, has a habit of classifying books. Dismissing the quantities of trash of all categories, there remain the entertaining books, the curently informative books, some books of more permanent worth, a few indispensable ones, and rarely a new one that tentatively may be called great.

"Now here is a book of such magnitude that it overlaps all these categories and goes into none. For three months I have been reading it with unflagging interest, with delight, amusement, excitement, profit, admiration and increasing dismay, for I must tell you about this book and I don't think I can.

"I have thought of comparing it to Plutarch's Lives, but then it more nearly resembles the History of the Father of History; yet it is American and contemporary, too . . .

"The author of the book is as difficult to classify as his work. Mr. J. A. Rogers is an American and a self-made scholar. He is an historian of enormous erudition. He is an anthropologist of no small caliber, elected in 1930 to membership in the Paris Society of Anthropologist. He has lectured at the Sorbonne and other leading European universities. He is a linguist, a world traveler, a journalist, an author, and, I would judge from references in his writings, a connoisseur of antique art. This book is a product of more than thirty years research in the world's libraries and museums, and of experience in many countries . . .

"I know no easier, more fascinating way to begin to acquire the world-view, innocent of propaganda or bias, based on fact, which no American learns from schools or the daily press, than reading World's Great Men of Color." From the Economic Council Review of Books, June 1947.

Rev. George S. Singleton, Editor, Christian Recorder, Philadelphia, Pa.: "I have read with avidity and profound interest your fascinating and scientific treatise, Sex and Race . . . You have made civilization and culture debtor to yourself. I can all the more appreciate what you have done because some years ago I taught anthropology and Negro history."

Louis A. Potter: "As a teacher in the Philadelphia schools I realize fully how great a need your contribution will fill. Not only in Philadelphia but throughout America and the world in general we suffer from an absymal lack of inspirational knowledge of our own. You bridge that gap in a grand manner.

"May I commend you for the effortless style that enables one to fairly flow through the book, making it possible thereby to devote one's entire attention to the absorption of the mass of material without the necessity of constant interpretation.

"Wishing you great success in your tremendous effort . . . May it be the dawn of an ever increasing wave of knowledge that must necessarily cause every Negro to hold his head a bit higher and all others who read your book to view the Negro with a loftier perspective."

Marcus Garvey's Negro World "From Superman to Man" is the greatest book on the Negro we have ever read. It gives the young Negro the historical authority that his race founded great civilizations, has ruled over areas as large as all Europe and was prolific in statesmen, scientists, poets, conquerors, religious and political leaders, arts, crafts, industry and commerce when the white race was wallowing in barbarity or sunk in savagery and cannibalism. 'From Superman To Man' was recommended for reading in the original Constitution and By-Laws of the Universal Negro Improvement Association."

Miss Z. Baber, Instructor, University of Chicago: " 'From Superman To Man' is the best literature I have read on the subject. I am placing it on the required reading list for my classes."

THE AUTHOR

J. A. Rogers has engaged continuously in research on race relations since 1915. Published himself his first book, "From Superman to Man," in 1917 after it was refused by the publishers.

Wrote and published his second book, "As Nature Leads," in 1919.

Began writing for the Negro press in 1920 and has been doing so since.

In 1924, '25, '26, toured the North and South, lecturing and selling "From Superman to Man" (4th edition).

In 1925 went to Europe for research in the libraries and museums there.

In 1927 returned for research lasting three years. Went to North Africa.

In 1930 went on his own initiative to the coronation of Haile Selassie, who presented him with the Coronation Medal. The same year published his "World's Greatest Men of African Descent."

From 1930 to 1933 continued his researches in Europe.

In 1934 published his "100 Amazing Facts About the Negro" which went into 19 editions.

In 1930, 1935 and '36 continued his researches in Egypt and the Sudan.

In 1935 published his "Real Facts About Ethiopia" and went the same year as war correspondent to Ethiopia for the Pittsburgh-Courier.

In 1940 began publication of his "Sex and Race" in three volumes.

In 1947 published his "World's Great Men of Color, 3000 B.C. to 1946 A.D." in two volumes.

In 1950 returned to Europe for further research on his "Nature Knows No Color-Line," an exposition of the Negro ancestry in the white race, which he published in 1952.

In 1956 and '57 studied black-white relations in England, Germany and other European countries with American troops.

Also author of several pamphlets, among them The Ku Klux Spirit, and the Real Facts About Ethiopia.

All books have been published by the author.

In 1930 was elected to membership in the Paris Society of Anthropology. Is now member of the American Geographical Society; the Academy of Political Science; the American Association For the Advancement of Society; and the Association Populaire des Amis Des Musees of France.

Sex and Race

Vol. I.   The Old World ....

Vol. II. The New World ....

Vol. III. Why White and Black Mate in Spite of Laws and Social
          Opposition. By Mail ....

From Superman To Man ....

100 Amazing Facts About The Negro ....

Nature Knows No Color-Line ....

AFRICA'S GIFT TO AMERICA ....

Five Negro Presidents ....

HELGA M. ROGERS

3806 48TH AVENUE SOUTH
ST. PETERSBURG, FL 33711